A Topical Guide to the Strategies Boxes

P9-AOE-485

General Skills

Global Technical Communication — 14
Analyzing Your Audience — 46
Persuasion — 51
Proofreading — 57
Avoiding Ethical Abuses — 67
Outlining — 75
Deciding about Tone — 98
Unbiased Usage — 99

Teamwork

Organizing a Team Project — 15
Running a Meeting — 17
Managing Team Conflicts — 18
Peer Review and Editing — 19

Doing Research

Thinking Critically about Research — 26
Finding Credible, Reliable Secondary Sources — 32
Informational Interviews — 34
Surveys — 36

Visuals and Document Design

Creating Tables — 108
Creating Graphs — 111
Creating Charts — 113
Illustrations, Diagrams, Photographs, Videos, Icons, and Symbols — 117
Designing: Consistency and Cohesiveness — 131
Designing: Navigation and Emphasis — 136

Getting a Job

Creating a Résumé — 146
Application Letters — 150
Digital Job Application Materials — 152
Dossiers, Portfolios, and E-portfolios — 155
Interviews and Follow-up Notes — 159

Memos and Letters

Memos — 172
Letters in General — 178

Inquiry Letters — 181
Claim Letters — 184
Sales Letters — 186
Adjustment Letters — 187

Reports and Proposals

Progress Reports — 265
Periodic Activity Reports — 269
Trip Reports — 269
Meeting Minutes — 272
Feasibility Reports — 275
Recommendation Reports — 277
Peer Review Reports — 279
Formal Reports — 291
Proposals — 317

Other Documents

Definitions — 202
Descriptions — 219
Specifications — 222
Readable Instructions — 236
Accessible Instructions — 239
Instructions and Procedures — 244
Summaries — 259

Digital Media and Presentations

Choosing and Using Email — 338
Email Style and Tone in the Workplace — 340
Blogs, Wikis, and Web Pages — 352
Social Media — 364
Preparing Oral Presentations — 379
Using Presentation Software and Video Conferencing — 381
Delivering Oral Presentations — 382

Avoiding Plagiarism

Taking Notes — 388
Quoting the Work of Others — 389
Paraphrasing the Work of Others — 390
Summarizing the Work of Others — 391

A Guide to the Checklists

Checklist for Effective Technical
Communication 21
Checklist for Doing Research 38
Checklist for Usability 57
Checklist for Ethical Communication 67
Checklist for Structuring Information 84
Checklist for Style 100
Checklist for Using Audience-Centered
Visuals 120
Checklist for Document Design 137
Checklist for Résumés 160
Checklist for Job Application Letters 160
Checklist for Supporting Materials 161
Checklist for Memos and Letters 189

Checklist for Definitions 202
Checklist for Descriptions
and Specifications 222
Checklist for Instructions
and Procedures 246
Checklist for Summaries 260
Checklist for Informal Reports 279
Checklist for Formal Reports 307
Checklist for Proposals 329
Checklist for Email 341
Checklist for Blogs, Wikis,
and Web Pages 353
Checklist for Social Media 365
Checklist for Oral Presentations 383

Strategies for Technical Communication in the Workplace

FOURTH EDITION

Laura J. Gurak
University of Minnesota

John M. Lannon
University of Massachusetts-Dartmouth

Pearson

330 Hudson Street, NY, NY 10013

Director of English: Karon Bowers
Executive Producer and Publisher: Aron Keesbury
Development Editor: Bruce Cantley
Marketing Manager: Nicholas Bolt
Program Manager: Rachel Harbour
Project Manager: Valerie Iglar-Mobley, Integra-Chicago

Text Design and Electronic Page Makeup: Integra
Cover Designer: Pentagram
Cover Illustration: Christopher DeLorenzo
Manufacturing Buyer: Roy L. Pickering, Jr.
Printer/Binder: LSC Communications/Crawfordsville
Cover Printer: Phoenix Color/Hagerstown

Acknowledgments of third-party content appear on page 438, which constitutes an extension of this copyright page.

PEARSON and REVEL are exclusive trademarks in the United States and/or other countries owned by Pearson Education, Inc., or its affiliates.

Unless otherwise indicated herein, any third-party trademarks that may appear in this work are the property of their respective owners and any references to third-party trademarks, logos, or other trade dress are for demonstrative or descriptive purposes only. Such references are not intended to imply any sponsorship, endorsement, authorization, or promotion of Pearson's products by the owners of such marks, or any relationship between the owner and Pearson Education, Inc., or its affiliates, authors, licensees, or distributors.

MICROSOFT®, WINDOWS®, and MICROSOFT OFFICE® are registered trademarks of the Microsoft Corporation in the U.S. and other countries. This book is not sponsored or endorsed by or affiliated with the Microsoft Corporation.

Microsoft and/or its respective suppliers make no representations about the suitability of the information contained in the documents and related graphics published as part of the services for any purpose. All such documents and related graphics are provided "as is" without warranty of any kind. Microsoft and/or its respective suppliers hereby disclaim all warranties and conditions with regard to this information, including all warranties and conditions of merchantability whether express, implied, or statutory, fitness for a particular purpose, title, and non-infringement. In no event shall Microsoft and/or its respective suppliers be liable for any special, indirect, or consequential damages or any damages whatsoever resulting from loss of use, data, or profits, whether in an action of contract, negligence, or other tortious action, arising out of or in connection with the use or performance of information available from the services.

The documents and related graphics contained herein could include technical inaccuracies or typographical errors. Changes are periodically added to the information herein. Microsoft and/or its perspective suppliers may make improvements and/or changes in the product(s) and/or the programs(s) described herein at any time. Partial screen shots may be viewed in full within the software version specified.

Library of Congress Cataloging-in-Publication Data
Library of Congress Cataloging-in-Publication Data can be found on file at the Library of Congress.

Copyright © 2019, 2016, 2013 by Pearson Education, Inc. All Rights Reserved. Printed in the United States of America. This publication is protected by copyright, and permission should be obtained from the publisher prior to any prohibited reproduction, storage in a retrieval system, or transmission in any form or by any means, electronic, mechanical, photocopying, recording, or otherwise. For information regarding permissions, request forms and the appropriate contacts within the Pearson Education Global Rights & Permissions Department, please visit www.pearsoned.com/permissions/.

1   17

Student Rental Edition ISBN-10:   0-13-466854-5
Student Rental Edition ISBN-13: 978-0-13-466854-3

A la Carte ISBN-10:   0-13-468006-5
A la Carte ISBN-13: 978-0-13-468006-4

Access Code Card ISBN-10:   0-13-467992-X
Access Code Card ISBN-13: 978-0-13-467992-1

Instructor's Review Copy ISBN-10:   0-13-467936-9
Instructor's Review Copy ISBN-13: 978-0-13-467936-5

www.pearsonhighered.com

Brief Contents

Preface   xv

Part 1   Foundations

1   Technical Communication: Global, Collaborative, and Digital   2

2   The Research Process in Technical Communication   24

3   Providing Audiences with Usable Information   40

4   Recognizing Ethical Issues in Technical Communication   60

Part 2   Blueprints

5   Structuring Information for Your Readers   70

6   Writing With a Readable Style   87

7   Using Audience-Centered Visuals   103

8   Designing User-Friendly Documents   123

Part 3   Documents

9   Résumés and Other Employment Materials   140

10   Memos and Letters   163

11   Definitions   191

12   Descriptions   204

13   Instructions and Procedures   225

14   Summaries   248

15   Informal Reports   262

16   Formal Reports   281

17   Proposals   309

Part 4   Digital Media and Presentations

18   Email   332

19   Blogs, Wikis, and Web Pages   343

20   Social Media   355

21   Oral Presentations and Video Conferencing   367

Appendix A   385
Appendix B   417
Works Cited   437
Credits   438
Index   439

Contents

Preface   xv

Part 1 Foundations

1 Technical Communication: Global, Collaborative, and Digital 2

What is Technical Communication?   3

Main Features of Technical Communication   4

Focus is on the Reader, Not the Writer   4

Document Design is Efficient and Accessible   5

Writing Style is Clear and Relevant   5

Information is Persuasive, Truthful, and Based on Research   6

Three Primary Purposes of Technical Communication   7

Informational Purpose   7

Instructional Purpose   7

Persuasive Purpose   7

Common Types of Technical Documents   12

Technical Communication is Global, Collaborative, and Digital   13

Technical Communication is Global   13

STRATEGIES for Global Technical Communication   **14**

Technical Communication is Collaborative   14

STRATEGIES for Organizing a Team Project   **15**

Running Successful Meetings   15

STRATEGIES for Running a Meeting   **17**

Identifying and Managing Group Conflicts   17

STRATEGIES for Managing Team Conflicts   **18**

Reviewing and Editing the Work of Others   19

STRATEGIES for Peer Review and Editing   **19**

Technical Communication is Digital   20

CHECKLIST for Effective Technical Communication   **21**

APPLICATIONS   **22**

2 The Research Process in Technical Communication 24

Thinking Critically About Research   25

STRATEGIES for Thinking Critically about Research   **26**

Primary Versus Secondary Sources   27

Exploring Secondary Sources   27

How to Locate Secondary Sources   27

Types of Secondary Sources   28

STRATEGIES for Finding Credible, Reliable Secondary Sources   **32**

Exploring Primary Sources   33

Unsolicited Inquiries   33

Informational Interviews   34

STRATEGIES for Informational Interviews   **34**

Surveys   35

STRATEGIES for Surveys   **36**

Observations and Experiments   36

CHECKLIST for Doing Research   **38**

APPLICATIONS   **38**

3 Providing Audiences with Usable Information 40

Analyze the Document's Audience   42

Primary and Secondary Audiences   42

Relationship with Audience   43

Audience's Technical Background   43

Audience's Cultural Background   45

STRATEGIES for Analyzing Your Audience   **46**

Determine the Document's Purpose   46

Primary and Secondary Purposes   47

Intended Use of the Document   47

Know How to Be Persuasive   47

Using Claims as a Basis for Persuasion   48

Connecting with Your Audience   48

STRATEGIES for Persuasion   51
Create a Task Analysis for the Document   51
Consider Other Related Usability Factors   53
 Setting   53
 Potential Problems   53
 Length   53
 Format   53
 Timing   54
 Budget   54
Develop an Information Plan for the Document   54
Write, Test, Revise, and Proofread the Document   56
 STRATEGIES for Proofreading   57
CHECKLIST for Usability   57
APPLICATIONS   58

4 Recognizing Ethical Issues in Technical Communication   60

Ethics, Technology, and Communication   61
 Types of Ethical Choices   62
How Workplace Pressures Affect Ethical Values   62
Recognizing and Avoiding Ethical Abuses   64
 STRATEGIES for Avoiding Ethical Abuses   67
CHECKLIST for Ethical Communication   67
APPLICATIONS   68

Part 2 Blueprints

5 Structuring Information for Your Readers   70

The Importance of an Understandable Structure   71
Outlining   72
 STRATEGIES for Outlining   75
Chunking   77
Sequencing   77
Paragraphing   78
 The Topic Sentence   79
 Paragraph Unity   79
 Paragraph Coherence   79
Clarifying Headings   81
Providing an Overview   81
CHECKLIST for Structuring Information   84
APPLICATIONS   86

6 Writing With a Readable Style   87

The Importance of a Readable Style   88
Writing Clearly   89
 Avoiding Ambiguous Pronoun References   89
 Avoiding Ambiguous Modifiers   90
 Using Active Voice Whenever Possible   90
 Using Passive Voice Selectively   91
 Avoiding Nominalizations   92
 Unstack Modifying Nouns   93
 Avoiding Unnecessary Jargon   93
Writing Concisely   94
 Avoiding Wordiness   94
 Eliminating Redundancy and Repetition   95
Writing Fluently   96
 Combining Related Ideas   96
 Varying Sentence Construction and Length   96
 Using Parallel Structure   97
Writing Personably   98
 Adjusting Your Tone   98
 STRATEGIES for Deciding about Tone   98
 Avoiding Biased Language   99
 STRATEGIES for Unbiased Usage   99
CHECKLIST for Style   100
APPLICATIONS   101

7 Using Audience-Centered Visuals   103

The Importance of Using Audience-Centered
Visuals   104
When to Use Visuals   106
 Using Visuals to Support Text   106
 Using Visuals on Their Own   107
Types of Visuals   107
 Tables   108
 STRATEGIES for Creating Tables   108
 Graphs   108
 STRATEGIES for Creating Graphs   111
 Charts   111
 STRATEGIES for Creating Charts   113
 Illustrations and Diagrams   114
 Photographs   115
 Videos   116

Icons and Symbols 116

STRATEGIES for Illustrations, Diagrams, Photographs, Videos, Icons, and Symbols **117**

Special Considerations When Using Visuals 118

Selecting Appropriate Visuals 118

Placing, Cross-Referencing, and Presenting Visuals 119

Using Color in Visuals 119

Using Visuals Fairly and Accurately 119

CHECKLIST for Using Audience-Centered Visuals **120**

APPLICATIONS **121**

8 Designing User-Friendly Documents 123

The Importance of User-Friendly Document Design 124

Characteristics of Well-Designed Documents 125

Specific Design Elements 128

Designing for Consistency and Cohesiveness 128

STRATEGIES for Designing: Consistency and Cohesiveness **131**

Designing for Navigation and Emphasis 133

STRATEGIES for Designing: Navigation and Emphasis **136**

CHECKLIST for Document Design **137**

APPLICATIONS **138**

Part 3 Documents

9 Résumés and Other Employment Materials 140

Assessing Your Skills and Aptitudes 142

Researching the Job Market 142

Engage in Active Networking 143

Résumés 143

Parts of a Résumé 144

Organizing Your Résumé 146

STRATEGIES for Creating a Résumé **146**

Application Letters 148

Solicited Application Letters 148

Unsolicited Application Letters 150

STRATEGIES for Application Letters **150**

Digital versus Print Job Application Materials 151

STRATEGIES for Digital Job Application Materials **152**

Dossiers, Portfolios, and E-portfolios 152

Dossiers 152

Portfolios and E-portfolios 154

STRATEGIES for Dossiers, Portfolios, and E-portfolios **155**

Interviews and Follow-up Letters 155

Interviews 156

Follow-up Communication 157

STRATEGIES for Interviews and Follow-up Notes **159**

CHECKLIST for Résumés **160**

CHECKLIST for Job Application Letters **160**

CHECKLIST for Supporting Materials **161**

APPLICATIONS **161**

10 Memos and Letters 163

Memo Basics, Parts, and Format 164

Parts and Format of Memos 165

Memo Tone 165

Types of Memos 168

Transmittal Memo 168

Summary or Follow-up Memo 168

Informational Memo 169

STRATEGIES for Memos **172**

Letter Basics, Parts, and Format 172

Letter Parts and Formats 172

Letter Tone 175

Establishing and Maintaining a "You" Perspective 175

Being Polite and Tactful 177

Using Plain English 177

Considering the Needs of International Readers 178

Being Direct or Indirect 178

STRATEGIES for Letters in General **178**

Types of Letters 179

Inquiry Letters 179

STRATEGIES for Inquiry Letters **181**

Claim Letters 181

STRATEGIES for Claim Letters **184**

Sales Letters 184

STRATEGIES for Sales Letters 186
Adjustment Letters 186
STRATEGIES for Adjustment Letters 187
CHECKLIST for Memos and Letters 189
APPLICATIONS 189

11 Definitions 191

Audience and Purpose of Definitions 192
Legal, Safety, and Societal Implications of Definitions 193
Types of Definitions 194
Parenthetical Definitions 194
Sentence Definitions 194
Expanded Definitions 195
Methods for Expanding Definitions 196
Etymology 196
History 197
Negation 197
Operating Principle 197
Analysis of Parts 197
Visuals 198
Comparison and Contrast 198
Required Conditions 198
Examples 199
Using Multiple Expansion Methods 199
Placement of Definitions 199
STRATEGIES for Definitions 202
CHECKLIST for Definitions 202
APPLICATIONS 203

12 Descriptions 204

Audience and Purpose of Descriptions 205
Objectivity in Descriptions 206
Elements of Descriptions 207
Title 207
Introduction 207
Sequence of Topics 207
Visuals 208
Conclusion 208
Product and Process Descriptions 209
A Complex Product Description 212
A Complex Process Description 216

STRATEGIES for Descriptions 219
Specifications 220
STRATEGIES for Specifications 222
CHECKLIST for Descriptions and Specifications 222
APPLICATIONS 223

13 Instructions and Procedures 225

Audience and Purpose of Instructions 227
Types of Instructional Formats 227
User Manuals 228
Quick Reference Materials 229
Assembly Guides 229
Web-Based Instructions 231
Online Instructions 232
Safety and Legal Implications 232
Elements of Effective Instructions 233
Title 233
Overview or Introduction 233
Body 233
Conclusion 233
Visuals 234
Notes, Cautions, Warnings, and Danger Notices 234
Content, Style, and Design Considerations 236
Detail and Technicality 236
Style 236
STRATEGIES for Readable Instructions 236
Design 237
STRATEGIES for Accessible Instructions 239
Procedures 239
Audience and Purpose Considerations 242
Types of Procedures 242
Conducting a Usability Survey 242
STRATEGIES for Instructions and Procedures 244
CHECKLIST for Instructions and Procedures 246
APPLICATIONS 246

14 Summaries 248

Audience and Purpose of Summaries 249
Elements of Effective Summaries 250
Accuracy 250

Completeness 251
Conciseness 251
Nontechnical Style 251
Writing Summaries Step by Step 251
Step 1: Read the Original Document 251
Step 2: Reread and Mark Essential Material 252
Step 3: Cut and Paste the Key Information 252
Step 4: Redraft the Information into Your
Own Organizational Pattern and Words 252
Step 5: Edit Your Draft 252
Step 6: Compare Your Version with the
Original Document 252
Special Types of Summaries 254
Closing Summaries 255
Informative Abstracts 256
Descriptive Abstracts 257
Executive Summaries 257
Summarizing Information for Social Media 259
STRATEGIES for Summaries 259
CHECKLIST for Summaries 260
APPLICATIONS 260

15 Informal Reports 262

Two Categories of Reports: Informational
and Analytical 264
Types of Informational Reports 264
Progress Reports 264
STRATEGIES for Progress Reports 265
Periodic Activity Reports 267
STRATEGIES for Periodic Activity Reports 269
Trip Reports 269
STRATEGIES for Trip Reports 269
Meeting Minutes 271
STRATEGIES for Meeting Minutes 272
Types of Analytical Reports 273
Feasibility Reports 273
STRATEGIES for Feasibility Reports 275
Recommendation Reports 275
STRATEGIES for Recommendation Reports 277
Peer Review Reports 278
STRATEGIES for Peer Review Reports 279
CHECKLIST for Informal Reports 279
APPLICATIONS 279

16 Formal Reports 281

Audience and Purpose of Formal Reports 283
Comparative Analysis 283
Causal Analysis 283
Feasibility Analysis 284
Elements of Effective Formal Reports 285
Accurate, Appropriate, and Clearly
Interpreted Data 286
Clearly Identified Purpose Statement 286
Understandable Structure 286
Readable Style 286
Audience-Centered Visuals 287
User-Friendly Design 288
Parts of Formal Reports 288
Letter of Transmittal 288
Front Matter 288
Text of the Report 290
End Matter 290
STRATEGIES for Formal Reports 291
A Sample Formal Report 292
CHECKLIST for Formal Reports 307
APPLICATIONS 307

17 Proposals 309

Audience and Purpose of Proposals 310
Types of Proposals 311
Planning Proposals 311
Research Proposals 313
Sales Proposals 313
Organization of Informal and Formal
Proposals 316
Clear Title or Subject Line 316
Background Information 316
Statement of Problem or Situation 316
Description of Solution or Resolution 317
Costs, Timing, and Qualifications 317
Conclusion 317
STRATEGIES for Proposals 317
A Sample Formal Proposal 318
CHECKLIST for Proposals 329
APPLICATIONS 329

Part 4 Digital Media and Presentations

18 Email 332

Workplace Email 333
  Audience and Purpose of Email 334
  Components and Organization of Email 334
Types of Workplace Email 335
  STRATEGIES for Choosing and Using Email 337
Appropriate Style for Workplace Email 338
  STRATEGIES for Email Style and Tone in the Workplace 340
Copyright and Privacy in Digital Communication 341
CHECKLIST for Email 341
APPLICATIONS 342

19 Blogs, Wikis, and Web Pages 343

Blogs 344
  Internal Blogs 344
  External Blogs 345
Wikis 345
  Internal Wikis 345
  External Wikis 346
Web Pages 346
Audience and Purpose of Web Pages 347
Elements of Effective Web Pages 348
  Structure 348
  Style 350
  Visuals 351
  Design 351
Web Page Credibility and Privacy Issues 352
  STRATEGIES for Blogs, Wikis, and Web Pages 352
  CHECKLIST for Blogs, Wikis, and Web Pages 353
APPLICATIONS 354

20 Social Media 355

Considering Audience and Purpose 357
  Audience as Contributor 358
  Personal versus Workplace Uses of Social Media 359

Social Media in Technical and Workplace Communication 359
  Customer Review Sites 359
  Facebook 360
  Google+ 360
  Instagram 360
  LinkedIn and Other Job Sites 360
  Twitter 361
  YouTube 362
  Other Popular Social Media Sites 363
Credibilty and Legal Issues 363
  STRATEGIES for Social Media 364
CHECKLIST for Social Media 365
APPLICATIONS 365

21 Oral Presentations and Video Conferencing 367

Audience and Purpose of Oral Presentations 369
Types of Oral Presentations 369
  Informative Presentations 369
  Training Presentations 371
  Persuasive Presentations 371
  Action Plan Presentations 371
  Sales Presentations 372
Parts of Oral Presentations 372
  Introduction 372
  Body 373
  Conclusion 373
Preparing Oral Presentations 373
  Research and Connect the Topic to Your Audience 373
  Create an Outline or Storyboard 373
  Determine a Delivery Style 374
  Choose Your Technology 376
  Plan the Use of Visuals 376
  Practice the Presentation 379
  STRATEGIES for Preparing Oral Presentations 379
Using Presentation Software 379
Video Conferencing 380
  STRATEGIES for Using Presentation Software and Video Conferencing 381

Delivering Oral Presentations 382
STRATEGIES for Delivering Oral
Presentations 382
CHECKLIST for Oral Presentations 383
APPLICATIONS 383

Appendix A:

Documenting Sources 385

What is Plagiarism? 385
Identifying Sources and Information
to be Documented 386
Taking Effective and Accurate Notes 387
STRATEGIES for Taking Notes 388
Quoting, Paraphrasing, and Summarizing
Properly 388
Quoting the Work of Others 388
STRATEGIES for Quoting the Work
of Others 389
Paraphrasing the Work of Others 389
STRATEGIES for Paraphrasing the Work
of Others 390
Summarizing the Work of Others 390
STRATEGIES for Summarizing the
Work of Others 391
Documentation: The Key to Avoiding
Plagiarism 391
Why You Should Document 391
What You Should Document 392
How You Should Document 392
MLA Documentation Style 393
MLA Parenthetical
References 393
MLA Works Cited Entries 394
APA Documentation Style 404
APA Parenthetical References 404
APA Reference Entries 405
Other Documentation Styles 414
Recognizing Copyright Issues 414
Works in the Public Domain 415
Fair Use 415
The Difference between
Plagiarism and Copyright
Infringement 415

Appendix B:

A Brief Handbook 417

Grammar 417
Sentence Fragments 417
Run-on Sentences 418
Comma Splices 419
Faulty Agreement—Subject and Verb 419
Faulty Agreement—Pronoun and Referent 420
Faulty Coordination and Subordination 420
Faulty Pronoun Case 422
Punctuation 422
Period 422
Question Mark 423
Exclamation Point 423
Semicolon 423
Colon 423
Comma 424
Apostrophe 426
Quotation Marks 427
Ellipses 428
Brackets 428
Italics 428
Parentheses 429
Dashes 429
Mechanics 429
Abbreviation 429
Hyphenation 430
Capitalization 430
Numbers and Numerals 431
Spelling 432
Usage 432
Transitions 432
Use Transitional Expressions 432
Repeat Key Words and Phrases 432
Use Forecasting Statements 434
Lists 434
Embedded Lists 434
Vertical Lists 435

Works Cited 437
Credits 438
Index 439

Preface

Overview

In today's workplace, professionals in all fields are expected to adapt to a variety of communication situations. Virtually everyone must be able to write routine workplace documents such as memos, emails, letters, and informal reports. In addition, employees must create more complex forms of communication such as formal reports and proposals, instructions, definitions and descriptions, Web pages, oral presentations, video presentations, and more. All the while, these professionals must also negotiate technological innovations, communicate in a global marketplace, work in teams, write persuasively, research effectively, and understand the ethical implications of the documents they produce.

We wrote *Strategies for Technical Communication in the Workplace* as a medium-length textbook that covers all the preceding topics thoroughly and concisely. Like the first three editions, this fourth edition of *Strategies* draws on the strengths of our other technical communication book, the best-selling *Technical Communication* (14th edition). We hope that students and faculty alike will appreciate the new edition of this distinctive textbook.

What's New in the 4th Edition

This fourth edition of *Strategies for Technical Communication in the Workplace* offers many new features, with an emphasis on updated discussions and examples of digital communication technologies and with a fresh new look and feel that students will appreciate. In addition, Learning Objectives at the outset of each chapter are now tied directly into the major sections of the chapter; model documents and pedagogical features have been revised or updated; and many new end-of-chapter Applications have been added. Another important update for this edition is the digital version of the text in an innovative platform called Revel that allows for interactivity, collaboration, and more. See page xix in this Preface for more information about Revel.

In detail, we have made the following chapter-by-chapter changes for this fourth edition of *Strategies*:

- **Chapter 1, "Technical Communication: Global, Collaborative, and Digital,"** features an updated introduction to the most common types of technical documents, as well as revised discussion of interpersonal and digital factors that can lead to team conflicts and a newly-written introduction to digital technical communication.

- **Chapter 2, "The Research Process in Technical Communication,"** has been thoroughly revised throughout to keep pace with the rapid changes in research technologies, placing less emphasis on the distinction between online and print sources and incorporating the latest information on locating secondary sources and using various types of secondary sources. A new figure provides an example of a cover email for an online survey.

- **Chapter 3, "Providing Audiences with Usable Information,"** includes revised discussion and examples to help students fully understand the process of analyzing an audience's technical background as well as expanded discussion of additional usability factors beyond audience and purpose that technical communicators must consider, such as length, format, and budget.

- **Chapter 4, "Recognizing Ethical Issues in Technical Communication,"** has been updated throughout to incorporate the latest information on how technology affects ethical issues in the workplace.

- **Chapter 5, "Structuring Information for Your Readers,"** features a new email example demonstrating an introduction-body-conclusion structure but also foregrounding the importance of social media in the workplace, discussed in more detail later in the book.

- **Chapter 6, "Writing with a Readable Style,"** provides a thoroughly revised section on the importance of using unbiased language, which incorporates rather than separates the discussion of nonsexist language.

- **Chapter 7, "Using Audience-Centered Visuals,"** includes a new section on using visuals fairly and accurately.

- **Chapter 8, "Designing User-Friendly Documents,"** provides new information on using templates and other digital design tools.

- **Chapter 9, "Résumés and Other Employment Materials,"** has been revised throughout to keep pace with new developments in the job search process, including using LinkedIn effectively, what to now include in the contact information portion of your résumé, adapting your résumé to the specifications of various job-search sites, interviewing via Skype, and using email for follow-up communication after an interview or job offer. In addition, all sample résumés in the chapter have been revised and updated.

- **Chapter 10, "Memos and Letters,"** now speaks to the increasing use of email rather than hard copy to send workplace memos and letters and how writers can make informed decisions as to when and how to send them over email. In addition, the chapter presents expanded discussion on the three most common types of memos, and most of the sample memos and letters have been revised and updated.

- **Chapter 11, "Definitions,"** includes a thoroughly revised section on legal, safety, and societal implications of definitions as well as discussion as to when to use a glossary or hyperlinked definitions.

- **Chapter 12, "Descriptions,"** features a revised complex product description as well as new discussion of the safety implications of descriptions.

- **Chapter 13, "Instructions and Procedures,"** has been thoroughly revised to provide several new sample instructions, as well as updated information on online versus print instructions, expanded discussion of user manuals and safety and legal implications of instructions, and a new section on assembly guides.

- **Chapter 14, "Summaries,"** includes a detailed new section on summarizing information for social media.

- **Chapter 15, "Informal Reports,"** provides new information on choosing an appropriate format when delivering informal reports. In addition, all of the sample informal reports in the chapter have been carefully revised and updated.

- **Chapter 16, "Formal Reports,"** features expanded discussion of the format of various portions of a formal report, as well as a sample formal report that has been thoroughly revised to conform to the latest APA style guidelines.

- **Chapter 17, "Proposals,"** includes a sample formal proposal that has been reformatted to conform to the latest MLA style guidelines.

- **Chapter 18, "Email,"** has been thoroughly revised. In addition to all new email samples throughout, the chapter now includes a new introductory discussion about the cautions of using email, a new section with examples on the three main types of workplace email, and a revised and expanded discussion of style and tone in email messages.

- **Chapter 19, "Blogs, Wikis, and Web Pages,"** now includes discussion of "universal design" of Web pages as well as a new section on fairness considerations in Web-based communication.

- **Chapter 20, "Social Media,"** has been thoroughly revised to include new discussions of personal versus workplace use of social media, using Instagram on the job, using other popular social media on the job (Reddit, Tumblr, Pinterest), and credibility and legal issues surrounding the use of social media on the job.

- **Chapter 21, "Oral Presentations and Video Conferencing,"** presents a thoroughly revised section on using presentation software, including new material on the individual benefits of using various presentation software programs such as PowerPoint, Apple Keynote, Prezi, and Google Slides.

Key Features

To help you get a better idea how *Strategies* works as a whole, following is a point-by-point discussion of the key features of this book.

Complete but Streamlined Coverage

Strategies includes all topics essential for an undergraduate technical communication course in a compact yet thorough format. The book covers everything technical communicators need to know—from writing basic letters and memos, to writing complex proposals and formal reports, to delivering oral presentations and writing for the Web—in roughly 500 pages. In addition, *Strategies* offers innovative coverage of emerging technologies used in the workplace, including text messages, social networks, and online videos.

Emphasis on Student Practice

This book is guided by the idea of providing students with practical, accessible concepts that are easy to follow and that get students writing and designing documents immediately. One key feature, as the title suggests, is the Strategies box, which provides step-by-step advice to follow in writing and discussing a given document. In addition, chapters in Parts 3 and 4 emphasize the importance of "doing" immediately via the Let's Get Started feature; students are asked to draft their best version of each chapter's document type or communication situation before they read the chapter. Then, as they work through the chapter content, students are encouraged to review and revise their original work. Finally, every chapter, including the foundational and "blueprints" chapters in Parts 1 and 2, includes Applications exercises, grouped into general, collaborative, global, digital, and social media categories.

Clear Explanations and Straightforward Organization

As we wrote and organized this book, we kept in mind five essential questions students most frequently ask: "What needs to be done?"; "What should it look like?"; "How do I do it?"; "What should be avoided?"; and "How well have I done it?". The features described previously focus on these questions. Also, marginal notes summarize and reinforce main points in each chapter.

The chapter sequence in *Strategies* proceeds from general foundational concepts and blueprints in Parts 1 and 2 to cumulatively more complex writing and communicating situations in Parts 3 and 4.

Practical Pedagogical Features

Strategies includes several practical, easy-to-access pedagogical tools. These features include:

- **Chapter Outlines and Learning Objectives.** On the opening page of each chapter, the outlines provide a quick orientation to the chapter topics and sequence, and they are tied into the learning objectives, which emphasize the practical skills students can expect to acquire.

- **Strategies boxes.** Featured in every chapter, the Strategies boxes summarize key strategies discussed in the text and provide additional pointers for approaching each communication situation.

- **Checklists.** End-of-chapter Checklists summarize each chapter, and more importantly, they emphasize "doing" by asking students to check off each item as they review their work.

- **Applications.** Called "applications" rather than "exercises" to emphasize applied learning, the end-of-chapter Applications fall into four categories: General Applications (for individual practice), Team Applications (for pair or group practice), Global Applications (for highlighting global issues in workplace communication), and Digital and Social Media Applications (for highlighting the use of technology in workplace communication).

Realistic and Accessible Annotated Model Documents

Model documents resemble the kinds of documents students will write in the workplace. Accessible, engaging, and easy to emulate, most of these documents are fully annotated.

Consistent Focus on Audience and Purpose

Technical communication in the workplace is more than a mere exercise in "information transfer"—it is also a social transaction involving individuals, teams, companies, and organizations that are national and international in scope. In the contemporary workplace, a one-size-fits-all approach to technical communication doesn't work. Effective communication must be tailored for different audiences and different purposes. Today's communicator must be smart about researching, summarizing, and customizing information to meet many different situations. *Strategies* has therefore been designed to provide much more than a "cookie cutter" approach to creating typical workplace documents and making presentations by focusing on key rhetorical principles of audience and purpose.

The Latest Technology and Global Issues Coverage

With the Internet and digital technology at our fingertips and with companies and teams spread across the world, communication reaches a wide audience and often is transmitted instantly. We receive or convey professional information in a variety of ways—handwritten, in word-processed documents, via email or text messaging; in video format; as a Web page; via blogs, wikis, or social networks; or as live presentations—and each medium and potential audience brings with it unique challenges about how to best present the information. *Strategies* incorporates relevant technology coverage and stresses the importance of thinking about global audiences wherever relevant.

Organization of the Book

Strategies begins with foundational concepts, then moves to "blueprints," and then applies the foundations and blueprints to increasingly complex documents and communication situations.

- **Part 1 ("Foundations")** introduces the underlying concepts for creating effective technical communication. This section provides a definition of technical communication (Chapter 1); coverage of research as a pivotal part of technical communication (Chapter 2); an introduction to the analysis of audience, purpose, and other factors (Chapter 3); and in-depth coverage of workplace ethics (Chapter 4).

- **Part 2 ("Blueprints")** builds on Part 1 by discussing four basic considerations for approaching each type of workplace document or communication situation: understandable structure (Chapter 5), readable style (Chapter 6), audience-centered visuals (Chapter 7), and user-friendly design (Chapter 8).

- **Part 3 ("Documents")** applies the previous foundations and blueprints, presenting increasingly complex types of print documents. This section begins with the types of documents students need to get hired and concludes with the two most complex types of documents: formal reports and proposals. Specific documents covered in Part 3 include résumés and other employment materials (Chapter 9), memos and letters (Chapter 10), definitions (Chapter 11), descriptions and specifications (Chapter 12), instructions and procedures (Chapter 13), summaries (Chapter 14), informal reports (Chapter 15), formal reports (Chapter 16), and proposals (Chapter 17).

- **Part 4 ("Digital Media and Presentations")** provides guidance for creating documents for digital media and for giving oral presentations. Included are chapters on email (Chapter 18); blogs, wikis, and Web pages (Chapter 19); social media (Chapter 20); and oral presentations and video conferencing (Chapter 21).

- **Appendices A ("Documenting Sources") and B ("A Brief Handbook")** offer guidance on citations and grammar. Appendix A includes guidelines for avoiding plagiarism and documenting sources completely and accurately in both MLA and APA format.

Appendix B provides a brief handbook of grammar, punctuation, mechanics, and usage. This appendix also includes useful advice on formatting lists and using transitions in written work.

REVEL™

Educational Technology Designed for the Way Today's Students Read, Think, and Learn

Revel is an interactive learning environment that deeply engages students and prepares them for class. Media and assessment integrated directly within the authors' narrative lets students read, explore interactive content, and practice in one continuous learning path. Thanks to the dynamic reading experience in Revel, students come to class prepared to discuss, apply, and learn from instructors and from each other.

The Revel features accompanying *Strategies* are as follows:

- **Journal Prompts** appear at the end of every major section in each chapter, encouraging hands-on practice through writing. Students are asked to perform brief writing activities that involve reflection, brainstorming, drafting a portion of a document, or analyzing a particular document.

- **Multiple-Choice Quizzes** help reinforce facts and concepts as students move through each major section in each chapter (the end of each major section quiz features three questions directly tied to that section) and then again at the end of the chapter (the end of chapter quiz provides five questions covering various sections of the chapter).

- **Table Drag-and Drop** activities help students remember information by matching terms with their descriptions or placing parts of complex documents in the right order.

- **Fill-in-the-Blank and True/False Quick Check** activities are directly tied to the

Strategies boxes that appear in every chapter and provide a quick means of remembering concepts presented in these important boxes.

- **Let's Get Started** activities, which appear at the beginning of each chapter in Parts 3 and 4, encourage students to begin "doing" immediately by producing the type of draft document or communication product discussed in the chapter based on their prior knowledge.

- **Shared Writing Activities** are tied to one or more of the chapter's Journal Prompts in Parts 1 and 2 and to the Let's Get Started activities in Parts 3 and 4, encouraging students to share, discuss, and critique each other's work.

Learn more about Revel
www.pearson.com/revel

Supplements

Make more time for your students with instructor resources that offer effective learning assessments and classroom engagement. Pearson's partnership with educators does not end with the delivery of course materials; Pearson is there with you on the first day of class and beyond. A dedicated team of local Pearson representatives will work with you to not only choose course materials but also integrate them into your class and assess their effectiveness. Our goal is your goal—to improve instruction with each semester.

Pearson is pleased to offer the following resources to qualified adopters of *Strategies*. Several of these supplements are available to instantly download from Revel or on the Instructor Resource Center (IRC); please visit the IRC at www.pearsonhighered.com/irc to register for access.

- **TEST BANK** Evaluate learning at every level. Reviewed for clarity and accuracy, the Test Bank measures this material's learning objectives with multiple-choice, true/false, fill-in-the-blank, short-answer, and essay questions. You can easily customize the assessment to work in any major learning management system and to match what is covered in your course. Word, Black-Board, and WebCT versions are available on the IRC, and Respondus versions are available on request from www.respondus.com.

- **PEARSON MYTEST** This powerful assessment generation program includes all of the questions in the Test Bank. Quizzes and exams can be easily authored and saved online and then printed for classroom use, giving you ultimate flexibility to manage assessments anytime and anywhere. To learn more, visit www.pearsonhighered.com/mytest.

- **INSTRUCTOR'S RESOURCE MANUAL** Create a comprehensive roadmap for teaching classroom, online, or hybrid courses. Designed for new and experienced instructors, the Instructor's Resource Manual includes overall teaching strategies (including general teaching ideas, advice on how to use the Revel features accompanying *Strategies*, and sample syllabi) and chapter-specific resources (including chapter overviews, Learning Objectives, teaching tips, additional exercises, and quizzes). Available within Revel and in the IRC.

- **POWERPOINT PRESENTATION** Make lectures more enriching for students. The PowerPoint Presentation includes a full lecture outline and figures from the textbook and Revel edition. Available in the IRC.

Acknowledgments

We appreciate the valuable advice from our reviewers who helped us determine the direction of this revision: Teresa Cook, University of Cincinnati; Nancy Martinez, Central New

Mexico Community College; Dianne Pearman, University of Texas at Arlington; and Matthew Specter, University of Cincinnati.

In addition, we thank the reviewers who helped shape the three prior editions of this book: Michael Avery, Jefferson Community College; Carol Ann Britt, San Antonio College; Sherry A. Cisler, Arizona State University at the West Campus; Teresa Foxworthy Cook, University of Cincinnati; Michael Creeden, Florida International University; Laura H. Davis, Cleveland Community College; Michael-John DePalma, University of New Hampshire; Carolyn Kusbit Dunn, East Carolina University; Sean Flannery, Immaculata University; Terri Gordon, Lake Michigan College; Leslie Janac, Blinn College-Bryan Campus; Michael F. Johanyak, The University of Akron; Barbara Rau Kyle, University of Central Florida; Christine Laursen, Red Rocks Community College; Nancy R. MacKenzie, Minnesota State University, Mankato; Lisa Meloncon, University of Cincinnati; Traci Nathans-Kelly, University of Wisconsin–Madison; Julianne Newmark, New Mexico Tech; Beata Peterson, Fayetteville Technical Community College; Lynnette Porter, Embry-Riddle Aeronautical University; Erin M. Price, Bismarck State College; Anne Regan, California Polytechnic State University; Rebecca Joy Ritzel, University of Maryland; Kelly Sassi, North Dakota State University; Clay Kinchen Smith, Santa Fe College; Carey E. Smitherman, Worcester State College; Betty H. Stack, Rowan Cabarrus Community College; Lisa Stanley-Smith, Forsyth Technical Community College; Karina Stokes, University of Houston–Downtown; Suba Subbarao, Oakland Community College; Scott Temple, Cleveland Community College; Barry Thatcher, New Mexico State University; Ronald J. Tulley, The University of Findlay; Candace A. Welhausen, The Georgia Institute of Technology; and Miriam F. Williams, Texas State University.

A special thanks to our students who allowed us to reproduce versions of their work and who are named in the text. From Cynthia Cox and Rachel Harbour, we received outstanding editorial guidance and support. Thank you to Lee Scholder for her work preparing the first and current edition of the Instructor's Manual and to Daun Daemon for her work revising the Instructor's Manual for its second and third editions. Many thanks to Bruce Cantley for his generous and unflagging development help and invaluable ideas and to Valerie Iglar-Mobley for expertly managing production.

—**Laura J. Gurak and John M. Lannon**

Part 1
Foundations

1 Technical Communication: Global, Collaborative, and Digital   2

2 The Research Process in Technical Communication   24

3 Providing Audiences with Usable Information   40

4 Recognizing Ethical Issues in Technical Communication   60

Chapter 1
Technical Communication: Global, Collaborative, and Digital

Learning Objectives

1.1 Define technical communication.

1.2 Describe the key characteristics of effective technical communication.

1.3 List the three main purposes of technical documents.

1.4 Recognize typical technical documents.

1.5 Understand the global, collaborative, and digital nature of technical communication.

Chapter Outline

What is Technical Communication? 3

Main Features of Technical Communication 4

Three Primary Purposes of Technical Communication 7

Common Types of Technical Documents 12

Technical Communication is Global, Collaborative, and Digital 13
    Strategies for Global Technical Communication 14
    Strategies for Organizing a Team Project 15
    Strategies for Running a Meeting 17
    Strategies for Managing Team Conflicts 18
    Strategies for Peer Review and Editing 19
    Checklist for Effective Technical Communication 21

Applications 22

What is Technical Communication?

1.1 Define technical communication.

Technical communication is the exchange of information that helps people interact with technology, advance workplace goals, and solve complex problems.

We live in a world where many of our everyday actions depend on complex but usable information. For example, when you purchase or install a new device, such as a DVD player or wireless speakers, you need clear, easy-to-use instructions. From banking systems to online courses to business negotiations, countless aspects of daily life are affected by technology, and we rely on usable technical information to answer questions such as these:

- How do I access my online bank statement?
- How do I connect my tablet with a conference room's projection system?
- How do I paste a digital photo into a document and resize the image?

Technical information is also used in more specialized settings. For example, a physician performing heart surgery must have clear information about how to install

Technical communication helps us interact with technology in our daily lives

Technical communication helps specialists solve complex problems

a pacemaker. A government research scientist must have accurate instructions about how to write a grant or how to perform a particular experiment. An engineer must have access to the correct specifications for designing a bridge or configuring a new app. In specialized settings, technical communication answers questions such as these:

Specialized questions

- Do the benefits of the Lyme disease vaccine outweigh its risks?
- What are the technical limits to wind energy?
- How effectively will the new heating system circulate in the top floors of the new office complex?

Technical communication helps advance workplace goals

In the workplace, we are not only consumers of technical communication but also producers. Virtually all professionals, at some point, function as technical communicators. Experts are often required to present their knowledge to nonexpert audiences. For instance, a nuclear engineer testifying before Congress would need to write a report explaining climate change data in nonscientific language to policy makers and the general public. Nurses and other medical professionals are often required to explain complex medical concepts to patients and families. Writers of instructions for uploading new software need to be sure that a wide range of readers can perform the task without having to call customer service.

Technical communication is global, collaborative, and digital

Technical communication is global, collaborative, and digital. Technical documents, including user manuals, instructions and procedures, online help, and other such materials, are accessible by people around the globe, created by teams from different countries and time zones, and available online in formats suitable for reading on a variety of devices from laptops to tablets to smartphones to print.

Main Features of Technical Communication

1.2 Describe the key characteristics of effective technical communication.

Technical communication differs from most academic writing

Technical communication differs from other communication and writing courses you take in college. In first-year writing (freshman composition) or expository writing, the emphasis typically is on one type of document: the traditional college essay. As you work on the assignments for this course, the skills you learned in previous writing classes will remain important, but the writing will often be different. Technical documents typically exhibit the following characteristics.

Focus is on the Reader, Not the Writer

Produce user-centered documents

Unlike poetry, fiction, or essays, technical documents rarely focus on the author's personal thoughts and feelings. This doesn't mean that technical documents should have no personality (or voice), but it does mean that the needs of your readers must come first. Users of technical communication are only interested in you, the communicator, to the extent that they want to know what you have done, what you recommend, or how you speak for your company or organization. This type of communication is called "user-centered communication" (see Figure 1.1). User-centered communication requires a focus on the people who will be *reading and using* the document. What do your readers need to know? What tasks are they trying to perform?

Placing the reader's needs and interests first takes practice because many of us are taught to write from our own perspectives. For instance, assume you've been asked to create a set of instructions that explain how people in the community can bring household hazardous waste (gasoline, paint) for recycling. Assume also that you live in the neighborhood near the recycling center and often visit that location. In this instance, you could easily forget to include a map and directions to the center, unless you focus consistently on your actual readers—people who are new in town, people who don't live close to the facility, and so on.

Learn to put yourself in the reader's place

Figure 1.1 User-centered communication

Document Design is Efficient and Accessible

Unlike college essays, which take essentially one shape (paragraphs of text), technical documents may take the form of a brochure, a memo, a report with different sections, a numbered set of instructions, a Web site, online help, a blog, a wiki, or an email with a PDF attachment. Regardless of format and media, the design must be efficient and accessible, making it easy for readers to find what they are looking for and use the content to perform a task or answer a question.

Produce documents that are easy for readers to use and navigate

Writing Style is Clear and Relevant

Technical communication uses clear language. For example, the instructions for using a fire extinguisher (Figure 1.4, page 9) are written for a wide range of readers. Likewise, the letter from the company's general manager to a potential client (Figure 1.5, pages 10–11) is another example of clear communication.

Write clearly

Provide only relevant information

Information is relevant if the audience can apply it to the task at hand. For instance, if someone needs to operate a fire extinguisher, that person needs clear, brief sentences listed numerically without a lot of unnecessary explanation. As shown in Figure 1.4, some limited background information may be required (by law or by code), but even that information must be clear, relevant, and to the point.

Information is Persuasive, Truthful, and Based on Research

Persuasion means trying to influence someone's actions, opinions, or decisions. In the workplace, we rely on persuasion daily: to win coworker support, to attract clients and customers, or to request funding. But changing someone's mind is never easy, and sometimes it is impossible. Your success will depend on who you are trying to persuade, what you are requesting, and how entrenched they are in their own views.

All documents are at least in part persuasive

All technical documents are persuasive, in some sense. Some documents, such as the letter in Figure 1.5, are explicitly persuasive, in that the writer is trying to convince the reader that the proposed project is the right choice. Other documents, such as the instructions in Figure 1.4, are mainly informative, but they are also implicitly persuasive: The writer is also trying to show readers that the fire extinguisher is easy to use and safe.

Balance information and persuasion

In short, a technical communicator is a problem solver and, as such, must be aware of the best balance between providing readers with the information they need and persuading them to respond as desired, as illustrated in Figure 1.2.

Technical documents should be truthful

Even when you need to be overtly persuasive, as in a sales proposal, honesty is essential. A document that is highly persuasive but in some way dishonest may influence readers in the short term but will lead to long-term problems. You will lose credibility with the client or your boss and could potentially damage a working relationship for life.

Figure 1.2 Balancing information and persuasion

Even routine technical documents produced on the job are based to some extent on research. For example, a routine email to employees about a new performance review system may not require extensive research, but the information must be accurate. Accuracy in this case may only involve double-checking meeting notes or asking a colleague in the human resources department for clarification on some point, but double-checking your facts is still research. With more complex documents, the research component of technical communication becomes more obvious. For more on research, see Chapter 2.

Base your documents on careful research

Three Primary Purposes of Technical Communication

1.3   **List the three main purposes of technical documents.**

Most technical communication seeks to address one of three primary purposes: to anticipate and answer questions (inform), to enable people to perform a task (instruct), or to influence people's thinking (persuade). Keep in mind that these purposes often overlap (as in the following sample documents). However, most documents have one *primary* purpose: to inform, to instruct, or to persuade.

Three purposes of technical documents: inform, instruct, and persuade

Informational Purpose

Figure 1.3 displays an *informational* document created by the U.S. Environmental Protection Agency. It is designed for a wide audience of readers who may know little about the topic (bioremediation), but the writer has kept audience diversity in mind by anticipating and answering likely questions.

Informational documents anticipate and answer questions

Instructional Purpose

Figure 1.4 is an *instructional* document. As we have all experienced, effective instructions can be a pleasure to work with because they help people do what they want to do. But poor instructions can create frustration, often causing people to return the product and to have second thoughts about purchasing that brand in the future.

Instructional documents help people perform a task

Persuasive Purpose

Figure 1.5 shows a *persuasive* document in the form of a letter from a company that distributes systems for generating electrical power from recycled steam. General Manager William Bullock writes a persuasive answer to a customer's question: "Why should I invest in the system you are proposing for my plant?" As you read the letter, note how the writer focuses on reasons that are important to the reader.

Persuasive documents encourage readers to take a desired action

Figure 1.3 An informational document

United States
Environmental Protection
Agency

Office of Solid Waste and
Emergency Response
(5102G)

EPA 542-F-01-001
April 2001
www.epa.gov/superfund/sites
www.cluin.org

⊕EPA A Citizen's Guide to Bioremediation

The Citizen's Guide Series

EPA uses many methods to clean up pollution at Superfund and other sites. Some, like bioremediation, are considered new or innovative. Such methods can be quicker and cheaper than more common methods. If you live, work, or go to school near a Superfund site, you may want to learn more about cleanup methods. Perhaps they are being used or are proposed for use at your site. How do they work? Are they safe? This Citizen's Guide is one in a series to help answer your questions.

What is bioremediation?

Bioremediation allows natural processes to clean up harmful chemicals in the environment. Microscopic "bugs" or microbes that live in soil and groundwater like to eat certain harmful chemicals, such as those found in gasoline and oil spills. When microbes completely digest these chemicals, they change them into water and harmless gases such as carbon dioxide.

Microbe eats oil | Microbe digests oil and changes it to water and harmless gases | Microbe releases water and harmless gases into soil or ground

How does it work?

In order for microbes to clean up harmful chemicals, the right temperature, nutrients (fertilizers), and amount of oxygen must be present in the soil and groundwater. These conditions allow the microbes to grow and multiply—and eat more chemicals. When conditions are not right, microbes grow too slowly or die. Or they can create more harmful chemicals. If conditions are not right at a site, EPA works to improve them. One way they improve conditions is to pump air, nutrients, or other substances (such as molasses) underground. Sometimes microbes are added if enough aren't already there.

The right conditions for bioremediation cannot always be achieved underground. At some sites, the weather is too cold or the soil is too dense. At such sites, EPA might dig up the soil to clean it above ground where heaters and soil mixing help improve conditions. After the soil is dug up, the proper nutrients are added. Oxygen also may be added by stirring the mixture or by forcing air through it. However, some microbes work better without oxygen. With the right temperature and amount of oxygen and nutrients, microbes can do their work to "bioremediate" the harmful chemicals.

SOURCE: U.S. Environmental Protection Agency Web site <www.epa.gov>.

Marginal annotations:

- The title is clear and easy to understand
- User-centered headings are phrased as questions that readers would need answered
- Illustrations combine text and visuals
- Headings and a clean layout make this document easy for readers to navigate
- Text provides the most relevant information without being too detailed

Figure 1.4 An Instructional Document

How to Operate a Portable Fire Extinguisher

The Occupational Health and Safety Administration (OSHA) requires employers to provide portable fire extinguishers in the workplace. This document illustrates the parts of a fire extinguisher and provides instructions for operating the extinguisher safely and effectively using the P.A.S.S. method: Pull, Aim, Squeeze, and Sweep.

> **WARNING**: At the first sign of fire, sound the alarm and call the fire department. Before approaching the fire, identify a safe evacuation path. **Never** allow the fire, heat, or smoke to come between you and your evacuation path. **If you have the slightest doubt about your ability to fight a fire...** EVACUATE **IMMEDIATELY!**

Parts of a Fire Extinguisher

Figure 1 illustrates the parts of a portable fire extinguisher. When the extinguisher handle is compressed, an inner canister of high-pressure gas forces the extinguishing agent from the main cylinder through a siphon and out the nozzle.

FIGURE 1

Using a Fire Extinguisher with the P.A.S.S. Method

1. **PULL** Pull the pin. This will also break the tamper seal.
2. **AIM** Aim low, pointing the extinguisher nozzle (or its horn or hose) at the base of the fire.
3. **SQUEEZE** Squeeze the handle to release the extinguishing agent.
4. **SWEEP** Sweep from side to side at the base of the fire until it appears to be out. Watch the area. If the fire reignites, repeat steps 2–4.

FIGURE 2

Introduction provides appropriate level of detail for first-time users

A prominent warning box alerts users before they take action

Clearly labeled illustration helps readers understand the product

Numbered steps and a complementary illustration make the instructions easy to navigate and use

SOURCE: Text and figures from the U.S. Occupational Safety and Health Administration <www.osha.gov>.

Figure 1.5 A persuasive document

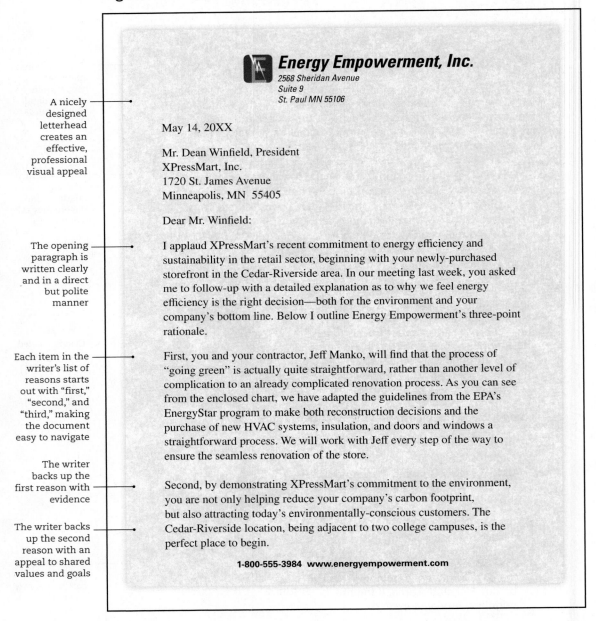

A nicely designed letterhead creates an effective, professional visual appeal

Energy Empowerment, Inc.
2568 Sheridan Avenue
Suite 9
St. Paul MN 55106

May 14, 20XX

Mr. Dean Winfield, President
XPressMart, Inc.
1720 St. James Avenue
Minneapolis, MN 55405

Dear Mr. Winfield:

The opening paragraph is written clearly and in a direct but polite manner

I applaud XPressMart's recent commitment to energy efficiency and sustainability in the retail sector, beginning with your newly-purchased storefront in the Cedar-Riverside area. In our meeting last week, you asked me to follow-up with a detailed explanation as to why we feel energy efficiency is the right decision—both for the environment and your company's bottom line. Below I outline Energy Empowerment's three-point rationale.

Each item in the writer's list of reasons starts out with "first," "second," and "third," making the document easy to navigate

First, you and your contractor, Jeff Manko, will find that the process of "going green" is actually quite straightforward, rather than another level of complication to an already complicated renovation process. As you can see from the enclosed chart, we have adapted the guidelines from the EPA's EnergyStar program to make both reconstruction decisions and the purchase of new HVAC systems, insulation, and doors and windows a straightforward process. We will work with Jeff every step of the way to ensure the seamless renovation of the store.

The writer backs up the first reason with evidence

Second, by demonstrating XPressMart's commitment to the environment, you are not only helping reduce your company's carbon footprint, but also attracting today's environmentally-conscious customers. The Cedar-Riverside location, being adjacent to two college campuses, is the perfect place to begin.

The writer backs up the second reason with an appeal to shared values and goals

1-800-555-3984 www.energyempowerment.com

Figure 1.5 (Continued)

 Dean Winfield, May 14, 20XX, page 2

Currently the storefront rates only a 42 on EnergyStar's performance scale. By improving that rating to 75 or above, this location will qualify for an EnergyStar display sticker, which, according to the EPA's Annual Report last year, increases retails sales in urban areas. Between the EnergyStar rating and your focus on sustainable products, expect to attract the interest of all residents of this forward-thinking community.

> The writer provides statistics to reinforce her point

Finally, and perhaps most importantly, rest assured that the costs you put into reconstruction, systems, and other materials will pay for themselves in less than two years. Jeff and I have assembled a preliminary proposal itemizing costs, to which I will add my estimates regarding cost recuperation. However, know that in Energy Empowerment's 12-year history, every store and office renovation project has paid for itself remarkably quickly. As a recent example, consider our recent small office renovation in Columbia Heights, which recouped its costs in only
14 months.

> The writer closes with the most important reason and backs it up with an appeal to a common financial goal

If I can answer any further questions, please do not hesitate to email me at rgarrido@esi.com or call me (extension 646). Again, we applaud your commitment to the environment and look forward to working with you and Jeff.

> The writer closes in a friendly manner but retains a persuasive tone

Best regards,

Rosemary Garrido
Executive Manager

cc: Jeff Manko, Manko Construction
Encl. Energy Star's performance chart

Common Types of Technical Documents

1.4 Recognize typical technical documents.

The variety of typical technical documents

Many of you probably encounter the following types of documents routinely, either through work or school. You may also be asked to produce such documents for a class, an internship, or your job.

- **Memos.** Organizations use memos as the primary means of internal written communication. Unlike a conversation, a memo leaves a record for future reference. An employee might write a memo to a manager requesting a pay raise; a team of students might write a memo to an instructor explaining their progress on a term project; or an office manager might write a memo to company employees to outline the new vacation policy. Most memos are sent out via email (either as an attachment or as a stand-alone email message).

- **Email.** Email is the main way people communicate in today's workplace. Email is used widely to communicate with clients, customers, suppliers, and associates worldwide. Email messages are sometimes written more informally than paper memos or letters, but in the workplace, most writers recognize that email must maintain a similar level of professionalism to other formats.

- **Letters.** Letters, especially on company letterhead, offer a more formal way to communicate than email or memos. As a student, you might write a letter to request research data or to apply for a summer internship. At work, you might use a letter format to persuade a client to invest in a new technology or to explain the delay in a construction project.

- **Instructions.** Instructions explain the steps or course of action for completing a specific task such as how to use a fire extinguisher. Instructions come in various formats: online instructions may be accessible from the help menu of an app; brief instructions may be written on single-page reference cards; longer instructions may be part of a more comprehensive user manual.

- **Procedures.** Procedures are similar to instructions in that they explain how to perform a task step by step; however, procedures are different in that they usually deal with matters of company or organizational policy. Many companies maintain standard operating procedures (SOPs) for tasks such as how to test soil samples or how to access corporate databases.

- **Manuals.** Almost every technology product or service comes with a manual. Manuals may include instructions on how to assemble, set up, and use a product, but they also include background information, such as technical specifications or lists of materials. Most people have used manuals to perform tasks such as connecting the components of your sound system or setting up the voice mail on your office phone system. Most manuals are available in hard copy and for digital download.

- **Brochures.** To market goods or services, companies produce brochures. Brochures from professional organizations such as the American Medical Association may define various medical conditions, explain the causes, and describe available treatments. Many government agencies create brochures to help with issues such as how to obtain student loans or how to start a small business.

- **Proposals.** Proposals offer solutions to problems and make specific recommendations for how to implement those solutions. A proposal's purpose is usually to persuade readers to improve conditions, accept a service or product, or otherwise support a plan of action. Proposals are often written in response to calls for proposals (CFPs) or requests for proposals (RFPs). For example, a nonprofit child-care facility may seek safer playground equipment, or a pharmaceutical company may wish to develop a new online education program for its employees. These organizations would issue RFPs, and each interested vendor would prepare a proposal that examines the problem, presents a solution, and defines the process and associated fees.

- **Reports.** Reports, both short and long, are generally based on the study of a specific problem or issue. Some reports are strictly informative ("Why Smartphone Batteries Can Explode"); other reports recommend solutions to urgent problems ("Recommended Security Measures for Airline Safety"); and still others have an overtly persuasive goal, advocating a particular course of action ("Why Voters Should Reject the Nuclear Waste Storage Facility Proposed for Our County").

Technical Communication is Global, Collaborative, and Digital

1.5 Understand the global, collaborative, and digital nature of technical communication.

In the workplace, the documents we create have global implications, are typically written not by one individual but in teams, and are created using digital technologies and distributed electronically. These concepts are described here and apply across all chapters and assignments in this book.

Technical Communication is Global

Employees who work across different continents, countries, and cultures must pay special attention to various customs and values. Key to this practice is the idea of "face saving." No one wants to be embarrassed in public, have his or her traditions or values criticized, or be treated with disrespect. (All these situations represent what is sometimes called a loss of "face.") But people in different cultures have different views about what is embarrassing or insulting. For example, in some cultures a "tell it like it is" approach is considered rude, while in others body language such as leaning back in your chair and crossing your arms signals disrespect.

Why global issues are important in today's workplace

Do your
research on
international
business culture

If you are working on a team project and the team spans different countries and cultures, do some research to learn about your team members, to appreciate their frame of reference, and to establish common ground. You may find, for example, that your team members in another country value a slower, more patient approach or put a value on oral communication (by phone or video conference) rather than written communication at certain stages of the project.

Remember
that any
document may
be transmitted
globally

Any document can reach across the globe. For example, the instructions you write for a new cell phone may well end up on a Web site, where they will be used by customers worldwide. Some international readers of your instructions may be offended by commands in strongly worded imperative forms, such as "STOP: Do not insert the storage card until you reach Step 3." Or they may be baffled by icons and other visuals that have no meaning in their culture.

Documents may originate in English but then be translated into many other languages. In these cases, writers must be careful to use English that is easy to translate. Idioms, humor, and analogies are often difficult for automated as well as human translators, and so these items should as a rule be avoided when writing technical documents

For more advice on global communication, see the following Strategies.

Strategies

for Global Technical Communication

- **Learn as much as possible about the culture and background of your team members or customers.** Search online for information from credible sources that can help you understand the communication norms for the countries or cultures with which you will be working.
- **Be respectful and considerate.** Do nothing that will cause anyone to feel embarrassed in front of the group.
- **Avoid the use of humor, slang, and idioms.** These items are culturally specific, do not translate well, and could be misunderstood by nonnative audiences.
- **Avoid stereotyping.** Violating a person's cultural frame of reference is offensive, but so is reducing individual complexity to a laundry list of cultural stereotypes. Any generalization about a culture is just that—a generalization. People are still individuals and should be respected as such.

Technical Communication is Collaborative

Teamwork is a
frequent part
of technical
communication

Complex technical documents (especially long reports, proposals, and manuals) are rarely created by one person working alone. In the workplace, such documents are typically produced by teams of writers, engineers, scientists, graphic artists, editors, reviewers, marketing personnel, lawyers, and other professionals.

Characteristics
of effective
in-person and
virtual teams

Teams can work in person or virtually. Usually, though, teamwork involves a combination of face-to-face meetings and technology-facilitated exchanges, such as those via the phone, email, or the Web. Whether the team shares information in person or virtually, members have to find ways of openly sharing their ideas, expressing their views persuasively, giving and accepting constructive criticism, and reaching agreement with others who hold different views. Teamwork is successful only when there is strong cooperation, a recognized team structure, and clear communication. The following Strategies explain how to work on a team project systematically.

Strategies

for Organizing a Team Project

- **Appoint a group manager.** The manager assigns tasks, enforces deadlines, conducts meetings, consults with supervisors, and "runs the show."
- **Define a clear and definite goal.** Compose a purpose statement that spells out the project's goal and the plan for achieving the goal. Be sure each team member understands the goal.
- **Identify the type of document required.** Is this a report, a proposal, a manual, or a brochure? Are visuals and supplements (abstract, appendices, and so on) needed? Will the document be made available online, in print, or both?
- **Divide the tasks.** Who will be responsible for which parts of the document or which phases of the project? Who is best at doing what (writing, editing, layout and graphics, oral presentation)? Which tasks will be done individually and which collectively? Spell out—in writing—clear expectations for each team member. Also keep in mind that the final version should display a consistent style throughout, as if written by one person only.
- **Establish a timetable.** A timetable will help the team visualize the whole project, each part of the project, and completion dates for each phase.
- **Decide on a meeting schedule.** How often, where, and for how long will the group meet?
- **Establish a procedure for responding to each other's work.** Will reviewing and editing be done in writing, face to face, as a group, one on one, or online?
- **Develop a file-naming system for various drafts.** Be careful about saving documents. It's too easy to save over a previous version and lose something important. Consider using a document sharing system such as Google drive or Dropbox.
- **Establish procedures for dealing with interpersonal problems.** How will disputes be discussed and resolved (by vote, by the manager, or by other means)? How will irrelevant discussion be curtailed?
- **Select a group decision-making style.** Will decisions be made by the group manager alone, by group input, or by majority vote?
- **Decide how to evaluate each member's contribution.** Will the manager assess each member's performance and in turn be evaluated by each member? Will members evaluate each other? What are the criteria?
- **Prepare a project planning form.** Figure 1.6 shows a sample form you can adapt for your team.
- **Submit regular progress reports.** These reports (see page 265) track activities, problems, and rate of progress.

Running Successful Meetings

Despite the many digital tools available for collaboration (see pages 20–21), if possible you should start your project with an in-person meeting for the entire team. Meetings are usually scheduled for one of two purposes: (1) to convey or exchange

Face-to-face meetings are either informational or decision based

Figure 1.6 Project planning form

Project Planning Form

Project title:
Audience:
Project manager:
Team members:
Purpose of the project:
Type of document required:

Specific Assignments
  Research:
  Planning:
  Drafting:
  Revising:
  Preparing final document:
  Presenting oral briefing:

Due Dates
  Research due:
  Plan and outline due:
  First draft due:
  Reviews due:
  Revision due:
  Progress report(s) due:
  Final document due:

Work Schedule

Team meetings:	Date	Place	Time	Note-taker
#1				
#2				
#3				
etc.				
Mtgs. w/instructor				
#1				
#2				
etc.				

Miscellaneous
  How will disputes and grievances be resolved?
  How will performances be evaluated?
  Other matters (online searches, email routing, online conferences, etc.)?

---

information or (2) to make decisions. Informational meetings tend to run smoothly because there is less cause for disagreement. But decision-based meetings often fail to reach clear resolution because the meeting leader fails to take charge. Running a meeting doesn't mean imposing one's views or stifling opposing views, but it does mean keeping the discussion moving and centered on the issue, as explained in the following Strategies.

Strategies

for Running a Meeting

- **Set an agenda.** Distribute copies of the agenda to participants beforehand: "Our 10 A.M. Monday meeting will cover the following items:..." Spell out each item, set a strict time limit for discussion of each item, and stick to this plan. Use Google drive or a similar document sharing app so everyone has access to the latest version of the agenda.
- **Ask each person to prepare as needed.** A meeting works best when each participant makes a specific contribution. Appoint someone to take notes or minutes, and appoint others to other roles, such as doing background research on a particular topic that will be discussed.
- **Appoint a different "observer" for each meeting.** This person's job is to take notes on what aspects of the meeting did or did not work well.
- **Begin by summarizing the minutes of the last meeting.** This process will ensure that the conversation in this meeting moves beyond what was concluded previously. (For preparing meeting minutes, see pages 272–273.)
- **Give all members a chance to speak.** Don't allow anyone to monopolize. At the same time, encourage quiet members to contribute. If someone is connecting via video or phone, reach out to that person to be sure they are still connected to the meeting.
- **Stick to the issue.** When the conversation strays, politely nudge members back on track.
- **Keep things moving.** Don't get hung up on a single issue. Work toward a consensus by highlighting points of agreement and pushing for a resolution.
- **Observe, guide, and listen.** As the meeting leader, don't lecture or dictate. Instead, take charge by steering the group discussion.
- **Summarize major points before calling for a vote.** Paraphrase what has been discussed to be sure everyone understands the major points and so that clarifications or corrections can be made before the vote.
- **End the meeting on schedule.** This is not a hard-and-fast rule. If you feel the issue is about to be resolved at the meeting's end time, continue. Understand, however, that some participants may need to leave for other appointments.

Identifying and Managing Group Conflicts

Even when all team members have good working relationships and positive attitudes, conflicts still can arise, usually because of the following factors:

- **Interpersonal styles.** People who work on teams often clash because of differences in a range of areas, including personality, working style, cultural norms (see page 18), or ability to take criticism. Some might disagree about exactly what or how much the group should accomplish, who should do what, or who should have the final say. Some might feel intimidated or hesitant to speak out. Certain people may be comfortable with a "just the facts" approach, while others on the team may interpret this style for rudeness.

  Differences that may lead to group conflict

- **Digital communication.** When we communicate via text or email, ideas can be easily misunderstood. The lack of vocal inflection and facial features (such as a smile or frown) can turn what you thought was a humorous comment into a serious insult. Also, because we write more quickly in digital settings, we may not proofread carefully and thus might leave out important information, causing the team to become confused and concerned.

- **Cultural differences.** According to one expert, some cultures value intuition and ambiguity more than hard evidence or data, or they prioritize politeness and personal relationships more than business relationships. Cultures also differ in their perceptions of time. Some are "all business" and like to get directly to the point; others take as long as they feel is needed to weigh the issues and come to carefully considered conclusions (Victor, 233). Finally, cultures differ in their accepted methods of communication, varying in their willingness to express disagreement, question or be questioned, leave things unstated, or use nonverbal language (Victor, 206).

When group conflicts do arise, deal with them directly and openly by using the following Strategies.

Strategies

for Managing Team Conflicts

- **Listen actively.** Perhaps the most constructive way to manage team conflict is to avoid it by *really* listening to others. Listening actively means focusing your attention when people speak, keeping your mind open to what they say, letting them finish before you interject, using direct eye contact and body language that communicates interest, and asking for clarification when genuinely needed. In short, observe the 90/10 rule: listen 90 percent of the time, and speak only 10 percent of the time. As President Calvin Coolidge once said, "Nobody ever listened himself out of a job."
- **Avoid gender and cultural bias.** Respect the fact that men and women must be treated equally as team members, and understand that assertiveness and reserve are qualities of both genders. Also, do not assume that one culture's approach to business, time, or communication is better than that of another.
- **Use technology wisely.** Email is the worst way to resolve a conflict. Find a time for the team to meet in person, or use a video chat or a group phone call.
- **Give everyone a chance to be heard.** Encourage quieter members to speak up, and curtail dominating members from speaking excessively.
- **Take everyone's feelings and opinions seriously.** Don't play favorites. Every team member has something valid to contribute.
- **Don't be afraid to disagree.** Politely let other team members know if you don't agree with their ideas or opinions. Your point of view is as important as anyone else's.
- **Offer and accept constructive criticism.** Criticism focused on helping reach the team's goal, as opposed to seeming like a personal attack, creates an atmosphere of open communication.
- **Find points of agreement with others who hold different views.** Although you might not agree with everyone in the group, find those points on which you do agree.
- **When the group makes a decision, support it fully.** At some point, decisions must be made. If you are outvoted, accept the fact that a vote is binding and that you represent the group as a whole, even if you disagree with the final decision.

Reviewing and Editing the Work of Others

Documents produced in teams must be reviewed and edited extensively. *Reviewing* means evaluating how well a document connects with its audience and meets its purpose. When reviewing, you explain to the writer how you respond as a reader; you point out what works or doesn't work. This commentary helps the writer think about ways of revising. Reviewers typically examine a document to make sure it includes these features:

> The process of reviewing a document

- accurate, appropriate, useful, and legal content
- material organized for the reader's understanding
- clear, easy-to-read, and engaging style
- effective visuals and page design

> Qualities reviewers look for

Editing means polishing a document by making it more precise and readable at the sentence and word level. Editing may happen simultaneously with reviewing, but usually it comes after a document has been reviewed and revised—when the more global considerations of content, organization, style, and design have already been resolved and the editor can focus on more particular details. Editors typically suggest improvements such as these:

> The process of editing a document

- rephrasing or reorganizing sentences
- clarifying a topic sentence
- choosing a better word or phrase
- correcting spelling, usage, punctuation, and so on

> Types of "fixing" that editors do

For a team project, at work or at school, you can each take turns reviewing and editing drafts of the document by using the following Strategies.

Strategies

for Peer Review and Editing

- **Read the entire piece at least twice before you comment.** Develop a clear sense of the document's purpose and audience. Try to visualize the document as a whole before you evaluate specific parts.
- **Focus first on the big picture.** Begin with the document's content and organization. Is the document appropriate for its audience and purpose? Is the supporting material relevant and convincing? Is the discussion easy to follow? Does each paragraph do its job? Do all the visuals serve a distinct and appropriate purpose? Is the design appropriate for this document?
- **Be honest but diplomatic.** Say what you think, but don't merely offer negative comments. Begin with something positive before moving to suggested improvements. Maintain a supportive tone.

- **Explain why something doesn't work.** Instead of "this paragraph is confusing," say "because this paragraph lacks a clear topic sentence, I had trouble discovering the main idea." Instead of "I don't like this visual," say "this visual doesn't work, not only because it is a little blurry, but also because it doesn't add to the discussion."
- **Make specific recommendations for improvements.** Write out suggestions in enough detail for the writer to know what to do. Don't just say "I think you should add a chart here." Instead offer "I think you should add a new chart here to show all the numerical information you've provided in an easy-to-understand visual way."
- **Don't expect everyone to agree with your suggestions.** Even professional editors can disagree. Offer your best advice but don't dictate—others may have better suggestions. If different readers offer conflicting opinions of what needs to be revised, seek your team leader's opinion or take it to a vote.
- **Understand the acceptable limits of editing.** Don't simply rewrite an entire document in your own words. Although changes can range from making a few suggestions and additions to closely editing every paragraph, always preserve the author's original vision and style.
- **Focus next on the particulars.** Once the document has been reviewed and revised for content, organization, style, and design, refine the sentences and word choice—and proofread several times.

Technical Communication is Digital

Digital technology helps teams collaborate

In today's workplace, teams are distributed across different locations, working hours, time zones, and countries. Even within the same local team, some people may work from home while others work mainly from the office. For a school project, you and other team members will probably have very different schedules. For these reasons, technical communication is heavily dependent on digital collaboration. For instance, a draft document might be created in Word and circulated via email. Or, team members may collaborate using a shared drive, such as Google Drive or Microsoft OneDrive. Some organizations use email to send attachments, but others prefer to make the document available on the company's internal server (intranet).

Digital technology combines text, visuals, and sound

Along with the use of digital technologies for collaboration, technical communication also involves the use of digital apps that combine words, images, and sounds effectively. Some documents, such as formal letters, rely heavily or solely on words; other documents, such as instructions, blend words with pictures or diagrams. Technical training documents, such as certain types of procedures, may contain embedded video links.

The following technologies are used regularly in technical communication:

Virtual collaboration technologies

- **Teleconferencing.** The oldest form of virtual collaboration—still very much in use—occurs when multiple callers hold a conference via the telephone.
- **Email.** The most popular app for workplace communication, email is used for sending attachments and keeping track of ideas and discussions among team members and individuals.
- **Instant messaging (IM).** IM is a fast and easy way to hold a real-time conversation among multiple people, as long as they are all logged in.
- **Project management software.** Most large organizations use dedicated software, such as Microsoft Project, to manage complex team projects.

- **Editing software.** Editing tools allow multiple users to see each other's edits (which are tagged by the user's initials) and to accept or reject those changes. An example is Microsoft Word's "track changes" feature.
- **Digital whiteboards.** These tools provide a large screen that allows participants to write, sketch, and erase from their own computers in real time.
- **Web conferencing.** A password-protected Web site provides the medium for this more contemporary version of teleconferencing.
- **Blogs.** Blogs allow people to create postings or add comments to previous postings as a way for teams to share and refine ideas.
- **Intranets.** Intranets are sites set up for internal company use only. Readers can access files, documents, and other content.
- **Wikis.** Wikis can be set up to allow access only to those directly involved in the project. When a team member edits a document, a new version is created and old versions saved.

For more on digital communication, see Chapters 18–21.

Checklist

for Effective Technical Communication

- ❑ Does my document focus on the reader, not the writer?
- ❑ Is the document efficient and accessible?
- ❑ Is the document clear and easy to understand?
- ❑ Does the document give readers what they need?
- ❑ Have I used the appropriate media to convey my message?
- ❑ Have I created the document to address a global audience as needed?
- ❑ Am I able to work as part of a team?
- ❑ Is the document sufficiently persuasive to get the response I want?
- ❑ Is the document based on careful research?
- ❑ Does the document achieve its primary purpose (i.e., inform, instruct, persuade)—or a combination of purposes?

Global Considerations

- ❑ Do I understand the communication customs of the international audience for my document?
- ❑ Is my writing clear and direct so that it is easy to translate?
- ❑ Have I avoided idioms, humor, and slang?
- ❑ Have I avoided stereotyping different cultures and groups of people?
- ❑ Is the communication about this project respectful to everyone?

Collaborative Considerations

- ❑ Has our team appointed a team manager?
- ❑ Does the team agree on the type of document required?

❑ Do we have a plan for how to divide the tasks?
❑ Have we established a timetable and decided on a meeting schedule?
❑ Do we have an agenda for our first meeting?
❑ Are we using the project planning form (page 16) to help us get organized?

Digital Considerations

❑ Have we decided which apps we will use for our collaboration (Google Drive; Microsoft OneDrive; other)?
❑ Do we know which digital features our document requires (text only; text plus images; video) and how it will be distributed (online as a downloadable PDF; as a Word file stored on the company Intranet)?

Applications

General Applications

1. Write an email to your boss, requesting that the company pay your tuition for this class. Explain how the class will help you be more effective on the job. Proofread your email: Is it too long or too short? Is the tone professional or demanding? Did you write from your perspective or the reader's (your boss)?

2. Find an example of an informational document or a set of instructions or a persuasive letter. Identify in your document the features of effective technical writing discussed in this chapter. Discuss your findings in class.

Team Applications

1. Class members will work together often this semester. So that everyone becomes acquainted, your task is to introduce to the class the person seated next to you. (That person, in turn, will introduce you.) Follow this procedure:
   a. Exchange with your neighbor whatever personal information you think the class needs: background, major, career plans, communication needs of your intended profession, and so on. Each person gets five minutes to tell her or his story.
   b. Take careful notes; ask questions if you need to.
   c. Take your notes home and select only what you think the class will find useful.
   d. Prepare a one-page memo telling your classmates who this person is. (See page 172 for memo elements and format.)
   e. Ask your neighbor to review the memo for accuracy; revise as needed.
   f. Present the class with a two-minute oral paraphrase of your memo and submit a copy of the memo to your instructor.

2. Write a short memo to your instructor describing the role of teams in a company, organization, or campus group where you have worked or volunteered. Your memo should address questions such as what type of projects your team worked on, how the teams were organized, what worked, and what did not work.

Global Application

Technical documents are often read by international audiences. Some companies handle this issue by translating their documentation into multiple languages; other companies use a combination of words and pictures or just pictures. Find an example of technical communication written for an international audience. You might look at the instructions that came with your computer, cell phone, unassembled bookshelves, or other products (or look online for similar instructions). Write a short memo explaining what techniques the writer used to make the information useful for people who may not speak English or who speak English as a second language.

Digital and Social Media Application

Use the Internet to research examples of technical communication that are common in your profession or major. For example, if you are studying electrical engineering, what are the typical types of reports you might need to write when you get a job? See if you can find a sample report or other document that relates to your major. Using the Checklist for Effective Technical Communication on pages 21–22, evaluate whether this document appears to be effective. Write a memo to your instructor explaining your findings. Include the Web address or other information about how to locate the document online.

Chapter 2
The Research Process in Technical Communication

 Learning Objectives

2.1 Apply critical thinking to every stage of the research process.

2.2 Understand the difference between primary and secondary research.

2.3 Locate, identify, and assess the reliability and credibility of secondary sources.

2.4 Consult primary sources via unsolicited inquiries, informational interviews, surveys, and observations.

Chapter Outline

Thinking Critically About Research   25
    Strategies for Thinking Critically about Research   26
Primary Versus Secondary Sources   27
Exploring Secondary Sources   27
    Strategies for Finding Credible, Reliable Secondary Sources   32
Exploring Primary Sources   33
    Strategies for Informational Interviews   34
    Strategies for Surveys   36
    Checklist for Doing Research   38
Applications   38

All technical communication requires some degree of research, even if that research merely entails checking a fact or consulting a colleague before writing a memo, letter, or email. This chapter explains how to conduct more complex research for such technical documents as long reports and proposals. As you read, consider how research in technical communication often differs from research conducted in an academic setting.

Thinking Critically About Research

2.1 **Apply critical thinking to every stage of the research process.**

Most major decisions in the workplace are based on careful research, often with the findings recorded in a written report, in a long memo, in some combination of documents typically available online (as a Web site or as a PDF document), in hard copy, or both. The types of research you will perform as a technical communicator depend largely on your workplace assignment.

Research is a vital part of technical communication

    Not all findings will be of equal value. For instance, if you really want to know how well the latest invention in robotic surgery works, you need to check with sources other than the inventor (from whom you could expect an overly optimistic or insufficiently critical assessment). Likewise, if you only consult material published more than 10 years ago and don't consult any updated sources, you are not likely to get a current and balanced view. Further, if you interpret your findings inaccurately—say, by ignoring a study that contradicts your viewpoint or claim—your research will be invalid.

Why critical
thinking is
essential in
research
Whether you work with your own findings or the findings of other researchers, you need to decide if the information is reliable. Then you need to decide what your information means. *Critical thinking* means that you test the quality of your information and the accuracy of your interpretations. Instead of accepting information at face value, you examine, evaluate, verify, analyze, and weigh alternatives during every stage of your research. You use critical thinking to examine your evidence and your reasoning to discover new connections and new possibilities and to test the soundness of your conclusions. Critical thinking is especially important when evaluating content from online sources (to be discussed later in this chapter). The following Strategies provide specific guidelines.

Strategies

for Thinking Critically about Research

- **Ask the right questions.** To get the right answers, start by asking the right questions. Instead of researching an overly general topic that will lead to an enormous variety of information, such as "genetically modified foods," ask a specific, narrowed question, such as "Are all genetically modified foods harmful to human health?"
- **Explore a balance of views.** Consider your research topic from a variety of angles. Don't just consult one expert because experts may disagree. Instead, find out what multiple experts say, and examine the points on which the experts agree and disagree.
- **Explore your topic in sufficient depth.** Different sources of information represent different levels of detail and dependability. At the surface layer is information that is widely available and designed for everyday readers, such as newspapers and news programming (on TV and online), most Twitter feeds, Facebook pages, and many Web sites. This surface information may be useful and valid, but you should also go further and explore deeper levels, such as trade and business publications, online resources intended for experts, and specialized literature (peer-reviewed journals as well as credible Web sites from professional associations and government sources).
- **Evaluate your sources.** The information you find may be incomplete or misleading. While you can't always verify that a source is trustworthy, you can weed out unreliable sources by looking for common ground among sources, by determining if any of these sources are driven by an agenda, and by checking the source's credentials. Increasingly, most online content will at first glance look and sound credible, but be sure to do more digging on the background of the organization that sponsors the content, the date of publication, and any reviews or commentary on this source and its underlying approach to facts and information.
- **Interpret your findings objectively.** Examine what you've uncovered from multiple angles. Do your findings support only one viewpoint, or are there several ways to interpret these findings? Remember that although our social media feeds often make it appear that there are only two sides to any issue ("us and them," for example), most topics, especially technical ones, can be viewed from more than two perspectives. If your research yields indefinite findings, don't try to force a definite conclusion. A wrong conclusion is worse than an indefinite one.

Primary Versus Secondary Sources

2.2 Understand the difference between primary and secondary research.

Primary research means getting information directly from the source by conducting interviews and surveys and by observing people, events, or processes in action. *Secondary research* means getting information secondhand by reading what other researchers have compiled in books and articles (in print or online or both). Most online information would be considered a secondary source. Online information requires increased scrutiny on the researcher's part; because almost anyone can create a Web page or online document that looks credible, researchers need to evaluate the source carefully. For instance, a Web site created by a high school student might be interesting but not overly reliable, whereas a site that is the equivalent of a traditional secondary source (research index, well-established news source, peer-reviewed journal, scientific or technical database or wiki) will be more reliable for your research.

How primary and secondary research differ

Whenever possible, combine primary and secondary research. Typically, you would start by using secondary sources because they are readily available and can help you get a full background understanding of your topic. However, don't neglect to add your own findings to existing ones by doing primary research. Working with primary sources can help you expand on what other people have already learned and add considerable credibility to your work. For instance, assume your boss asks you to write a report about how successfully your company's new product is being received in the marketplace: you might consult sales reports and social media (Yelp, Facebook) reviews of the product (secondary research), but you might also survey actual product users and interview some of them individually (primary research).

Why you should combine primary and secondary research

Exploring Secondary Sources

2.3 Locate, identify, and assess the reliability and credibility of secondary sources.

Research assignments begin more effectively when you first uncover and sort through what is already known about your topic before attempting to add to that knowledge yourself. To locate existing research and information on your topic, start with secondary sources such as books; journal, magazine and news media articles; government publications and other public records; professionally conducted surveys and interviews; blogs and wikis; and Web sites. These sources may be available online, in print, or both. Make sure the sources are credible and reliable (see the Strategies box on pages 32–33).

Types of secondary sources

How to Locate Secondary Sources

Secondary sources such as the ones described above can be located by using various search tools. The two most common ways of locating secondary sources are searches done through a library and searches done using Google.

Locate
secondary
sources by using
the library

- **Library searches.** Public libraries as well as college and university libraries offer a range of search tools you can use to find secondary sources related to your topic. It can be helpful to start by meeting with a librarian to get an overview of how to use the library's online public access catalog (OPAC) and to get some help in narrowing your search. Library searches will yield books, articles, and other materials available in that library as well as from other libraries via interlibrary loan. You can access the library's OPAC from a computer located at the library or, if the library is set up for remote access, via the Web.

Locate
secondary
sources by using
Google

- **Google searches.** Google searches through millions of pages of content, including Web pages, government documents, online news sites, blogs, wikis, Twitter feeds, social media pages, and more. Google also has a large collection of digitized books (Google Books) and a specialized search for academic articles (Google Scholar). Google is a good way to start your search, but be careful to narrow your findings to credible, reliable sources and then to use these sources as a basis for more focused research (such as library research for books and peer reviewed reports or articles).

Types of Secondary Sources

GENERAL COMMERCIAL, ORGANIZATIONAL, AND ACADEMIC WEB SITES. Google and other search engines locate a wide range of material, most of which will be commercial (.com), organizational (.org), and academic (.edu) Web sites. If the content within a commercial site looks directly relevant to your search, consider using it, but think critically about the information presented. Does the fact that the company is likely trying to sell you something affect the content? Be careful also of organizational Web sites that may be well researched but have a particular social or political agenda. Are the opinions expressed by the organization designed to sway you to their agenda? Academic Web sites tend to be credible. However, some academics may also have biases, so never stop thinking critically about what you find on the Web.

GOVERNMENT WEB SITES.   Most government organizations (local, state, and federal) have a Web site and online access to research and reports. Examples include the Food and Drug Administration's Web site, which offers information on food recalls, clinical drug trials, and countless related items. State and local sites provide information on auto licenses, state tax laws, and local property and land issues. From some of these sites you can link to specific government-sponsored research projects. Be sure to check the dates of reports or data you locate on a government Web site, and find out how often the site is updated.

ONLINE NEWS OUTLETS AND MAGAZINES.   Most major news organizations offer online versions of their broadcast and print publications. Examples include online versions of newspapers such as the *New York Times* and the *Wall Street Journal*, CNN, and National Public Radio. Major magazines, such as *Time, Newsweek, Forbes*, and other more specialized magazines also offer Web versions. Some news is available online only, as in the online magazines *Slate* and *Salon*. To locate these publications, do a Google search on the publication name.

Make sure you understand how the publication obtains and reviews information. Is it a major news site with careful editorial scrutiny and wide respect, or is it a less reputable site that looks great on the surface but is run by a special-interest group that takes wide liberty with the facts?

BLOGS.   *Blogs* are used by journalists, commentators, and others to post ideas and opinions about a wide range of topics. Postings and replies are displayed in reverse chronological order, with the newest topic first. Older posts can usually be viewed via an index or link. Links chosen by the owner also supply ways to connect to other blogs on the same or similar topics. Blogs are great for finding current information from individuals, companies, and nonprofit organizations that are knowledgeable about particular topics. You will find more blogs than you can use, so you need to evaluate the information on individual blogs carefully and decide which ones are most relevant and reliable.

Keep in mind that blogs nearly always represent the particular views of the blog author (whether an individual, company, organization, or academic institution) and of those who reply to the blog postings. Check any information you find on a blog against a professionally edited or peer-reviewed source.

WIKIS.   *Wikis* are sites that are used to collect information and keep this information updated. Most wikis allow readers to add to or edit content. The most popular wiki is *Wikipedia*; the theory behind Wikipedia is that if the information from one posting is wrong, someone else will correct it, and over time the site will reach a high level of accuracy and reliability. Keep in mind, however, that many wikis have no oversight. Aside from a few people who determine whether to delete articles based on requests from readers, wiki content may not be checked by editors for accuracy. Always confirm information you find on a wiki against several other peer-reviewed or traditional sources. See Chapter 19 for more on blogs and wikis.

ONLINE FORUMS AND EMAIL LISTS.   For almost any topic imaginable, you will find a forum or discussion group, either on the Web site for the company or organization or on sites such as Reddit, Google groups, Yahoo groups, or even some Facebook pages. Large technology companies such as Apple and Microsoft offer Web-based discussion forums to help customers solve technical problems; health-related sites such as WebMD offer forums on specific illnesses and conditions. Email lists allow you to subscribe to a discussion related to a specific topic and receive regular emails in your inbox. As with blogs, you will find more forums and email lists than you could ever possibly use, so choose with care, especially when reviewing forums that are not moderated or subject to other editorial scrutiny.

DIGITAL LIBRARIES AND COLLECTIONS.   Entirely searchable online, digital libraries and collections can be excellent research tools. Aside from the online sites sponsored by most public libraries, one notable digital library is the Internet Public Library, a partnership between seven major research universities. HathiTrust, also a partnership between several major research libraries, offers millions of digitized books and other documents. The Internet Archive is another site offering digitized and archived materials, including its "WayBackMachine," which searches through all current and past versions of Web pages and other online materials. Balance your use of digital libraries with your own college or university or public library to be sure your search is yielding all possible findings related to your topic.

PERIODICAL DATABASES. Almost all libraries have their own Web site where, if you are a library cardholder or a student, you can access a wide variety of periodical databases. Periodical databases are electronic collections of articles from newspapers, magazines, journals, and other publications. You can search these databases by title, author, keyword, and so on.

When searching a periodical database, narrow your search when you get too many hits or expand your search if you don't find enough relevant material. Once you have typed in your keyword(s), you will be presented with a citation page that includes some or all of the following information: author(s), title, source, subject area, abstract (a brief summary of the article), ISSN (International Standard Serial Number—an identifier for the article much like a book's ISBN), and DOI (or Digital Object Identifier—where the article can be found in digital format).

Some of the most popular general periodical databases include *InfoTrac, NewsBank, ProQuest*, and *EBSCOHost*, but there are also many specialized periodical databases in a variety of subject areas to which your library may also subscribe.

Before initiating a periodical database search, try to meet with your local reference librarian for a tour of the various databases and the instructions for searching them effectively. Also, be aware that some databases may not be accessible from school or home—you may need to visit your library in person.

HARD COPY BOOKS AND PERIODICALS. Any library will be well stocked with books as well as numerous print copy magazines, journals, and newspapers. The smaller and more general the library you visit, the less likely you are to find highly specialized print sources; the larger or more specialized the library, the more likely you are to find books by specialist publishers and periodicals that delve into more specific subject areas. Some older publications may be available on CD-ROMs and microfiche, but as time goes on, these publications continue to be digitized.

When consulting books and periodicals, be sure to check the copyright date and supplement the source with additional information from more recent sources, if necessary.

REFERENCE WORKS. Reference works are general information sources that provide background and can lead to more specific information. Reference works may be available in hard copy but increasingly these publications are also (or only) available online. Because most of these secondary sources are available only by subscription, you'll most likely need to access these at the library (although a number of the reference works mentioned here are accessible for free via the Internet Public Library or other sites, so be sure to check). Always look for the copyright date to make sure you are accessing the most current information available. The following items represent typical reference works you might access.

- **Bibliographies.** Bibliographies are lists of books or articles by subject field. To locate bibliographies in your field, begin by consulting the *Bibliographic Index Plus*, a list (by subject) of major bibliographies, which indexes more than 500,000 bibliographies worldwide. You can also consult such general bibliographies as *Books in Print* or the *Reader's Guide to Periodical Literature*. Once you have narrowed your topic, you can consult specific subject area bibliographies topics ranging from engineering to medicine to history (and more).

- **Indexes.** Book and article bibliographies may also be referred to as indexes. However, other types of indexes collect information not likely to be found in standard bibliographies, such as indexes to conference proceedings (e.g., the *Index to Scientific and Technical Proceedings*), which collect the most current information in various fields not yet published in book or periodical form; patent indexes (e.g., the *Index of Patents Issued from the United States Patent and Trademark Office* and the *World Patents Index*), which collect cutting-edge technological descriptions not yet widely available to the public; and technical report indexes (e.g., *Scientific and Technical Aerospace Reports*), which also collect current information unavailable elsewhere.

- **Encyclopedias.** Encyclopedias are alphabetically arranged collections of brief articles. Wikipedia, discussed previously, is the most popular online encyclopedia; its entries are edited by a wide range of readers, both expert and nonexpert. Other encyclopedias, such as *Encyclopedia Britannica* or the *Columbia Electronic Encyclopedia*, are subject to a more traditional editorial process and are not always available online except with a subscription. Once you've narrowed your idea, you can consult more specific subject-focused encyclopedias, such as *Encyclopedia of Nutritional Supplements* or the *Encyclopedia of Business and Finance*.

- **Dictionaries.** Dictionaries are alphabetically arranged lists of words, including definitions, pronunciations, and word origins. If you can't locate a particular word in a general dictionary (e.g., a highly specialized term or jargon specific to a certain field), consult a specialized dictionary, such as *Dictionary of Engineering* or the *Dictionary of Media and Communication Studies*. Online dictionaries vary widely in their currency and detail; most researchers prefer the *Merriam-Webster* version.

- **Handbooks.** Handbooks offer condensed facts (formulas, tables, advice, examples) about particular fields. Examples include the *Civil Engineering Handbook* and *The Electrical Engineering Handbook*.

- **Almanacs.** Almanacs are collections of factual and statistical data, usually arranged by subject area and published annually. Examples include general almanacs such as the *World Almanac and Book of Facts* or subject-specific almanacs such as *Baer's Agricultural Almanac*.

- **Directories.** Directories provide updated information about organizations, companies, people, products, services, or careers, often listing addresses and phone numbers. Examples include *The Career Guide: Dun's Employment Opportunities Directory*; *Hoover's Company Capsules* (for basic information); and *Hoover's Company Profiles* (for detailed information).

- **Abstracts.** Abstracts are collections of summaries of books or articles, as you might find when searching a periodical database, but collected in one place. Abstracts can save you from having to track down a journal before deciding whether to read or skip the article. Abstracts usually are titled by discipline: *Biological Abstracts, Computer Abstracts,* and so on. For current research, you might consult abstracts of doctoral dissertations in *Dissertation Abstracts International.*

GRAY LITERATURE. Some useful printed information may not be available at any library. This content is known as "gray literature"—content that is not formally published and not usually catalogued in the library. Examples include pamphlets and brochures (e.g., medical pamphlets or company marketing materials); unpublished government documents (available under the Freedom of Information Act, with the exception of classified documents); papers presented at professional conferences; and self-published works. You can track down gray literature by looking at the Web sites for various organizations to see if brochures or the like are accessible and downloadable. You can also contact organizations to ask if they have anything available in your subject area. For instance, you might email a professional organization asking for papers on your topic delivered at its recent annual conference. Before doing so, know your research topic well and know specifically whom to contact and what you are looking for. Keep in mind that similar to some Web sites, gray literature is often not carefully scrutinized for content by editors. Therefore, the material may not be reliable and should be backed up by information from other sources.

Strategies

for Finding Credible, Reliable Secondary Sources

- **Use more than one approach when searching.** Google is a good starting point, but as you search, continue to narrow your topic and refine your search terms. Try Google Scholar, Google Books, and Google Images. Balance these searches with focused searches using the library's tools and apps, and be sure to work with a reference or research librarian: These highly skilled professionals can help you understand what you are finding and teach you a thing or two about searching through the many, many sources you will find and determining what's credible and reliable versus what is not.
- **When searching, select keywords or search phrases that are varied and technical rather than general.** Some search terms generate more useful hits than others. In addition to "electromagnetic radiation," for example, try "electromagnetic fields," "power lines and health," or "electrical fields." Specialized terms (say, "vertigo" versus "dizziness") offer the best access to reliable sites. Still, check the source of the site and look for peer-reviewed or edited content (journal articles; reporting from credible news sites) to corroborate your findings.
- **Consider the domain type (where the site originates).** Standard domain types in the United States include .com (commercial organization), .edu (educational institution), .gov or .mil (government or military organization), .net (general usage), and .org (organization). A commercial site may be biased and thus not as credible as, say, an educational or research site. By finding and comparing information across different domains, you can begin to determine where the information is in conflict and where the information tends to agree.

- **Identify the source's purpose and sponsor.** Is the intent of a particular source merely to relay information, to sell something, or to promote an ideology or agenda? The purpose and sponsor might alert you to a bias or a hidden agenda. A .com site might provide accurate information but also some type of sales pitch. An .org site might reflect a political or ideological bias. Looking for a source's sponsor can also help you evaluate the content. For example, a Web site about genetically modified organisms (GMOs) by an organization called the Non-GMO Project may contain useful information but may also be biased toward one point of view, so you would want to balance this source with other information.

- **Look beyond the style of a source or site.** Sometimes, the most reliable material resides in less attractive, text-only publications, such as very plain Web sites or text-based books. Even though we tend to evaluate source credibility based on the way information looks, remember that a highly professional looking Web site, report, news item, or book is easy to create but that the look of the information does not necessarily indicate reliable content.

- **Assess the currency of the source and its materials.** When was the material created, posted, and updated? Many Web sites have not been updated in months or years. On social media, old news stories are often recirculated and people are all too willing to share the post before checking to discover that the story is actually from many years ago. Less credible online news sites bury the date at the bottom of the page, or in small print, so that readers are drawn into the headline and pictures and do not notice that the story is too old to be credible.

- **Assess the author's credentials and assertions.** Check the author's reputation, expertise, and institutional affiliation (university, company, environmental group). For Web-based sources, follow links to other sites that mention the author. Check to see if this author is only published in small, niche publications that cater to extreme viewpoints or if the author is widely published in edited, peer-reviewed sources. Where, on the spectrum of expert opinion and accepted theory, does this author fall? Is each assertion supported by solid evidence? Verify any extreme claim through other sources, such as a professor or expert in the field. Consider whether your own biases might predispose you to accept certain ideas.

- **Don't discount social media but don't rely on it, either.** Facebook, Twitter, Reddit, and other social media sites may provide some credible secondary source content (for instance, if a company representative makes a statement about a new product release), but typically these sources are more like starting points—places where you might read about a topic and get the gist of what people are discussing. You should then use these insights to research a balance of solid, credible secondary sources.

Exploring Primary Sources

2.4 **Consult primary sources via unsolicited inquiries, informational interviews, surveys, and observations.**

Once you have explored your research topic in depth by finding out what others have already uncovered (secondary sources), supplement that knowledge with information you uncover yourself by doing primary research. Primary sources include unsolicited inquiries, informational interviews, surveys, and observations or experiments.

Types of primary sources

Unsolicited Inquiries

The most basic form of primary research is making simple unsolicited inquiries. Letters, phone calls, or email inquiries to experts can yield information that adds to, clarifies, or supplements information you already have. When making an unsolicited

Unsolicited inquiries uncover basic but important information inquiry, be sure you contact the right individual or individuals. Don't just contact a company or department. Also, prepare your ideas in advance, and ask exactly what you need to know rather than vague, general questions. As best as you can determine, ensure that what you ask is not confidential or otherwise sensitive.

Unsolicited inquiries by phone can be intrusive. Therefore, start with a polite, professionally worded email or private social media message (such as via LinkedIn or Facebook) to ask if the person would be interested in communicating with you about your research. If the person says *yes*, ask their preference for the communication (email, phone, Skype). Be prepared to limit yourself to one or two questions that don't require extensive research or thought on the part of the person or persons you contact.

Informational Interviews

Informational interviews provide original source material

An excellent primary source of information is the informational interview, a solicited and extended form of inquiry. Much of what an expert knows may never be published. Therefore, you can uncover highly original information by spending time with someone and asking pertinent questions. In addition, an interviewee might refer you to other experts or sources of information.

Expert opinion should be balanced with a range of views

Of course, an expert's opinion can be mistaken or biased to some extent. Like patients who seek second opinions about serious medical conditions, researchers should seek a balanced range of expert opinions about complex problems or controversial issues—not only from a company engineer and environmentalist, for example, but also from independent and presumably more objective third parties such as a professor or credible, experienced journalist who has studied the issue. See the following Strategies for advice on effective interviews.

Strategies

for Informational Interviews

- **Know exactly what you're seeking.** Write out a purpose statement. For example, "The purpose of my interview with Leslie Brown, clinical nutritionist, is to ask about her latest research on the possible links between certain genetically modified foods and childhood attention deficit disorder."
- **Do your homework.** Learn all you can about the topic beforehand. Conduct a search about the person's professional credentials and his or her area of expertise. If the interviewee has published anything relevant, read it. Be sure your questions don't simply repeat the questions already answered in this person's published materials.
- **Request the interview at your respondent's convenience.** Find a time, location, and method (Skype; Google chat; phone; in person) that works best for your respondent. Ask whether the person objects to being quoted or recorded. If possible, email your questions beforehand.
- **Make each question clear, specific, and open-ended.** Don't ask vague or general questions, and avoid questions that can be answered with a mere *yes* or *no*. Get the benefit of the interviewee's elaboration.

- **Avoid loaded questions.** A loaded question invites or promotes a particular bias. For example, don't ask, "In what ways do you think the hazards of genetically modified foods have been overstated?" Ask impartial questions instead, such as "In your opinion, have the hazards associated with genetically modified food been accurately stated, overstated, or understated?"

- **Save the most difficult, complex, or sensitive questions for last.** Leading off with your toughest questions might annoy interviewees, making them uncooperative for the remainder of the interview.

- **Be polite and professional.** If you are meeting in person, arrive on time, express your gratitude, and explain why you believe the interviewee can be helpful and how you will use the information. If you are meeting via Skype or another form of online communication, test your settings beforehand and make sure your technology is working properly.

- **Let your interviewee do most of the talking.** Be a good listener. This courtesy ensures that the interviewee will provide the most information with the least interruption or leading from you.

- **Ask for clarification if needed, but do not put words in the respondent's mouth.** Questions such as "Could you go over that again?" or "What did you mean by that word?" are fine, but do not impose erroneous conclusions. Instead, paraphrase what the interviewee said so that she or he can verify your interpretation.

- **Stick to your interview plan.** If the interviewee wanders off topic, politely nudge him or her back on track (unless the information is useful).

- **Ask for closing comments.** Questions such as "Would you care to add anything?" or "Do you feel you've said what you wanted to say?" give the interviewee a chance to elaborate and clarify, and you may end up with useful additional information.

- **Ask for permission to follow up.** Additional questions may come to mind later, so find out if your interviewee would be willing to help with those new questions and, if so, what method is best (email, for example).

- **Invite the interviewee to read your version of the interview.** Inviting feedback in this way prevents you from possibly misquoting or misinterpreting the answers.

- **End on time and thank the interviewee.** Don't drag the interview on longer than the interviewee expected. Be sure to thank the interviewee for his or her time (and follow up with an email doing the same).

- **As soon as possible, transcribe your notes or recordings.** Get the interview down in writing before you forget important details.

Surveys

Surveys help you form impressions of the concerns, preferences, attitudes, beliefs, or perceptions of a large, identifiable group (a *target population*) by studying representatives of that group (a *sample*). While interviews allow for greater clarity and depth, surveys offer an inexpensive way to get the viewpoints of a large group. Respondents can answer privately and anonymously—and often more candidly than in an interview.

Surveys provide multiple fresh viewpoints on a topic

The tool for conducting surveys is called a *questionnaire*. When you send the questionnaire, include a cover memo. See Figure 2.1 for an email cover memo that is professionally worded, concise, and brief. Using email allows you to attach the questionnaire as an attachment.

Use the following Strategies to plan a survey and to develop a questionnaire.

Strategies

for Surveys

- **Seek out expert assistance to design the questionnaire.** A subject matter expert (for example, a professor of soil science if your topic is about groundwater levels) can help you create questions that are technically accurate. A survey design expert (for example, a researcher in the social sciences who designs questionnaires for a living) can help ensure that you have the right number of questions and the right sample size (see next item).
- **Define the survey's purpose and target population.** Ask yourself, "Why is this survey being performed?" "What, exactly, is it measuring?" "How much background research do I need?" "How will the survey findings be used?" and "Who is the exact population being studied?"
- **Identify the sample group.** Determine how many respondents you need. Generally, the larger the sample surveyed the more dependable the results (assuming a well-chosen and representative sample). Also determine how the sample will be chosen. Will participants be randomly chosen? In the statistical sense, *random* does not mean "haphazard." A random sample means that each member of the target population stands an equal chance of being in the sample group.
- **Define the survey method.** Decide how the survey will be administered—by phone, by mail, or online. Each has its benefits and drawbacks. Phone surveys yield fast results and high response rates; however, they take longer than written surveys, many respondents find them annoying, and respondents tend to be less candid when speaking with someone in person. Mail surveys are less expensive than phone surveys and promote candid responses, but many people won't bother taking a trip to the mailbox or post office to return the survey, and results can be slow to arrive. Online surveys, conducted via sites such as SurveyMonkey or by emailing an attachment, are the least expensive and yield quick results, but you need to build in features to be sure the same person only responds to the survey one time (online survey tools are helpful with this aspect).
- **Decide on the types of questions.** Questions can be open-ended or closed-ended. Open-ended questions ("How much do you know about genetically modified food products?") allow respondents to answer in any way they choose. Data gathered from open-ended questions are time-consuming to measure, but they provide rich information. Closed-ended questions ("Are you concerned about genetically modified food products? Yes/No") do not allow respondents to elaborate on their responses. Data from closed-ended questions are easily measured but more limited in value.
- **Develop an engaging and informative introduction.** Thank the respondents; persuade them that the questionnaire relates to their concerns and that their answers matter; provide directions for completing the survey; and ensure the anonymity of respondents. See Figure 2.1.
- **Phrase questions precisely.** Vague phrasing will only lead to inaccurate answers and findings. Avoid combining questions or asking the same basic question more than once.
- **Avoid loaded questions.** Do not invite or advocate a particular point of view or bias.

Observations and experiments offer proof to back up assumptions about a topic

Observations and Experiments

Observations or experiments should be your final step because you now know exactly what to look for.

Observations are firsthand examinations of people, processes, places, and so on, using only your senses. When you make observations, have a plan in place. Know

Figure 2.1 A Questionnaire Cover Email for a Questionnaire

Dear Mr. Duda:

Thank you for responding to my previous email and agreeing to participate in my research project. I am exploring ways to enhance relationships between the University of Massachusetts Dartmouth (UMD) Professional Communication Program and our local business community. Specific areas of inquiry include the following:

— Keep the introductory sentence short

- the communication needs of local companies and industries
- the feasibility of on-campus and in-house seminars for employees
- the feasibility of expanding communication course offerings at UMD

— Use bullets or a numbered list for ease of reading

Please take a few minutes to complete the attached questionnaire; it is formatted as an interactive PDF file. If you have any problems with the file, please let me know and I will provide the document in a different format. You may return the document to me at lstaylor@umd.procom.edu

Your response will provide an important contribution to my study. All respondents will receive a copy of my final report, scheduled to appear in the fall issue of *The Business and Industry Newsletter*. Thank you.

— Be polite and professional in tone

L.S. Taylor, Technical Communication Student, UMD

SOURCE: Microsoft Outlook 2013.

how, where, and when to look, and jot down your observations immediately. If you are observing in a public setting, you may wish to take photos or videos of what you observe.

Experiments are controlled forms of observations designed to verify assumptions (e.g., the role of fish oil in preventing heart disease) or to test something untried (e.g., the relationship between background music and productivity). Each field has its own guidelines for conducting experiments (e.g., you must use certain equipment, scrutinize your results in a certain way), and you must follow those guidelines to the letter when you conduct your own experiments.

Remember that observations and experiments are not foolproof. When making an observation or performing an experiment, you may be biased about what you see (focusing on the wrong events, ignoring something important). In addition, if you are observing people or experimenting using people as subjects, they may be conscious of being observed and may alter their normal behaviors.

Checklist

for Doing Research

- ❏ Have I maintained a high level of critical thinking while researching?
- ❏ Have I asked the right questions?
- ❏ Have I considered a balance of views?
- ❏ Have I explored my topic in sufficient depth?
- ❏ Have I evaluated each source for credibility and reliability?
- ❏ Have I interpreted my sources objectively?
- ❏ Have I conducted searches effectively, combining Google searches with library searches?
- ❏ Have I used critical thinking to assess online secondary sources?
- ❏ Have I supplemented findings from secondary sources with primary research whenever possible?
- ❏ Have I added my own findings to existing findings whenever possible?
- ❏ Have I kept careful and precise track of each source I am using?

Applications

General Applications

1. Locate an expert in your field or your major for an upcoming project (such as a long report). Email that person and arrange for an interview. Follow the Strategies on pages 34–35. Discuss your interview experiences and your findings with classmates.

2. Use the following two approaches to locate research articles for your field or topic. First, conduct a Google search and then narrow your search using Google Scholar. Next, use your library's search tools to locate two to three of the articles you found; download PDF versions of these articles if possible. Write a one-page summary describing your search process and your findings. Cite your sources and create a Works Cited (MLA) or References (APA) page (see Appendix A).

Team Application

In groups of three people, select a topic that might be suitable for one of the later assignments in this class (for example, a topic that could be used for the final proposal or formal report). Individually, each person should start a search using Google, then Google scholar, then your college or university's online library search tool. Keep track of the time spent in each search, compare the ease of searching and quality of results obtained from each type of search on your group's selected topic. Which approach yielded the most current sources? Which provided abstracts and full texts as well as bibliographic data? Which provided the most dependable sources? Which provided the most diverse or varied sources? Prepare a short report, and present your findings to the class.

Global Application

Global research can be easy to locate using social media. For example, you can visit the Facebook page and Twitter feed for the World Health Organization (WHO) and look for links to recent publications and studies. See if you can locate an actual study (hint: you will probably end up at the WHO Web site and their publications section). Download the information and review it carefully. With a focus on the international scope of the issue addressed in the study, create a list of questions you might ask of the publications' author(s) during an informational interview. Write a cover email that you would use to request that interview.

Digital and Social Media Application

Select two to three Web or social media sites related to a research project for this or another class. Compile a working list of criteria based on these sites, then work as a group to expand your list. For example, do you consider good design to be an indicator of credibility? What else do you look for when assessing the relevance, currency, and validity of information on a particular site? How do you know if a site is commercially or politically biased? Present your results in class and compare the findings of the different small groups.

Chapter 3
Providing Audiences with Usable Information

3.1 Analyze a document's audience.

3.2 Determine a document's purpose.

3.3 Identify the persuasive elements involved.

3.4 Write a task analysis for a document.

3.5 Consider a document's setting, potential problems, length, format, timing, and budget.

3.6 Create an information plan for a document.

3.7 Understand the stages in writing, testing, revising, and proofreading a document.

Chapter Outline

Analyze the Document's Audience   42
    Strategies for Analyzing Your Audience   46
Determine the Document's Purpose   46
Know How to Be Persuasive   47
    Strategies for Persuasion   51
Create a Task Analysis for the Document   51
Consider Other Related Usability Factors   53
Develop an Information Plan for the Document   54
Write, Test, Revise, and Proofread the Document   56
    Strategies for Proofreading   57
    Checklist for Usability   57
Applications   58

A document's *usability* is a measure of how well that document fulfills the information needs of its audience. Whatever their specific goals and concerns in using a particular document, readers must be able to do at least three things (Coe, *Human Factors* 193; Spencer 74):

Definition of usability

- Locate the information they need easily.
- Understand the information immediately.
- Use the information safely and successfully.

What a usable document enables readers to do

To assess the usability of a manual that comes with your new gas grill, for instance, you would ask: "How well do these instructions enable me to assemble, operate, and maintain the grill safely and effectively?" To prepare a usable document, follow these six steps:

1. Analyze the document's audience.
2. Determine the document's purpose.
3. Create a task analysis for the document.
4. Consider the setting, potential problems, length, format, timing, and budget.
5. Develop an information plan for the document.
6. Write, test, and revise the document.

Steps in preparing a usable document

Analyze the Document's Audience

3.1 Analyze a document's audience.

You cannot create an effective document until you first explore all you can about *who* will use your document. In other words, understand your audience. Ask these questions:

Questions to ask to analyze a document's audience

- Who is the main audience for this document?
- Who else is likely to read it?
- What is your relationship with the audience? Are there multiple types of relationships involved?
- How familiar might the audience be with technical details?
- What culture or cultures does your audience represent?
- What media format (printed manual; PDF available online; interactive Web page) is best for this audience?

Answer these questions by considering the suggestions in the sections that follow, and by filling in the audience portion of the Audience and Purpose Profile Sheet shown in Figure 3.1 before writing any technical documents. Also, have a look at the Strategies for Analyzing Your Audience on page 46.

Primary and Secondary Audiences

Determine the primary and secondary audiences

When writing a technical document, keep two audiences in mind. Most documents are geared to an immediate audience. This is your *primary audience*. For instance, a set of instructions for installing new project management software for an office might

Figure 3.1 Audience and purpose profile sheet

Audience

Primary audience:_____(name, title)

Secondary audience(s): _____

Relationship with audience members: _____

_____(client, employer, other)

Technical background of audience: _____

_____(layperson, expert, other)

Cultural background of audience:_____

Purpose

Primary purpose: _____(inform, instruct, persuade)

Secondary purpose(s): _____

Intended use of document: _____

_____(master concepts, follow directions, other)

be directed primarily at the information technology (IT) support staff who would be doing the installing. But most documents also have a *secondary audience*—those outside the immediate circle of people who will be needing the information directly. For example, a secondary audience for software instructions might be managers, who will check to see if the instructions comply with company policy, or lawyers, who will make sure the instructions meet legal standards.

Relationship with Audience

Besides identifying the primary and secondary audiences in a general way, you also need to understand your relationship with everyone involved. Are the primary readers of your document going to be superiors, colleagues, or subordinates? Determining which will help you decide the level of formality and authority to use in the document. Are they going to be from inside or outside your organization? Answering this question will help you to decide how confidential you need to be. Do you know your readers personally? This information can help you decide if you can adopt a more informal tone. Are they likely to welcome or reject your information? Knowing the answer will help you decide how persuasive you need to be. Are they a combination of people from various levels, both inside and outside the company? This knowledge will help you to determine how evenhanded your writing needs to be. Also, how might you speak to the needs of secondary audience members, who may be interested in or affected by your document?

Determine your relationship with the audience or audiences

Audience's Technical Background

Any message can be conveyed in numerous ways, depending on how it is written and designed for different audiences. For example, information about a new cancer treatment may appear in a medical journal for health care professionals, in a textbook for nursing or medical students, or in a newspaper article for the general public. In each of these situations, a document's technical level needs to use words and images at the right level for the intended audience.

Be aware of your audience's technical background

For example, an audience of medical professionals will understand technical terms readily; an audience of medical and nursing students will have some familiarity with such terms but will be in the process of learning; and the general public may not understand technical terminology at all. Thus, articles written for each of these audiences will differ in terms of word choice, content, organization, illustrations, and page design.

Consider the technical level of your general target audience

The broader the audience, the more you must consider the various levels of expertise and language differences. For example, medical professionals can be divided into subgroups of specialists and general practitioners; medical and nursing students can be divided into subgroups based on years of training; and the general public can be divided into subgroups who read popular medical journals and those who have little or no familiarity with medical information. For the general public, even highly technical information is increasingly accessible online. Readers with little to no training may access specialized research reports and other information once available only to experts. In cases where you can't be certain about the range of audiences who might read your document online, you can provide links directing readers to information written for people with different levels of technical expertise.

Consider the technical level of your specific target audience. One example of how to write and structure technical information for different audiences is visible on the Web site for the U.S. Food and Drug Administration (FDA). Figure 3.2 shows the main FDA page, which, in the upper right corner, offers links for readers from a wide range of backgrounds and levels of technical expertise ("For Consumers;" "For Patients;" "For Health Professionals;" "For Scientists and Researchers;" "For Industry"). People who click on "For Consumers" can search through many options on topics of importance, written using non-technical language. For example, consumers who click on links about childhood vaccinations will encounter the information you see in Figure 3.3, which is written in nontechnical language, uses short sentences, and refers to ideas that most if not all consumers will understand. But people who click on the "For Scientists and Researchers" icon will instead see information using more technical, expert language including a "compendium of analytical laboratory methods for food safety" or "health informatics." Drilling down further into these categories, scientists will find even more technical information. In this way, the writers for this Web site have adapted the information to the different technical levels and needs of specific audiences.

Figure 3.2 FDA main page

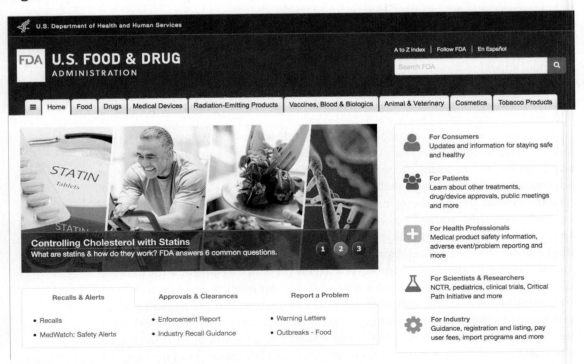

SOURCE: U.S. Department of Health and Human Services.

Figure 3.3 Excerpt of an article on the FDA "for Consumers" page

Steps to Take When Your Child Is Vaccinated

Review the vaccine information sheets

These sheets explain both the benefits and risks of a vaccine. Healthcare professionals are required by law to provide them.

Talk to your healthcare professional about the benefits and risks of vaccines.

Learn the facts about the benefits and risks of vaccines, along with the potential consequences of not vaccinating against diseases. Some parents and caregivers are surprised to learn that children can be harmed or die of measles, diphtheria, pertussis, and other vaccine-preventable diseases.

Before vaccination, inform your healthcare professional of these conditions.

This might include being sick or having a history of certain allergic or other adverse reactions to previous vaccinations or their components. For example, eggs are used to produce many influenza (flu) vaccines; therefore, it is important to inform your healthcare professional if your child is severely allergic to eggs.

The packaging of some vaccines that are supplied in vials or prefilled syringes may contain natural rubber latex, which may cause allergic reactions in latex-sensitive individuals. Let your healthcare professional know about an allergy to latex. It is also extremely important to discuss with your healthcare professional which vaccines should or should not be given to children who have a weakened immune system.

Report adverse reactions

Adverse reactions and other problems related to vaccines should be reported to the Vaccine Adverse Event Reporting System, which is maintained by FDA and the Centers for Disease Control and Prevention (CDC). For a copy of the vaccine reporting form, call 1-800-822-7967, or report online to www.vaers.hhs.gov

This article appears on FDA's Consumer Updates page, which features the latest on all FDA-regulated products.

SOURCE: U.S. Department of Health and Human Services.

Audience's Cultural Background

Information needs and preferences often are culturally determined. Although it is not possible to generalize about an entire group of people from a particular culture or country, international communication experts have noted some characteristics can be helpful. German audiences, for example, often value thoroughness and complexity with detail included and explained in a businesslike tone. Japanese audiences generally prefer multiple perspectives on the material, plenty of graphics, and a friendly, encouraging tone (Hein 125–26). Western business culture generally values plain talk that gets right to the point, but Eastern cultures may consider this rude, preferring indirect, more ambiguous messages that leave interpretation up to the reader. The more you can learn about your specific readers for your specific document or information, the more you can consider how cultural differences might create misunderstanding in your situation and seek an approach that bridges these differences.

Consider the audience's cultural background

Strategies

for Analyzing Your Audience

- **Picture your readers and exactly what they need and expect.** Whether your audience is the company president or the person next to you in class, that person has specific concerns and information needs. Your readers may need to complete a task, solve a problem, make a decision, evaluate your performance, or take a stand on an issue.

- **Identify the primary and secondary audiences, your relationship to them, and their technical and cultural background.** Remember that if your document will be widely available via the Internet, you may need to add an explicit audience statement ("this material is written for the following audiences…") and/or provide links that direct people of different technical backgrounds to information suited for their background and needs.

- **When you don't know exactly who will be reading your document, picture the "general reader."** General readers are impatient with abstract theories yet expect enough background to help them grasp your message. They are bored or confused by excessive detail and frustrated by raw facts left unexplained or not interpreted. Instead of trying to show readers how smart you are, make *them* feel smart. Whoever they are, readers need enough material to understand your position and to react appropriately.

- **Anticipate readers' questions.** Based on their needs and concerns, readers have questions: What is it? What does it mean? What happened? Who was involved? When, where, and why did it happen? What might happen? How do I do it? How did you do it? Why is X better than Y? Can you give examples? Says who? So what? Give readers what they need to know.

- **Recognize that audiences are not merely passive recipients of information.** Technical communicators and their audiences should overlap and interact. Therefore, as you analyze and learn about your audience, remember that the communication process works both ways, especially in online settings where readers are invited to leave feedback and ask questions. Use this information to refine and update your document based on what you learn from these readers.

Determine the Document's Purpose

3.2 Determine a document's purpose.

To create an effective technical document you need to understand *how* readers will use it. In other words, determine your purpose. Ask these questions:

Questions to ask to determine a document's purpose

- What is the main purpose of the document?
- What other purpose or purposes does the document serve?
- What will readers do with this information?

Answer these questions by considering the suggestions in the sections that follow and by filling in the purpose portion of the Audience and Purpose Profile Sheet shown in Figure 3.1 before writing any technical document. You can revise this Audience and Purpose Profile Sheet to suit your particular project, situation, and document.

Primary and Secondary Purposes

All forms of technical communication are intended to fulfill a specific *primary purpose*. As discussed in Chapter 1, the primary purpose (to inform, to instruct, or to persuade) will affect the document's overall shape and substance.

Many documents have a primary purpose and one or more *secondary purposes*. For example, the primary purpose in most instruction manuals is to instruct; that is, to teach an audience how to assemble or use the product. But for ethical and legal reasons, companies also want people to use the product safely. A manual for a power tool or a lawnmower, for instance, typically begins with a page that spells out safety hazards before instructing readers how to assemble and use the mechanism.

In planning a document, work from a clear statement of purpose that takes into account both the primary and secondary purposes. For example, "The purpose of my document is to inform my readers of the new absentee policy and to instruct them on how to follow the procedures properly," or "The purpose of my document is to inform my readers about the new antivirus software as well as to instruct them on how to install the software and to persuade them of the importance of running weekly virus scans."

Decide if the primary purpose of the document is to inform, instruct, or persuade

Determine if the document serves any secondary purposes

Always write a comprehensive purpose statement

Intended Use of the Document

In addition to determining purposes of a document from your own perspective, also consider how and why it will be used by others. Answer a variety of questions: Do my readers simply want to learn facts or understand concepts? Will they use my information in making some decision? Will people act immediately on the information? Do they need step-by-step instructions? In my audience's view, what is most important about this document? How and where will they use the document (outdoors while trying to assemble a new gas grill or tool shed? On their computer or phone as a PDF document while trying to fix a flat tire or install new software?) In addition to asking yourself these questions, try asking members of your audience directly, so you can verify what they want to know and where and how they will use the document.

Determine how the document will be used

Know How to Be Persuasive

3.3   Identify the persuasive elements involved.

In the workplace, we rely on persuasion daily: to win coworker support, to attract clients and customers, to request funding. An email, a memo, a product description, or a set of instructions can be an implicitly persuasive document. Even the most complex report, which at first glance may appear to be "all facts," can be persuasive because the writer probably shaped the report to favor a particular interpretation of the data.

Changing someone's mind is never easy—in fact, sometimes it is impossible. Your success will depend on what you are requesting, who you are trying to persuade, and how entrenched those people are in their own views.

Why persuasion is difficult

Using Claims as a Basis for Persuasion

Explicit persuasion is required whenever you tackle an issue about which people disagree. Assume, for example, that you are Manager of Employee Relations at Softbyte, a software developer whose recent sales have plunged. To avoid layoffs, the company is trying to persuade employees to accept a temporary cut in salary. As you plan your various memos and presentations on this volatile issue, you must first identify your major claim or claims (a claim is a statement of the point you are trying to prove).

For example, in the Softbyte case, you might first want employees to recognize and acknowledge facts about which they may have been unaware or have ignored:

A claim about
what the facts
are

Because of the global recession, our software sales in two recent quarters have fallen nearly 30 percent, and earnings should remain flat all year.

Even when a fact is obvious, people often disagree about what it means or what should be done about it. And so you might want to influence their interpretation of the facts:

A claim about
what the facts
mean

Reduced earnings mean temporary layoffs for roughly 25 percent of our staff. But we could avoid layoffs entirely if each of us at Softbyte would accept a 10 percent salary cut until the market improves.

And eventually you might want to ask for direct action:

A claim about
what should be
done

Our labor contract stipulates that such an across-the-board salary cut would require a two-thirds majority vote. Once you've had time to examine the facts, we hope you'll vote "yes" on next Tuesday's ballot.

As you present your case, you will offer support for your claims before you finally ask readers to take the action you favor.

Whenever people disagree about what the facts are or what the facts mean or what should be done, you need to make the best case for your own view by presenting an argument that is not only well supported but that also connects with your audience.

Connecting with Your Audience

Determine how best to connect with your audience. Persuasive people know when to simply declare what they want (get the reader to *comply* with what you say), when to reach out and create a relationship (get the reader to *identify* with what you say), when to appeal to reason and common sense (get the reader to *internalize* what you say), and when to employ some combination of these approaches (Kipnis and Schmidt 40–46). These three approaches, respectively, can be labeled the *power connection*, the *relationship connection*, and the *rational connection*, as illustrated in Figure 3.4.

To get a better understanding of these three different approaches, consider the following scenario: Your Company, XYZ Engineering, has just developed a fitness program based on findings that healthy employees work better, take fewer sick days, and cost less to insure. This program offers clinics for smoking cessation, stress reduction, and weight loss, along with group exercise.

Figure 3.4 Three approaches for connecting with an audience

In your second month on the job, you read this notice in your email:

TO: Employees at XYZ.com

FROM: GMaximus@XYZ.com

DATE: June 6, 20xx

SUBJECT: Physical Fitness

On Monday, June 10, all employees will report to the company gymnasium at 8:00 a.m. for the purpose of choosing a walking or jogging group. Each group will meet for 30 minutes three times weekly during lunch time.

Power connection

How would you react to the previous notice? Despite the reference to "choosing," the recipients of this memo are given no real choice. They are simply ordered to show up at the company gymnasium. Typically used by bosses and other authority figures, this type of approach does get people to comply, but it also almost always alienates them.

Suppose instead you receive this next version of the memo. How would you react in this instance?

TO: Employees at XYZ.com

FROM: GMaximus@XYZ.com

DATE: June 6, 20xx

SUBJECT: An Invitation to Physical Fitness

I realize that most of you spend your lunch hour on your phone, reading, or just enjoying a bit of well-earned relaxation in the middle of a hectic day. But I'd like to invite you to join our lunchtime walking/jogging club.

Relationship connection

We're starting this club in the hope that it will be a great way for us all to feel better. Why not give it a try?

This second version conveys the sense that "we're all in this together." Instead of being commanded, readers are *invited* to participate in the exercise program. Someone who seems likable and considerate offers readers a real choice.

Often, the biggest variable in a persuasive message is the reader's perception of the writer. Readers are more open to people they like and trust. The relationship connection often works for this reason, and it is especially vital in cross-cultural communication—as long as it does not sound too "chummy" and informal to carry any real authority.

Of course, you would be unethical using a relationship connection merely to hide the fact that you have no evidence to support your claim (R. Ross 28). People need to find the claim believable ("Exercise will help me feel better") and relevant ("I personally need this kind of exercise").

Here is a third version of the memo. As you read, think about the ways in which its approach differs from the first two examples.

TO: Employees at XYZ.com

FROM: GMaximus@XYZ.com

DATE: June 6, 20xx

SUBJECT: Invitation to Join One of Our Jogging or Walking Groups

Rational connection

I want to share a recent study from the *New England Journal of Medicine*, which reports that adults who walk two miles a day could increase their life expectancy by as much as three years.

Other research shows that 30 minutes of moderate aerobic exercise, at least three times weekly, has a significant and long-term effect in reducing stress, lowering blood pressure, and improving job performance.

As a first step in our exercise program, XYZ Engineering is offering a variety of daily jogging groups: The One-Milers, Three-Milers, and Five-Milers. All groups will meet at designated times on our brand-new quarter-mile, rubberized clay track.

For beginners or skeptics, we're offering daily two-mile walking groups. For the truly resistant, we offer the option of a Monday–Wednesday–Friday two-mile walk.

Coffee and lunch breaks can be rearranged to accommodate whichever group you select.

Why not take advantage of our hot new track? As small incentives, XYZ will reimburse anyone who signs up as much as $100 for running or walking shoes and will even throw in an extra 15 minutes for lunch breaks. And with a consistent turnout of 90 percent or better, our company insurer may be able to eliminate everyone's $200 yearly deductible in medical costs.

This version conveys respect for the reader's intelligence and for the relationship. With any reasonable audience, the rational connection stands the best chance of success.

For more on persuasion, see the Strategies that follow.

Strategies

for Persuasion

- **Identify your specific goal.** What exactly do you want readers to do: change their opinion, change their behavior, or take specific action?
- **Anticipate your audience's reaction.** Typically, when you try to change people's minds or get them to do something, they will naturally resist. Try to address their biggest objections beforehand. Will people be surprised, annoyed, or angry at your attempt? Will they agree with you in essence but want to know further details? Be careful to express your arguments ("We could do better") without making people defensive ("It's all your fault"). Also, be prepared to field negative reactions after your message is delivered and to back off if your message is rejected.
- **Don't ask for too much.** No matter how persuasive you are, if you ask for what seems like too much, your argument will fail. Ask for what your audience will consider reasonable, not outlandish. Consider what is achievable in this situation.
- **Allow for give-and-take.** Be flexible in your argument. Indicate you are able to see your argument from the recipient's point of view, and offer possible alternatives or compromises along with what you want to accomplish.
- **Recognize constraints.** For various reasons other than their personal opinions, recipients may be unable to comply with your request. For example, readers may have time constraints, organizational constraints (deadlines, budgets), legal constraints (agreements, laws), ethical constraints (when the request is legal but not necessarily ethical), and social and psychological constraints (shyness, fear of failure, fear of disruption, fear of the unknown).
- **Consider the cultural context.** How people react to your persuasive appeals may be culturally based. Will some audience members feel that your message ignores customs? Will they be offended by too many facts and figures without a relationship connection? Will they be offended by a direct approach? Remember that cultural groups consist not only of racial and ethnic groups but also groups connected by religious or spiritual views, sexual orientation, physical ability, and so on.
- **Choose the right time and the right medium.** Consider how the timing of your message (just prior to a vacation, during the busy season, during a period of optimism) and the way in which it is delivered (in person, over email, in a printed memo) will affect how positively it is received.
- **Connect with your audience.** Using the power connection may work but will likely alienate your audience; using the relationship connection may appeal to readers but fail to convince them. Whenever possible, use the rational connection or, even better, a rational connection combined with a relationship connection.

Create a Task Analysis for the Document

3.4 Write a task analysis for a document.

Most technical documents entail a series of tasks to be completed, tasks most evident in a set of instructions: If people want to change an oil filter, assemble a new gas grill, or install a new project management app, they must follow a step-by-step procedure. Less obvious is that other documents, such as reports, memos, and brochures, also involve a series of tasks. For instance, when reading a report, a manager may need to extract information and write a response. Similarly, a technician may need to make a persuasive argument as to why the company should purchase new equipment. In short, most technical communication is task-oriented. People come to the information wanting to *do* something, and you want to ensure they achieve their goal; therefore, you need to think through the step-by-step nature of your document before you write it by creating a *task analysis*.

Define main tasks, then subtasks

For your task analysis, you can create a worksheet similar to the one shown in Figure 3.5. Begin by defining the main tasks. For example, in planning an instruction manual to accompany a gas grill, you might start your task analysis by defining the main tasks as "assemble the grill," "use the grill," and "maintain the grill" and then divide these larger tasks into several smaller tasks, or subtasks ("locate all parts," "get the required tools," "lay out parts in order," etc.). Note that both the tasks and subtasks should be listed using active verb forms (*assemble, locate, get,* and so on).

You can determine these tasks by interviewing customers and watching them perform each step to complete the project (Figure 3.6). Your document will be most useful if you know what your audience needs to *do* in order to produce the desired results.

Figure 3.5 Sample task analysis for an instructional manual

Main task: Assemble the grill.
Subtasks
1. Locate all parts.
2. Get the required tools.
3. Lay out parts in order.
4. Assemble parts into smaller units.
5. Assemble these smaller units into large units.

Main task: Use the grill.
Subtasks
1. Attach the gas canister.
2. Turn on the main gas valve.
3. Turn on the individual burners.
4. Press button to ignite.

Main task: Maintain the grill.
Subtasks
1. Turn off the main gas valve when not in use.
2. Cover to protect from rain.
3. Clean the grate regularly.

Consider Other Related Usability Factors

3.5 **Consider a document's setting, potential problems, length, format, timing, and budget.**

Once you've answered questions about audience (*Who?*), purpose (*Why?*), and tasks (*How?*), it's time to consider smaller but no less important factors that influence the usability of your document: setting (*Where?*), potential problems (*What are the hazards?*), length (*How much information?*), format (*Print? PDF? Interactive Web page or app?*), timing (*When?*), and budget (*How much money?*).

Think about setting, potential problems, length, format, timing, and budget

Setting

Will distractions or interruptions make it hard for people to pay attention? Will readers always have the document in front of them? Will they be scanning the document, studying it, or memorizing it? Will they read page by page or consult the document randomly?

Determine where your document will be used

Potential Problems

How might the document be misinterpreted or misunderstood? Are there potential "trouble spots" (material too complex for this audience, hard to follow, or packed with information)? Are any important points missing? Anticipating problems is important in creating any technical document but especially in a set of instructions; therefore, when preparing instructions plan on background research. In planning the gas grill instruction manual, for example, learn all you can about the typical audience for this information (age, education, and so on). If possible, observe first-time operators using the instructions for a previous model and then ask for their feedback. Also, find out how most injuries occur, check company records for customer complaints, get feedback from dealers, and ask your legal department about prior injury claims by customers.

Anticipate what might go wrong

Length

How much information is enough? This depends on what you can learn about your audience's needs. Were you asked to "keep it short" or to "be comprehensive"? Are people more interested in conclusions and recommendations, or do they want everything spelled out? If you can observe people using draft versions of your document, you will quickly be able to see when a section is too long versus when you have not included enough information.

Decide on an acceptable length

Format

Does your audience expect a letter, a memo, a short report, or a long, formal report with supplements (title page, table of contents, appendices, and so on—see pages 294–306)? Can visuals and page layout (charts, graphs, drawings, headings, lists) make the material more accessible? Should the document be made available only in PDF format, online, where readers can make print copies if they wish? Or is there a legal or other reason why you need to include a print copy?

Decide on your document's format

Timing

Consider due
dates and
timing

Does your document have a deadline? Workplace documents almost always do. Is there a best time to submit it? Do you need to break down the deadline into a schedule of milestones? Will any of your information become outdated if you wait too long to complete the document?

Budget

Consider the
budget and
costs

Does your document have a budget? If so, how much? Where can you save money? How much time can your company afford to allot you for creating the document? How much money can you spend obtaining permission to use materials from other sources? How much can you spend on printing, binding, and distributing your document? How much of the budget is dedicated to creating digital documents or a Web site or app to go along with (or take the place of) the document?

Develop an Information Plan for the Document

3.6   **Create an information plan for a document.**

Write out your
plan

Once you have a clear picture of the audience, purpose, tasks, and related factors, you can draft an *information plan:* an outline based on the previous considerations in this chapter. Information plans can be as short as a two- to three-page memo or as long as a multipage report, depending on your project. Begin with a clearly stated purpose statement ("People will be able to assemble a gas grill within 30 minutes") so you can measure when a task has been successfully completed (Rubin 97). Also include information about the audience, tasks, setting, potential problems, length, format, timing, and budget.

Figure 3.6 is a sample information plan created in a short-memo format for the gas grill instructions. Note how this plan takes into account not just audience, purpose, and tasks (each get their own section), but also all the related factors (some of which are implied):

- **Setting.** Although not spelled out, it is understood that people will be reading the instructions while assembling their grills, which the authors have accounted for via the document's simple, lightweight design.

- **Potential problems.** Although safety issues are not given their own subheaded section, the authors have considered safety measures at a number of points.

- **Length.** In the "Rough outline" section, the authors have determined that the instructions will be four pages long.

- **Format.** In the "Rough outline" section, both text and visuals have been carefully considered, page by page.

Figure 3.6 Sample information plan

GrillChef Corporation

To: Technical writing design team
From: Erin Green and Geoff Brannigan, team leaders
Date: January 21, 20XX
Re: Information plan for gas grill manual

As you know, our team recently performed an analysis of user needs as we prepare to design and write the new User Manual for the new GrillChef Model GC-23 double-burner grill. This memo summarizes our findings and presents a plan for proceeding.

Part One: Audience, Purpose, and task analysis

Primary audience: Consumers with a wide range of technical backgrounds (general audience). Most are existing users of gas grills but some are making the switch from charcoal. Audience analysis revealed that regardless of technical background, the majority of customers are nervous about grill assembly. This grill ships to the U.S. and Canada.

Purpose: The primary purpose of this manual is to instruct customers in safely assembling and using their new grill. Secondary purposes include providing customers with adequate safety instructions and all required legal notices, as well as providing contact information (customer support Web site and phone number).

Task analysis: The primary task is grill assembly. In addition, customers need to know how to operate and maintain their grill.

Part Two: Design Plans based on the above analysis

Features: The manual should be easy to use in an outdoor setting and written for a general audience, with technical terms defined and with a balance of text and visuals (line drawings). We can use the older grill model GC-22 manual as a template but revise as per below.

Outline: Cover with drawing of grill, model number, company name.
Inside front cover: safety and legal notices. Note that this page will differ based on shipments to the U.S. or to Canada.
First section: "Assembling Your Grill"—exploded diagram, list of parts, numbered instructions (each instruction accompanied by a visual).
Second section: "Using Your Grill"—Numbered instructions with line drawings as appropriate.
Third section: "Maintaining Your Grill"—List of maintenance tasks based on time (annual and monthly maintenance); Frequently Asked Questions.
Final page: Contact information (company name and address; Web site with link for PDF version of manual).

Production schedule: Manual must be ready for shipment on April 1, 20XX. See project management spreadsheet (on our technical writing Intranet) for breakdown of key deliverable dates. PDF version can be made available prior to print copies. User testing is scheduled for one month prior to final deadline.

- **Timing.** In the "Schedule" section, the authors have not only accounted for the due date but also the various milestones to be reached along the way.
- **Budget.** Under the "Production guidelines" section, the authors note that the budget will not allow for color printing or photographs but that color can be used in the online, PDF version.

Write, Test, Revise, and Proofread the Document

3.7   **Understand the stages in writing, testing, revising, and proofreading a document.**

When your planning is completed, you will be ready to write, test, revise, and proofread your document. For a gas grill manual, you would write the instructions and design the graphics as you've planned and select a medium (print, CD, Web—or some combination) for distributing the information.

Once you have a workable draft, test the document on potential readers, if possible. Ask people what they find useful and what they find confusing. If you have created a draft set of instructions, watch people use the document and measure their ability to perform the task based on what you have written. If someone trying to assemble the gas grill, for instance, could not locate a part because of unclear instructions, knowing about this would be valuable as you revise your material. Ask respondents to identify specific difficulties they encountered in reading the instructions and in performing the task:

Questions for assessing a document's usability

- **Content.** Are there any inaccuracies? Is the level of technicality appropriate to this audience? Are claims, conclusions, or recommendations supported by evidence? Are all key terms defined? Is the material free of gaps, foggy areas, or needless details?
- **Organization.** Is the structure of the document visible at a glance? Is anything out of order or hard to find or follow? Is the material "chunked" into easily digestible parts? Is the material organized in a logical sequence?
- **Style.** Is anything hard to understand, imprecise, too complex, or too wordy? Are sentences put together with enough variety? Is the tone appropriate for the situation? Are words chosen for exactness, not for camouflage?
- **Layout and visuals.** Are there adequate aids to navigation (heads, numbered lists, bullets, type styles)? Are there any excessively long paragraphs, lists, or steps? Are any visuals overly complex or misleading? Could anything be clarified by a visual? Is anything cramped and hard to read?
- **Ethical, legal, and cultural considerations.** Is there any distortion or misrepresentation of facts? Are there any potential legal or safety concerns?

All technical documents should be proofread carefully

Based on feedback, revise your plan and your draft document. Finally, proofread your document carefully. Regardless of how engaging and informative a document is, basic errors distract the reader and make the writer look careless. Proofreading is vital in detecting easily correctable errors such as these:

- Sentence errors, such as fragments, comma splices, or run-ons
- Punctuation errors, such as missing apostrophes or excessive commas
- Usage errors, such as "it's" for "its"; "lay" for "lie"; or "their" for "there"
- Mechanical errors, such as misspelled words, inaccurate dates, or incorrect abbreviations
- Formatting errors, such as missing page numbers, inconsistent spacing, or incorrect form of documenting sources
- Typographical errors (typos), such as repeated or missing words or letters, missing word endings (say, *-s* or *-ed* or *-ing*), or an omitted quotation mark

Follow these Strategies for proofreading and refer to the Brief Handbook (Appendix B) for more information:

Strategies

for Proofreading

- **Save it for the final draft.** Proofreading previous drafts might cause writer's block and distract you from the document's rhetorical features (content, organization, style, and design).
- **Take a break before proofreading your final document.** Revisit your document with a fresh, rested pair of eyes.
- **Work from hard copy.** Research indicates that people read more perceptively (and with less fatigue) from a printed page than from a computer screen.
- **Keep it slow.** Read each word—don't skim. Slide a ruler under each line or move backward through the document, sentence by sentence. For a long document, read only small chunks at one time.
- **Be especially alert for problem areas in your writing.** Do you have trouble spelling? Do you get commas confused with semicolons? Do you make a lot of typos? Make one final pass to check on any problem areas like these.
- **Proofread more than once.** The more often you proofread, the more likely you will catch all errors.
- **Never rely only on autocorrect.** A synonym found by your app's autocorrect function may distort your meaning, and a spell checker cannot differentiate among correctly spelled words such as "their," "they're," and "there" or "nope" versus "hope." In the end, nothing can replace your own careful proofreading.

Checklist

for Usability

- ❏ Have I identified my exact audience (primary and secondary)?
- ❏ Have I identified my relationship with this audience?
- ❏ Have I identified this audience's technical background?

❏ Have I identified the exact purpose of this document (primary and secondary)?
❏ Am I seeking an outcome that is achievable in this situation?
❏ Have I anticipated my audience's reaction?
❏ Have I stated my claim clearly?
❏ Have I supported my claim with convincing evidence?
❏ Have I considered the various constraints and the cultural context?
❏ Have I chosen the approach most likely to connect with my audience?
❏ Have I written a purpose statement?
❏ Do I know exactly how this information will be used and in what format (digital, print, both)?
❏ By creating a task analysis, have I identified the steps involved?
❏ Have I pinpointed the main tasks and the subtasks?
❏ Have I considered the document's setting, potential problems, length, format, timing, and budget?
❏ Have I developed an information plan that outlines all the preceding factors?
❏ After drafting the document, have I tested it with potential readers?
❏ Have I identified any problems in terms of content, organization, style, layout and visuals, and ethical/legal/cultural/persuasive considerations?
❏ Did I make needed revisions based on testing?
❏ Have I proofread the document carefully?

Applications

General Applications

1. Identify an activity that could require instructions for a nonexpert to complete (for instance, someone who has no automotive repair experience might need to change a tire). Prepare a task analysis for this activity similar to the one in Figure 3.6. Exchange your task analysis with another student in your class, and critique each other's work. With your class, discuss the challenges of doing such an analysis and identify strategies for performing a task analysis effectively.

2. Online, find a set of instructions that appear easy to use. Identify specific characteristics of the document, including any persuasive elements, that make it usable. (Refer to the usability questions on page 56 to guide your assessment.) Then find a set of instructions that is hard to use. What characteristics make it unusable? In a memo to your instructor, define specific changes you would make in revising the documents. Submit both examples with your memo.

Team Application

Bring in some children's connecting blocks, such as TinkerToys or Legos. Form teams of four to six people, and assign two people as technical writers. The technical writers should assemble a few of the pieces into a simple design (don't use more than three or four pieces). Then the technical writers should write up a quick instruction card explaining how to assemble the pieces into the design they've created. For example, the card for Lego blocks might read like this:

1. Select two large red blocks and two small green blocks.
2. Place one red block on its side.
3. Attach one green block to the red block.

...and so on. Then present the "parts" and your instructions to team members. Watch as your team tries to assemble the blocks according to your instructions. Assess the instructions for usability. Were all tasks accounted for? Did any terms or language confuse the readers? Would the addition of visuals help? Go back and perform a task analysis, and discuss what you could do to improve the usability of your instruction card.

Global Application

Astronomy and planetary science have become truly global sciences, and space exploration is now conducted by multinational teams. Knowledge about astronomy belongs to everyone, regardless of nationality or language. Do the Web sites representing these disciplines succeed in making themselves accessible to and useful for a global audience?

Explore Web sites such as the Planetary Society, NASA, and the European Space Agency, and assess their usability for international audiences. Would non-English speakers be able to access the information on these sites? What efforts are made to inform and persuade international readers? Are language and cultural differences accounted for in the design, content, and interface?

Draw up a list of key elements and features of each site that contribute to or detract from usability for international audiences. What changes would you recommend to make each site more accessible, usable, and persuasive for non-English readers? Summarize your assessment in a brief memo, including printed copies of specific pages from each Web site that you discuss.

Digital And Social Media Application

Locate a Web site that accommodates various audiences at various levels of technicality. For instance, the U.S. Food and Drug Administration (FDA) is a good source of both general and specialized information, with links for general readers and medical experts alike.

On this or a similar site, locate (a) material aimed at a general audience and (b) material on the same topic aimed at a specialized or expert audience. First, list the features that enabled you to identify each piece's level of technicality. Next, using the Audience and Purpose Profile Sheet, record assumptions about the audience made by the author of the nontechnical version. See if the agency or organization you selected also has a Facebook page; if so, compare the content on Facebook to what you noted for the Web site, and discuss what audience assumptions seem to be involved in changes in word choice, images, and other features.

Chapter 4
Recognizing Ethical Issues in Technical Communication

 Learning Objectives

4.1 Recognize ethical dilemmas and appreciate that they involve many considerations.

4.2 Realize how ethics are often compromised by workplace pressures.

4.3 Avoid various types of ethical abuses.

Chapter Outline

Ethics, Technology, and Communication   61

How Workplace Pressures Affect Ethical Values   62

Recognizing and Avoiding Ethical Abuses   64
  Strategies for Avoiding Ethical Abuses   67
  Checklist for Ethical Communication   67

Applications   68

Technical communication does not occur in a void. It happens in the world of human beings, politics, and social conditions, a world in which we regularly face ethical dilemmas that balance our sense of what is right against a decision that may be more efficient, profitable, or better for the company.

Ethics, Technology, and Communication

4.1   Recognize ethical dilemmas and appreciate that they involve many considerations.

Imagine the following scenario: You work for a company that makes apps to help travelers locate restaurants and hotels. Your team of engineers and technical writers decides that linking the app to a smartphone's maps or GPS would be great for customers. To operate most effectively, however, the app must continue collecting location information in the background, even when the app itself is switched off. Customers could opt out of this feature, but the default setting is for the feature to be on. Your company's legal department has approved. The team wants customers to keep the setting on so that the app works properly. As a technical communicator, your decision becomes less a legal one than an ethical one about customer privacy. Communication about this app (a press release announcing it or online help via the company Web site) plays a central role in this dilemma. Should you, as the technical writer, include this information where it is easily visible to customers (such as on the first page of the user manual), exclude the information completely, or deemphasize this feature by using a small font?

A sample ethical dilemma

These are not simple questions. Taking an ethical stance requires a personal decision on your part as to how to weigh your ethical and moral beliefs against the realities of the job. This stance requires you to consider the effects of your decisions on the people who use your product, on your company, on society at large, and on your job. Sometimes standing your ground on an ethical issue may mean losing your job or suffering retaliation from coworkers.

Ethical decisions involve many considerations

Types of Ethical Choices

Virtually all areas of science and technology are involved in issues of communication and ethics. Here are a few examples:

- *Medical technologies*, such as genetic testing, raise questions about personal privacy and medical insurance.
- *Banking and retail operations*, which increasingly collect personal information on consumers, raise concerns about how this information is used and who has access to it.
- *Environmental pollutants*, such as pesticides or smokestack output, raise serious questions about the long-term health of the planet.

In your own communication, you will often face ethical decisions—about how much information to include, how much to leave out, how to word an issue, or how to shape the information for your audience. Note how the memo from David Michem in Figure 4.1 sounds completely well-reasoned and persuasive. An employee reading the memo, especially one with an existing medical condition, might go straight to the company Web site and sign up for a Medical History Card. But in his desire to make the card program a success, Michem's memo offers employees no information about confidentiality and privacy. Will the company have access to personal and medical information when employees sign up via the Web site? Will the information be encrypted? Will third parties have access to this information? By omitting this information from the memo, Michem has been misleading, as reasonable as his memo may sound. In the end, communication is never neutral but instead always carries some type of consequence.

How Workplace Pressures Affect Ethical Values

4.2   Realize how ethics are often compromised by workplace pressures.

Ethics are often compromised by outside pressure

In the workplace, ethical rules are broken not because people are dishonest but because they feel pressure (about deadlines or sales targets, for example) to bend or break the rules. To save face, escape blame, or get ahead, people often feel obliged to say what other people want to hear or to suppress or downplay bad news. Figure 4.2 depicts how workplace pressures to "succeed at any cost" can influence ethical values.

Why ethics matter

Despite outside pressures, however, it is critical to maintain workplace ethical standards at all times. Unethical decisions can harm a company's reputation and bottom line. More importantly, unethical decisions can compromise the safety and welfare of workers and customers. When an instruction manual is written and vital safety information is purposely omitted to downplay any safety concerns, for example, people can be injured.

Figure 4.1 A document that raises ethical concerns

MEMORANDUM

To: All Employees
From: David Michem, Health Benefits Manager
Date: November 10, 20XX
Subject: Medical history card program

Last week, you received a brochure about the new Medical History Cards (MHCs) available
through the Human Resources Department. I encourage you to enroll in the card program for
a variety of reasons:

- **MHCs ensure that all employees receive safe and efficient health care.** Whether you have
  a serious medical condition, take a prescription medication, have an allergy, or none of the
  above, MHCs instantly provide medical personnel with personalized medical data during an
  emergency or routine visit.

- **The cards are free to all Andrews and McNeel employees.** Any employee at Andrews and
  McNeel—whether full-time, part-time, or contract—may enroll in the program and receive a
  card free of charge.

- **Enrolling in the MHC program is easy.** Simply go to www.andrews-mcneel.com/hr/mhc
  to enroll in the program and fill out the requested personal and medical information to be
  uploaded to your card.

- **MHCs contain much more information than standard medical ID bracelets.** While an
  emergency bracelet may only provide basic information, such as the fact that a person is
  diabetic, MHCs hold your complete medical data, including emergency contact information,
  prescription information, and so on.

- **MHCs are easy to update.** If your medical information changes (for example, you are
  prescribed a new medication or your emergency contact information changes) simply update
  that information online. You will receive a replacement card within 5 business days.

Please take advantage of this program by re-reading your brochure or simply going to the Human
Resources MHC Web page above to learn more. This is an excellent benefit not offered at many
companies. We strongly encourage you to participate.

cc: Elizabeth Sanchirico-Edwards, Director of Human Resources

Note the
misleading
omission of
information
about employee
confidentiality

Figure 4.2 How workplace pressures can influence ethical values

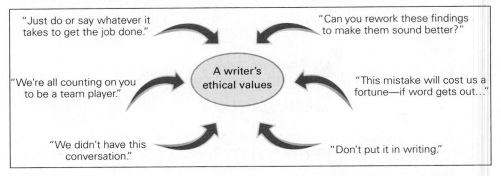

Recognizing and Avoiding Ethical Abuses

4.3   Avoid various types of ethical abuses.

Following are some of the major examples of unethical communication in the workplace.

- **Plagiarizing the work of others.** Technical communicators may feel pressure to produce results quickly and thus may be tempted to cut corners. Workplace plagiarism occurs when a person claims the work of someone else as one's own, without citing or even mentioning the original source. Plagiarism may also happen in collaborative work, as when a team leader claims all the credit for the work of team members.

- **Falsifying or fabricating information.** Outside pressure to produce results may tempt people to distort information. For example, research data might be manipulated or invented by a scientist seeking grant money; researchers whose studies could benefit human health (for instance, studies about new drugs or medical innovations) might feel pressured to release their findings before the data is verified by peer review or additional testing.

- **Suppressing or downplaying information.** Withholding information is just as unethical as supplying false information. For example, a report author may purposely fail to mention an important study that contradicts what he or she wants to prove. Or a company may fail to inform the public about a safety hazard in one of its products—or, if the hazard is revealed, may downplay its importance.

- **Exaggerating claims.** Organizations that have a stake in a particular technology (e.g., bioengineered foods) may be especially tempted to exaggerate its benefits, potential, or safety and to downplay its risks. If your organization depends on outside funding (e.g., the defense or space industry), you might find yourself pressured to make unrealistic promises.

- **Using visual images that conceal the truth.** Images are generally more powerful than words and can easily be created to distort the real meaning of a message. For example, an individual might create a pie chart that paints a more optimistic picture than the data indicate by distorting the sizes of the pie pieces. Or an online ad for a prescription drug may list drastic side effects while showing images of smiling, healthy people, thus downplaying the dangers. Photo editing software makes it especially easy to manipulate images.

- **Stealing or divulging proprietary information.** Information that originates in a specific company is typically the exclusive intellectual property of that company. In theory, such information is legally protected, but it remains vulnerable to sabotage, theft, or leaks to the press. Fierce competition among rival companies for the very latest intelligence gives rise to theft or unethical divulging of such information.

- **Misusing electronic information.** Ever-increasing amounts of personal information are stored in databases (by schools, governments, credit card companies, insurance companies, pharmacies), and all employers, of course, keep data about their employees. How we combine, use, and share all of this electronic information raises questions about privacy. If you are designing a Web site, for example, should you create a page that asks customers for personal information without providing information about how your company intends to use that information? The lack of an easy-to-access privacy policy could be considered an ethical breach.

- **Exploiting cultural differences.** Both individuals and organizations can exploit the vulnerabilities of various cultural groups through manipulation or deception. For instance, one employee of a company might exploit another's English-language limitations for personal gain. So too, an organization might exploit clients for whom the culture places greater emphasis on interpersonal trust than on lawyers or legal wording.

Types of ethical abuses

To avoid ethical abuses, follow the guidelines provided by professional organizations in your field (e.g., see the American Medical Writers Association Code of Ethics in Figure 4.3), and use the Strategies on page 67.

Figure 4.3 A code of ethics from a professional organization

SOURCE: Courtesy of American Medical Writers Association. Used with permission.

Strategies

for Avoiding Ethical Abuses

- **Always cite your sources if the information or data are not your own.** For specific advice on avoiding plagiarism and citing outside sources, see Appendix A.
- **Give the audience everything it needs to know.** Don't bury readers in needless details, but do make sure they get all the facts, including information about online privacy, data sharing practices, sources of the information you publish, and dates of publication.
- **Give people a clear understanding of what the information means.** Even when all the facts are known, facts can be misinterpreted. Try to ensure that readers understand the facts clearly. Provide links to other credible sources if you think people need more information. If you are not certain about your own understanding, say so.
- **Never manipulate information or data in your writing or in your visuals.** If you encounter data that contradict what you want to say, include and interpret those data honestly. Likewise, do not make your case via exaggeration, understatement, sugarcoating, or any other distortion or omission.
- **Follow your company's confidentiality guidelines.** If you suspect information may be confidential, assume it is or ask the appropriate personnel to clarify.
- **Do not exploit cultural inequalities or manipulate international readers.** Try to be fair. When producing a document for an international audience, be especially careful about using simple and honest language and visuals.
- **Constantly ask yourself, "Would I stand behind what I have created if I were held publicly accountable for it?"** If you would not, then chances are what you have written is unethical to some degree. It may be not entirely honest, fair, confidential, or safe.
- **Consult the ethical guidelines for your profession.** Every profession, from the law to medicine to technical writing to engineering, has a professional society and a set of guidelines for ethical behavior. Figure 4.3 presents just one example.

Checklist

for Ethical Communication

Use this checklist for any document you prepare or for which you are responsible.
- ❏ Are the statements in this document fair, accurate, and clear?
- ❏ Will the document be reviewed by the company or organization's legal department?
- ❏ Am I familiar with my company or organization's ethics and privacy standards?
- ❏ Have I researched and reviewed the ethical guidelines for the profession or subject matter area (health, medicine, engineering, banking, manufacturing, other)?
- ❏ Have I avoided exaggerating, distorting, or leaving out any important information?
- ❏ Do I have a clear understanding of the audience for this document (see Chapter 2)?
- ❏ Am I creating a document that represents what these readers need to know or do?
- ❏ Have I conducted enough research (see Chapter 3) to ensure that the document is fact-based and presents a range of perspectives?
- ❏ Have I informed readers about safety and other precautions related to this product or service?
- ❏ Have I avoided plagiarizing or taking credit for the work of others?

- ❏ Has anyone on the team felt pressure to fabricate or falsify information?
- ❏ Do the document's visuals convey information in a truthful way, avoiding any sort of distortions?
- ❏ Have I considered the digital and social media outlets where this document might be published and looked into those sites' privacy policies?
- ❏ Does the document provide contact information (Facebook page, Web site, toll free phone number), in case readers have questions or want more information?

Applications

General Application

Do an online search to locate the professional code of ethics for your major or career. Divide into groups of three or four students, each of whom has a different major. Compare your professional codes, noting similarities and differences. Discuss why each code seems appropriate for that profession. Discuss any recent ethical situations or cases you know about and review how the professional code of ethics may not have been adequate enough to address these situations.

Team Application

In groups of two or three, locate a piece of technical communication (such as an online user manual or a Web site about vaccines or a study about climate change) and evaluate the document's ethical stance. Is the information presented in such a way that ideas or facts are exaggerated or suppressed? Are any cultural issues exploited? Share your thoughts in class, and explain how your team would revise, rewrite, and redesign the information.

Global Application

Counterfeiting, sometimes known as "intellectual property piracy," has become a major point of tension between the United States and many developing nations. Counterfeit products ranging from consumer products (such as high fashion purses and jeans) to cigarettes to cell phones can be found in markets across the globe.

Use the Internet to do some preliminary reading about the problems of counterfeit products. What are the advantages and disadvantages, both economically and politically, of trying to crack down on unauthorized copycat products? Why do some countries do little to police such piracy while others, including the United States, view it as a major priority?

Write a brief report analyzing the ethical issues involved and how these issues influence economic and political settings. Present your findings in a brief oral presentation to your class.

Digital and Social Media Application

Social media creates ethical challenges for the workplace. For example, people use Facebook to post about personal activities and assume this information is only viewable by friends. But during a job interview, a person may be surprised to discover that a posting intended for friends was also discovered by the potential employer. Should the employer have looked at a person's social media postings? Also, the use of content from Twitter or blogs as the basis for workplace decisions could result in unintended consequences if that information turns out to be inaccurate.

Do an online search on "ethics and social media." Select two or three articles or sources from credible sites about workplace communication (for instance, LinkedIn has lots of great articles about how to use social media effectively in the job market). Meet with two other students in class and share your findings. Give a brief presentation in class describing the main points made in these sources.

Part 2
Blueprints

5 Structuring Information for Your Readers 70

6 Writing with a Readable Style 87

7 Using Audience-Centered Visuals 103

8 Designing User-Friendly Documents 123

Chapter 5
Structuring Information for Your Readers

 Learning Objectives

5.1 Recognize the necessity of a standard or varied introduction/body/conclusion structure.

5.2 Create a brief or formal outline.

5.3 Chunk information into discrete units.

5.4 Determine the best sequence for your material.

5.5 Shape each paragraph for effectiveness.

5.6 Create clear headings.

5.7 Provide overviews of longer documents.

Chapter Outline

The Importance of an Understandable Structure 71

Outlining 72

Strategies for Outlining 75

Chunking 77

Sequencing 77

Paragraphing 78

Clarifying Headings 81

Providing an Overview 81

Checklist for Structuring Information 84

Applications 86

To use a familiar architectural metaphor, Part I of this book has focused on the *foundations* of technical communication—the underlying supports on which the technical communication "building" stands. To review, these foundations include: 1) a definition of technical communication; 2) teamwork, ethics, persuasion, and global issues as cornerstones; 3) research as a vital part of the technical communication process; and 4) usability as a key feature of technical communication.

Before producing specific technical documents, you need a set of *blueprints*. This section, Part II, discusses the four components of technical communication blueprints: an understandable *structure* (Chapter 5), a readable *style* (Chapter 6), audience-centered *visuals* (Chapter 7), and a user-friendly *design* (Chapter 8). This chapter focuses on the first of these blueprint components: structure.

> Structure, style, visuals, and design as technical communication blueprints

The Importance of an Understandable Structure

5.1 **Recognize the necessity of a standard or varied introduction/body/ conclusion structure.**

Structure your information in a way that readers can easily grasp. To follow your thinking, readers need a clear path from point *a* to point *b*. This path needs to be obvious as readers scan through your document, looking for its overall structure.

> Your audience comes first

Unfortunately, information rarely materializes—and thinking rarely occurs—in neat, predictable sequences. As you look over your collected information and begin to think about how you will structure it for your readers, you will face questions such as these:

- What relationships do the collected data suggest?
- What should I emphasize?
- In which sequence will readers approach this material?
- What belongs where?
- What do I say first? Why?
- What comes next?
- How do I end?

Although a great deal of thinking goes into the process of answering these types of questions, the result will be worth the effort, as Figures 5.1 and 5.2 illustrate.

Figure 5.1 depicts the standard structure of a workplace document, one that readers will instantly recognize: introduction, body, and conclusion. The introduction attracts the reader's attention, announces the writer's viewpoint, and previews what will follow. The body delivers on the promise implied in the introduction. The body explains and supports the writer's viewpoint, achieving *unity* by remaining focused on that viewpoint and *coherence* by carrying a line of thought from sentence to sentence in a logical order. Finally, the conclusion has various purposes: It might reemphasize key points, take a position, predict an outcome, offer a solution, or suggest further action. Good conclusions give readers a clear perspective on what they have just read and invite readers to do something.

There are, however, many ways of adapting this standard structure: For example, Figure 5.2 provides visual features (columns, colors), headings, and an engaging layout. Although organized differently from the email in Figure 5.1, Figure 5.2 does provide an introduction, a body, and a conclusion: The heading "What is arsenic?" represents a form of introduction. The next several headings answer the question posed in the introduction, forming in essence the body of the document. The final heading, asking about EPA standards, represents a form of conclusion, moving beyond data and description to the topic of policy and use.

Beyond the introduction/body/conclusion structure and its variations, there are other ways to structure information, as discussed below.

Outlining

5.2 Create a brief or formal outline.

Even basic documents require at least an introduction-body-conclusion outline done in your head and/or a few ideas jotted down in list form. Longer documents require

Figure 5.1 Workplace email with a standard introduction/body/conclusion structure

To: Department managers email list
From: Jill McCreary, General Manager
Date: December 8, 20XX
Subject: Social media training initiative

As part of our ongoing efforts to improve Powell & Rabkin's corporate use of social media, we recently conducted an online customer survey to determine what features of our Facebook page were most useful and why. The survey results have been compiled, and we'd like to share a few key results with you in this email.

> *Introduction: announces the topic and provides an overview*

The most important survey result indicates that overwhelmingly (92%), customers state that our Facebook page is the first place they look when checking for special pricing events, sales, and announcements of new product lines. A second reason for checking our Facebook page, stated by 60% of those surveyed, is to find out how other customers are using the products. Those surveyed were particularly interested in learning about innovative solutions that other customers have come up with. A third reason involves checking for recalls or documentation updates. Customers appreciate the feedback they receive from other customers and our company representatives.

> *Body: provides details to support the main topic*

The take-away from this survey is that our Facebook page is now the key component in our marketing and customer service communication. Please review the survey data more closely; you will find this data on the secure server under the "Marketing and Analysis" folder. During next month's annual budget review meetings, we will look for proposals to expand our use of Facebook and other social media platforms.

> *Conclusion: summarizes the main points and asks readers to take action*

a more detailed outline so you can visualize your document overall and ensure that ideas flow logically from point to point.

Start by searching through the information you have gathered and creating a random list of key topics your document should include. For instance, in preparing the arsenic document in Figure 5.2, you might start by simply listing all the information you think readers need or expect:

- explain what the EPA is doing about arsenic in drinking water
- define arsenic
- explain how arsenic gets into drinking water
- list some of the effects of arsenic (stomach, heart, cancer)
- include specific data
- mention/explain the Safe Water Drinking Act
- refer to/define MCLGs

> *Start by creating a list of essential information*

Figure 5.2 Document with a nonstandard but well-organized structure

Visuals, color, and columns make the structure clear

"What is arsenic?" is placed above subsequent sections, indicating that it is the introduction

Three lengthier sections—all of equal importance—are balanced in the middle of the page to indicate the body

"What is EPA's standard" section is placed at the bottom of the page, indicating that it is the conclusion

JUST THE FACTS FOR CONSUMERS

ARSENIC IN YOUR DRINKING WATER

What is arsenic?

Arsenic is a toxic chemical element that is unevenly distributed in the Earth's crust in soil, rocks, and minerals.

How does arsenic get into my drinking water?

Arsenic occurs naturally in the environment and as a by-product of some agricultural and industrial activities. It can enter drinking water through the ground or as runoff into surface water sources.

How is arsenic in drinking water regulated?

In 1974, Congress passed the Safe Drinking Water Act. This law directs EPA to issue non-enforceable health goals and enforceable drinking water regulations for contaminants that may cause health problems. The goals, which reflect the level at which no adverse health effects are expected, are called maximum contaminant level goals (MCLGs). The MCLG for arsenic is 0 parts per billion (ppb).

The enforceable standard for arsenic is a maximum contaminant level (MCL). MCLs are set as close to the health goals as possible, considering cost, benefits, and the ability of public water systems to detect and remove contaminants using suitable treatment technologies.

Why should I be concerned about arsenic in my drinking water?

Although short-term exposures to high doses (about a thousand times higher than the drinking water standard) cause adverse effects in people, such exposures do not occur from public water supplies in the U.S. that comply with the arsenic MCL.

Some people who drink water containing arsenic in excess of EPA's standard over many years could experience skin damage or problems with their circulatory system, and may have an increased risk of getting cancer. Health effects might include:

- Thickening and discoloration of the skin, stomach pain, nausea, vomiting, diarrhea, and liver effects;

- Cardiovascular, pulmonary, immunological, neurological (e.g., numbness and partial paralysis), reproductive, and endocrine (e.g., diabetes) effects;

- Cancer of the bladder, lungs, skin, kidney, nasal passages, liver, and prostate.

What is EPA's standard for arsenic in drinking water?

To protect consumers served by public water systems from the health risks of long-term (chronic) arsenic exposure, EPA recently lowered the arsenic MCL from 50 ppb to 10 ppb.

SOURCE: U.S. Environmental Protection Agency www.epa.gov.

Now you can reorganize this list.

A simple list like the one above usually suffices for organizing a short document like the memo in Figure 5.1. However, for a more complex document, transform your list into a deliberate map that will guide readers from point to point. Create an introduction, body, and conclusion and then decide how you will divide each of these parts into subtopics. An outline for Figure 5.2 might look like this:

I.   INTRODUCTION—Define arsenic.

II. BODY

    A. Explain how arsenic gets into drinking water.

    B. Explain how it is regulated (1974 Safe Drinking Water Act/MCLGs; Maximum Contaminant Levels).

    C. List some of the health effects of arsenic (visible effects; diseases, cancers).

III. CONCLUSION—Describe the EPA's standards.

Then organize the information into an outline

For a long, complex document, you will want a formal outline to keep you organized as you write (Figure 5.3).

For a long document, create a formal outline

Notice a few key characteristics of formal outlines:

- Roman numerals indicate the three main sections (introduction/body/conclusion).

- The first level of subtopics under each main section is indented and preceded by capital letters; the next level is further indented and preceded by Arabic numerals; and the third level is again indented three spaces and preceded by lowercase letters. This format is known as *alphanumeric notation*.

An alternate system, *decimal notation*, appears in Figure 5.4. The decimal outline makes it easier to refer readers to various sections in your final document. But both systems achieve the same organizing objective.

- Each level of division must yield at least two subtopics—if you cannot divide a larger topic into at least two subtopics, retain only your larger topic.

- A formal outline typically undergoes changes as you write. Expect to adjust it as needed. When the document is complete, you can use the formal outline to create a table of contents for the document.

See also the Strategies for Outlining box (below) for more advice.

Strategies

for Outlining

- **List key topics and subtopics to be included in your document.** Gather your information, determine what information is important to include, decide what information is superfluous, and make a list of the topics to be included.

- **Set up a standard outline.** Start with a typical introduction, body, and conclusion structure—even if you plan to vary the structure later.

- **Place key topics and subtopics where they fit within your standard outline.** Keep your introduction brief, using it to set the stage for the rest of your document. Include your specific data in the body section to back up what you promised in your introduction. Do not introduce new data in the conclusion.
- **Use alphanumeric or decimal notation consistently throughout the outline.**
- **Avoid excessive subtopics.** If your outline is getting into multiple levels of detail too often, think of ways to combine information. Do not go to another level unless there are at least two distinct subtopics at that level.
- **Refine your outline as you write your document.** Continue revising your outline until you complete your document.

Figure 5.3 A formal outline using alphanumeric notation

Converting the Office Building from Oil to Gas Heating: A Feasibility Analysis

I. INTRODUCTION
   A. Background
   B. Purpose of the Report
   C. Intended Audience (usually for in-school reports only)
   D. Information Sources
   E. Limitations of the Report
   F. Scope (list of major topics)

II. DATA (BODY)
   A. Description of Our Present Heating System
      1. Physical condition
      2. Required yearly maintenance
      3. Fuel supply problems
         a. Overworked distributor
         b. Varying local supply
      4. Cost of operation
   B. Removal of the Oil Burner and Tank
      1. Data from the oil company
      2. Data from the salvage company
         a. Procedure
         b. Cost
      3. Possibility of private sale
   C. Installation of a Gas Pipe from the Street to the Building
      1. Procedure
      2. Cost of installation
      3. Cost of landscaping

III. CONCLUSION
   A. Summary of Findings
   B. Comprehensive Interpretation of Findings
   C. Recommendations

Figure 5.4 Part of a formal outline using decimal notation

```
2.0 Data (Body)
    2.1 Description of Our Present Heating System
        2.1.1 Physical condition
        2.1.2 Required yearly maintenance
        2.1.3 Fuel supply problems
            2.1.3.1 Overworked distributor
            2.1.3.2 Varying local supply
        2.1.4 Cost of operation
    2.2 Removal of the Oil Burner and Tank
        2.2.1 Data from the oil company
        2.2.2 (and so on)
```

Chunking

5.3 Chunk information into discrete units.

Outlining helps to illustrate the importance of *chunking*: breaking information down into discrete, digestible units, based on the readers' needs and the document's purpose. When you chunk information into smaller portions, you help readers to see which pieces of information belong together and how the various pieces are connected.

Chunking: Breaking information down into smaller units

Chunking requires careful decisions about exactly how much information is enough for each portion and what constitutes sensible proportions among the parts. For example, note how in the outline in Figure 5.3 the writer plans to break up the information for readers in a variety of ways. First, the planned report is divided into three general sections, or chunks: introduction, data section (body), and conclusion. Then, each of those sections is broken into as many smaller chunks as appropriate to help the reader see how this discussion breaks into parts and yet each of these parts fits together to form a whole.

Chunking information is handled differently online than on the printed page. On Web sites, readers expect information in very short chunks because they don't like reading large portions of text on a computer screen, and they want the option of zeroing in on various parts of the page and moving from link to link. When documents are printed on paper, however, readers can handle longer passages of text because the printed page is easier on the eyes and because the expectation of reading a printed page is to read sequentially rather than jump from section to section.

Chunking on the Web versus chunking on a printed page

Sequencing

5.4 Determine the best sequence for your material.

In addition to chunking information, you also need to show readers the logical progression of information. The specific information sequence will depend on the type of document. For instance, a mechanism description usually follows a *spatial sequence* (What are the parts, and how do they fit together?); a progress report or set of instructions

Sequencing: ordering information to follow a logical progression

usually follows a *chronological sequence* (In what order have things happened/should things happen?); a feasibility, recommendation, or justification report would follow a *problem-solution sequence* (What was/is the problem or goal and how was it/can it be fixed or achieved?); and an analytical report describing an incident and the reasons for the incident would follow a *cause-and-effect sequence* (What caused something to happen, or what were the effects of something?). Examples later in this book illustrate these four sequential approaches:

- Figure 12.2 (page 210) uses a spatial sequence to describe a stethoscope.
- Figure 15.2 (page 267) uses a chronological sequence to provide a progress report on a student's term project.
- Figure 17.4 (pages 319–328) uses a problem-solution sequence to propose a solution to budgetary issues with a college campus newspaper.
- Figure 16.4 (pages 293–306) uses a cause-effect sequence to show a correlation between periodontal disease in mothers and low birth weight babies.

Paragraphing

5.5   Shape each paragraph for effectiveness.

Paragraphing: the process of shaping information within paragraphs

The preceding three strategies for structuring information (outlining, chunking, and sequencing) enable you and your readers to see the "big picture" of the document. Once you have thought through the document's larger structure, you need to consider how smaller-scale but no less important strategies will help readers follow your message. The first of these strategies, *paragraphing*, is the process of shaping your information within paragraphs.

Why paragraphing is important

In most documents, different types of paragraphs have different shapes and purposes. For example, introductory paragraphs set the stage for the discussion that follows; transitional paragraphs (usually brief) help hold the discussion together; concluding paragraphs wrap up the discussion. But the focus here is on standard *support paragraphs*, typically found in the document's body section. Each support paragraph advances one aspect of the main point made in the document's introduction, and each usually can stand alone in meaning.

Readers look for structures they can recognize both in the document as a whole and within individual paragraphs. Just as the document as a whole needs to have an introduction-body-conclusion structure, so must each paragraph. Most of the standard support paragraphs in a technical document begin with a clear *topic sentence*, stating a generalization. Details in the body section support that generalization. These paragraphs also display *unity* (each sentence in the paragraph's body section must relate to and expand on the topic sentence). Finally, these paragraphs display *coherence* (all sentences form a connected line of thought, leading from the topic sentence to the conclusion).

The Topic Sentence

Readers look to a paragraph's opening sentences for the main idea. Unless you have good reason to place it elsewhere, the topic sentence should appear first (or at least early) in the paragraph; it should focus and forecast what will come in the remainder of the paragraph. In some instances, the main idea may require a "topic statement" consisting of two or more sentences, but usually a single sentence will do, as in the following example:

> Solar power offers the most efficient, economical, and safe solution to the Northeast's energy problems.

An effective topic sentence

Note that key words in the topic sentence signal that the paragraph's next sentences (the body section) will describe how solar energy is *efficient, economical*, and *safe*.

Paragraph Unity

The body of the paragraph must deliver on the topic sentence's promise. A paragraph is unified when all its material belongs there—when each and every sentence directly expands on the topic sentence. Here, for example, is the complete version of the solar energy paragraph, fully unified:

> *Solar power offers an efficient, economical, and safe solution to the Northeast's energy problems*. To begin with, solar power is highly efficient. Solar collectors installed on fewer than 30 percent of roofs in the Northeast would provide for more than 70 percent of the area's heating and air-conditioning needs. Moreover, solar heat collectors are economical, operating for up to 20 years with little or no maintenance. These savings recoup the initial cost of installation within only ten years. Most important, solar power is safe. It can be transformed into electricity through photovoltaic cells (a type of storage battery) in a noiseless process that produces no air pollution—unlike coal, oil, and wood combustion. In contrast to its nuclear counterpart, solar power produces no toxic waste and poses no catastrophic danger of meltdown. Thus, massive conversion to solar power would ensure abundant energy and a safe, clean environment for future generations.

A unified paragraph

Note how the body of the previous paragraph tackles each of the benefits of solar energy introduced in the topic sentence, sometimes devoting two or more sentences to each benefit, but nonetheless staying on track. One way to damage unity in the paragraph above would be to veer from the focus on the key words *efficient, economical*, and *safe* into a discussion about the differences between active and passive solar heating or the advantages of solar power over wind power, neither of which was introduced in the topic sentence.

Paragraph Coherence

The body of the paragraph must deliver on the promise of the topic sentence through paragraph unity and lead to a conclusion via a connected line of thought, like links in a chain. This feature is called paragraph coherence. Paragraph coherence can be damaged by 1) sentences in the wrong order; 2) insufficient transitions and connectors for linking related ideas; or 3) an inaccessible line of reasoning and lack of conclusion. Here is how the solar energy paragraph might become incoherent:

An incoherent paragraph

> Solar power offers an efficient, economical, and safe solution to the Northeast's energy problems. Unlike nuclear power, solar power produces no toxic waste and poses no danger of meltdown. Solar power is efficient. Solar collectors could be installed on fewer than 30 percent of roofs in the Northeast. These collectors would provide for more than 70 percent of the area's heating and air-conditioning needs. Solar power is safe. It can be transformed into electricity. This transformation is made possible by photovoltaic cells (a type of storage battery). Solar heat collectors are economical. The photovoltaic process produces no air pollution.

In the above paragraph, the second sentence, about safety, belongs near the end because it was introduced as the third of the three benefits of solar energy. Also, because of insufficient links between ideas, the paragraph reads more like a list than like a flowing discussion. Finally, a concluding sentence is needed to complete the chain of reasoning and to give readers a clear perspective on what they've just read.

Here, in contrast, is the original, coherent paragraph with sentences numbered for later discussion and with transitions and connectors shown in boldface. Notice how this version reveals a clear line of thought:

A coherent paragraph

> [1]Solar power offers an efficient, economical, and safe solution to the Northeast's energy problems. [2]**To begin with,** solar power is highly efficient. [3]Solar collectors installed on fewer than 30 percent of roofs in the Northeast would provide for more than 70 percent of the area's heating and air-conditioning needs. [4]**Moreover,** solar heat collectors are economical, operating for up to 20 years with little or no maintenance. [5]**These savings** recoup the initial cost of installation within only ten years. [6]**Most important,** solar power is safe. [7]It can be transformed into electricity through photovoltaic cells (a type of storage battery) in a noiseless process that produces no air pollution—unlike coal, oil, and wood combustion. [8]**In contrast** to its nuclear counterpart, solar power produces no toxic waste and poses no danger of catastrophic meltdown. [9]**Thus,** massive conversion to solar power would ensure abundant energy and a safe, clean environment for future generations.

We can easily trace the sequence of thoughts in the previous paragraph:

Sentence 1.	The topic sentence establishes a clear direction.
Sentences 2–3.	The first reason is given and then explained.
Sentences 4–5.	The second reason is given and explained.
Sentences 6–8.	The third and major reason is given and explained.
Sentence 9.	The conclusion reemphasizes the main point.

To reinforce the logical sequence, related ideas are combined in individual sentences, and transitions and connectors signal clear relationships between ideas. The whole paragraph sticks together.

Clarifying Headings

5.6   Create clear headings.

One of the final steps in structuring information is to make sure you have used clear headings. Use your outline as a guide. Headings may not be appropriate for all documents, such as short documents (e.g., the email in Figure 5.1), but most technical material relies on some use of headings as a way to break up long passages of text and give readers guideposts throughout the document.

Headings often follow standard formats, such as "Introduction," "Methods," "Findings," "Conclusion," and so forth. In certain cases, the type of document (a scientific paper, a report for a company that always follows the same format) will dictate the headings you need to use.

You may use single words, phrases, brief statements, or questions as headings, as long as the headings signal to readers exactly what to expect in the section that falls under the heading's umbrella.

When used consistently, questions are often the most helpful way to construct headings. In effect, the question in the heading is answered by the material that falls under that heading. The author of Figure 5.2 has taken this reader-friendly approach, anticipating questions ("What is arsenic?" "How does arsenic get into my drinking water?" "How is arsenic in drinking water regulated?" "Why should I be concerned about arsenic in my drinking water?" and "What is the EPA's standard for arsenic in drinking water?") and answering each in turn.

Figure 5.5 is an example of a short report that uses clear, concise, and accurate headings to break up the material into logical sections. Because it is a progress report, the introductory heading gets right to the point of progress, and the concluding heading gets directly to the topic of work remaining. Meanwhile, the headings in the middle section directly signal the key topics the reader needs to know about.

For more on the use of headings, see pages 133 and 136.

Create headings as one of the final steps in the structuring process

Heading format and purpose

Providing an Overview

5.7   Provide overviews of longer documents.

The last step in structuring information for your readers is providing an overview. An overview may not be necessary for all technical documents, particularly short documents and reports. However, if you are writing a longer, more complex document, help your readers by providing a brief (usually paragraph-length) preview of what they can expect. This will help readers get the most out of the document by answering several key questions at the outset:

Provide an overview as the last step in the structuring process

- What is the purpose of this document?
- Why should I read it?
- What information can I expect to find here?

Figure 5.5 A short report with clear headings

Four headings divide the report into distinct, logical sections

Information in each headed section is brief and does not stray from the heading topic

Progress Report: Equipment for New Operations Building

Work Completed

Our training group has met twice since our May 12 report. In our first meeting, we identified the types of training we anticipate.

Types of Training Anticipated

- Loan Officer Work Experience
- Divisional Systems Training
- Divisional Clerical Training (Continuing)
- Divisional Clerical Training (New Employees)
- Divisional Management Training (Seminars)
- Special/New Equipment Training

In our second meeting, we considered various areas for the training room.

Training Room Assignment and Equipment

The frequency of training requires us to have a training room available daily. The large training room in the Corporate Education area (10th floor) would be ideal. Before submitting our next report, we need your confirmation that this room can be assigned to us.

To support the training programs, we purchased this equipment:

- Audioviewer
- Large flat screen monitor
- Digital video camera and tripod
- Software for computer-assisted instruction

This equipment will allow us to administer training in a variety of modes, ranging from programmed and learner-controlled instruction to group seminars and workshops.

Figure 5.5 (Continued)

Work Remaining •————————————————————————————————•   Final heading clearly signals that this section is the conclusion

To support the training, we need to furnish the room appropriately. Because the types of training will vary, the furniture should provide a flexible environment. Outlined here are our anticipated furnishing needs.

- Tables and chairs that can be set up in many configurations. These items would allow for individual or group training and large seminars.
- Portable room dividers. Dividers would allow study space for training with programmed instruction and allow for simultaneous training.
- Built-in storage space for audiovisual equipment and training supplies. Ideally, this storage space should be multipurpose, providing work or display surfaces.
- A flexible lighting system for audiovisual presentations and individualized study.

The project is on schedule. As soon as we receive your approval of these specifications, we will send out bids for room dividers and have plans drawn for the built-in storage.

cc. R. S. Pike, SVP

Think about it this way: If you were taking a long trip, you would probably use Google Maps or a GPS system to get the big picture of your journey and to know exactly where you were headed. Overviews provide a similar type of road map.

An overview should be placed at the beginning of a document, but you may also want to provide section overviews at the beginning of each section in a long document. The following is an example of an overview paragraph that comes at the beginning of a long report on groundwater contamination.

A report overview

> **About This Report**
>
> This report contains five sections. The first section describes the scope and scale of groundwater contamination in Jackson County. The second section offers background on previous legislation related to groundwater. Section Three shows the most recent data from the Jackson County Groundwater Project, and Section Four compares those data to national averages. Section Five offers recommendations and ideas for next steps.

In addition to helping readers negotiate longer reports, overviews are also extremely helpful in longer instruction and user manuals so that readers will know immediately what to expect in the longer document.

Figure 5.6 is an example of an overview page from a user guide designed to help people find and apply for federal grants. This overview (titled "Introduction" in this document) provides a short, simple introductory paragraph—explaining the context for this user guide. Additional paragraphs describe what is contained in the guide, and a bulleted list provides a streamlined, easy-to-read visual overview of what is contained in the rest of this 60-page document.

Checklist

for Structuring Information

- ❏ Am I structuring my document with readers in mind?
- ❏ Does my document employ a standard or varied introduction/body/conclusion structure?
- ❏ Have I created an outline that allows me to include all the necessary data for my document?
- ❏ Have I organized my outline using alphanumeric or decimal notation?
- ❏ Have I chunked my information into discrete, digestible units and for the proper medium (print or online)?
- ❏ Am I using the right sequence?
- ❏ Do each of my paragraphs include these features?
  - Topic sentence (introduction)
  - Unity (body that supports the topic sentence)
  - Coherence (connected line of thought leading to a conclusion)
- ❏ Have I used headings that are clear and addressed the sections or questions readers expect?
- ❏ If appropriate, does my document include an overview, helping readers understand what will follow?

Figure 5.6 Overview page from a user guide summarizes the contents of the full document

Introduction

Grants.gov has been designed to make it easier for organizations to find and apply for more than $500 billion in federal grants. With electronic access to more than 1,000 grant programs offered by all federal grant-making agencies, Grants.gov leverages the power of the Web to streamline your grant acquisition process.

This user guide has been developed to help you navigate the Grants.gov environment more easily. In it, you'll find detailed instructions for every step of the process – whether you're an applicant or grant-making agency.

From getting started and registration to viewing and tracking completed applications, this user guide offers clarification throughout the entire process.

Provided information in this user guide:
- How To Register Your Organization
- How To Register As An Authorized Organization Representative
- How To Register As An Individual
- Find and Search Grant Opportunities
- Download Application Packages
- Apply For Grants
- Track Your Application
- And How To Stay Connected

Heading lets readers know that this page will give them an overview of the user guide

Introductory paragraph provides background information in brief format

Second paragraph explains the purpose of the user guide

Bulleted list outlines the major sections in the user guide

Applications

General Application

Locate a set of instructions for something you have purchased. Identify specific features of how this material is organized and written. Are the paragraphs chunked into discrete units? Are headings used, and if so are they in question format? Is the material sequenced in a standard way? Do all of the paragraphs include topic sentences, and are they unified and coherent? Write a brief memo explaining why you think the technical writers who wrote the instructions made the decisions they did.

Team Application

With a team of two to three other students, consider the following documents and discuss the most logical sequence. (For instance, a description of a proposed podcasting computer lab would follow a spatial sequence.)

- a set of instructions for operating a power tool
- a campaign report describing progress in political fund-raising
- a report analyzing the desirability of a proposed oil refinery in your area
- a detailed breakdown of your monthly budget to trim excess spending
- a report investigating the reasons for student apathy on your campus
- a proposal for a no-grade policy at your college

Global Application

Find a document that presents the same information in several languages (assembly instructions, for example). Even if you don't understand all of the languages used, see if you can spot any changes made in the use of headings, the length of paragraphs, or the extent to which information is chunked. Interview a language professor on campus to find out why these choices may have been made.

Digital and Social Media Application

Locate a Web page and a print document (brochure, booklet, user guide) about the same product or service. Compare these, looking for the different ways in which material is written and organized online versus in print. Compare the use of headings, length of sentences, length of paragraphs, and balance of text and visuals, looking for any differences between the two. In class, give a short presentation on these differences, noting the advantages and disadvantages of each format.

Chapter 6
Writing With a Readable Style

 ## Learning Objectives

6.1 Appreciate the importance of a readable style in any document.

6.2 Understand the strategies for writing clearly.

6.3 Practice the strategies for writing concisely.

6.4 Recognize the strategies for writing fluently.

6.5 Follow the strategies for writing personably.

Chapter Outline

The Importance of a Readable Style   88

Writing Clearly   89

Writing Concisely   94

Writing Fluently   96

Writing Personally   98

    Strategies for Deciding about Tone   98

    Strategies for Unbiased Usage   99

    Checklist for Style   100

Applications   101

Definition of style

While *structure* has to do with the reader's ability to understand the document as a whole, including paragraphs, *style* has to do with readability at the sentence and word level.

The Importance of a Readable Style

6.1   **Appreciate the importance of a readable style in any document.**

Style emphasizes the audience's needs first

No matter how technical your document, your audience won't understand the content unless your sentences are easy to understand and your words are chosen precisely. Your style is a blend of these elements:

What determines your style

- the way in which you construct each sentence
- the length of your sentences
- the way in which you connect sentences
- the words and phrases you choose
- the tone you convey

Whether you are writing content for an email, a memo, a Web site, a report, or any other form of technical communication, these elements are always important in creating professional, usable workplace communication. Too often, tone and style, especially in email, become sloppy and casual. See Chapter 18 for more on email tone and style.

Style is more than correct grammar, usage, mechanics, and spelling

Readable style, of course, also requires correct grammar, usage, mechanics, and spelling. But correctness alone is no guarantee of readability. For example, the following response to a job application follows the rules of grammar, usage, mechanics, and spelling, but it is dense, stuffy, and hard to read:

> We are in receipt of your recent correspondence indicating your interest in securing the advertised position. Your correspondence has been duly forwarded for consideration by the personnel office, which has employment candidate selection responsibility. You may expect to hear from us relative to your application as the selection process progresses. Your interest in the position is appreciated.

Inefficient style

Notice as a reader how hard you have to work to extract information from the previous paragraph. This information could be expressed clearly and concisely, as in the following paragraph:

> Your application for the advertised position has been forwarded to our personnel office. As the selection process moves forward, we will be in touch. Thank you for your interest.

Readable style

Inefficient style makes readers work harder than they should. Style can be inefficient for many reasons but especially when it does the following:

- makes the writing impossible to interpret
- takes too long to make the point
- reads like a story from primary school
- sounds stuffy and impersonal

Ways in which style goes wrong

Regardless of the cause, inefficient style results in writing that is less informative and less persuasive than it should be. Also, inefficient style can be unethical when it confuses or misleads the audience, whether intentionally or unintentionally. Therefore, take the time to write with a readable style, using the strategies described in the following sections: writing clearly, writing concisely, writing fluently, and writing personably. For advice regarding correct grammar, usage, and mechanics, see Appendix B.

Inefficient style can be uninformative, unpersuasive, and even unethical

Writing Clearly

6.2   Understand the strategies for writing clearly.

Clear writing enables people to read each sentence only once to fully grasp its meaning. Strategies for writing clearly include avoiding ambiguous pronoun references, avoiding ambiguous modifiers, using active voice whenever possible, using passive voice selectively, avoiding nominalizations, unstacking nouns, and avoiding unnecessary jargon.

Why writing clearly is important

Avoiding Ambiguous Pronoun References

Pronouns (*he, she, it, their*, and so on) must clearly refer to the nouns they replace; otherwise, the sentence will be ambiguous and readers will puzzle over your intended meaning. For example, consider the following sentence, in which the reader is unable to discern whether Jack *or* his assistant is competitive:

> Jack resents his assistant because he is competitive.

Unclear referent

Depending on whether the referent for "he" is Jack or his assistant, the sentence can be clarified:

Clear referent
> Because his assistant is competitive, Jack resents him.
> *or*
> Because Jack is competitive, he resents his assistant.

Exercise 1

Edit each sentence below to eliminate ambiguities in pronoun reference.

    a. Bill told Darius that he was working too hard.
    b. Janice dislikes working with Magdalena because she's impatient.
    c. Our patients enjoy the warm days while they last.
    d. They couldn't start their cars because they were too cold.
    e. Celia can't talk to Betsy because she's still too angry.

Avoiding Ambiguous Modifiers

A *modifier* is a word (usually an adjective or adverb) or a group of words (usually a phrase or clause) that provides information about other words or groups of words. If a modifier is too far from the words it modifies, the message can be ambiguous. For instance, in the following sentence, the reader cannot discern whether "only" modifies "press" or "emergency":

Ambiguous modifier
> Only press the red button in an emergency.

If, however, the writer repositions the modifier, the sentence becomes clear:

Clear modifier
> Press only the red button in an emergency.
> *or*
> Press the red button in an emergency only.

In your own writing, position modifiers to reflect your meaning as accurately as possible.

Exercise 2

Edit each sentence below to clarify ambiguous modifiers.

    a. Just place the dishes back in the cabinets after 8 p.m.
    b. He purchased a ticket for his wife from Carnegie Hall.
    c. I almost sat there waiting for Gino for 45 minutes.
    d. Before she passed away, Philippa told her mother she admired her.
    e. Only use this phone in a red alert.

Using Active Voice Whenever Possible

In general, readers understand the meaning more quickly and clearly when the writer uses active voice ("I did it") rather than the passive voice ("It was done by me"). In active voice sentences, a clear agent performs a clear action on a recipient, as in the following example:

| Felix lost your report.

Active voice

Passive voice, by contrast, reverses this pattern, placing the recipient of the action (i.e., *report*, in the previous example) in the subject slot, as in the following sentence:

| Your report was lost by Felix.

Passive voice

Note that passive voice adds a form of the verb "be" ("was") next to the actual verb.

Some writers mistakenly rely on passive voice because they think it sounds more objective and important. But passive voice makes sentences wordier and harder to understand.

In addition, passive voice sometimes obscures the subject of the sentence, as in the following example:

| Your report was lost.

Inappropriate use of passive voice (no subject identified)

Passive voice is unethical if it obscures the person or other agent who performed the action when the person or agent responsible should be identified. In the above example, "Your report was lost" leaves out the responsible party. (Who lost the report?) For these reasons, favor the active voice in most writing situations.

Exercise 3

Convert these passive voice sentences to concise, forceful, and direct expressions in the active voice.

   a. The evaluation was performed by us.
   b. Unless you pay me within three days, my lawyer will be contacted.
   c. Hard hats should be worn at all times.
   d. The due date was delayed.
   e. Our test results will be sent to you as soon as verification is completed.

Using Passive Voice Selectively

There are times when the passive voice is appropriate: for instance, when the subject is not known or when the object is more important than the subject. For example, if a group of scientists performed an experiment and wanted to explain the results, they might write the following:

| The data were analyzed, and the findings were discussed.

Appropriate use of passive voice

Even here, active voice ("We analyzed the data…") would be preferable. But if it is clear who analyzed the data or truly not important who did the work, passive voice might be acceptable.

Passive voice can also ease the blow a direct sentence might deliver:

<small>Blunt use of
active voice</small>

| You have not paid your bill.

To be indirect and less offensive, the writer may choose passive voice instead:

<small>Appropriate
(indirect) use of
passive voice</small>

| Your bill has not been paid.

Consider this technique when you want to avoid a blunt or hostile tone. But in general, to convey clear, readable technical information, use active voice.

Exercise 4

The sentences below represent blunt uses of active voice. Convert each to passive voice.

    a. Joe's company fired him.
    b. Cecelia's coworkers accused her of being lazy.
    c. You are paying inadequate attention to worker safety.
    d. You are checking temperatures too infrequently.
    e. You did a poor job editing this report.

Avoiding Nominalizations

A nominalization is a noun that would be easier to understand as a verb. Verbs are generally easier to read because they signal action that can be visualized. You can usually spot a nominalization in two ways. First, look for words with *-tion* endings. Second, look for sentences in which the "[noun] of [noun]" formula appears. Following is an example of each type of nominalization:

<small>Unclear (*-tion*
ending)</small>

| My recommendation is for a larger budget.

<small>Unclear ("[noun]
of [noun]")</small>

| The managing of this project is up to me.

To fix the *-tion* problem, strike the ending to find the root verb ("recommend") and rewrite the sentence in a more direct form. To fix the "[noun] of [noun]" problem, identify the root verb form ("manage") and create a more accessible sentence. Following are improved versions of the above sentences:

<small>Clear verb form
(*-tion* removed)</small>

| I recommend a larger budget.

<small>Clear verb
form ("[noun]
of [noun]"
removed)</small>

| I manage this project.

Exercise 5

Make these sentences clearer by eliminating nominalizations.

    a. Our acceptance of the offer is a necessity.
    b. Your assertion is that we spend too much time in meetings.

    c. We ask for the cooperation of all employees.
    d. My validation of the report is required.
    e. Please provide a description of the problem.

Unstack Modifying Nouns

Too many nouns in a row can create confusion for readers. One noun can modify another (as in "software development"). But when two or more nouns modify a noun, the string of words becomes "stacked"—in other words, hard to read and ambiguous. For example:

| Be sure to leave enough time for today's training session participant evaluation.

Ambiguous use of stacked nouns

In the previous sentence, the reader is left unsure whether evaluation is of the session or of the participants. With no articles, prepositions, or verbs to unstack the nouns, readers cannot sort out the relationships among the nouns. To fix the problem, separate the stacked nouns by changing some nouns into verb forms where appropriate, as in the following example:

| Be sure to leave enough time for participants to evaluate today's training session.
| *or*
| Be sure to leave enough time to evaluate the participants in today's training session.

Clear sentence with nouns unstacked

Exercise 6

Make these sentences clearer by unstacking the nouns.
    a. They developed online editing system documentation.
    b. I recommend these management performance improvement incentives.
    c. Sarah's job involves fault analysis systems troubleshooting handbook preparation.
    d. Constantine read through the strategic implementation status guidelines.
    e. You should think about providing employees with memory recall stimulus devices.

Avoiding Unnecessary Jargon

Every profession has its own shorthand and accepted phrases and terms. Among specialists, these terms are an economical way to communicate. For example, "stat" (from the Latin *statim*, "immediately") is medical jargon for "drop everything and deal with this emergency." Jargon can be useful in communications among specialists. However, to avoid confusion, use jargon only when you know your audience will understand it and not simply to sound important or pretentious. Consider the following sentence:

| We will bilaterally optimize our efforts on this project.

Needless jargon

Clearly, that writer meant to sound important, but to most readers, the sentence is simultaneously meaningless and pretentious.

    Following is a clear and simple version:

| We will cooperate on this project.

Jargon-free version

Exercise 7

Edit these sentences to eliminate useless jargon.

- **a.** To optimize your financial return, prioritize your investment goals.
- **b.** The use of this product engenders a 50 percent repeat consumer encounter.
- **c.** Unless all parties interface synchronously within given parameters, the project will fail.
- **d.** Acoustically attenuate our company's food consumption area.
- **e.** We need to formulate a workable paradigm for this project.

Writing Concisely

6.3 **Practice the strategies for writing concisely.**

Why writing concisely is important

Concise writing provides readers with all of the information they need but without any needless filler. Strategies for writing concisely include avoiding wordiness and eliminating redundancy and repetition.

Avoiding Wordiness

Wordiness is often unavoidable in a first draft, when a writer is simply trying to get thoughts down on the page. For your readers, however, wordiness is distracting and detracts from a writer's credibility. When you edit your document, go through each sentence and work to eliminate excess words.

Wordiness has multiple causes: First, some writers habitually use needless phrases that can be reduced to one word:

Wordy phrases and their one-word substitutes

at a rapid rate = rapidly
due to the fact that = because
aware of the fact that = know
in close proximity to = near
the majority of = most

Second, many writers tend to start sentences with "there is," "there are," and "it is," which can often be eliminated:

Needless "there is," "there are," and "it is" sentence openers and their corrections

There is a danger of explosion in Number 2 mineshaft. = Number 2 mineshaft is in danger of exploding.

It is necessary to complete both sides of the form. = Please complete both sides of the form.

Third, writers often gravitate to weak verbs, such as all forms of the verb "to be" ("am," "are," "is," etc.), "give," "make," "come," and "take." These verbs need to be combined with other words to express fuller meaning, but they can easily be replaced with stronger verbs that can stand on their own:

Weak verbs and their replacements

has the ability to = can
make an assumption = assume

come to the conclusion that = conclude
give a summary of = summarize
take action = act

Fourth, writers often overuse prepositional phrases, which can easily be reduced to one or two words:

with the exception of = except for
in the near future = soon
at the present time = now
in the course of = during
in the process of = during (*or* in)

Prepositional
phrases
and their
replacements

Finally, many writers pad their writing by using clutter words (such as "very," "quite," "somewhat," "really," "actually"), needless qualifiers ("I think," "in my opinion," "it seems"), and unnecessary prefaces ("As far as I am concerned," "the purpose of this is") that add no meaning to a sentence. Of course, if you are expressing a tentative position on a complex issue, do use a qualifier ("I think," "it seems") as appropriate.

Exercise 8

Eliminate wordiness from the following sentences.

- **a.** Our lateness was due to the fact that we ran into traffic.
- **b.** I have come to the realization that I was mistaken.
- **c.** It seems as if I have just wrecked the company car.
- **d.** It is essential that we act immediately.
- **e.** A malfunction occurred during the process of rebooting.

Eliminating Redundancy and Repetition

A redundant expression says the same thing twice, in different words, whereas a repetition says the same thing twice or more in the same words. Following are examples of each, which can be fixed simply through cutting out the bracketed words.

[completely] eliminate   [mental] awareness

[end] result   [utter] devastation

enter [into]   [mutual] cooperation

consensus [of opinion]   [fellow] colleagues

Redundant
phrases

Techniques of artificial respiration include mouth-to-mouth [respiration] and mouth-to-nose [respiration].

Needlessly
repetitious
sentence

Exercise 9

Make these sentences more concise by eliminating redundancy and repetition.

- **a.** Igor's fellow colleagues are ambitious.
- **b.** We ask for everyone's mutual cooperation during this busy time.

c. This report is the most informative report on the project.
d. The consensus of opinion is that we agree with Tanisha's idea.
e. Sam agrees, Tanya agrees, and Soon-ye agrees too.

Writing Fluently

6.4   Recognize the strategies for writing fluently.

Why writing fluently is important

When you write fluently, you will hold your readers' interest and attention by making clear connections between ideas and by reducing monotony. Strategies for writing fluently include combining related ideas, varying sentence construction and length, and using parallel structure.

Combining Related Ideas

Readers who are forced to trudge through a series of short, choppy sentences will not only lose interest but will also fail to see how ideas are meant to be related or which ideas should receive emphasis. For example, the following string of five short sentences makes for dull reading. In addition, it forces readers to invent transitions between ideas and decide which points are most important:

Disconnected series of ideas

> Running can be healthful. You need the right equipment. Well-fitting shoes are important. You take the chance of injuring your legs. Your knees are especially prone to injury.

In contrast, the following two-sentence revision reads more smoothly and places a stronger emphasis on the importance of having the right jogging shoes:

Fluent combination of ideas

> Running can be healthful if you have the right equipment. Shoes that fit well are particularly important because they prevent injury to your legs, especially your knees.

Exercise 10

Combine the following sentences three times, each time creating one fluent sentence that places emphasis in a different place. For the first combination, emphasize the negative aspects of the job. For the second combination, emphasize the positive aspects. For the third combination, emphasize the salary.

> The job offers an attractive salary. It demands long work hours. It can be stressful. Promotions are rapid.

Varying Sentence Construction and Length

While you should combine short, choppy sentences into longer, more fluid versions, you don't want to create a string of unvaried longer sentences. Readers will find these just as monotonous, and they will also have a hard time determining which points are meant to receive emphasis. For example, the following two longer sentences are unvaried and dull, and at the same time the reader is forced to decide which of the five points made is the most important:

> Two drawbacks of diesel engines are that they are difficult to start in cold weather and cause sulfur dioxide pollution. In addition, they give off noise, emit an unpleasant odor, and cause vibrations.

In contrast, the following two-sentence revision reads less monotonously and incorporates one short sentence to place special emphasis on sulfur dioxide pollution:

> Diesel engines have a number of drawbacks, including cold weather starting difficulties, noisiness, odor, and vibrations. More seriously, they also cause sulfur dioxide pollution.

Exercise 11

Add variety to the following string of similar sentences.

> Because people are busy these days, DVRs are unsurprisingly popular. Because you can record while you are at work, you don't have to worry about missing your favorite programs. In addition, because you can record programs that show late at night, you don't have to stay up late to catch your favorite programs. Finally, in case you are on vacation, you can set the DVR to record your favorite shows automatically every week.

Using Parallel Structure

Parallel structure is a fancy way of saying that similar items should be expressed in similar grammatical form. Without parallelism, readers will lose attention, being mentally forced to "fix" the grammatical fluency of your sentence. For example, the structure of the following sentence is not parallel:

> She likes many outdoor activities, including running, kayaking, and to design new hiking trails.   Not parallel

This sentence is essentially a list of items. The first two items, "running" and "kayaking," are expressed as gerunds (verbs converted into nouns by using *-ing* endings). The third item, "to design," is not a gerund but a verb followed by an object. To make this sentence parallel and increase its fluency you would revise as follows:

> She likes many outdoor activities, including running, kayaking, and designing new hiking trails.   Parallel

Exercise 12

Make these sentences clearer by eliminating faulty parallelism.

- **a.** The weather today is going to be cold, rainy, and without much sun.
- **b.** My television picture is cloudy and I can see pixellation.
- **c.** My car needs a tune-up, an oil change, and the tires should be replaced.
- **d.** The new tutor is enthusiastic, skilled, and you can depend on her.
- **e.** In his new job, Ramon felt lonely and without a friend.

Writing Personably

6.5 **Follow the strategies for writing personably.**

Why writing personably is important

When you write in a personable manner, you connect directly with your readers and avoid inadvertently offending them. Strategies for writing personably include adjusting your tone and avoiding sexist and biased language.

Adjusting Your Tone

Your tone is your personal stamp—the personality that takes shape between the lines. The tone you create depends on 1) the distance you impose between yourself and the reader, and 2) the attitude you show toward the subject. To increase the likelihood of bringing readers over to your side, see the Strategies that follow.

Exercise 13

Adjust the tone of the following sentences to improve the connection between the writer and the reader.

    a. The writer of this letter would like a refund.
    b. The requested report will be sent next week.
    c. Students at this college will find the faculty always willing to help.
    d. No way am I going to approve this dog of a proposal.
    e. Because of your division's lagging productivity, a management review may be needed.

Strategies

for Deciding about Tone

- **Determine if you want a formal, semiformal, or informal tone.** You may prefer a formal tone when writing to superiors, professionals, or academics (depending on what you think they expect), a semiformal tone for colleagues and subordinates (depending on how close you feel to your readers), or a slightly informal tone when you want your writing to be conversational.
- **Remain consistent.** Once you've determined the appropriate overall tone of the document, stay with it throughout.
- **Address readers directly.** Prefer the personal pronouns "you" and "your" to connect with readers.
- **Use "I" and "we" when appropriate.** Instead of disappearing behind your writing, use "I" and "we" to connect with your readers.
- **Prefer the active voice.** Show confidence and directness by using active rather than passive voice.
- **Emphasize the positive.** Avoid a negative tone when conveying unpleasant information.
- **Always avoid an overly informal tone.** Achieving a conversational tone does not mean relying on substandard usage ("He ain't got none"), profanity ("This idea sucks"), and colloquialisms ("OK," "a lot," "snooze"). Pay special attention to tone when using email (see Chapter 18 for more on email tone and style).

Avoiding Biased Language

Language that is offensive or makes unwarranted assumptions is inappropriate for workplace communication and may harm the reputation of a company or organization. For example, letters addressed to "Dear Sir" may leave an unfavorable impression of the company on all readers but especially on women. Unnecessary mention of gender, marital status, physical appearances, and ethnicity may also alienate readers.

References to individuals and groups should include only as much detail as necessary for the particular point you are trying to make. The *Publication Manual of the American Psychological Association* (APA), 6th edition, says it well, stating that "[p]art of writing without bias is recognizing that differences should be mentioned only when relevant. Marital status, sexual orientation, racial and ethnic identity, or the fact that a person has a disability should not be mentioned gratuitously" (71).

When such items are important to the document and need to be included, the APA recommends that writers pay special attention to how individuals and groups are labeled (72) and recognize that "[p]references for terms referring to racial and ethnic groups change often" (75). They recommend that, if uncertain, writers consider "two basic guidelines of specificity and sensitivity"—in other words, how specific does the writer need to be and how can the language be as unbiased and sensitive as possible (75).

Exercise 14

The sentences below suffer from sexist or biased expressions. Adjust the tone.

a. The group's spokesman demanded salary increases.
b. The explosion left me blind as a bat for nearly two hours.
c. While the girls played football, the men waved pom-poms to cheer them on.
d. The Latino mechanic fixed the problem in under an hour.
e. Lame excuses for late papers will not be tolerated.

Strategies

for Unbiased Usage

- **Use neutral expressions.** Use "chair" or "chairperson" rather than "chairman" and "postal worker" rather than "postman."
- **Don't mention gender if it is not relevant.** Don't use "the female police officer" unless you are talking about police officers in the context of gender.
- **Avoid sexist pronouns.** You can avoid using a sexist pronoun by revising the sentence ("A writer who revises will succeed" rather than "A writer will succeed if he revises"), by using a plural form ("Writers will succeed if they revise"), or by occasionally using paired pronouns ("A writer will succeed if he or she revises").
- **Drop condescending diminutive endings.** Avoid words such as "poetess" and "majorette" and simply use "poet" and "major" instead.
- **Use "Ms."** Unless you know that a person prefers a traditional title, avoid "Mrs." and "Miss." Males are not identified by marital status, nor should females have to be.

- **Avoid potentially judgmental expressions.** For example, instead of "Third World" or "underdeveloped" use "newly industrialized" or "developing."
- **Never use demeaning expressions.** Avoid expressions such as "lame excuse," "the blind leading the blind," or "that's queer."
- **Use person-first language for people with disabilities or medical conditions.** Avoid terms that place the disability over the person or that suggest pity. Use "person with a disability" rather than "disabled person" and "person with AIDS" rather than "AIDS victim."
- **Use age-appropriate designations.** The APA recommends that when age is an important and relevant part of the discussion, use "girl" and "boy" to refer to people under age 12; use "young woman" and "young man" for people ages 13–17; use "women" and "men" for those ages 18 and over (76).

Checklist

for Style

Clarity

❑ Have I ensured that each pronoun clearly refers to the noun it replaces?
❑ Have I placed each modifier close enough to the word(s) it explains?
❑ Have I used active rather than passive voice (unless the agent is immaterial)?
❑ Have I restored nominalizations to their verb forms?
❑ Have I unstacked modifying nouns?
❑ Have I avoided needless jargon?

Conciseness

❑ Have I avoided needless sentence openers?
❑ Have I traded weak verbs for verbs that express a definite action?
❑ Have I avoided needless prepositional phrases?
❑ Have I avoided clutter words and needless qualifiers?
❑ Have I eliminated redundancy and needless repetition?

Fluency

❑ Have I combined related ideas appropriately?
❑ Have I varied sentence construction and length?
❑ Have I used parallel structure?
❑ Have I used short sentences for special emphasis?

Tone

❑ Is my tone appropriate and consistent for the situation and audience?
❑ Is the level of formality what the intended audience would expect?
❑ Is my writing free of implied bias or offensive language?
❑ Does the piece display sensitivity to cultural differences?
❑ If using email, is my tone professional and polite?

Applications

General Application

Using the Checklist for Style, revise the following selections. (Hint: Use the example on page 89 as a model for revision.) If available, use the "track changes" or "comments" function in your word processing software to record your suggested revisions and to identify the specific style problems in the original selection.

a. Letter to a local newspaper

In the absence of definitive studies regarding the optimum length of the school day, I can only state my personal opinion based upon observations made by me and upon teacher observations that have been conveyed to me. Considering the length of the present school day, it is my opinion that the day is excessive length-wise for most elementary pupils, certainly for almost all of the primary children.

To find the answer to the problem requires consideration of two ways in which the problem may be viewed. One way focuses upon the needs of the children, while the other focuses upon logistics, transportation, scheduling, and other limits imposed by the educational system. If it is necessary to prioritize these two ideas, it would seem most reasonable to give the first consideration to the primary reason for the very existence of the system, i.e., to meet the educational needs of the children the system is trying to serve.

b. Memo to employees

We are presently awaiting an on-site inspection of the designated chemistry lab location by corporate representatives relative to electrical adaptations necessary for the laboratory installation. Meanwhile, all staff members are asked to respect the off-limits designation of the aforementioned location, as requested, due to the liability insurance provisions in regard to the laboratory equipment.

Team Application

Locate a document (from a brochure, report, or Web site) that you feel is difficult to read. In groups of four, look for problems of tone and style. Each person in the group should be assigned to identify a problem section of the document and to improve a different stylistic area in that part of the document. The first person should improve clarity; the second, conciseness; the third, fluency; and the fourth should make the document more personable. Keep track of the improvements each team member makes, and present your edits and final version to the class. Note how each group will have revised the document differently.

Global Application

The style guidelines in this chapter apply specifically to Standard English in North America, but technical communication is a global activity. Practices and preferences differ widely. For example, some cultures prefer long sentences and elaborate language to convey an idea's full complexity. Others expect lengthy introductions and expressions of politeness and praise rather than clarity or directness. Certain documents may originate in English but then be translated into other languages or read by audiences for whom English is a second language. In such cases, writers must be careful to use language that is easy to translate. Idioms ("cutthroat competition," "over the top,"), cultural references ("the Bronx Bomber," "the Deep South"), and humor ("heads I win; tails you lose") are often difficult to translate. Some words may carry insulting connotations, as in cultures in which the terms "male" and "female" refer only to animals.

Your assignment is to search online using the keywords "international business culture" to learn about the writing style preferences of one particular culture. Then, in a one-page memo to your instructor and classmates, describe the style preferences of that culture, and give examples of how these preferences differ from the style guidelines (i.e., for North American English) in this chapter.

Digital and Social Media Application

Do an online search for the phrase "writing for social media." Look for Web sites from professional organizations such as major news media, colleges and universities, government agencies, and corporations. Compare the advice given on these Web sites with the strategies offered in this chapter, particularly about sentence length, word choice, audience, tone, and formality. Make a list of items that are important regardless of the format (print or digital) and another list of style and tone considerations specific to social media. Discuss your findings with two or three other students, then share your findings in a brief in-class presentation.

Chapter 7
Using Audience-Centered Visuals

 ## Learning Objectives

7.1 Appreciate the role of visuals in technical communication.

7.2 Decide when to use visuals with text or on their own.

7.3 Identify, create, and use different types of visuals.

7.4 Understand how to select and place visuals, use color appropriately, and use visuals fairly and accurately.

Chapter Outline

The Importance of Using Audience-Centered Visuals   104

When to Use Visuals   106

Types of Visuals   107
   Strategies for Creating Tables   108
   Strategies for Creating Graphs   111
   Strategies for Creating Charts   113
   Strategies for Illustrations, Diagrams, Photographs,
   Videos, Icons, and Symbols   117

Special Considerations When Using Visuals   118
   Checklist for Using Audience-Centered Visuals   120

Applications   121

In addition to structure and style, the use of audience-centered visuals is one of the four essential elements in technical communication.

The Importance of Using Audience-Centered Visuals

7.1   Appreciate the role of visuals in technical communication.

Visuals help readers interpret and remember complex information

Visuals are important in print or digital documents, in oral presentations, and on Web sites and apps for several reasons: They help readers interpret and remember complex information, they show how items look or work, and they show how items are organized or actions are performed.

Because they focus and organize complex information into more simplified form, visuals make data easier for readers to interpret and remember. Visuals work because readers want more than just raw information; they want the information presented so they can understand it at a glance. Consider, for example, how the following passage might be better presented using a visual:

Technical data in prose form can be hard to interpret

> The time required for the global population to grow from 5 to 6 billion was shorter than the interval between any of the previous billions. It took just 12 years for this to occur, just slightly less than the 13 years between the fourth and fifth billion and the 15 years between the third and fourth billion, but much less time than the 118 years between the first and second billion. . . .

Now consider this same information presented as a graph in Figure 7.1.

Figure number and informative title
Caption explains the visual's overall meaning

Labels identify key elements (in this case, units of measure)

Figure 7.1 A graph that simplifies complex information

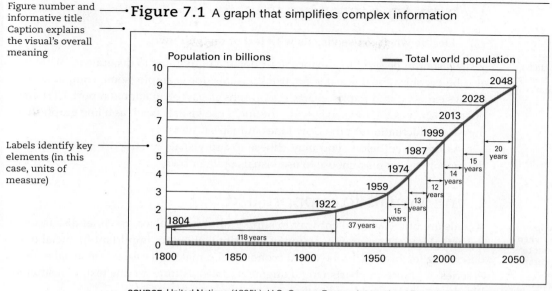

SOURCE: United Nations (1995b); U.S. Census Bureau; International Programs Center, International Database and Unpublished Tables.

Notice how Figure 7.1 makes it easier to understand and remember the upward population trend and the numerous facts and figures described in the paragraph that precedes it.

Not all visuals are designed to convey numeric or other data. A second reason visuals are important is that they can show readers at a glance what something looks like and/or how it works—as opposed to lengthy descriptions in prose form.

Visuals show readers how items look or work

Visuals that show how items look include illustrations and photographs, while visuals that show how items work include diagrams. For example, the diagram in Figure 7.10 (page 114) illustrates how a safety belt locking mechanism operates. Notice how this diagram is much easier to understand than if the idea were described using text only.

Finally, visuals are important because they can quickly and efficiently show how items are organized or actions are performed, without resorting to long and difficult-to-follow textual explanations. Such visuals include organizational charts and flowcharts. For example, imagine the dense and wordy paragraphs that would be needed to describe the process for helping an adult choking victim, as shown in the flowchart in Figure 7.6 on page 112.

Visuals show readers how items are organized or actions are performed

When to Use Visuals

7.2   Decide when to use visuals with text or on their own.

Use visuals to enhance, not decorate

Visuals should be used to enhance your document, not just to decorate it. There may also be organizational reasons for using visuals; for example, some companies may always expect photographs, charts, and graphs as part of an annual report. Certain industries, such as the financial sector, routinely use visuals (such as a line graph showing recent fluctuations in the Dow Jones Industrial Average).

As discussed below, you may choose to use visuals to support the text of your document, or you may choose to use visuals on their own.

Using Visuals to Support Text

Use supporting visuals when you want to add to important textual discussion

Visuals are often an excellent way to support, but not replace, essential discussion in the actual text. For example, you may be writing about an important financial trend, describing features about the world economy, and making a case for financial reforms. A series of graphs or charts would augment, not substitute for, the text. In a situation like that, visuals would add to your discussion.

Be sure to refer to each visual by number ("see Figure 1") in the text. Explain what the visual means, supply a caption for it, and place the visual as close as possible to the text it supports.

For captions, use "Table" for tables; for all other visuals, use "Figure." See, for example, Tables 7.1 and 7.2 versus Figure 7.2 or any of the other figures in this chapter.

Table 7.1 A numerical table

Years of Potential Life Lost Before Age 75					
(Per 100,000 population under age 75)					
	Heart Disease		Unintentional Injuries		
Year	Male	Female	Male	Female	
1990	2356.0	948.5	1162.1	607.4	
2000	1766.0	774.6	1026.5	573.2	
2005	1559.0	680.2	1137.2	647.9	
2009	1399.2	606.5	1028.2	604.6	
2010	1370.8	593.6	1025.2	616.4	
% change, 1990–2010	−41.8	−37.4	−11.8	+1.5	

Title explains the table's purpose

Each column has a clear heading

Numbers are aligned properly for ease of reading

Where helpful, data are tallied

This table compares years of potential life lost before age 75 due to heart disease and unintentional injury in males and females. In both males and females, years lost due to heart disease decreased between 1990 and 2010. Years lost due to unintentional injury decreased only slightly in males and increased very slightly in females.

A caption explains the numerical relationships

SOURCE: *Health, United States 2012*, from the U.S. National Center on Health Statistics.

Table 7.2 A textual table

Radon Risk if You Smoke			
Radon level	**If 1,000 people who smoked were exposed to this level over a lifetime . . .**	**The risk of cancer from radon exposure compares to . . .**	**WHAT TO DO: Stop smoking and . . .**
20 pCi/L[a]	About 135 people could get lung cancer	←100 times the risk of drowning	Fix your home
10 pCi/L	About 71 people could get lung cancer	←100 times the risk of dying in a home fire	Fix your home
8 pCi/L	About 57 people could get lung cancer		Fix your home
4 pCi/L	About 29 people could get lung cancer	←100 times the risk of dying in an airplane crash	Fix your home
2 pCi/L	About 15 people could get lung cancer	←2 times the risk of dying in a car crash	Consider fixing between 2 and 4 pCi/L
1.3 pCi/L	About 9 people could get lung cancer	(Average indoor radon level)	
0.4 pCi/L	About 3 people could get lung cancer	(Average outdoor radon level)	(Reducing radon levels below 2 pCi/L is difficult)

Title explains the table's purpose

Each column has a clear heading that leads readers into the information

Phrases are brief and aligned for ease of reading

Numbers enhance the verbal information

A footnote provides more detail

Note: If you are a former smoker, your risk may be lower.
[a]picocuries per liter

SOURCE: *Home Buyer's and Seller's Guide to Radon*, by the U.S. Environmental Protection Agency.

Using Visuals on Their Own

In some cases, visuals may work well on their own, as when they make your point more clearly than text can. In situations like these, you can refer to the visuals that show readers what they need to see. For instance, to show how customers who have purchased your company's new UHD televisions break out by age group, don't list the percentages in a lengthy paragraph. Instead, supply a chart or graph that conveys these data visually.

Use visuals on their own when textual discussion is not necessary

When you use stand-alone visuals, make sure these visuals tell the whole story that you want readers to understand. In any text preceding the visual, make sure you introduce the visual clearly. If you need to explain how the visual should be interpreted, do so briefly in a figure caption.

Types of Visuals

7.3 Identify, create, and use different types of visuals.

The most commonly used types of visuals are tables, graphs, charts, illustrations, diagrams, photographs, videos, symbols, and icons. The following sections describe each type.

Tables

Tables display organized data or information across columns and rows for easy comparison. Tables can be used to display quantitative information (*numeric tables*) or qualitative information (*textual tables*) or sometimes both. For specific advice on creating tables, see the annotations to Tables 7.1 and 7.2 (page 106 and 107) and the Strategies below.

Numeric tables focus on quantitative information

NUMERIC TABLES. Numeric tables simplify complex quantitative information. Although text may be used in headings to organize the table, the primary purpose of the table is to show numbers and their relationships. Note in Table 7.1 how the data are compared in a variety of ways and how a tally of the numbers and an explanatory caption further help readers understand and interpret the data.

Textual tables focus on qualitative information

TEXTUAL TABLES. Textual tables simplify complex qualitative information. Numbers may be used to help organize the textual information, but the primary purpose of the textual table is to show written information and relationships. Note how Table 7.2 simplifies written information that would be difficult to explain in paragraph form and uses a footnote to explain a nuance to the reader.

Strategies

for Creating Tables

- **Don't include too much information in a single table.** Overly complex tables are confusing. Limit your table to two or three areas of comparison. Or use multiple tables.
- **Provide a brief but descriptive title.** Announce exactly what is being compared.
- **Label the rows and columns.**
- **Line up data and information clearly.** Use neat columns and rows and plenty of white space between items.
- **Keep qualitative information and quantitative data brief.** When including high numbers (more than three digits), abbreviate the numbers and indicate "in thousands," "in millions," and so on. When using text in a table, limit the number of words.
- **Provide additional information, if necessary.** Add footnotes or a caption at the bottom of the table to explain anything readers may not understand at first glance.
- **Credit your sources.** Unless you collected the data or information yourself, always credit the source (see pages 385–386 for advice on avoiding plagiarism).

Graphs

Graphs translate numbers into shapes, shades, and patterns. At a glance, graphs display the approximate values, the point being made about those values, and the relationship being emphasized. Typically, a graph's horizontal axis shows categories to be compared, such as time periods, while the vertical axis shows the range of values, such as numbers. The most common types of graphs are *bar graphs* (simple or multiple) and *line graphs* (simple or multiple). For specific advice on creating graphs, see the annotations to Figures 7.2 through 7.5 and the Strategies on page 111.

BAR GRAPHS. Bar graphs present data using colored (or shaded) bars, usually lined up along the horizontal axis. Simple bar graphs depict changes over time, patterns, or trends for a single category. For instance, the simple bar graph in Figure 7.2 shows one trend extracted from Table 7.1, male deaths from heart disease between 1970 and 2006.

Multiple bar graphs, meanwhile, compare two or more categories. For example, the multiple bar graph in Figure 7.3 (also extracted from Table 7.1) shows not only a trend in male deaths from heart disease between 1990 and 2010 but also from cancer during that same period.

Bar graphs depict changes over time, patterns, and trends

Figure 7.2 A simple bar graph

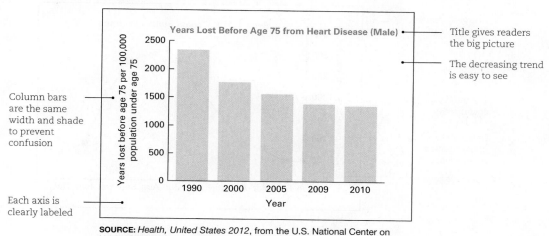

Column bars are the same width and shade to prevent confusion

Each axis is clearly labeled

Title gives readers the big picture

The decreasing trend is easy to see

SOURCE: *Health, United States 2012*, from the U.S. National Center on Health Statistics

Figure 7.3 A multiple bar graph

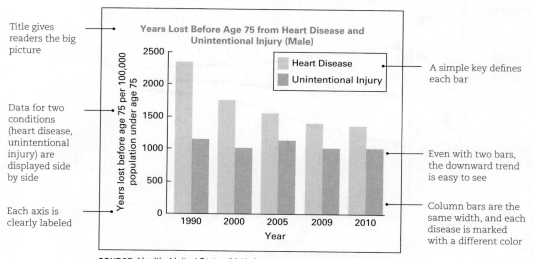

Title gives readers the big picture

Data for two conditions (heart disease, unintentional injury) are displayed side by side

Each axis is clearly labeled

A simple key defines each bar

Even with two bars, the downward trend is easy to see

Column bars are the same width, and each disease is marked with a different color

SOURCE: *Health, United States 2012*, from the U.S. National Center on Health Statistics.

Line graphs can synthesize large quantities of data

LINE GRAPHS.   Line graphs present data using colored (or shaded) lines, marked at regular intervals so that the data points line up with the items on the horizontal axis. A line graph can accommodate and display more data points than a bar graph. Simple line graphs show changes, patterns, or trends for a single category. In Figure 7.4, the single line tracks the number of building permits issued during the year, showing how permit requests are more common between May and October.

Multiple line graphs display several relationships simultaneously, as in Figure 7.5.

Figure 7.4 A simple line graph

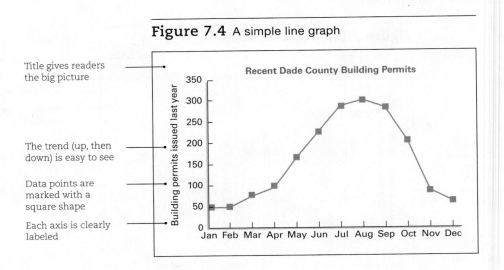

Figure 7.5 A multiple line graph

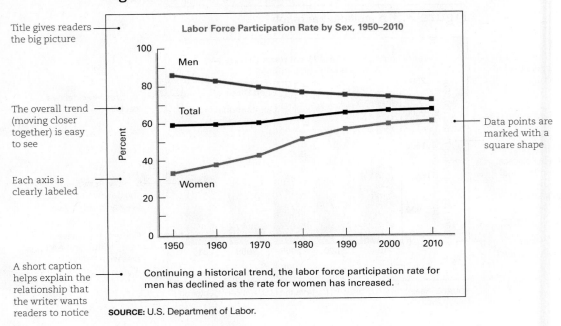

SOURCE: U.S. Department of Labor.

Strategies
for Creating Graphs

Tick marks

- **Use a graph only to compare values that are noticeably different.** A bar graph in which all bars are about the same height or a line graph depicting a single straight line (or overlapping multiple lines) serves no purpose.
- **Provide a clear title.** Announce exactly what is being displayed.
- **Label both the purpose and divisions of each axis.** Use numbers or gradations that are evenly divided (e.g., multiples of 10, spans of 5 years, months of the year), and add tick marks next to each number/gradation.
- **Keep the graph simple and easy to read.** Use no more than three bars (bar graph) or three to four lines (line graph) per graph. Avoid needless details; readers should understand the graph at a glance.
- **Make each bar or line distinct.** In multiple bar or line charts, use different colors or shades for each bar or line. Provide a key or label that indicates what each bar or line represents.
- **Use consistent format for bars and lines.** In a bar graph, bars should all be of the same width. In a line graph, lines should all be of the same thickness, and all data points (those points at which a line intersects with gradations on the horizontal axis) should be marked.
- **Credit your sources.** As always, avoid plagiarism by citing the sources of your information or data.

Charts

Charts depict relationships via shapes, arrows, lines, and other design elements. The terms "chart" and "graph" are often used interchangeably; technically, however, a chart displays relationships (quantitative or cause-and-effect) that are not plotted on vertical and horizontal axes. Commonly used charts include *flowcharts, pie charts,* and *organization charts.* For more specific advice on creating charts, see the annotations to Figures 7.6 through 7.8 and the Strategies on page 113.

FLOWCHARTS. A flowchart traces a process or procedure from beginning to end, moving from top to bottom or from left to right and using connector bars to show relationships, as in Figure 7.6.

Flowcharts show processes and procedures

PIE CHARTS. Easy for almost anyone to understand, pie charts are circular diagrams that display the status of each "piece" of the "pie"—the percentage of the whole pie (which totals 100%) that each piece represents. Readers can compare the differently colored (or shaded) pieces to each other and to the whole. Figure 7.7 shows a basic pie chart comparing major food sources of trans fat for American adults.

Pie charts show proportions among the segments

ORGANIZATION CHARTS. An organization chart shows the hierarchy and relationships between different departments and other units in an organization, using a top-down series of boxes connected by arrows, as in Figure 7.8.

Organization charts show relationships between departments or units

Figure 7.6 A flowchart

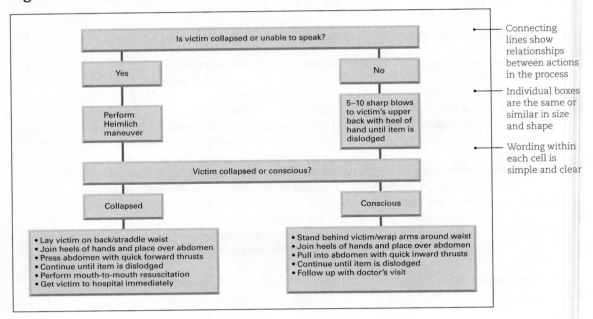

Figure 7.7 A pie chart

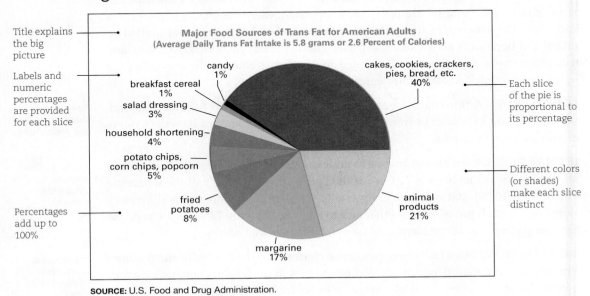

SOURCE: U.S. Food and Drug Administration.

Figure 7.8 An organization chart

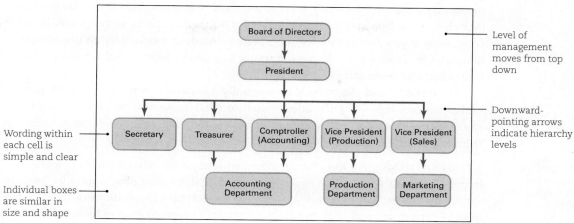

Level of management moves from top down

Downward-pointing arrows indicate hierarchy levels

Wording within each cell is simple and clear

Individual boxes are similar in size and shape

Strategies

for Creating Charts

For all types of charts, provide a clear title and credit your sources.

- **Flowcharts**
  - **Move from top to bottom or left to right.** The process must start at the top (top-to-bottom chart) or left (left-to-right chart).
  - **Use connector lines.** Show relationships between parts of the process.
  - **Keep boxes uniform and text brief.** See the tips for organization charts below.
- **Pie charts**
  - **Make sure the parts of the pie add up to 100%.**
  - **Differentiate and label each slice clearly.** Use different colors or shades for each slice, and label the category and percentage of each slice.
  - **Keep all labels horizontal.** Make the chart easy to read.
  - **Combine very small pie slices.** Group categories with very small percentages under "other."
- **Organization charts**
  - **Move from top to bottom or left to right.** Place the highest level of hierarchy at the top (top-to-bottom chart) or at the left (left-to-right chart).
  - **Use downward- or rightward-pointing arrows.** Arrows show the flow of hierarchy from highest to lowest.
  - **Keep boxes uniform and text brief.** Shape may vary slightly according to how much text is in each box. Maintain a uniform look. Avoid too much text in any box.

Illustrations and Diagrams

Illustrations and diagrams rely on drawings and sketches rather than data or words, though some words may be needed to point out names, parts, or purposes. In some cases, even if you attempt the most accurate prose description, only an illustration or diagram can show what it is you are trying to explain. Technical illustrations accomplish what text alone cannot.

Illustrations and diagrams are especially valuable when you need to convey spatial relationships or help readers visualize what an item or process actually looks like. For specific advice on creating illustrations and diagrams, see the annotations to Figures 7.9 and 7.10 and the Strategies on page 117.

Illustrations show what something looks like

ILLUSTRATIONS. An illustration shows with accuracy what something looks like. Impressive visuals are easy to create by using digital drawing programs or by locating clip art and other images online. However, more complex illustrations or those suited to your exact needs generally require the services of graphic artists or technical illustrators. See, for example, how the illustration in Figure 7.9 (taken from the document in Figure 1.3) provides a clear visual of the bioremediation process.

Figure 7.9 An illustration

Microbe eats oil

Microbe digests oil and changes it to water and harmless gases

Microbe releases water and harmless gases into soil or ground

SOURCE: Environmental Protection Agency. Information available at <www.epa.gov/superfund/sites> or <www.cluin.org>.

Figure 7.10 A diagram

Simple line drawings make the diagram easy to understand

All parts are clearly labeled

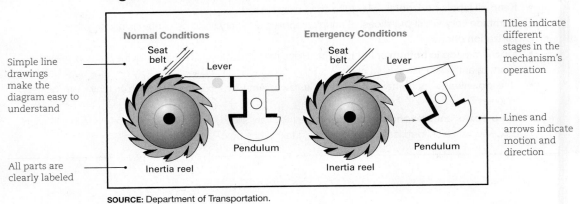

Normal Conditions
Seat belt
Lever
Pendulum
Inertia reel

Emergency Conditions
Seat belt
Lever
Pendulum
Inertia reel

Titles indicate different stages in the mechanism's operation

Lines and arrows indicate motion and direction

SOURCE: Department of Transportation.

If you are unable to locate an illustration that points out just the parts of a product, process, or other item you want to display, you may need a professional illustrator. However, the variety of illustrations available online grows every day.

DIAGRAMS.   Unlike illustrations, which simply show what something looks like, diagrams show how parts of an object fit together or how mechanisms operate. For example, the diagram of a safety belt locking mechanism in Figure 7.10 portrays the mechanism in operation by juxtaposing "normal conditions" and "emergency conditions."

> Diagrams show how parts fit or operate

Among the many types of diagrams, three of the most common are *exploded diagrams* (which separate parts of an object while showing how the parts fit together), *cutaway diagrams* (which show the interior of an object by "cutting away" the shell), and *maps*.

Photographs

Although photographs (Figure 7.11) are obviously more realistic than illustrations and diagrams (which often highlight certain parts of an object), photographs can provide *too much* detail or fail to emphasize the parts you want viewers to focus on.

> Photographs show an ultra-realistic view

Many people take their own digital photographs and then use software to crop the image for proper emphasis. For basic documents circulated to a small group inside a department or organization, this can be fine. But for important documents circulated to high-level audiences inside or outside an organization, use professionally taken photographs.

If you locate photographs online, be sure to credit your sources. You also need to request permission if your document will be printed and circulated. For more advice on taking and altering photographs, see the Strategies on page 117.

Figure 7.11 A photograph

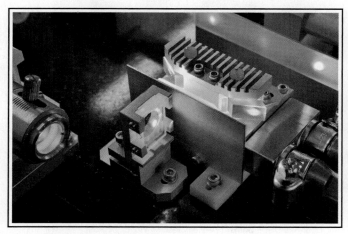

SOURCE: YuryZap/Shutterstock.

Videos

Videos show a full-motion view

Until recently, workplace videos were typically used for training and safety purposes only and were filmed by professionals. Today, videos are easy to create (even phones take great video), and sites like YouTube and Vimeo provide accessible platforms for delivery. So, increasingly, organizations are using videos to supplement or even replace traditional documents (such as user manuals). For instance, the frame captured in Figure 7.12 is from video instructions for a product called Dust-Aid (used to clean dust from the camera sensor of a digital SLR camera). The principles for using videos are similar to those for photographs, except that videos are altered via editing rather than cropping. For more advice, see the annotations to Figure 7.12, the Strategies on page 117, and Chapter 20.

Icons and Symbols

Icons are simple concrete illustrations; symbols are simple abstract illustrations

Icons and symbols use simple illustrations that reduce a concept or item to its most basic, understandable level. The words *icon* and *symbol* are often used interchangeably. But icons resemble the items they represent (for instance, an icon of a file folder on your computer that looks like a real file folder), whereas symbols get the meaning across without resembling the items they represent (for example, a skull-and-crossbones warning symbol broadly represents the idea of danger or death, making clear the "do

---

Figure 7.12 A video frame

Video is taken from an angle that simulates the angle of vision of an in-person learner

Video shows both the object and the person using it, for a sense of scale

Full motion helps people see how to perform a task

SOURCE: From "Dust-Aid: DSLR Camera Sensor Cleaning Video" by Ross Wordhouse from www.youtube.com. Reproduced by permission.

Figure 7.13 Internationally recognized icons and symbols

Simplicity of the drawings reduces any chance for confusion

The first three images are icons (representative); the last two are symbols (abstract)

not ingest/poison" message). Because these types of illustrations generally do not rely on text, they are more easily understood by international audiences, children, and people who have difficulty reading. For specific advice on using icons and symbols, see the annotations to Figure 7.13 and the Strategies below.

Strategies

for Illustrations, Diagrams, Photographs, Videos, Icons, and Symbols

For all such visuals, always credit the source if not self-created, and seek permission if reproduced and circulated.

- **Illustrations**
  - **Use illustrations that are easy to interpret.** Avoid illustrations that distort an object's actual appearances.
  - **Show only those parts that your viewers need to see.**
  - **Label each important part.**
- **Diagrams**
  - **Provide clear explanations.** Explain how diagram parts fit together or operate.
  - **Use lines and arrows to indicate direction and motion.** For diagrams that show action, directional markers help viewers understand the action.
  - **Keep diagram illustrations simple.** Merely show viewers what they need to see.
  - **Label each important part.**
- **Photographs**
  - **Provide a sense of scale.** Try to show the object and a person using it, a ruler, or a hand.
  - **Simulate the viewer's angle of vision.** Consider how your readers would need to view the item.
  - **Crop out needless details.**
  - **Label key parts.** A simple photograph may not need labels, but a more complicated photograph should have essential parts labeled.
- **Videos**
  - **Provide a sense of scale.** Try to show the object and a person using it (or a ruler or a hand).
  - **Show only what the viewer needs to see.** For example, in a video of a long procedure, focus on just the part of the procedure that's most relevant.
  - **Edit out needless detail.** If you have editing software, shorten the video to include only the essentials.
  - **Avoid excess outside or office noise when recording sound.**

- **Icons and Symbols**
  - **Use icons and symbols sparingly.** Use them only when directly appropriate, say, to supplement textual warnings or instructions.
  - **Use internationally recognized icons and symbols.** Some icons and symbols may not convey your intended meaning in other cultures.

Special Considerations When Using Visuals

7.4 **Understand how to select and place visuals, use color appropriately, and use visuals fairly and accurately.**

Once you are aware of the variety of visuals at your disposal, select those most appropriate for your audience and purpose, and consider how to integrate them within your document.

Selecting Appropriate Visuals

When selecting visuals for any document, first ask yourself this question: Who is my audience, and what do audience members need to know?

Special audience considerations

Generally speaking, expert audiences tend to prefer numerical tables, complex graphs and charts, and diagrams they can interpret for themselves. Nonexpert audiences tend to prefer basic tables, graphs, and charts, uncomplicated illustrations and diagrams, and other visuals that direct their focus and interpret key points for them. If your audience is a combination of experts and nonexperts, you should err on the side of the nonexperts.

Also, be aware that your audience may include international readers or North American readers from different cultural backgrounds. When choosing icons or symbols, use those that are internationally recognized (when in doubt, check the International Organization for Standardization's Web site). Also keep your visuals (including text within visuals) simple and basic and avoid images and colors that might unintentionally offend people from other cultures. If you are knowingly writing to members of a particular culture or nationality, search online for more background on that audience.

Consider how each visual advances your purpose. For example, don't decide to use a bar chart just because you like its professional appearance; make sure the information or data you want to present are best served via a bar chart. Following are additional suggestions for fitting a visual to its purpose:

Consider the purpose of each visual

- To simplify complex numerical data or textual information, use a table.
- To get your audience to draw conclusions from facts and figures, use a graph or a chart that shows comparisons.

- To show how parts make up the whole, use a pie chart.
- To show hierarchy and relationships in an organization, use an organization chart.
- To show steps in a process from beginning to end, use a flowchart.
- To show what something looks like, use an illustration or photograph.
- To show how parts fit together or operate, use a diagram or a photograph that depicts a process.

Placing, Cross-Referencing, and Presenting Visuals

Place your visuals where they best serve the needs of your readers: as close as possible to the related discussion if they are central to that discussion or in an appendix if they are peripheral to your discussion. Introduce your visuals within the text by referring to them by number (Figure 1, Table 4, etc.) and explaining what they mean (e.g., "As Figure 3.4 shows…"), making sure the figure and table numbers match the cross-references in the text. See the sample formal report on page 293 for an example of a table used as part of a larger document. Make your visuals user-friendly in their presentation by framing them with plenty of white space, eliminating visual "noise" (excessive lines, bars, numbers, and inessential information), and sizing each visual for the right proportion and emphasis on the page.

Place visuals close to their related topic in the text

Using Color in Visuals

Color focuses reader attention and helps readers identify various elements of a visual. Most of the software you will use to create visuals (e.g., Excel, PowerPoint) automatically adds color to charts and graphs. In an illustration or diagram, you can highlight particular areas by using color against a more subdued background. When color is not available, try using grayscale shades. In some visuals, however, grayscale may not be effective; for example, in a pie chart with numerous "slices" (see Figure 7.7), using slight gradations of gray may cause the slices to blend too closely. Likewise, in a multiple bar chart or multiple line chart (see Figures 7.3 and 7.4), you will want to sharply differentiate bars and lines. For more information on using color, see Chapter 8.

Color helps focus your reader's attention

Using Visuals Fairly and Accurately

As a technical communicator, you are responsible for creating documents that are fair and that present information accurately. Visuals are powerful forms of communication: one quick glance, and readers are left with a strong impression of a trend, idea, or interpretation. Online, visuals are often the reason why stories "go viral," sometimes with the visual having little or nothing to do with the story (or with the visual being very distorted). The golden rule of using visuals fairly and accurately is to always present the real and complete picture.

Always present the real and complete picture

Some of the ways in which visuals can be distorted or misused include using inaccurately sized slices in a pie chart to misrepresent the true percentages; leaving out

Some ways in which visuals can be distorted

essential information from a table, chart, or graph; inflating or reducing the size of illustrations or photographs to make items appear more or less important than they actually are; and including a visual unrelated to the story or report. When creating visuals, take care to convey and explain information accurately.

Checklist

for Using Audience-Centered Visuals

❑ Have I looked for parts of the document that contain numeric or other data that would be best conveyed as a visual?

❑ Is the visual located near the text, and have I referenced the visual within the text (for example, "See Figure 1 on page 9")?

❑ Are my visuals easy to understand at a glance?

❑ Are my visuals accurate and not distorted in any way?

❑ Have I considered each type of visual and determined the most appropriate?

❑ If the visual is part of an item to be circulated on social media, have I made certain that the visual is related directly to the story or report's data, conclusions, and outcomes?

Tables

❑ Am I using a table to compare data or other information?

❑ Is the table clear and uncluttered?

❑ Can readers make easy comparisons of the data in the table?

❑ Are rows and columns clearly labeled?

Graphs

❑ Am I using a graph to depict patterns, trends, or changes over time?

❑ Will a bar graph or a line graph be more effective for these data?

❑ Am I using color effectively but not overwhelmingly?

❑ Is each bar or line distinct and easy to distinguish?

Charts

❑ Am I using a chart to illustrate relationships of parts to a larger whole?

❑ In a flowchart, is the flow easy to follow and are all boxes connected?

❑ In an organization chart, are the titles/names clear and easy to read?

❑ In a pie chart, do the slices of the pie add up to 100%?

Illustrations, Diagrams, and Photographs

❑ Are the illustrations sufficiently clear without being too detailed?

❑ Do all illustrations and diagrams have a title or explanation?

❑ Is the quality of my photographs sufficient for viewers to see what I am trying to illustrate?

❑ Am I using any symbols or icons sparingly?

Applications

General Applications

1. You have been asked to create a visual about the historic uses of various energy sources in the U.S. during the latter part of the 20th century. Display the following information in the visual format most appropriate for a semi-technical audience (engineers but also some managers at the company who are technically adept but are not engineers). Describe your assumptions about this audience, and explain why you selected the type of visual as most effective for these readers. Include with the visual a caption that interprets and explains the data.

   Data: Assume that the Department of Energy breaks down energy consumption in the United States (by source) into these percentages: **In 1970**, coal, 18.5; natural gas, 32.8; hydro and geothermal, 3.1; nuclear, 1.2; oil, 44.4. **In 1980**, coal, 20.3; natural gas, 26.9; hydro and geothermal, 3.8; nuclear, 4.0; oil, 45.0. In **1990**, coal, 23.5; natural gas, 23.8; hydro and geothermal, 7.3; nuclear, 4.1; oil, 41.3. In **2000**, coal, 20.3; natural gas, 25.2; hydro and geothermal, 9.6; nuclear, 6.3; oil, 38.6.

2. Find an article in a journal or newspaper (print or online) that lacks the visuals necessary to support the purpose of the article or the needs of its readers. Analyze the article and identify where visuals would be helpful. Make a list of the visuals you would recommend. Pick one visual from your list and create it. Does the article contain all the data or information you need to create the visual?

3. Devise a pie chart to depict your yearly expenses. Title the chart and be prepared to discuss it in class. (Hint: you can use Excel, Quicken, or other apps to convert your data to a pie chart. But remember that the data you input must be correct or your pie chart won't be accurate.)

Team Applications

1. As a team, obtain enrollment figures at your college for the past five years by gender, age, race, or any other pertinent category. Construct a bar graph to illustrate one of these relationships over the five years.

2. As a team, decide what would be the most appropriate visual for illustrating this relationship: a comparison of three top models of flat screen televisions, according to cost, size, brand repair records, and picture quality. In groups of two, create this visual, then compare approaches. Why did one group choose one type of visual over another?

Global Application

The International Organization for Standardization (ISO) is a group devoted to standardizing a range of material, including technical specifications and visual information. If you've ever been in an airport and seen the many international signs directing travelers to the restroom or informing them not to smoke, you have seen ISO signs. Go to the ISO Web site to learn about ISO icons and symbols. Show some of the icons and symbols, and explain why these work for international audiences.

Digital and Social Media Application

Social media relies heavily on the use of images. Look for a news story or meme, preferably from a business or technical site, that recently appeared on your Facebook, LinkedIn, or Twitter feed. First, analyze the visual in relation to the text/headline. Next, open up the link and read the story or report. Is the visual authentic to the story (for instance a chart or graph based on the data in the article), or did the writer select an unrelated visual to enhance a particular point of view? What features of the story or report does the visual enhance? How does this visual increase the chances that this item will be reposted? What could the writer have done to create a better connection between the visual and the story or report's findings? Write a memo to your instructor with answers to these questions. Include a screen capture of the item and a link to the original meme or story.

Chapter 8
Designing User-Friendly Documents

 Learning Objectives

8.1 Understand the importance of document design.

8.2 Appreciate the role of accessibility, cohesiveness, hierarchy, and inclusiveness in document design.

8.3 Use design elements for consistency, coherence, navigation, and emphasis.

Chapter Outline

The Importance of User-Friendly Document Design   124

Characteristics of Well-Designed Documents   125

Specific Design Elements   128
> *Strategies for Designing: Consistency and Cohesiveness*   131
> *Strategies for Designing: Navigation and Emphasis*   136
> *Checklist for Document Design*   137

Applications   138

Design, the layout of words and graphics, determines the look of a document. Whether hard copy or digital, well-designed pages invite readers in, guide them through the material, and help them understand and remember the information.

This chapter provides principles and guidelines that are generally applicable across many media types (print, digital). See Chapter 19 for more on blogs, wikis, and Web pages.

The Importance of User-Friendly Document Design

8.1   Understand the importance of document design.

Design affects a document's usability

Like all decisions about technical communication, document design consists of a series of informed choices. You need to decide about fonts, typography, white space, and other visual elements, based on the document's audience and purpose. These decisions affect the usability of the document.

Imagine you are asked to produce a heart surgery brochure for a hospital. The brochure's intended audience consists of patients who have a particular heart condition and may need to undergo a specific type of heart surgery. The brochure's purpose is to explain the procedure, answer frequently asked questions, and review the risks—while reassuring patients.

Begin by analyzing your audience and purpose

Before you would even begin to think about what to write or how to design the document, you would need to do an audience and purpose analysis (see Chapter 3). If the brochure also needed to include a list of tasks, such as a checklist of actions patients must take, you might also conduct a task analysis (explained in Chapter 3). Your analysis would yield much important information. For example, you are likely to determine the following as the most important outcomes for the document:

1. To reassure fearful patients that the surgery is safe and that the recovery rate is quicker than that of many other types of heart surgery.

2. To ensure that readers are able to understand what they need to do before, during, and after the surgery.

3. To make certain that older patients—who make up the largest population of candidates for this surgery and who sometimes have poor eyesight—are able to read the document.

To reassure fearful patients, you could choose a comforting typeface, a warm color scheme, and plenty of white space to give the brochure an unimposing look. To ensure that patients understand the steps involved, you could use numbered and bulleted lists to break up and simplify the various procedures. To make the document more readable for older patients, you could use a large font size. To make the document accessible to as many readers as possible, you could design print copies for a doctor's waiting room and a PDF version for the Web site.

Design the document to meet reader needs

Document design, like all aspects of technical communication, puts audience and purpose first.

Characteristics of Well-Designed Documents

8.2 **Appreciate the role of accessibility, cohesiveness, hierarchy, and inclusiveness in document design.**

Readers appreciate documents that are well designed because such documents make it easy and pleasant for people to access and use the information they need. Well-designed documents typically have four characteristics: they are inviting and accessible; they flow well as a single, cohesive unit; they provide a visual hierarchy, displaying information in the right order; and they address a diversity of readers. Figure 8.1 does not meet those requirements, while Figure 8.2 (a revision of the same document) does.

Four audience expectations of a document's design

People generally read technical documents only because they have to. They may pick up a document because they need information, as in the heart surgery brochure described above, or they may be presented with a document they are required to read for work. Either way, readers will resist a document that is intimidating or hard to read and will try to get the information in some other way (e.g., going online to find a more straightforward presentation or asking a colleague or the writer for clarification).

Readers expect an inviting and accessible design

Word processing, page layout, and other apps can help you with document design, but all the software in the world won't make a difference unless you first understand the basic principles of visual appeal and accessibility.

Notice how Figure 8.1 presents a barrage of information with absolutely no design elements, making the information needlessly intimidating, unappealing, and hard to grasp. In contrast, Figure 8.2 uses a clear title, margins, white space, bullets,

Figure 8.1 Ineffective page design

Mold is a public health problem. Molds are simple organisms that are found virtually everywhere, indoors and outdoors. The potential health effects of indoor mold are a growing concern. Mold can cause or worsen certain illnesses (e.g., some allergic and occupation-related diseases and infections in health care settings). There is not conclusive evidence, however, about whether indoor mold is associated with a multitude of other health problems, such as pulmonary hemorrhage, memory loss, and lack of energy.

The Centers for Disease Control has accomplished much on the problem. The CDC has a mold Web site (http://www.cdc.gov/nceh/airpollution/mold) that provides information on molds and health and links to resources. In conjunction with the Council of State and Territorial Epidemiologists, the CDC has created an inventory of state indoor air quality programs which is available at http://www.cdc.gov/nceh.airpollution/indoor_air.htm. The CDC assists states in responding to mold-related issues, including offering technical assistance with assessment, cleanup efforts, and prevention of further mold growth and unnecessary exposure. The CDC is strengthening state, local and tribal capacity to respond to mold-related issues, including: determining the extent to which state programs establish coordinated responses to indoor mold exposures, working with federal and other organizations to coordinate plans related to indoor air and mold, developing a coordinated public response strategy, and identifying resources for developing and implementing responses. The CDC is also developing an agenda for research, service, and education related to mold. As a first step, the CDC contracted with the Institute of Medicine (IOM) to conduct a study on the relationship between damp or moldy indoor environments and the manifestation of adverse health effects and to provide recommendations for future research. The CDC's mold-related agenda is expected to address subjects such as the following: characterizing environmental conditions that allow mold growth indoors and the association between indoor mold and disease or illness; improving the capacity of state, local, and tribal health departments to prevent, investigate, and control mold exposures; and conducting and supporting research to define the association between damp or moldy indoor environments and harmful health effects.

The next steps the CDC will take include assisting states and others in responding to mold issues and developing an agenda for research, service, and education related to mold as described above. For more information, visit http://www.cdc.gov/nceh/airpollution/mold.

Document is untitled and provides no visual hierarchy: everything looks equal

Small margins make the document look crowded

Unbroken paragraph looks dense and intimidating

Inadequate white space makes this version hard on the eye

headings, and color to present the same information in a much more open, inviting, and accessible manner.

Generally, readers view a document first as a whole unit, scanning the page quickly to get a sense of the overall layout. Even from a distance, without being able to read the text, readers should be able to answer the question "How is this document structured?" Design elements help readers answer that question.

Readers appreciate a design that works as a single, cohesive unit

Consider how Figure 8.1 tells readers nothing about how the document works as a unit—it is simply a page full of text. Figure 8.2, on the other hand, has a purpose (as indicated by a title), moves from point A to point B (as indicated by the headings), and presents a list of specific facts (as indicated by the bullets).

Readers appreciate a design that forms a visual hierarchy

Readers also expect the document to highlight the most important information. In other words, they expect the document's design to help them determine the *visual*

Figure 8.2 Effective redesign of Figure 8.1

Even from a distance, readers can see the document as a cohesive, single unit

CDC™   **PROGRAM IN BRIEF**

Title, headings, and bullets provide a visual hierarchy

Mold

Ample margins and white space give the document an open, accessible look

WHAT IS THE PUBLIC HEALTH PROBLEM?
Molds are simple organisms that are found virtually everywhere, indoors and outdoors. The potential health effects of indoor mold are a growing concern. Mold can cause or worsen certain illnesses (e.g., some allergic and occupation-related diseases and infections in health care settings). There is not conclusive evidence, however, about whether indoor mold is associated with a multitude of other health problems, such as pulmonary hemorrhage, memory loss, and lack of energy.

WHAT HAS CDC ACCOMPLISHED?

Bulleted list breaks up dense paragraphs

- CDC's Mold Web site (http://www.cdc.gov/mold) provides information on molds and health and links to resources. In conjunction with the Council of State and Territorial Epidemiologists, CDC has created an inventory of state indoor air quality programs, which is available at http://www.cdc.gov/nceh/airpollution/indoor_air.htm.
- CDC assists states in responding to mold-related issues, including offering technical assistance with assessment, cleanup efforts, and prevention of further mold growth and unnecessary exposure.
- CDC is strengthening state, local, and tribal capacity to respond to mold-related issues, including (1) determining the extent to which state programs establish coordinated responses to indoor mold exposures; (2) working with federal and other organizations to coordinate plans related to indoor air and mold; (3) developing a coordinated public response strategy; and (4) identifying resources for developing and implementing responses.

Document is available in PDF and can be viewed on a screen or printed on paper

- CDC is developing an agenda for research, service, and education related to mold. As a first step, CDC contracted with the Institute of Medicine (IOM) to conduct a study on the relationship between damp or moldy indoor environments and the manifestation of adverse health effects and to provide recommendations for future research. CDC's mold-related agenda is expected to address subjects such as the following:
  o Characterizing environmental conditions that allow mold growth indoors and the association between indoor mold and disease or illness;
  o Improving the capacity of state, local, and tribal health departments to prevent, investigate, and control mold exposures;
  o Conducting and supporting research to define the association between damp or moldy indoor environments and harmful health effects.

Simple use of second color for Web address and headings helps readers focus on essential information

WHAT ARE THE NEXT STEPS?
CDC will continue to assist states and others in responding to mold issues and develop an agenda for research, service, and education related to ***mold*** as described above.

Hyperlink allows readers of a PDF version to navigate to more information

For more information, visit http://www.cdc.gov/mold.

DEPARTMENT OF HEALTH AND HUMAN SERVICES
CENTERS FOR DISEASE CONTROL AND PREVENTION
SAFER · HEALTHIER · PEOPLE™

SOURCE: Centers for Disease Control and Prevention.

hierarchy of the information, displayed primarily through the level and design of the headings and the inclusion of numbered or bulleted lists.

Notice how Figure 8.1 provides no visual hierarchy. It simply offers a series of paragraphs, each seemingly offering information of equal importance. In contrast, Figure 8.2 offers a clear hierarchy of information. All three headed sections are of equal importance, and so the headers are designed identically (same font, font size, and color). The bulleted items fall into two levels of detail: general and specific (the more specific bulleted items are indented further in a different style of bullet).

A document's design can also affect its multicultural appeal. For instance, a certain color might be interpreted differently by different readers. As a rule, use subtle and varied colors, standard fonts and font sizes, and appropriate white space.

Readers appreciate a design that takes a wide range of people into account

Specific Design Elements

8.3   **Use design elements for consistency, coherence, navigation, and emphasis.**

The elements of document design comprise two categories: those that give a document a consistent and cohesive look and those that aid navigation and add emphasis. No design elements should be merely decorative; all should enhance the reader's orientation and understanding.

Designing for Consistency and Cohesiveness

Elements that provide consistency and cohesiveness include grid patterns, margins, paragraphs, justification, white space, line spacing and indentation, font style, and font size. Each element is described below and summarized in the Strategies on pages 131–132.

GRID PATTERNS.   Grid patterns help readers make sense of a document as a single unit because they create an underlying structure throughout the document. Figure 8.3 shows a sampling of grid patterns. Most documents follow a standard horizontal grid pattern, as, for example, a memo or letter. A vertical grid is commonly used in manuals, brochures, or newsletters. In rare cases, you may want to use a combined grid pattern. Word processing and page layout software let you choose from templates that offer different combinations of grid patterns, appropriate for different formats (brochure versus newsletter, for example).

MARGINS.   Consistent margins give the document a unified appearance. Margins must not only be the same width throughout a document but also wide enough. Narrow margins crowd the page and make the material look harder than it probably is. On your 8½-by-11-inch page, provide margins of at least 1 or 1½ inches on each side, as well as at the top and bottom, of every page. If the manuscript is to be bound in a cover, increase the left (inside) margin to 2 inches.

Figure 8.3 Grid patterns

Vertical Grid
(2 columns)   Horizontal Grid   Combined Grid

PARAGRAPHS. Whereas ordering information within paragraphs (as discussed in Chapter 5) affects a document's overall structure, the shape of each paragraph serves a design function. Use a long paragraph (but try to keep it to 15 lines or less) for clustering material that is closely related or best understood in one block; use short paragraphs for making complex material more digestible (as in step-by-step instructions or for emphasizing vital information). At the same time, try to vary the lengths of your paragraphs. Readers are likely to resist a document that consists primarily of long or short paragraphs only. Also, avoid "orphans" (one line of a paragraph at the bottom of a page) and "widows" (one line of a paragraph at the top of a page).

JUSTIFICATION. Text is always automatically flush left (lined up evenly along the left margin). However, along the right margin, you have a choice between *justified* text (even right margins) or *unjustified* text (uneven or "ragged" right margins). Each arrangement creates its own feel.

In justified text, blocks of text look clean and even on either side, but spacing varies between words and letters on a line, and you may need to frequently hyphenate words. Justified text is generally used in books, annual reports, and other formal materials. In unjustified text, text is ragged on the right side of text blocks, but spacing between words and letters on a line is even, and you can avoid overuse of hyphenation. Unjustified text is appropriate for more personal forms of communication, such as letters, memos, and in-house reports. Whichever justification you choose, be consistent throughout the document. Figure 8.4 illustrates justified and unjustified text.

WHITE SPACE. Sometimes, it's what's *not* on the page that makes a difference. Whereas margins are the empty spaces along the left, right, top, and bottom of a document, white space is any empty space surrounding figures and tables, between columns, and between paragraphs. Areas of text or visuals surrounded by appropriate white space draw the reader's eye to those areas. Well-designed white space is used evenly throughout an entire document, orienting readers by keeping related elements

Figure 8.4 Justified and unjustified text

According to the chart in Figure 3, the population of Queens County, New York, remains the most diverse in the United States. Historically, particular populations have been concentrated in particular areas. For example, Long Island has long been known as a largely Latino area, Woodside as mostly Asian and Middle eastern, and Jamaica as primarily African and Caribbean. However, over the last 15 years, these concentrations have become less cogent.

—Right and left justified text (from a formal report)

In order for this new initiative to be a success, we ask for the support and participation of every employee of the company. Please take a moment to review the enclosed list of training sessions, which will begin on August 24th. We strongly suggest that you sign up for at least one session during the first month to get an overview of the initiative, then take intermediate and advanced sessions in the upcoming months.

—Left-only justified text (from a memo)

together, isolating and emphasizing important elements, and providing breathing room between blocks of information, as in Figure 8.5.

LINE SPACING AND INDENTATION. Always be consistent about line spacing. In most technical documents, use double spacing for ease of reading. When inserting a long quotation, indent the quotation, use single spacing within the quotation only, then return to double spacing for regular text. Also, be consistent about indentation. As a general rule, indent each paragraph unless you insert an extra line space between paragraphs.

Figure 8.5 White space

White space in example #1 equates the two visuals and isolates them from the paragraph

1.

White space in example #2 equates all three paragraphs and provides breathing room between them

2.

FONT STYLE.   Font style refers to the typeface used and the personality that each typeface conveys. Fonts fall into several categories: *Serif* fonts (such as Times New Roman and Palatino) include serifs, or fine lines that extend horizontally from the main strokes of a letter. Serif fonts are generally considered more formal. *Sans serif* fonts (such as Helvetica and Arial) do not include these fine lines ("sans" is French for "without"). They tend to look professional without being quite as formal as serif fonts and are appropriate for most other types of technical documents. *Decorative fonts* are often used in advertising and marketing but should be avoided in technical documents. Figure 8.6 shows the differences between these font styles. Pick an appropriate font and stick with it throughout a document. For headings, you might select a different font (and a larger size); be sure to use those heading fonts consistently.

Figure 8.6 Sample font styles

Italics, **boldface**, and ALL CAPS are another element of font style you need to consider. Sometimes, people use italics much as they would use a highlighter or marker to set words apart and draw attention to these words. But excessive use of italics can make it hard for your audience to decide which information is truly important. The same is true for boldface: too much bold will lose its appeal. Bold is good for headings, subheadings, or terms or concepts that you want to emphasize in a sentence. Within text, use bold selectively. Use all capital letters for a few words only or when creating short headings. Long strings of capital (uppercase) letters and words are hard to read.

FONT SIZE.   Use font sizes that are easy to read. Standard guidelines suggest using between a 10-point and 12-point font size for the text of most documents (usually erring to the side of 12-point). Use a 2-point larger font for each level of headings (see page 132). Most important, be consistent throughout the document.

Strategies

for Designing: Consistency and Cohesiveness

Grid Patterns

- **Select an appropriate grid pattern.** Use a horizontal grid pattern for most basic documents (memos, letters, reports). Use a vertical grid pattern for specialized documents (manuals, brochures, and newsletters). Use a combined pattern rarely.
- **Use the same grid pattern throughout the document.**

Margins

- **Use adequate margins.** Use a 1-inch to 1½-inch margin along the top, bottom, left, and right of the page. For bound documents, use a 2-inch inside margin.
- **Use the same margins throughout the document.**

Paragraphs

- **Vary the length of paragraphs.** Use long and short paragraphs as appropriate to keep blocks of related text together.
- **Avoid orphans and widows.** Add extra space to bump orphans to the next page, and reduce space (or shorten paragraph content) to pull widows to the previous page.

Justification

- **Determine if your text will be justified on one or both margins.** Use justified left and right for formal documents, and use left-only justified (ragged right margin) for less formal documents (memos, letters, in-house reports, and so on).
- **Use the same justification throughout the document.**

White Space

- **Use plenty of white space.** Use white space between paragraphs and/or columns and around visuals, when appropriate.
- **Use white space consistently.** If you include white space between paragraphs or columns, use the same amount throughout the document. Include the same amount of white space around each visual in the document.

Line Spacing and Indentation

- **Decide how you want to use line spacing and indentation.** Use single, double, or other (for instance, 1½) line spacing. Indent all paragraphs or none.
- **Stick with your original plan.** Don't vary the line spacing or paragraph indentation. Be consistent.

Font Style

- **Use either a serif or sans serif font.** Use a serif font for formal reports and a sans serif font for most other documents.
- **Decide which serif or sans serif font to use.** Some of the most popular serif fonts are Times New Roman and Times. The most popular sans serif font is Helvetica.
- **Stay with the same font throughout.** You might choose a different font for any headings in your document.
- **Use *italics*, boldface, and ALL CAPS selectively and sparingly.**

Font Size

- **Use a standard font size.** Generally, a 10-point to 12-point size (depending on the font style) should be used for text and a slightly larger size for each level of heading.
- **Use a consistent font size.** Stay with the font size you've chosen for each element (text, headings, notes) throughout the document.

Designing for Navigation and Emphasis

Elements that aid navigation and add emphasis include headings; color, shading, bold-face, italics, and underlining; bulleted and numbered lists; running heads and footers; and tables of contents and indexes.

HEADINGS. Headings not only help chunk information into easily digestible parts (structure, see Chapter 5) but also guide readers through a page and signal the relative importance of topics. Readers often will move back and forth in a document, searching for the sections that seem most relevant, or they will scan only the main headings, skipping the lower-level headings. To help readers navigate, design your headings consistently.

Headings generally break down into A-level (major headings), B-level (secondary headings, which always fall beneath A-level headings), and C-level (minor headings, which always fall beneath B-level headings). Each higher level of heading should encompass at least two heads at the next lower level. Lower levels of headings (D-level, etc.) make a document appear hard to navigate. Use bulleted or numbered lists instead. *Levels and design of headings*

Always use the same font style, size, and color at each level. Avoid orphans (headings that stand alone at the bottom of a page without any text beneath them). Notice how the headings are set up in Figure 8.2 (page 127). The A-level heading ("Mold") uses a bold font, larger than the other fonts. B-level heads are in all caps and boldface and italics, set above each paragraph. Instead of using headings, C-level entries use bullets and are indented. These C-level entries could also be set up as actual headings by creating a short title for each and using boldface along with the bullets and indentations.

COLOR, SHADING, BOLDFACE, ITALICS, AND UNDERLINING. Color can help readers move through the text and can draw attention to particular areas. For example, you can use color for headings, tabs, sidebars, callouts (labels that identify parts of a figure), and leader lines (dotted, dashed, or solid lines that connect labels with their objects), as in Figure 8.7. To highlight important information, you can use color for screens, horizontal and vertical rules, type, cross-references, and ruled boxes, as in Figure 8.8.

Use color sparingly and use colors that aren't overly bright, that don't obscure the text they cover, and that contrast well with black print. You may also use shading, bold, italics, or underlining.

BULLETED AND NUMBERED LISTS. Whenever you include a series of similar or step-by-step items within a sentence or paragraph, consider using a bulleted or numbered list. Bulleted and numbered lists help readers navigate through dense information and emphasize the information by separating it from the text. However, don't overuse; don't use fancy icons when a plain round dot will do; and don't confuse the functions of bulleted and numbered lists. Bullets separate and highlight equally weighted items. Numbers enumerate the fixed sequence of steps in a process. Figure 8.9 compares in-text lists to bulleted and numbered lists. (For more on using lists, see Appendix B.)

Figure 8.7 Using color for navigation

Color headings   Color tabs   Color sidebars, callouts,
and leader lines

Figure 8.8 Using color for emphasis

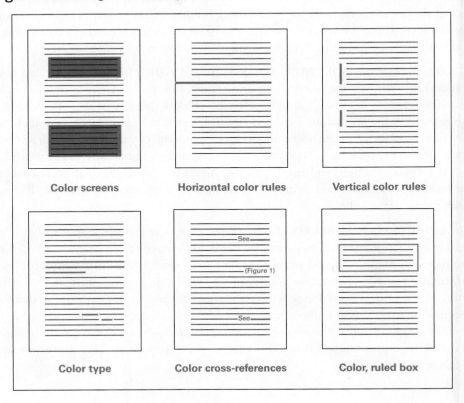

Color screens   Horizontal color rules   Vertical color rules

Color type   Color cross-references   Color, ruled box

Figure 8.9 Bulleted versus numbered lists

Text	Bulleted list	
The fire ant has now spread to three regions: the Galapagos Islands, the South Pacific, and Africa.	The fire ant has now spread to three regions: • The Galapagos Islands • The South Pacific • Africa	To organize and highlight similar items, use a bulleted list

Text	Numbered list	
There are three steps to installing your graphics card: Open the computer case, insert the graphics card in the slot, and close the case.	To install your graphics card: 1. Open the computer case. 2. Insert the graphics card in the slot. 3. Close the case.	To enumerate a fixed sequence of steps, use a numbered list

RUNNING HEADERS AND FOOTERS. Running heads and footers in longer printed documents help readers find material. They also help readers stay oriented to their location in the document. Typically, a running head includes section- or chapter-specific information (as in this book) and running footers are reserved for book titles. However, page numbers may be included either in a running head or footer. In a document with single-sided pages, running heads or footers should be placed consistently, typically flush right. In a document with double-sided pages, the running heads or footers should appear flush left on left-hand pages and flush right on right-hand pages, as in Figure 8.10.

Figure 8.10 Running heads and footers

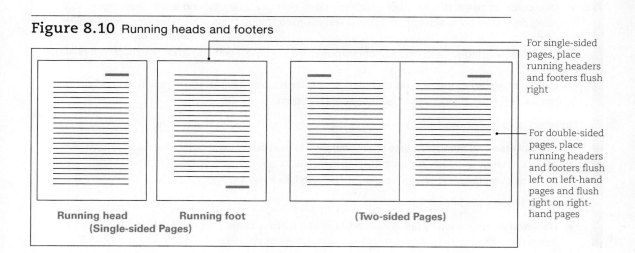

Running head (Single-sided Pages)   Running foot   (Two-sided Pages)

For single-sided pages, place running headers and footers flush right

For double-sided pages, place running headers and footers flush left on left-hand pages and flush right on right-hand pages

TABLES OF CONTENTS AND INDEXES. In a longer document, a table of contents and an index help readers find the information they need. In addition, the table of contents signals the relationship between topics and subtopics. Make sure your table of contents matches the heading structure of your document exactly.

Most of us have had the frustrating experience of trying to look something up in an index and discovering that the term we use is not the term the index uses. A successful index depends on knowing what categories, terms, and topics your readers are likely to look up when searching for what they need. For longer, more complex documents, consider hiring a professional indexer.

Strategies

for Designing: Navigation and Emphasis

Headings

- **Design headings consistently.** Always use the same font style, size, and color for the same level of headings. A-level headings are typically in all caps, boldface, and rest above paragraphs; B-level headings are usually in initial caps, boldface, and rest above paragraphs; and C-level heads are typically in initial caps, boldface, and run into paragraphs (whether or not the paragraphs are indented).
- **Divide headings logically.** Make each higher level head yield at least two heads at the next level. B-level headings always fall within A-level headed sections, and C-level headings always fall within B-level headed sections.
- **Avoid excessive headings.** Try to avoid D-level headings and never move to a level beyond that.
- **Avoid orphans.** If a heading stands alone at the bottom of a page, without at least two lines of text beneath, add more space to bump the heading to the next page.

Color, Shading, Boldface, Italics, and Underlining

- **Use color as needed.** Use color headings, tabs, sidebars, callouts, and leader lines (page 133) for navigation. Use color screens, horizontal/vertical rules, type, cross references, and ruled boxes for emphasis.
- **Use color sparingly.** Color should not overpower the document and should complement, not obstruct, the text.
- **Use shading, bold, italics, and underlining.** If color is unavailable or you prefer to aid navigation and provide emphasis in other ways, use these design options.

Bulleted and Numbered Lists

- **Use bulleted and numbered lists appropriately.** Bulleted lists show a series of similar items, while numbered lists show a sequence of step-by-step items.
- **Don't overuse lists.** Otherwise, your document might look like a shopping list.

Running Heads and Footers

- **Decide if running footers are necessary.** Usually, running footers are used only for full-length books, though you may use them in documents to place page numbers.

- **Always include page numbers.** Whether you put them in running heads or running footers, page numbers are essential. For a long document, count your title page as page i, without numbering it, and number all front matter pages, including the table of contents and abstract, with lowercase roman numerals (ii, iii, iv). Number the first and subsequent text pages with Arabic numerals (1, 2, 3, and so on).
- **Include section- or chapter-specific information in running heads.**
- **Format running heads and footers correctly.** See Figure 8.10.

Tables of Contents and Indexes

- **Use tables of contents and indexes for longer documents.**
- **Make sure tables of contents match document headers exactly.**
- **Use standard index categories and topics.** Try to accurately anticipate which terms readers will look up in searching for what they need.

Checklist

for Document Design

Consistency and Cohesiveness

- ❏ Does my grid structure provide a consistent visual theme?
- ❏ Are margins ample?
- ❏ Is each paragraph tailored to suit its purpose?
- ❏ Is the document's right margin unjustified?
- ❏ Does the white space create areas of emphasis?
- ❏ Is the document's line spacing and indentation effective?
- ❏ Have I chosen readable and appropriate font sizes and styles?
- ❏ In general, have I used versions of a single typeface throughout?
- ❏ If different typefaces *are* used, are they used consistently?
- ❏ Have I used *italics*, **boldface**, and ALL CAPS sparingly?

Navigation and Emphasis

- ❏ Do headings clearly announce the document's large and small segments?
- ❏ Are headings sized to reflect their specific level in the document?
- ❏ Are headings visually consistent and grammatically parallel?
- ❏ Have I formatted a series of parallel items as a list (numbered or bulleted, as appropriate)?
- ❏ Do running headers and footers announce sections of the document?
- ❏ Have I used page numbers appropriately?
- ❏ Are the table of contents and the index complete and easy to navigate?

Applications

General Application

With a partner, find two printed documents: one that demonstrates good use of design elements and another that demonstrates confusing or inconsistent use. Imagine you and your partner are a team of technical communication consultants. Write a memo to the manager of the organization that produced the effective document, explaining its positive features. Write a memo to the manager of the organization that produced the confusing document, making suggestions for improvement.

Team Application

Working in teams of three or four people, find a document (print or online) intended to answer a question—a patient brochure about an illness or medical procedure, a reference guide for new students on campus, or a personnel document from your company, for example. Your team's goal is to redesign the document so that it uses an appropriate grid design; makes effective use of white space; and uses formatting, fonts, headings, and other page design elements consistently and clearly.

Appoint one member of your group to serve as editor. The editor is responsible for making sure the design elements are used consistently throughout the redesigned document. Ask each team member to work on one section of the document. Assemble all the redesigned sections, and ask your editor to review the materials. The editor should check your work against the Checklist for Document Design.

Global Application

Find a document that presents the same information in several languages (assembly instructions for various products are often written in two or three languages, for example). Evaluate the design decisions made in these documents. For example, are the different languages presented side by side or in different sections? Write a memo to classmates and your instructor evaluating the document and making recommendations for improvement.

Digital and Social Media Application

Technical documents are often created using templates, which are readily available in word processing and page design programs. Templates allow you to create sophisticated, attractive documents quickly and easily. But this ease of use can restrict your options to change or customize a design for a specific audience and purpose. In groups of two, consider the heart surgery brochure described on the first page of this chapter. Find a few brochure templates, either in Microsoft Word, Google docs, or the Adobe Digital Publishing Suite, and compare your findings to the design principles presented in the Strategies boxes (pages 131–132 and 136–137). What are the pros and cons of using a template for this situation? How much are you able to manipulate the template's settings? For example, can you change an all caps heading to upper- and lowercase? Can you change the colors? Which programs are easier to use, and can you find any online tutorials to learn more?

Part 3
Documents

9   Résumés and Other Employment Materials   140

10   Memos and Letters   163

11   Definitions   191

12   Descriptions   204

13   Instructions and Procedures   225

14   Summaries   248

15   Informal Reports   262

16   Formal Reports   281

17   Proposals   309

Chapter 9
Résumés and Other Employment Materials

 Learning Objectives

9.1 Focus on what you can offer an employer.

9.2 Research jobs and narrow your job search.

9.3 Create an effective reverse chronological or functional résumé.

9.4 Write a persuasive solicited or unsolicited job application letter.

9.5 Submit appropriate digital job application materials.

9.6 Compile a dossier, portfolio, or e-portfolio.

9.7 Prepare for job interviews and write professional follow-up communication.

Chapter Outline

Assessing Your Skills and Aptitudes   142

Researching the Job Market   142

Résumés   143
  Strategies for Creating a Résumé   146

Application Letters   148
  Strategies for Application Letters   150

Digital versus Print Job Application Materials   151
  Strategies for Digital Job Application Materials   152

Dossiers, Portfolios, and E-portfolios   152
  Strategies for Dossiers, Portfolios, and E-portfolios   155

Interviews and Follow-up Letters   155
  Strategies for Interviews and Follow-up Notes   159
  Checklist for Résumés   160
  Checklist for Job Application Letters   160
  Checklist for Supporting Materials   161

Applications   161

This chapter highlights the importance of using the skills you have learned thus far and encourages you to create a portfolio of sample documents that will help you on the job market.

Enhance your job search by relying on key principles from earlier chapters. For example, research each specific position for which you apply (see Chapter 2). Show that you communicate persuasively, present yourself honestly, and understand team-work (see Chapters 1, 3, and 4). Also, prepare all application materials with a clear sense of audience and purpose (see Chapter 3).

Review the basics of effective communication

In today's job market, there is strong competition for jobs at all levels. Whether you are applying for your first professional job or changing careers, you need to mar-ket your skills effectively. At each stage of the job search, you must stand out among the competition.

Assessing Your Skills and Aptitudes

9.1   Focus on what you can offer an employer.

Begin your job search by assessing the qualities and skills you can offer a potential employer:

Identify your assets

- Do I communicate well, and am I a good listener?
- Do I work well in groups and with people from different backgrounds?
- Do I have experience or aptitude for a leadership role?
- Can I solve problems and get things done?
- Can I perform well under pressure?
- Can I work independently, with minimal supervision?
- Do I have any special skills (public speaking, working with people, technical skills, aptitude with writing and editing, analytical skills, second or third languages, artistic/musical talent, mathematical aptitude)?
- Do I have any hobbies that could improve my job prospects?
- Would I prefer to work at a large company or a small one? At a for-profit or a non-profit organization?
- Do I like to travel, or would I prefer working in a single location?

Besides helping to focus your job search, your answers to these questions will come in handy when you write your résumé and prepare for job interviews.

Researching the Job Market

9.2   Research jobs and narrow your job search.

Search within a reasonable range

Narrowing your search does not mean limiting yourself to one or two types of job, but instead giving yourself a measure of realistic focus. Try to stick to those fields that interest you most and fit you best.

Don't just dive in; work step by step

Begin your research well in advance of the time you need to have a job lined up. If you've never done job research, the question "Where do I start?" can be daunting. More than ever, seemingly endless sources of information are available to job seekers. Try to proceed in a step-by-step, logical way, as described below, rather than immediately going online and trying to navigate random Web sites.

Consult industry-specific resources

Before you apply for specific jobs, learn more about the industry or area where you'd like to work. Consult reference materials (such as books, magazines, and Web sites) that provide background information about working in this field. Join a professional group related to your industry, study the information on its Web site, and attend local meetings where you can speak with people already working in this area. (Note that many professional societies offer reduced membership rates for students.) Learn about the key companies in your industry of choice—find out who they are, make a list, and research those particular companies. Finally, set up an informational interview with someone at a company in this field. Even busy professionals are usually willing to speak with students who want to learn more about a particular company or area of employment. These professionals can offer general advice about the industry as a whole and about their own company.

Engage in Active Networking

Once you've narrowed down your job search, go to your campus job placement office and meet with a career counselor. Ask about any upcoming on-campus job fairs, alumni networks, résumé workshops, and other campus resources. Go to the library and speak with a reference librarian who can point you to helpful library resources, too. Contact acquaintances and colleagues who may know someone else you can contact.

> Network in person and online

In addition, use online networking to your advantage. Set up a LinkedIn account and begin going through your contact list to connect with everyone you know who might be of assistance in the job search. Look for communities of interest related to your field, see what jobs are available in your preferred field and location, search for people you know and connect with them, then see what other connections LinkedIn might recommend. In certain fields, such as engineering, science, and management, you might also look for ways to connect to a recruiter on LinkedIn. Remember that the human connection, both in person and facilitated by LinkedIn and similar sites, is a very powerful way to find a job.

Job postings can be located in a variety of places. Use LinkedIn and other sites such as Monster.com, Careerbuilder.com, and the *Riley Guide* to find jobs across the country or specific to your location; consult the Help Wanted sections of your local newspapers; locate industry-specific jobs on professional organization Web sites; or find jobs advertised only on human resources Web sites of particular companies. You don't have to limit your search options to advertised jobs, however. Another approach is to send an unsolicited application letter to a company that interests you (for more on unsolicited application letters, see page 150).

> Look for specific job postings or send out unsolicited application letters

Résumés

9.3 **Create an effective reverse chronological or functional résumé.**

Before applying for any job, you should create an effective résumé. A *résumé* is essentially an applicant's personal advertisement for employment. It lists (in a standard format) education and employment history, along with other relevant information, providing a snapshot of the person's qualifications.

> Definition and function of a résumé

A résumé is designed to give an employer an instant overview. In fact, employers initially spend only 15 to 45 seconds looking at a résumé; during this scan, they are looking for a persuasive answer to the bottom-line question: "What can you do for us?"

Employers are impressed by a résumé that looks good, reads easily, appears honest, and provides only the relevant information an employer needs to determine if the applicant should be interviewed. Résumés that are mechanically flawed, cluttered, sketchy, hard to follow, or seemingly dishonest simply get discarded.

Parts of a Résumé

What to include—and not include—in a résumé

All résumés contain standard parts. Every résumé must include contact information, career objectives, education, work experience, and references. A résumé is not the place to include such items as your desired salary and benefits or your requirements for time off. In addition, do not include irrelevant personal information, your photograph, or information that employers are not allowed to legally ask (such as your race, age, or marital status). As you read through this section, refer to Figure 9.1, which includes all the typically required parts.

CONTACT INFORMATION.   Tell prospective employers where they can reach you. If you are between addresses, use the address where your mail is being delivered. Be especially sure that your email address and phone number are accurate. For your phone's voice mail, record a message that is both friendly and professional. If you have a LinkedIn page, include the Web address for your profile page. Remember: Employers may be able to view your Facebook or other social networking pages, so keep those sites professional in tone and content.

CAREER OBJECTIVES.   Spell out the job you want. Avoid vague statements such as "A position in which I can apply my education and experience." Instead, be specific: "An intensive-care nursing position in a teaching hospital, with the eventual goal of supervising and instructing." Tailor your career objective statement as you apply for different jobs, in order to match yourself with each position.

EDUCATION.   Begin with your most recent schooling and work backward. Include the name of the school, degree completed, year completed, and your major and minor. Omit high school, unless the high school's prestige or your achievements there warrant its inclusion. List courses that have directly prepared you for the job you seek. If your class rank or grade point average is favorable, list it. Include specialized training during military service. If you finance your education by working, say so, indicating the percentage of your contribution.

WORK EXPERIENCE.   If your experience relates to the job, list it before your education. List the most recent job and then earlier jobs. Include employers' names and dates of employment. Indicate whether a job was full-time, part-time (hours weekly), or seasonal. Describe your exact duties for each job, indicating promotions. If it is to your advantage, state why you left each job. Include military experience and relevant volunteer work. If you lack paid experience, emphasize your education, including internships and special projects.

LEADERSHIP OR OTHER ACTIVITIES.   By law, you are not required to include a photograph or reveal your sex, religion, race, age, national origin, disability, or

Figure 9.1 Standard Résumé

James David Purdy
203 Elmwood Avenue
San Jose, CA 95139
Phone: (555) 316-2419
Email: jpur@valnet.net

Contact information includes full name and address, phone, and email address

Objective
Customer relations for a hospitality chain, leading to management.

Career objective is specific and tailored to the job

Education
2014–2016
San Jose City College, San Jose, CA
Associate of Arts Degree in Hotel and Restaurant Management, May 2009. Grade point average: 3.25 of a possible 4.00. All college expenses financed by scholarship and part-time job (20 hours weekly).

Education section lists school, location, degree earned, and other relevant information

Employment
2014–2016
Pretalo Lodge and Convention Center, San Jose, CA
Began as desk clerk, promoted to desk manager (part-time) of this 200-unit resort. Responsible for scheduling custodial and room service staff, planning conventions, and handling customer relations.

Work experience section lists most recent jobs first and includes relevant skills applied on the job

2013–2014
Teo's Restaurant, Pensacola, FL
Beginning as waiter, advanced to cashier and finally to assistant manager. Responsible for preparing weekly payroll, making banquet arrangements, and supervising dining room and lounge staff.

2012–2013
Encyclopaedia Britannica, Inc., San Jose, CA
Sales representative (part-time). Received top bonus twice.

2011–2012
White Family Inn, San Luis Obispo, CA
Worked as bus-person, then server (part-time).

Leadership
Awards
Captain of basketball team, 2009; Lion's Club Scholarship, 2011.

Leadership section combines awards, skills, and activities that may be relevant to a job

Languages
Committee chair for student French club; fluent French speaker.

Activities
High school basketball and track team (3 years); college student senate (2 years); Innkeepers' Club—prepared and served monthly dinners at the college (2 years).

References
Available on request.

When no references are included, an "available on request" statement substitutes marital status. List any awards, skills, activities, and interests that are *relevant* to the given position (e.g., memberships, demonstrations of leadership, languages, and special skills that may be of interest to the employer).

REFERENCES. If the employer has requested references, list three to five people who have agreed to provide strong assessments of your qualifications and who can speak on your behalf. Never list as references people who haven't first given you express permission. Your references should not be family members or non-work-related friends; instead, list former employers, professors, and community figures who know you well. If the employer does not request references as part of the initial application, simply state at the end of your résumé: "References available upon request." If you don't list references, prepare a separate reference sheet that you can provide on request. Include each person's job title, company address, and contact information.

Organizing Your Résumé

Reverse chronological versus functional résumés

Organize your résumé to convey the strongest impression of your qualifications, skills, and experience. A standard résumé, like the one in Figure 9.1, is also known as a *reverse chronological résumé*, listing the most recent school and job first. If you have limited experience or education or gaps in your work history (e.g., due to illness, raising children) or if you have frequently switched career paths, create a *functional résumé* (Figure 9.2) to highlight skills relevant to a particular job.

Strategies

for Creating a Résumé

- **Begin your résumé well before your job search.**
- **Tailor your résumé for each job.** Read the advertised job requirements, and adjust your career objective accordingly. Tailor your work experience, personal data, and personal interests to emphasize certain areas for certain jobs. Follow the instructions given on the job application or site.
- **Try to limit your entry-level résumé to a single page.** For entry-level employees, the single page résumé is standard and will help employers get a quick but complete feel for your potential. Experienced professionals will usually have a résumé that fits on two pages.
- **Stick to experience relevant to the job.** Don't list everything you've ever done.
- **Use action verbs and key words.** Action verbs (*supervised, developed, built, taught, installed, managed, trained, solved, planned, directed*) stress your ability to produce results. If your résumé is likely to be scanned electronically or if you post it online, list keywords as nouns (*leadership skills, software development, data processing, editing*) below your contact information and your statement of objective (see Figure 9.4).
- **Use bold, italic, underlining, colors, fonts, bullets, and other devices thoughtfully, for emphasis.** Do not use these features to be artsy.
- **Never invent or distort credentials.** Make yourself look as good as the *facts* allow. Companies routinely investigate claims made in résumés, and people who lie will certainly not be hired.
- **Proofread, proofread, proofread.** Don't rely on autocorrect or spell check alone. Infamous résumé mistakes include winning a "bogus award" instead of a "bonus award" and "ruining" rather than "running" a business.

Figure 9.2 Functional Résumé

Carol R. Chasone
642 Eagle Lane
Eugene, OR 97405
(503-314-5555)
crchasone@eor.edu

OBJECTIVE	Position in marketing/communications with opportunity for advancement

Includes contact information and objective

SALES/ MARKETING SKILLS
- Wrote recruiting letter currently used by the Eugene Chamber of Commerce
- Designed posters for promotion of industrial development in Central Oregon
- Assisted Chamber President in promoting the organization's activities
- Recruited 7 speakers for Chamber meetings
- Wrote 3 public-relations pieces about a local hospital, for area newspapers

COMMUNICATION AND DOCUMENT DESIGN SKILLS
- Conducted demographic study of small businesses in Southwestern OR
- Presented study findings to Eugene Chamber of Commerce
- Wrote 15-page report on results of demographic study
- Designed and wrote two brochures to promote the Small Business Institute
- Designed *Patient Care*, in-house hospital newsletter (print and online)
- Wrote 8 articles and conducted 3 interviews for the newsletter
- Designed 6 posters for in-service hospital programs

Emphasizes three skills areas appropriate to the job, with specific accomplishments in bulleted-list format

ORGANIZATIONAL/ MANAGEMENT SKILLS
- Coordinated weekly Chamber meetings each Fall
- Attended 2 seminars (Houston, Seattle) for hospital public relations
- Trained and supervised 3 new interns at the Small Business Institute
- Scheduled and chaired weekly intern meetings

EDUCATION
Eastern Oregon University
B.S. in Marketing; Graphic Design minor—May 2016
GPA: 3.3/4.0; Dean's List, 5 semesters
Contract Learning: Eugene Chamber of Commerce, Fall 2015
Internships: EOU's Small Business Institute, Spring 2014;
Mercy Hospital, Fall 2015

Includes but deemphasizes education

EMPLOYMENT
Personal trainer (part-time 2012–2013)—Acme Gym, Eugene
Pro Shop salesperson—Eugene Golf Club, summers, 2010–2012

REFERENCES
Available on request

Application Letters

9.4 **Write a persuasive solicited or unsolicited job application letter.**

Definition and
function of an
application
letter

An *application letter*, also known as a *cover letter*, complements your résumé when you apply for a job. The letter's main purpose is to explain how your credentials fit the particular job and to convey a sufficiently informed, professional, and likable persona for the prospective employer to decide that you should be interviewed. Another purpose of the letter is to highlight specific qualifications or skills; for example, you might have listed "Java programming" on your résumé, but for one particular job application, you may wish to call attention to this item in your cover letter:

> My résumé notes that I am experienced with Java programming. In fact, I also tutor Java programming students in our school's learning center.

Solicited and
unsolicited
application
letters

Sometimes, you will apply for positions advertised in print or by word of mouth or where you have been invited to apply (for example, by a recruiter who visits your campus) (*solicited applications*). At other times, you will write prospecting letters to organizations that have not advertised an opening but that might need someone like you (*unsolicited applications*). In either case, tailor your letter to the situation.

Solicited Application Letters

An application letter—whether solicited or unsolicited—consists of an introduction, body, and conclusion as in Figure 9.3.

Use the
introduction to
get right to the
point

In your brief introduction (generally, five lines or fewer), do these things: Name the job you're applying for and where you have seen it advertised; identify yourself and your background; and, if possible, establish a connection by naming the person who encouraged you to apply—but only if that person has given you permission.

Use the body
to demonstrate
your
qualifications

Use the body of your letter to detail your case. Without merely repeating your résumé, relate your qualifications specifically to this job. Be specific. Instead of referring to "much experience" or "increased sales," state that you have "three years of experience" or that you helped create "a 35 percent increase in sales between June and October 2013." Support all claims with evidence. Instead of saying, "I have leadership skills," say, "I served as student senate president during my senior year and was captain of the lacrosse team."

Use the
conclusion to
restate interest

In the conclusion, restate your interest and emphasize your willingness to retrain or relocate if necessary. If the job is nearby, request an interview; otherwise, request a phone call, suggesting a time you can be reached.

Figure 9.3 Solicited Application Letter

203 Elmwood Avenue
San Jose, CA 10462

April 22, 20XX

Sara Costanza
Personnel Director
Liberty International, Inc.
Lansdowne, PA 24153

Dear Ms. Costanza:

Please consider my application for a junior management position at your Lake Geneva resort, as advertised on April 19 on Monster.com. I will graduate from San Jose City College on May 30 with an Associate of Arts degree in hotel and restaurant management. Dr. H. V. Garlid, my nutrition professor, described his experience as a consultant for Liberty International and encouraged me to apply.

As you can see from my enclosed résumé, for two years I worked as a part-time desk clerk, and I was promoted to manager, at a 200-unit resort. This experience, combined with earlier customer relations work in a variety of situations, has given me a clear and practical understanding of customers' needs and expectations.

As an amateur chef, I'm well aware of the effort, attention, and patience required to prepare fine food. Moreover, my skiing and sailing background might be assets to your resort's recreation program.

I have worked hard to hone my hospitality management skills. My experience, education, and personality have prepared me to work well with others and to respond creatively to challenges, crises, and added responsibilities.

If my background meets your needs, please phone me any weekday after 4:00 p.m. at (555) 316-2419.

Sincerely,

James D. Purdy

James D. Purdy

Annotations (right margin):

- Writer identifies self and purpose
- Establishes a connection
- Relates specific qualifications from his résumé to the job opening
- Applies relevant personal interests to the job
- Expresses confidence and enthusiasm throughout
- Makes follow-up easy for the reader

Unsolicited Application Letters

Advantages and disadvantages of unsolicited application letters

Do not limit your job search to advertised openings. In fact, only between 20 and 30 percent of all job openings are advertised. Unsolicited application letters are a good way to uncover possibilities. They do have drawbacks, however: You may waste time writing to organizations that have no openings, and you cannot tailor your letter to advertised requirements. But there are also advantages: Even employers with no openings often welcome and file impressive unsolicited applications or pass them on to another employer who has an opening.

Use the introduction to spark reader interest

Because an unsolicited letter arrives unexpectedly, you need to get the reader's immediate attention. Don't begin, "I am writing to inquire about the possibility of obtaining a position with your company." Instead, open forcefully by establishing a connection with a mutual acquaintance or by making a strong statement or asking a persuasive question as in the following example:

A forceful opening

> Does your hotel chain have a place for a junior manager with a college degree in hospitality management, a proven commitment to quality service, and customer relations experience that extends far beyond textbooks? If so, please consider my application for a position.

Address your letter to the person most likely in charge of hiring. Consult company Web sites for names of company officers. Then call the company to verify the person's name and title.

Strategies

for Application Letters

- **Use caution when adapting sample application letters.** Plenty of free, online sample letters can provide ideas for your own situation. But never borrow them whole. Most employers can spot a "canned" letter immediately.
- **Create a dynamic tone with active voice.** Instead of saying, "More and more management responsibilities were steadily given to me," say, "I steadily assumed ever-greater management responsibilities."
- **Never be vague.** Paint a clear picture for employers who may not be familiar with what you describe. Instead of saying, "I am familiar with the 1022 interactive database system and RUNOFF processing system," say, "As a lab grader, I kept grading records on the 1022 database management system and composed lab procedures on the RUNOFF text processing system."
- **Avoid being overly informal or overly stiff.** Avoid informal terms that sound unprofessional ("Your company sounds like a cool place to work") as well as stuffy language ("Hitherto, I request the honor of your acquaintance").
- **Never settle for a first draft—or even a second or third.** The application letter is your one chance to introduce yourself to a prospective employer. Make it perfect by trimming excess wording, double-checking the tone, and making sure you have connected your qualifications directly to the job. After you are satisfied with the content, proofread repeatedly to spot any factual errors or typos.

Digital versus Print Job Application Materials

9.5   Submit appropriate digital job application materials.

Résumés and cover letters today are typically submitted as PDF or Word documents and uploaded to the online job application site for a particular organization. Career networking sites like LinkedIn or Monster.com allow you to upload your résumé and other materials and connect these to your online profile. Some employers may also ask you to submit your materials as email attachments, especially if you were solicited to apply. Whenever possible, use PDF; these files retain the look and feel (fonts, page breaks, line breaks) of the résumé you worked so hard to create. PDF files also make it more difficult for a reader to accidentally insert a stray keystroke or change your formatting while reading your materials.

Using PDF files for digital résumés

A printed résumé is important to have on hand, especially in certain situations. Although increasingly rare, for some job applications you may still be asked to mail printed copies of your application materials. Also, if you attend a campus career fair or similar in-person event (for instance, a company holds an information session or comes to campus to recruit), having print copies of your résumé ready to hand to recruiters is invaluable. You can point out items of interest on the spot and make a lasting impression. Be sure to use high-quality white stationery paper, available at most copy shops.

Print résumés are still important

If you do hand out or mail print copies of your materials, keep in mind that prospective employers will probably end up digitizing your résumé by scanning a copy for their job database systems. Digital résumés become part of a much larger database of applicants (for current or later job openings). Digital résumés are easier for employers to search via computer, looking for keywords to help them narrow down the application pool.

Scanned résumés

To create a print résumé that can be scanned easily and accurately, keep the formatting as simple as possible. Figure 9.4 provides one example of a résumé suitable for scanning.

LinkedIn, Monster.com, and other job networking sites offer templates for various types of résumés. Microsoft Word and other word processing programs also offer résumé templates. Use these templates carefully, always keeping audience and purpose in mind. Adapt templates as needed for the particular job, using the guidelines suggested in this chapter.

Use résumé templates carefully

Strategies

for Digital Job Application Materials

- **Follow the instructions of the job application site.** Employer job sites will tell you what format to use, how large the file size can be, whether to upload just the résumé or the résumé and cover letter, and so forth.
- **Unless otherwise noted, use PDF.** PDF files retain the formatting of the original, no matter what computer platform a reader is using.
- **Use templates carefully.** If you start off using a template (from LinkedIn or other site or from Microsoft Word), consider editing the formatting and layout to comply with the potential employer's guidelines (for instance, page count) and advice from a career counselor. Adapt the template based on the advice you receive and on the strategies discussed in this chapter.
- **Use a simple font.** Stick with fonts that are easy to scan, such as Times New Roman or Helvetica.
- **Use simple formatting.** Especially for print résumés that may be scanned, avoid fancy fonts, tables, and too much formatting. You may substitute ALL CAPS instead of boldface, for example. But even with digital résumés (PDF or Word), keep the design simple and clean (see Figure 9.2 for an example).
- **Use keywords.** Use words that are likely to get hits if the document is searched. You may want to create a "qualifications" section at the top of your résumé. Include keywords for general skills (conflict management, report and proposal writing), specialized skills (graphic design, Java programming), credentials (B.S. in electrical engineering, Phi Beta Kappa), and job titles (manager, technician, intern). Use nouns for keywords.
- **Avoid personal information for job materials that are widely available to the public.** For résumés uploaded to secure job application sites, you will want to use your actual address, phone number, and email address. But for materials you upload to a site that is more widely accessible (such as your e-portfolio) or even to job networking sites (where you can't predict who will see it), you may wish to avoid the potential for identity theft by leaving off your home address and just listing the city and state.

Dossiers, Portfolios, and E-portfolios

9.6   Compile a dossier, portfolio, or e-portfolio.

Definitions and purposes of dossiers and portfolios

An employer impressed by your résumé and application letter will likely have questions about your credentials and your past work. These questions will be answered, respectively, by your dossier and your portfolio (or e-portfolio).

Dossiers

What a dossier contains

Your dossier contains your credentials: college transcript, recommendation letters, and other items (such as a scholarship award or commendation letter) that document your achievements. Prospective employers who decide to follow up on your application may request your dossier. By collecting recommendations in one folder, you spare your references from writing the same letter repeatedly.

Your college placement office will usually keep the dossier (or placement folder) on file and send a secure digital copy or mail a print copy to employers. Always keep your own copy, including any nonconfidential recommendation letters. Then, if an employer requests your dossier, you can photocopy and mail it, advising your

Figure 9.4 Résumé That Can Be Scanned, Emailed, or Posted Online

KAREN P. GRANGER
P.O. Box 6772
New Bedford, MA 02720
Phone: (555) 864-9318
Email: kgrang@swis.net

OBJECTIVE
A summer internship in software documentation.

QUALIFICATIONS
Software and hardware documentation. Editing. Desktop publishing. Usability testing.
Web collaboration. Networking technology. Instrutor-led training.
Framemaker, RoboHelp, Web Works ePublisher, JavaScript, and Adobe Flash.

EDUCATION
University of Massachusetts at Dartmouth (UMD): B.A. expected May 2017. English and
Communications major. Computer Science minor. GPA 3.54. Class rank top 7 percent.

EXPERIENCE
Conway Communications, Inc., Marlboro, MA: Intern technical writer. LAN
technology. Writing, designing, and testing hardware upgrade manuals. Designing
and publishing of installation and maintenance manual. Specifying art and
illustrations. Designing a fully linked home page and online help for the company
intranet Summers 2014 and 2015.

Writing and Reading Center, UMD: Tutor. Individual and group instruction. Training
new tutors. Newsletter editing. Scriptwriting and acting in a training video.
Designing home page. Fall 2014–present.

THE TORCH, UMD weekly newspaper: Managing editor. Conducting staff meetings.
Generating story ideas. Writing editorials and articles. Supervising page layout,
paste-up, and copyediting. Fall 2014–Present.

ACHIEVEMENTS AND AWARDS
Writing samples published in TECHNICAL COMMUNICATION, 13th ed. (Pearson, 2014).

Massachusetts State Honors Scholarship, 2014–2015.

Dean's list each semester.

ACTIVITIES
Student member, Society for Technical Communication and American Society for
Training and Development.

Student representative, College Curriculum Committee. UMD Litetary Society.

REFERENCES AND WRITING PORTFOLIO
Available on request.

For online confidentiality, use a P.O. box, rather than a street address

Uses nouns instead of verb forms for keywords most likely to generate "hits" during scanning

Uses a simple font and format

All text is flush to the left margin

recipient that the official placement copy is on the way, as sometimes dossiers may not be mailed immediately.

Portfolios and E-portfolios

What a portfolio contains

Portfolios, whether print or digital (e-portfolios, Figure 9.5), allow you to provide a potential employer with additional information and examples pertinent to your job search, such as copies of documents from your dossier as well as writing samples, more information about honors and awards, and multimedia or visual design projects. Your portfolio or e-portfolio would normally contain an introduction or mission statement explaining what you've included and why. Do not include items unrelated to the

Figure 9.5 An e-portfolio

Email address provided but street address and phone omitted to avoid identity theft

Introduction or mission statement page orients readers

Clearly labeled file folders make the e-portfolio easy to navigate

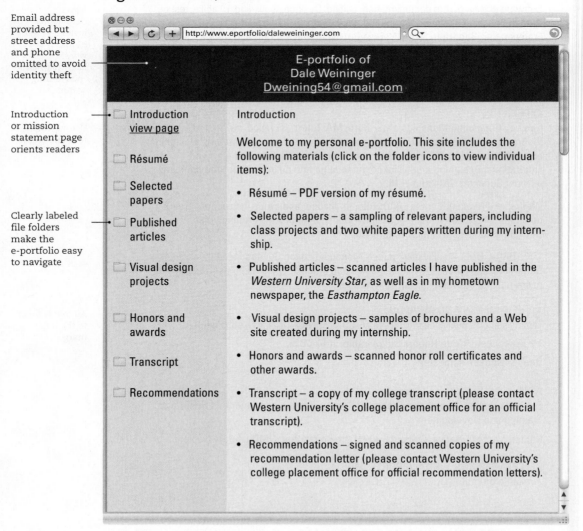

http://www.eportfolio/daleweininger.com

E-portfolio of
Dale Weininger
Dweining54@gmail.com

Introduction
view page

Résumé

Selected papers

Published articles

Visual design projects

Honors and awards

Transcript

Recommendations

Introduction

Welcome to my personal e-portfolio. This site includes the following materials (click on the folder icons to view individual items):

• Résumé – PDF version of my résumé.

• Selected papers – a sampling of relevant papers, including class projects and two white papers written during my internship.

• Published articles – scanned articles I have published in the *Western University Star*, as well as in my hometown newspaper, the *Easthampton Eagle*.

• Visual design projects – samples of brochures and a Web site created during my internship.

• Honors and awards – scanned honor roll certificates and other awards.

• Transcript – a copy of my college transcript (please contact Western University's college placement office for an official transcript).

• Recommendations – signed and scanned copies of my recommendation letter (please contact Western University's college placement office for official recommendation letters).

job search or your qualifications. An organized, professional portfolio or e-portfolio shows that you can apply your skills and makes you stand out as a candidate. It also gives you concrete material to discuss during job interviews.

As you create your portfolio or e-portfolio, seek advice and feedback from professors in your major and from other people in the field. If you have a portfolio or e-portfolio, indicate this on your résumé, followed by "Available on request" or a link to the Web address for access. If you have an e-portfolio, bring printed copies of the more relevant contents (for instance, your résumé and one writing or design sample) to your interview. Many colleges and universities offer e-portfolio services via their career and student placement centers. You can also find e-portfolio software and templates online; many of these are quite simple to use. LinkedIn and other job sites also offer ways to create e-portfolios. Always check the privacy settings when using a social network or online portfolio site.

Strategies

for Dossiers, Portfolios, and E-portfolios

- **Consider an introduction or mission statement.** Place this page at the beginning to introduce and explain the contents.
- **Collect relevant materials.** Gather documents or graphics you've prepared in school or on the job, presentations you've given, and projects or experiments you've worked on. Possible items: campus newspaper articles, reports on course projects, papers that earned an "A," examples of persuasive argument, documents from an internship, or visuals you've designed for an oral presentation.
- **Include copies of dossier materials.** Although they won't be official unless they go directly from your campus placement office to your prospective employer, have copies of your college transcript and recommendations on hand to give to employers during the waiting period and/or to post on your e-portfolio.
- **Assemble your items.** Place your résumé first (after your introduction/mission statement), and use divider pages to separate groups of items. Follow the same structure for an e-portfolio. Position your résumé file immediately below the introduction/mission statement file, and group similar items into appropriate files. In either case, aim for a professional look.
- **Omit irrelevant items.** Personal photographs and other items more appropriate for a Facebook page do not belong in your portfolio or e-portfolio.
- **Omit your street address or phone number from your e-portfolio.** If your e-portfolio is available to the public, post only your email address to avoid identity theft. If you post your references, include only their names and comments, not their contact information. Always check the privacy settings with any e-portfolio software.

Interviews and Follow-up Letters

9.7   **Prepare for job interviews and write professional follow-up communication.**

All of your preparation leads to the last stages of the hiring process: the interview and follow-up to the interview.

Interviews

Purpose of
interviews

An employer who is impressed by your credentials will arrange an interview. The interview's purpose is to confirm the employer's impressions from your application letter, résumé, references, and dossier. If you have an e-portfolio and have shared it with the employer, they will probably have reviewed its contents in advance. But you may also be asked to present portions of your portfolio at the interview. If possible, bring print copies of the most relevant documents, such as your résumé and one of your papers or projects. Offer to leave these copies with the interviewer.

Types of
interview
situations

Interviews come in various shapes and sizes. Initial screening interviews are often conducted by phone or Skype. In these cases, if you make the "first cut," you will be invited to meet with your potential employer. You might meet with a single interviewer, a hiring committee, or several people or committees in succession. You might be interviewed alone or as part of a group of candidates. Interviews can last an hour or less, a full day, or several days. The interview can range from a pleasant chat to a grueling interrogation. Many companies ask questions that may not seem related to the job but are included to observe your critical thinking skills, technical aptitude, or approach to interpersonal conflicts.

The importance
of preparing for
an interview

Careful preparation is the key to a productive interview. If you haven't already done so, learn what you can about the company from trade journals, industrial indexes, business magazines (like *Forbes, Fortune,* and *Business Week*), and other resources. Request company literature, including the most recent annual report. Speak with people who know about the company, or (well in advance) arrange an informational interview with someone at the company. In addition, visit the company's Web site. Once you've done all this, ask yourself, "Does this job seem like a good fit?" Many organizations use an approach and set of questions that you can research in advance by asking others who have interviewed there, looking around on career networking sites, or by searching online for more information.

In addition to knowing about the company and its interview process, be prepared in other ways. Dress and present yourself appropriately. Be psychologically prepared and confident (but not arrogant). Follow the rules of business etiquette. Unprepared interviewees make mistakes such as the following:

How people fail
job interviews

- They know little about the company or what role they would play as an employee in this particular division or department.
- They have inflated ideas about their own worth.
- They have little idea of how their education prepares them for work.
- They dress inappropriately.
- They exhibit little or no self-confidence.
- They have only vague ideas of how they could benefit the employer.
- They inquire only about salary and benefits.
- They speak negatively of former employers or coworkers.

Perhaps the most important way to prepare for an interview is to practice answering typical questions. Think about how you would answer the following:

Practice answering interview questions

- Why does this job appeal to you?

Questions to expect during a job interview

- What do you know about our company? About this division or unit?

- What do you know about our core values (for example, informal management structure, commitment to diversity or to the environment)?

- What do you know about the expectations and demands of this job?

- What are the major issues affecting this industry?

- How would you describe yourself as an employee?

- What do you see as your biggest weakness? Biggest strength?

- Can you describe an instance in which you came up with a new and better way of doing something?

- What are your short-term and long-term career goals?

Don't forget to prepare your own list of well-researched questions about the job and the organization. You will be invited to ask questions, and what you ask can be as revealing as any answers you give.

Prepare your own questions, too

Finally, tell the truth during the interview—doing so is both ethical and smart. Companies routinely verify an applicant's claims about education, prior employment, positions held, salary, and personal background. Perhaps you have some past infraction (such as a bad credit rating or a brush with the law) or some pressing personal commitment (such as caring for an elderly parent or a disabled child). Experts suggest that it's better to air these issues up front—before the employer finds out from other sources. The employer will appreciate your honesty, and you will know exactly where you stand before accepting the job (Fisher 292).

Be truthful

Follow-up Communication

You need to follow up after your interview to (1) thank the potential employer for meeting with you and (2) to accept the job if offered or to refuse the job (because you feel it is a bad fit or because you have accepted a different offer). Traditionally, a handwritten thank you note is considered the most professional way to follow up after a job interview. However, if email has been the primary way you and the potential employer have been communicating, it is fine to email a brief note of thanks. (You can always follow up with a thank you card by mail.) When offering a job, many companies like to call the employee with the good news, then follow up with an email that outlines the offer, usually with attachments (a contract, terms of the offer, salary, and benefits). Whether you decide to accept or you decide to refuse, and whether you choose to do so via a letter or an email, your response should be professionally written, checked for spelling and grammar, and formal in tone. (See Chapter 18 for more on this topic related to the use of email.)

Types of follow-up communication

THANK YOU NOTE. Within a day or so after the interview, send a thank you note to the person who interviewed you. If you were interviewed by multiple people, send each one an individual thank you note. Not only is this courteous, but it also reinforces a positive impression. Keep your email or note brief, but try to personalize your connection with the reader (Crosby 20).

Purpose and content of thank you notes

Open by thanking the interviewer and reemphasizing your interest in the position. Then refer to some details from the interview or some aspect of your visit that would help the interviewer reconnect with the interview experience. If you forgot to mention something important during the interview, include it here—briefly. Finally, close with genuine enthusiasm, and provide your contact information again to make it easy for the interviewer to respond. Following is the text of an effective thank you note from James Purdy, the entry-level candidate in hotel-restaurant management whose résumé and cover letter appeared earlier:

> Thank you for your hospitality during my Tuesday visit to Lake Geneva Resort. I am very interested in the restaurant-management position and was intrigued by our discussion about developing an eclectic regional cuisine.
>
> Everything about my tour was enjoyable, but I was especially impressed by the friendliness and professionalism of the resort staff. People seem to love working at the Resort, and it's not hard to see why.
>
> I'm convinced I would be a productive employee at Lake Geneva Resort and would welcome the chance to prove my abilities. If you need additional information, please call me at (555) 316-2419.

Content and approach of acceptance notes

ACCEPTANCE OR REFUSAL NOTE. You may receive a job offer by phone, email, or hard copy (or all three). If by phone, ask when you will receive a written offer and then respond with a formal letter or email of acceptance. The employer may also ask you to sign and return a form indicating your acceptance; be sure to check that the outlined terms match what you discussed by phone. Remember to accept a job offer with enthusiasm. Here is James Purdy's note of acceptance, sent, as requested by this employer, as an email:

> I am delighted to accept your offer of a position as assistant recreation supervisor at Liberty International's Lake Geneva Resort, with a starting salary of $44,500.
>
> As you requested, I will phone Bonnie Dunn in Human Resources for instructions on reporting date, physical exam, and employee orientation.
>
> I look forward to a long and satisfying career with Liberty International.

Content and approach of refusal notes

You may also have to refuse a job offer, for example, if you receive a preferable offer or decide that the position is not the right fit for you. Even if you refuse by phone, write a prompt and cordial note of refusal, explaining your reasons and allowing for future possibilities. Remember to be diplomatic when refusing a job. A courteous refusal and explanation can let the employer know why you have chosen a competing employer or why you have decided against taking the job for other reasons. Purdy handled one job refusal this way:

> Although I thoroughly enjoyed my visit to your company's headquarters, I have to decline your offer of a position as assistant desk manager of your London hotel.
>
> I've decided to accept a position with Liberty International because the company has offered me the chance to participate in its manager-trainee program. Also, Liberty will provide tuition for courses in completing my B.S. degree in hospitality management.
>
> If any future openings should materialize at your Aspen resort, however, I would appreciate your considering me again as a candidate.
>
> Thank you for your confidence in me.

Strategies
for Interviews and Follow-up Notes

- **Confirm the interview's exact time and location.** Arrive early but no more than 10 minutes.
- **Don't show up empty-handed.** Bring a briefcase, pen, and notepad. Have your own questions written out. Bring extra copies of your résumé (unfolded) and a portfolio (if appropriate).
- **Make a positive first impression.** Come dressed as if you already work for the company. Learn the name of your interviewer beforehand so you can greet this person by name—but never by first name unless invited. Extend a firm handshake, smile, and look the interviewer in the eye. Wait to be asked to take a chair. Maintain eye contact much of the time, but don't stare.
- **Don't worry about having all the answers.** When you don't know the answer to a question, say so, and relax. Interviewers typically do most of the talking.
- **Avoid abrupt yes or no answers—as well as life stories.** Just saying yes or no doesn't leave any impression—elaborate on your answers, but also keep them short and to the point.
- **Don't answer questions by merely repeating the material on your résumé.** Instead, explain how specific skills and types of experience could be assets to this particular employer.
- **Remember to smile often and to be friendly and attentive throughout.** Qualifications are not the only reason a person gets hired. People often hire the candidate they *like* best.
- **Never criticize a previous employer.** Above all, interviewers like positive attitudes. Complaining about a former employer, whether or not your criticisms are legitimate, only makes you look negative.
- **Prepare to ask intelligent questions.** When questions are invited, focus on the nature of the job: travel involved, specific responsibilities, typical job assignments, opportunities for further training, types of clients, and so on. Avoid questions that could easily have been answered by your own prior research.
- **Take a hint.** When your interviewer hints that the meeting is ending (perhaps by checking a watch), restate your interest, ask when a hiring decision is likely to be made, thank the interviewer, and leave.
- **Follow up as soon as possible.** Send a thank you note to each person with whom you interviewed. Be sure to get the spelling right for each person's name. You can use email but also follow up with a hard copy thank you note if you feel this is appropriate for the situation.

Checklist

for Résumés

- ❏ Does my résumé's organization (reverse chronological or functional) emphasize my best characteristics?
- ❏ Is my contact information accurate?
- ❏ Does my objective show a clear sense of purpose?
- ❏ Have I included a summary of skills or qualifications, as needed?
- ❏ Is my educational background clear and complete?
- ❏ Have I accurately but briefly described my previous jobs?
- ❏ Have I presented education versus experience in the appropriate sequence?
- ❏ Have I included personal data and interests, as appropriate?
- ❏ Have I listed references or offered to provide them?
- ❏ Have I offered to provide a portfolio, if appropriate?
- ❏ Have I used action verbs and keywords?
- ❏ Have I limited the résumé to a single page, if possible?
- ❏ Is the résumé uncluttered and tasteful?
- ❏ For print copies, have I used quality (white) paper?
- ❏ If I have a scannable résumé, does it use keywords and effective formatting?
- ❏ Am I being scrupulously honest?
- ❏ Have I proofread exhaustively?

Checklist

for Job Application Letters

- ❏ Is my letter addressed to a specific person?
- ❏ If my letter is *solicited*, do I indicate how I heard about the job?
- ❏ If my letter is *unsolicited*, does it have a forceful opening?
- ❏ Does my introduction get directly to the point?
- ❏ Does the body section paint a clear picture of qualifications sketched in the résumé?
- ❏ Does the conclusion restate my interest and encourage specific action?
- ❏ Have I made my case without merely repeating the résumé?
- ❏ Is my letter free of "canned" expressions?
- ❏ Is my tone confident without being arrogant?
- ❏ Have I avoided a tone that is overly formal or overly stiff?
- ❏ Have I avoided flattery and exaggeration?
- ❏ Have I proofread exhaustively?
- ❏ Am I being scrupulously honest?

Checklist

for Supporting Materials

- ❏ Is my dossier complete, with letters of recommendation and other supporting materials?
- ❏ Is my portfolio or e-portfolio up to date?
- ❏ If my portfolio has hyperlinks, are they all functioning?
- ❏ Have I prepared for interviews?
- ❏ Have I sent the appropriate follow-up correspondence?

Applications

General Applications

1. If you have not already prepared a standard résumé, prepare one following the guidelines in this chapter. If you already have a résumé, revise it not only to follow this chapter's guidelines but also to update your work experience, educational background, and other details. Remember to include persuasive action verbs, design the résumé in an efficient but attractive way, and include all relevant experience.

2. Write an application letter applying for a part-time or summer job in response to a specific ad and tailor your résumé for the job. Choose an organization related to your career goals. Identify the exact hours and calendar period during which you are free to work. Submit a copy of the ad along with your letter and résumé.

3. A friend has asked you for help with the following application letter. Read it carefully, evaluate its effectiveness, and rewrite it as needed.

> Dear Ms. Brown,
>
> Please consider my application for the position of assistant in the Engineering Department. I am a second-year student majoring in electrical engineering technology. I am presently an apprentice with your company and would like to continue my employment in the Engineering Department.
>
> I have six years' experience in electronics, including two years of engineering studies. I am confident my background will enable me to assist the engineers, and I would appreciate the chance to improve my skills through their knowledge and experience.
>
> I would appreciate the opportunity to discuss the possibilities and benefits of a position in the Engineering Department at Concord Electric. Please phone me any weekday after 3:00 P.M. at (555) 568-9867. I hope to hear from you soon.
>
> Sincerely,

4. Write an unsolicited application letter to the human resources director of a company that interests you. Go to the company's Web site to research the various positions for which you may be qualified. Select one, and name that position in your letter. Also learn the name of the human resources director and address your letter to that person. Be sure to grab the reader's attention, remain persuasive throughout, and conclude with a call to action.

Team Application

Divide into groups and prepare a list of five blogs or news articles written by career professionals that students and other job seekers should visit for advice about application letters and résumés. Write a one-paragraph summary of the ideas found on each site, and include the Web address for that site. Compare the findings of your group with others in your class. See if you can find at least two resources specific to your city, town, or state. If your class is using a learning management system or has a class Wiki, ask your instructor if you can upload your findings to that site.

Global Application

Assume that you and other students in your major would like to work in a particular country after graduation. Select a country and do some research on the economy, culture, and travel issues. Then see what you can learn about job application materials for that country (for instance, are résumés a universal requirement?). Write a short memo that tells prospective students what they need to know about finding employment abroad.

Digital and Social Media Application

Career networking sites usually provide advice for creating résumés, including samples for different careers. Such sites also offer résumé templates and samples. Start with LinkedIn and Monster.com and review the information about how to write a résumé suitable for your career stage and desired profession. Then, set up your own LinkedIn account and begin creating an online profile, based on the content of your résumé. Connect to six or more people on LinkedIn and see what other connections come up. Write a one-page memo for your instructor explaining what you learned about résumés and about LinkedIn in general. Include the Web address for your new profile page.

Chapter 10
Memos and Letters

 ## Learning Objectives

10.1 Explain the importance of a workplace memo and identify its parts and format.

10.2 Determine when to take a direct or indirect approach in a memo.

10.3 Write an effective transmittal, summary/follow-up, or informational memo.

10.4 Describe the importance of a workplace letter and identify its parts and formats.

10.5 Understand the aspects of good letter tone, including maintaining a "you" attitude and using plain English.

10.6 Write an effective inquiry, claim, sales, or adjustment letter.

Chapter Outline

Memo Basics, Parts, and Format   164

Memo Tone   165

Types of Memos   168
    Strategies for Memos   172

Letter Basics, Parts, and Format   172

Letter Tone   175
    Strategies for Letters in General   178

Types of Letters   179
    Strategies for Inquiry Letters   181
    Strategies for Claim Letters   184
    Strategies for Sales Letters   186
    Strategies for Adjustment Letters   187
    Checklist for Memos and Letters   189

Applications   189

Memos and letters are the most frequently used forms of workplace communication. Many memos and short letters are written directly into the body of an email message; for more formal situations, a memo or letter is sent via email as a PDF attachment, typically on company letterhead. You need to consider audience, purpose, formality, and workplace guidelines when choosing between an email on its own versus a memo or letter attachment or print copy. This chapter considers memos and letters, discussing these as stand-alone documents that might be delivered in print and digital formats. Chapter 18 ("Email and Text Messages") builds on the concepts from this chapter but provides more detail about using email.

Memo Basics, Parts, and Format

10.1 **Explain the importance of a workplace memo and identify its parts and format.**

Definition and importance of memos

"Memo" (short for "memorandum") is derived from the same Latin roots as the words "memorize," "remember," and "remind." Memos remind readers about important events, give directives, provide instructions and information, and make requests. Memos are typically distributed to employees within an organization, not to people outside the company. Memos are important in the workplace because they are easy to distribute via email or interoffice mail (print copies) and because they provide written documentation about an event or issue.

Informal memos and day-to-day exchanges are typically written as email messages. (See Chapter 18.) More formal memos would typically follow the strategies discussed in this chapter. These memos can then be delivered as print documents and/or as PDF attachments via email. (PDF is preferable to Word or other word processing formats because with PDF files, the formatting and layout can't change.)

Memos versus email

Parts and Format of Memos

A standard memo has the word "Memo" or "Memorandum" centered or set flush left at the top of the page and includes a header (flush to the left margin) identifying the recipient(s), sender, date, and subject. (Subject line can be set in italic for added emphasis.) If anyone is copied on the memo, use the abbreviation "cc" (for "courtesy copy") followed by a colon and the name of each recipient. Because memos are often read rapidly by busy recipients, they should follow a consistent, predictable format. Figure 10.1 shows a standard memo with all parts labeled. Typically, you would double space between the header and the opening paragraph and between the paragraphs. For printed memos, top and bottom margins are typically set to 1 inch; left and right margins are typically set to anywhere from 1 inch to 1.25 inches.

Standard parts and layout of a memo

The body copy (main text portion) of a memo should focus on one topic. Content should be complete yet compact, providing all the information readers need but not going into unnecessary detail. Organize the body of your memo by starting with a short introduction, then writing a paragraph or two to address the main issue, and then concluding by suggesting a course of action or asking your readers to follow up.

Memo format: introduction, body, conclusion

Memo Tone

10.2 **Determine when to take a direct or indirect approach in a memo.**

Memos are typically distributed in-house and circulated among colleagues, subordinates, and superiors. Memo topics often involve evaluations or recommendations about policies, procedures, and, ultimately, the people with whom you work. Because people are sensitive to criticism (even when it is merely implied) and often resistant to change, an ill-conceived memo tone can create problems. So, be particularly careful about your tone.

The importance of memo tone

Achieving the right tone in your memos involves using some common sense. Put yourself in the shoes of your recipients and write accordingly. Be polite and avoid sounding bossy, condescending, and aggressive or deferential and passive. Don't criticize, judge, or blame any individual or department. Don't resort to griping,

Achieving the right tone

Figure 10.1 A properly formatted memo

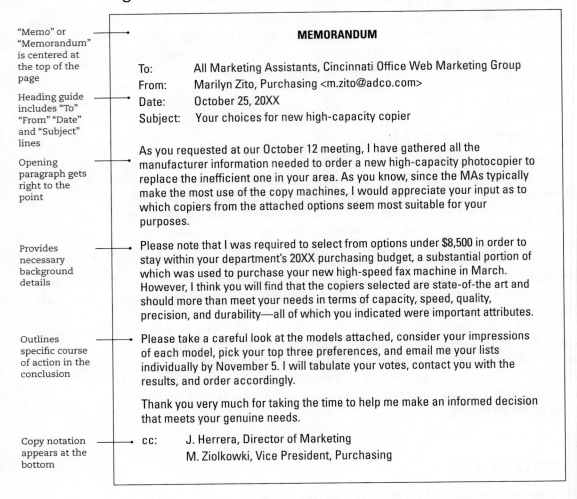

"Memo" or "Memorandum" is centered at the top of the page

Heading guide includes "To" "From" "Date" and "Subject" lines

Opening paragraph gets right to the point

Provides necessary background details

Outlines specific course of action in the conclusion

Copy notation appears at the bottom

MEMORANDUM

To: All Marketing Assistants, Cincinnati Office Web Marketing Group
From: Marilyn Zito, Purchasing <m.zito@adco.com>
Date: October 25, 20XX
Subject: Your choices for new high-capacity copier

As you requested at our October 12 meeting, I have gathered all the manufacturer information needed to order a new high-capacity photocopier to replace the inefficient one in your area. As you know, since the MAs typically make the most use of the copy machines, I would appreciate your input as to which copiers from the attached options seem most suitable for your purposes.

Please note that I was required to select from options under $8,500 in order to stay within your department's 20XX purchasing budget, a substantial portion of which was used to purchase your new high-speed fax machine in March. However, I think you will find that the copiers selected are state-of-the art and should more than meet your needs in terms of capacity, speed, quality, precision, and durability—all of which you indicated were important attributes.

Please take a careful look at the models attached, consider your impressions of each model, pick your top three preferences, and email me your lists individually by November 5. I will tabulate your votes, contact you with the results, and order accordingly.

Thank you very much for taking the time to help me make an informed decision that meets your genuine needs.

cc: J. Herrera, Director of Marketing
        M. Ziolkowski, Vice President, Purchasing

---

complaining, and other negative commentary. Try to emphasize the positive. Finally, approach difficult situations reasonably. Instead of taking an extreme stance or suggesting ideas that will never work, be practical and realistic.

Being direct or indirect

The tone of a memo also comes across in the sequence in which you deliver the information. Depending on the sensitivity of your memo's subject matter, you may want to take a direct or indirect approach. A direct approach (as in Figure 10.1) begins with the "bottom line" in the first sentence (and in the subject line) and then presents the details or analysis that support your case. An indirect approach lays out the details of the case over several sentences (and leaves the subject l ine vague) before delivering the bottom line later in the paragraph.

Readers generally prefer the direct approach because they want to know the bottom line without being told in advance how to feel about it. Assume, for example, that a company Payroll Manager has to announce to employees that their paychecks will be delayed by two days: This manager should take a direct approach, announcing the unpopular news in the subject line and in the opening sentence and then explaining the causes of the problem:

MEMO

To: All employees
From: Meredith Rocteau, Payroll Manager
Date: May 19, 20XX
Subject: Delay in paychecks

I regret to inform you that those employees paid by direct deposit will experience a two-day delay in receiving their paychecks.

This delay is due to a virus that infiltrated the primary computer server for our payroll system. Although we hired consultants to identify the virus and clean out the server, the process took nearly 48 hours.

We apologize for the inconvenience.

> Direct approach: Subject line gets right to the main point
>
> Opening paragraph starts with the bottom line

However, when you need to convey exceedingly bad news or make an unpopular request or recommendation (as in announcing a strict new policy or employee layoffs), you might consider an indirect approach; this way you can present your case and encourage readers to understand your position before announcing the unpopular bottom line. The danger of the indirect approach, though, is that you may come across as evasive.

MEMO

To: All employees
From: J. Travis Southfield, Director of Human Resources
Date: September 19, 20XX
Subject: Difficult economic times

Each employee of the AutoWorld family is a valued member, and each of you has played an important role in our company's expansion over the past 10 years.

Yet as you all know, times are difficult right now for the automobile industry. Sales are down, financing is hard to obtain, and consumers are holding back on major purchases.

In order to keep the company solvent, we must consider all options. Therefore, I have been informed by our company president, John Creaswell, that we must downsize. We will begin with options for retirement packages, but please be prepared for the possibility that layoffs may follow.

We will have more information for you at an all-hands meeting tomorrow.

> Indirect approach: Subject line is not specific about bottom line
>
> Opening paragraph starts with an explanation before delivering the bottom line
>
> The bottom line

Delivering
memos in the
right medium to
the right people

Finally, a memo's tone comes across in the way you handle its distribution. Use the appropriate delivery medium. If your topic is very short, timely, not overly formal and the message needs to reach everyone quickly, consider sending the memo as an email. But if your topic is more formal and more detailed, use an email to send a PDF attachment, and consider following up with a printed memo. Be careful about who receives the memo. Don't send a memo to everyone at work when the content is only appropriate for a few, and don't leave vital people off your distribution list.

Types of Memos

10.3   **Write an effective transmittal, summary/follow-up, or informational memo.**

Memo format can also be used for distributing short reports, discussed in Chapter 15. However, for the purposes of this chapter, consider the following common and more basic types of memos. Whether sent on paper, as an email message, or as an attachment, the purpose of these memo types, and the suggestions for composing your memo's content and message, would remain the same as discussed here. Formatting your message as an email can also follow the samples and guidelines in this chapter, although some email programs may not allow all of the visual features shown here. (See Chapter 18 for more examples of memos and other workplace documents sent as email.)

Transmittal Memo

Transmittal
memos explain
package
contents
or email
attachments

A transmittal memo accompanies a package of materials, such as a long report, a manuscript, or a proposal. Its purpose is to signal that the information is being sent from one place to another (providing a paper trail), to introduce the material, and to explain what is enclosed. A transmittal memo may be as simple as a sentence or a paragraph with a bulleted list describing the package, as in Figure 10.2. Transmittal memos may also be used to send these materials as email attachments. Figure 10.2, for example, could also be used as a cover email, noting that the report is attached as a PDF file, available for download from the company file server, or available on a shared site such as Google Drive or Dropbox.

Summary or Follow-up Memo

Summary
or follow-up
memos provide
written records

A summary or follow-up memo provides a written record of a meeting or conversation or just a topic during the meeting or conversation that was not resolved at the time. In addition to providing documentation that the meeting or conversation took place, summary and follow-up memos also ensure that each recipient has the same understanding of what was decided. Figure 10.3 shows a memo that performs both a

Figure 10.2 A transmittal memo

Greentree
Bionomics, Inc.

MEMORANDUM

To: D. Spring, Director of Human Resources
From: M. Noll, Head, Biology Division
Date: January 16, 20XX
Subject: Hiring of new laboratory manager

As you know, each unit manager has been asked to prepare a hiring plan for the coming year. Attached to this memo please find a brief report outlining the biology division's need for a new laboratory manager.

The attached report includes

• an overview of needs

• a job description

• a budget

Please let me know if you require any additional information. I look forward to hearing from you.

summary and follow-up function. As noted with the transmittal memo, this summary and follow-up memo is very short and to the point and could easily be sent out as an email message.

Informational Memo

Informational memos, such as the one shown in Figure 10.4, typically contain some type of announcement or update. For instance, you may receive a memo announcing the closure of a parking ramp over the holidays for repair or an upcoming awards ceremony on Friday. Given the timely nature of most informational memos, email is probably the best way to circulate this information, either as an email message or, for more formality, as a memo attachment on company letterhead.

Informational memos make announcements or provide updates

Figure 10.3 A summary or follow-up memo

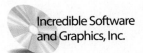

Incredible Software
and Graphics, Inc.

MEMO

To: Elaine Lamer and Mitchell Dramson, Software Development Team
From: Christopher Felts, Manager
Date: June 19, 20XX
Subject: Follow-up to today's meeting

Thank you for meeting today to discuss next steps to complete the next version of our animation software package.

As you noted, the original release date of October 1 is probably too optimistic given the latest hiring freeze. Yet, as I mentioned, we can't afford to go beyond a date of October 15 if we are to make our fourth-quarter sales goals. So, let's agree on October 15 as the new due date.

Please communicate this information to the other members of your team.

cc: E. Hearly, Division Chief

Figure 10.4 An informational memo

MEMORANDUM

To: All employees
From: Jorge Gonsalves, Human Resources
Date: January 12, 20XX
Subject: 401K matching policy

As the new year begins, we in Human Resources would like to remind you about the company's generous 401K matching policy. We will match your 401K contributions 100% when you roll up to 10% of your salary into your 401K.

Many companies will match only up to 5% of an employee's salary and usually not at a 100% rate, so please take advantage of this program by enrolling now. Enrollment is only open until March 1 and will not be open again until next January.

Please drop by the Human Resources office on the 6th floor to get a handout that provides more detailed information or to speak with an HR representative in person.

Thanks.

cc: Alison Sheffield, Manager, Human Resources

Strategies

for Memos

- **Focus on one topic.** If you need to address more than one topic, consider a format other than a memo (for instance, a report).
- **Be brief.** People expect memos that are short and to the point.
- **Use the appropriate organizational format (direct or indirect).** Consider the direct format when you need people to get the point quickly and the indirect format when you have something difficult to say that needs to be softened.
- **Use white space, headings, and bullets.** These features provide visual structure to your memo. But if your memo will be sent as the body of an email message, don't get too fancy with formatting.
- **Distribute to the right people.** Whether you are sending the memo via email or on paper, be sure it reaches only those who need the information. At the same time, don't leave out anyone who needs to read your message.
- **Consider when to use an email, email with attachment, paper, or some combination.** Most organizations have guidelines on their preferences. Email is suitable for short memos that need to be sent in a timely manner; email with an attachment is also quick but more formal; paper memos are perhaps the most formal of all, but increasingly, PDF attachments are preferred to actually printing and sending paper.

Letter Basics, Parts, and Format

10.4 **Describe the importance of a workplace letter and identify its parts and formats.**

Importance of letters

A well-crafted workplace letter conveys a formal, professional impression. It presents a reasoned, carefully constructed case and represents not only you but also your company or organization. Letters also serve as an official notice or record. Your signature on a letter certifies your approval of the message. Letters often serve as legal documents, and so precision is crucial. As noted above with memos, letters can be sent as attachments to an email or as print or even as both. For example, often when a person receives a job offer, the offer letter will come as a PDF attachment to an email, but then a print copy (along with other materials) will be sent through the mail.

Letter Parts and Formats

All letters contain various parts (date line, return address, signature line), which are formatted in a standard way. Companies and organizations have differing rules and guidelines for how they want letters formatted, when to use letterhead, and how to circulate letters both internally and to clients. Also, most word processing programs (like Word) offer letter templates; these templates will contain pre-set formatting options. Be careful when choosing a template, especially ones with fancy formatting and atypical margins or layouts. Use the guidelines and strategies in this chapter as a basis for your decisions.

The parts of a letter include the sender's address/heading, date, inside address, salutation, body text, complimentary closing, and signature. In addition, a letter may include such optional parts as a company logo, typist's initials, enclosure notation, and/or copy notation. Figure 10.5 shows a workplace letter with the standard parts (as well as optional typist's initials and enclosure notation) labeled.

Standard and optional parts of a letter

SENDER'S ADDRESS.   The sender's address appears at the top of the letter in the form of either company letterhead or the sender's mailing address. When you use your personal address, omit your name because that will appear below your signature at letter's end. On the first line, include the full street address, and on the next line, include the city, state (abbreviated), country (if applicable), and postal code (ZIP code or other postal code).

DATE.   The date appears below the sender's address. Spell out the month completely.

INSIDE ADDRESS.   Use between two and four spaces between the date and the inside address (the address of the recipient). Include the courtesy title ("Mr.," "Ms.," "Dr.") and the full name of the recipient on the first line; the person's job title (if applicable) on the second line; the name of the company (if applicable) on the next line; the full street address on the next line; and the city, state, country (if applicable), and postal code on the last line.

SALUTATION.   Double space between the inside address and the salutation. The salutation includes a greeting (usually "Dear"), followed by a courtesy title and the recipient's last name. If you don't know the person's gender, use the full name ("Dear Sandy Martin:"). In a business letter, use a colon at the end of the salutation, not a comma.

Use an *attention line* when you write to an organization and do not know your recipient's name but are directing the letter to a specific department or position. Place the attention line flush with the left margin two line spaces (returns) below the inside address ("Attention: Director of Research and Development").

Typically, *subject lines* are used with memos, but if the recipient is not expecting your letter, a subject line can be a good way of catching a busy reader's attention ("Subject: New patent for hybrid wheat crop"). Place the subject line below the inside address or attention line. You can italicize the subject to make it more prominent.

BODY TEXT.   Double space between the salutation and the body text; double space between body text paragraphs. The introductory paragraph should get right to the point. The middle paragraph(s) should support the introduction without straying off topic. The concluding paragraph should summarize and call for further action.

COMPLIMENTARY CLOSING.   Double space between the body text and the complimentary closing. Use a standard, businesslike closing such as "Sincerely," "Respectfully," or "Best regards."

Figure 10.5 A workplace letter

Heading (sender's address) ————→

LEVERETT LAND & TIMBER COMPANY, INC.
18 River Rock Road
Leverett, MA 01054

creative land use
quality building materials
architectural construction

Date ————→ January 17, 20XX

Inside address ————→ Mr. Thomas E. Muffin
Clearwater Drive
Amherst, MA 01022

Salutation ————→ Dear Mr. Muffin:

Body text ————→ I have examined the damage to your home caused by the ruptured water pipe and consider the following repairs to be necessary and of immediate concern:

Exterior:
Remove plywood soffit panels beneath overhangs
Replace damaged insulation and plumbing
Remove all built-up ice within floor framing
Replace plywood panels and finish as required

Northeast Bedroom—Lower Level:
Remove and replace all sheetrock, including closet
Remove and replace all door casings and baseboards
Remove and repair windowsill extensions and moldings
Remove and reinstall electric heaters
Respray ceilings and repaint all surfaces

This appraisal of damage repair does not include repairs and/or replacements of carpets, tile work, or vinyl flooring. Also, this appraisal assumes that the plywood subflooring on the main level has not been severely damaged.

Leverett Land & Timber Company, Inc., proposes to furnish the necessary materials and labor to perform the described damage repairs for the amount of six thousand one hundred and eighty dollars ($6,180).

Complimentary closing ————→ Sincerely,

Signature ————→ *P.A. Jackson*

Gerald A. Jackson, President

Typist's initials ————→ GAJ/ob

Enclosure notation ————→ Encl. Itemized estimate

Phone: 410-555-9879   Fax: 410-555-6874   Email:

SIGNATURE.   Type your name four lines beneath the complimentary closing and sign in the space between the complimentary closing and typed name.

OPTIONAL PARTS.   Most company letters will feature a preprinted logo at the very top of the page, providing the name and address of the company along with contact information. You may also need a *typist notation*: If someone other than the author types the letter, place the author's capitalized initials first, followed by a slash and the typist's lowercase initials. If anything was sent in the same envelope provide an *enclosure notation*: Use the abbreviation "Encl." and briefly describe the contents. If anyone is copied on the letter, provide a *copy notation*. Use the abbreviation "cc" followed by a colon and the name of each recipient. Multiple notations would appear in this order: typist, enclosures, and then copy.

Although several formats are acceptable and your company may have its own, the most popular format for workplace letters is *block format*, illustrated by Figures 10.5 and 10.6.

Block format

Letter Tone

10.5 **Understand the aspects of good letter tone, including maintaining a "you" attitude and using plain English.**

Letters are typically written from one individual to another. But unlike a face-to-face conversation, video chat, or phone call between two people, letters lack important nonverbal cues (smiles, frowns, vocal expressions of agreement or disagreement) to help clarify what's being said. These nonverbal cues in a phone call or a meeting allow you to modify your comments and your vocal tone.

The importance of a letter's tone

When writing a letter, however, you can easily forget that a flesh-and-blood person will be reacting to what you say—or seem to say. You will receive no visual or auditory clues to alter what you write before you send the letter. As a result, the tone of a letter, like that of a memo, is especially important to get right.

To achieve an appropriate tone, consider the factors discussed below that affect the relationship between sender and recipient. As you read through this section, refer to Figure 10.6, which maintains an appropriate tone in conveying bad news.

Establishing and Maintaining a "You" Perspective

A letter displaying a "you" perspective puts the reader's interest and feelings first. To convey a "you" perspective, put yourself in the place of the person who will read your correspondence, and ask yourself how this recipient will react to what you have written. Even a single word or sentence, carelessly chosen or phrased, can offend. Consider the following sentence in a letter to a customer:

Prioritize the readers' needs, wants, and feelings

Our record keeping is very efficient and we have looked into it, so this is obviously your error.

Offensive

Figure 10.6 Appropriate tone in conveying bad news

LEVERETT LAND & TIMBER COMPANY, INC.
18 River Rock Road
Leverett, MA 01054

creative land use
quality building materials
architectural construction

January 17, 20XX

Mr. Thomas E. Shaler
19 Clearwater Drive
Amherst, MA 01022

Dear Mr. Shaler:

Thank you for bringing the matter of the ruptured water pipe to my attention. I was pleased to hear from you again these months after our firm completed construction of your living room addition, though I was of course sorry to hear about the water damage not only to the new construction but to the living room as a whole.

Naturally, I understand your desire to receive compensation for your home's damage, especially taking into account how recently the extension was completed. In reviewing the blueprints for the extension, however, I find that the pipes were state-of-the-art and were fully insulated. In fact, it is the practice of Leverett Land & Timber not only to use the best materials available but also to exceed piping insulation requirements by as much as 50 percent. For this reason, we cannot fulfill your request to replace the piping at no cost and repair the water-damaged areas.

Undoubtedly, your insurance will cover the damage. I suspect that the rupture was caused by insufficient heating of the living room area during this unusually cold winter, but homeowner's insurance will cover damages resulting from cold-ruptured pipes 95 percent of the time.

Our policy is to make repairs at a 20 percent discount in situations like this. Though the pipe rupture was not our fault, we feel personally close to every project we do and to every client we serve. Please get in touch if you would like to discuss this matter further. I would also be happy to speak with your insurance company if you wish.

Sincerely,

P.A. Jackson

Gerald A. Jackson

Annotations (left margin):

- Establishes "you" perspective immediately
- Takes an indirect approach to bad news by easing into it and saving the bad news until end of second paragraph
- Speaks clearly and directly to the reader
- Remains polite and tactful, despite delivery of bad news
- Maintains the "you" perspective through to the end

This self-centered tone might be appropriate after numerous investigations into the customer's complaint and failed attempts to communicate your company's perspective to the customer, but in your initial correspondence it would be offensive. The example below shows a more considerate version. Instead of expressing only the writer's point of view, this second version conveys respect for the reader's viewpoint.

> Although my paperwork shows that you were charged correctly, I will investigate this matter immediately by checking my files against our records.

Considerate and respectful

The "you" perspective is appropriate not only at the beginning of a letter but also throughout. Do not sign and send the letter until you are certain that the needs, wants, and feelings of your reader consistently get top billing, even when you simultaneously must assert your own perspective.

Being Polite and Tactful

If you must express criticism, do so in a way that conveys good will and trust in the recipient. Avoid the following type of expression:

Be courteous and emphasize good will

> I am shocked that your company lacks the standards to design and manufacture an alarm clock that actually works.

Tactless

Although a company representative would be required to write a polite and thoughtful response to the above complaint, he or she might be inclined to look closely at the clock's warranty, offer only the most basic reimbursement, and not seek the customer's future business via an incentive.

In contrast, a polite and thoughtful letter might yield a full refund, a brand-new replacement, or an attractive incentive:

> Although your clock worked reliably for several months, one of the internal mechanisms recently malfunctioned. I would appreciate your contacting me about an exchange or refund.

Polite

Using Plain English

Avoid the stuffy, puffed-up phrases some writers think they need to make their communications sound important. Even though a letter is more formal than a memo or an email, plain English can still get your point across. For example, consider the following closing section to an inquiry letter asking for help:

Be professional without being stuffy

> Humbly thanking you in anticipation of your kind assistance, I remain
>
> Faithfully yours,

Stuffy

The reader of this letter might feel spoken down to and decide not to respond. However, in this revised version, the reader would likely perceive the writer as a straight-talking equal and be more inclined to follow up:

Clear and direct | I would greatly appreciate any help you could offer me.

Best wishes,

Here are a few stuffy phrasings, with clearer, more direct translations:

Stuffy, unclear	Clear and direct
As per your request	As you requested
Contingent upon receipt of	As soon as we receive
Due to the fact that	Because

Be natural. Write as you would speak in a classroom or office: professionally and respectfully but clearly and directly.

Considering the Needs of International Readers

Any letter might be read by international readers

In the global marketplace, you will often find that you need to communicate with readers outside the United States. In many of these settings, formality may be highly valued, and so at some point, instead of just using email, you may need to write a formal letter. Some of your readers may speak English as a first language. To ensure your letter is appropriate for an international reader, avoid being overly informal, use plain English, and avoid idiomatic expressions such as "in the ball park" or "under the weather."

Being Direct or Indirect

Determine if the direct or indirect approach is preferable

During your career, you will have to write letters that convey bad or unwelcome news. For example, you may have to say no to customers, employees, and job applicants. You may have to make difficult requests, such as asking employees to accept higher medical insurance premiums or seeking an interview with a beleaguered official. You may have to notify consumers or shareholders about accidents or product recalls. You may have to apologize for errors—and so on. In each instance, you will have to decide whether to build your case first (indirect approach) or get right to the point (direct approach).

When to be direct or indirect

Try to anticipate your readers' reaction. Generally speaking, when you have good news use the direct approach; readers will appreciate your getting right to the point. When presenting bad news, you may prefer the indirect approach; by presenting your rationale beforehand, you give readers the chance to adjust to the bad news.

Strategies

for Letters in General

- **Determine whether the situation calls for a letter, memo, or email.** Letters are the most formal of these three choices.
- **Use an appropriate letter format and include all the required parts.** Unless your organization has its own guidelines, use the block format and the parts discussed earlier.

- **Place the reader's needs first.** Always write from the "you" perspective, putting yourself in your reader's place.
- **Decide on the direct or indirect approach.** Generally speaking, take the direct approach for good news and the indirect approach for bad news.
- **Maintain a courteous, professional tone.** A professional tone creates goodwill and is more effective in the long run.
- **Avoid stuffy language.** Use plain English, no matter how formal or important the letter. Stuffy language only comes across as phony.
- **Keep international readers in mind.** Don't assume every letter you write is directed at a recipient whose first language is English.
- **Use PDF for digital delivery.** If your letter will be sent as an email attachment, use PDF rather than a word processing format for your attachment. (PDF will retain the formatting and layout more precisely and can't be edited or modified as easily.)

Types of Letters

10.6 **Write an effective inquiry, claim, sales, or adjustment letter.**

There are many types of business letters. Among the most common types you can expect to write on the job are inquiry letters, claim letters, sales letters, and adjustment letters.

Inquiry Letters

Inquiry letters ask questions and request a reply. They may be solicited (in response to an advertisement or announcement) or unsolicited (to request some type of information you need for your job). For example, a manager at a computer repair company might write a solicited inquiry to a manufacturer that offers free troubleshooting guides for repair specialists. If there has been no such advertised offer, the manager might write an unsolicited inquiry to the same company asking if any troubleshooting information is available.

In a solicited inquiry, be brief and make sure to reference the advertisement, social media post, or other announcement that prompted you to write. In an unsolicited inquiry, you are asking a busy person to read your letter, consider your request, collect the information, and write a response. Therefore, keep your request reasonable and state the purpose clearly and concisely. Express your appreciation. Avoid long, involved inquiries that are unlikely to be answered.

Figure 10.7 is an example of an unsolicited letter requesting information. Research consultant Alan Greene is preparing a report on the feasibility of harnessing solar energy for home heating in Alaska. After learning that a nonprofit research group has been experimenting with solar applications, Alan decides to write for details. Notice how Greene tries to make the respondent's task as easy as possible. If this letter were sent as an attachment to an email, Greene could set up a link to an online survey or form, making the reader's task even easier.

Solicited and unsolicited inquiry letters ask questions

Figure 10.7 An unsolicited inquiry letter

Solar Solutions, Inc.
234 Western Road
Fargo, ND 27116

March 10, 20XX

Rachel Cowans
Director of Energy Systems
The Earth Research Institute
Persham, ME 04619

Dear Ms. Cowans:

States the purpose — As a Research Consultant at Solar Solutions, Inc., I am preparing a report (April 15 deadline) on the feasibility of solar energy for home heating in Arctic regions.

Makes a reasonable and courteous request — While gathering data on home solar heating, I encountered references (in *Scientific American* and elsewhere) to your group's pioneering work in solar energy systems. Would you please allow me to benefit from your experience? Your answers to the following questions would be a great help.

Presents a list of specific questions —
1. At this stage of development, do you consider active or passive heating more practical? (Please explain briefly.)
2. Do you expect to surpass the 60 percent limit of heating needs supplied by the active system? If so, at what level of efficiency and how soon?
3. What is the cost of materials for building your active system, per cubic foot of living space?
4. What metal do you use in collectors to obtain the highest thermal conductivity at the lowest maintenance costs?

Provides complete contact information — Please write your answers on the back of this page and return in the enclosed envelope. If email or phone are more convenient, feel free to contact me at agreene@solarsolutionsND.com or 555-986-6578.

Offers to share findings — I would be glad to send you a copy of the final document. Thank you in advance.

Sincerely,

Alan Greene

Alan Greene
Research Consultant

Strategies

for Inquiry Letters

- **Don't wait until the last minute.** Provide ample time for a response.
- **Whenever possible, write to a specific person.** If you need the name, call the organization and ask to whom you should address your inquiry.
- **Do your homework to ask the right questions.** A vague request such as "Please send me your data on..." is likely to be ignored. Don't ask questions for which the answers are readily available elsewhere.
- **Explain who you are and how the information will be used.** If you appear to be from a competing company, your request will likely be ignored. But in other situations, you still need to explain what you plan to do with the requested data.
- **Write specific questions that are easy to understand and answer.** If you have multiple questions, put them in a numbered list to increase your chances of getting all the information you want.
- **Provide alternate contact information.** If you can also be reached by email or phone, provide that information.
- **Include a stamped, self-addressed envelope or provide an online option, such as a clickable survey or form.** These gestures will increase the likelihood of a response.
- **Say thank you and offer to follow up.** Even if you said it at the beginning, say thank you again at the end. Offer to send a copy of the document in which you plan to use the information, if appropriate.

Claim Letters

In the workplace, things do not always run smoothly. Sometimes people make mistakes, systems break down, or companies make promises that can't be kept. Claim (or complaint) letters request adjustments for defective goods or poor services, or they complain about unfair treatment or the like. Such letters fall into two categories: *routine claims* and *arguable claims*. Each calls for a different approach. Routine claims typically take a direct approach because the customer's claim is not debatable. Arguable claims present more of a persuasive challenge because they convey unwelcome news and are open to interpretation; arguable claims, therefore, typically take an indirect approach.

Routine and arguable claim letters request adjustments

Figure 10.8 shows a routine claim letter. Writer Jeffrey Ryder does not ask whether the firm will honor his claim; he assumes that it will and asks directly how to return his defective skis for repair. Notice that, in place of a salutation, an attention line directs the claim to the appropriate department, while a subject line (and its reemphasis in the first sentence) makes clear the nature of the claim.

Figure 10.9 shows an arguable claim letter. Because the reply may not necessarily be in her favor, writer Sandra Alvarez uses a tactful and reasonable tone and an indirect approach to present her argument. Although she is courteous, she is also somewhat forceful to reflect her insistence on an acceptable adjustment. For example, the attention line creates an immediate businesslike tone.

Figure 10.8 A routine claim letter

Ryder's Ski Shop
Box 2641-A
Pocatello, ID 83201

April 13, 20XX

Star Ski Manufacturing Company
P.O. Box 3049
St. Paul, MN 55165

Attention: Consumer Affairs Department

Subject: *Delaminated skis*

States problem and action desired → This winter, four of the pairs of Tornado skis I purchased for rental at my ski shop began to delaminate. I want to take advantage of your lifetime guarantee to have them relaminated.

Provides details → I purchased the skis via your St. Paul Sales Representative in November 1989. Although I no longer have the sales slip, the registration numbers are P9906, P9961, P9965, and P9978.

Explains basis for claim → I'm aware that you no longer make metal skis, but as I recall, your lifetime guarantee on the skis I bought was a major selling point. Only your company and one other were backing their skis so strongly.

Courteously states desired action → Would you please let me know how to go about returning my delaminated skis for repair?

Yours truly,

Jeffrey Ryder

Jeffrey Ryder

Figure 10.9 An arguable claim letter

OFFICE SYSTEMS, INC. 657 High Street Tulsa, OK 74120
(302) 655-5550 (v)(302) 655-5551 (fax) osys@sys.com (email)

January 23, 20XX

Consumer Affairs Department ETC.
Hightone Office Supplies
93 Cattle Drive
Houston, Texas 77028

Attention: Ms. Dionne Dubree

Dear Ms. Dubree:

Your company has an established reputation as a reliable wholesaler of office supplies. For eight years we have counted on that reliability, but a recent episode has left us annoyed and disappointed. — Establishes early agreement

On January 29, we ordered 5 cartons of 700 MB HP CDs (#A74-866) and 13 cartons of Epson MX 70/80 black cartridges (#A19-556).

On February 5, the order arrived. But instead of the 700 MB HP CDs ordered, we received 650 MB Everlast CDs. And the Epson cartridges were blue, not the black we had ordered. We returned the order the same day. — Presents facts to support claim

Also on the 5th, we called John Fitsimmons at your company to explain our problem. He promised delivery of a corrected order by the 12th. Finally, on the 22nd, we did receive an order—the original incorrect one—with a note claiming that the packages had been water damaged while in our possession. — Offers more support

Our warehouse manager insists the packages were in perfect condition when he released them to the shipper. Because we had the packages only five hours and had no rain on the 5th, we are certain the damage did not occur here. — Includes all relevant information — Sticks to the facts

Responsibility for damages therefore rests with either the shipper or your warehouse staff. What bothers us is our outstanding bill from Hightone ($2,049.50) for the faulty shipment. We insist that the bill be canceled and that we receive a corrected statement. Until this misunderstanding, our transactions with your company were excellent. We hope they can be again. — Requests a specific adjustment

We would appreciate having this matter resolved before the end of this month. — Stipulates a reasonable response time

Yours truly,

Sandra Alvarez

Sandra Alvarez
Manager, Accounting

Strategies

for Claim Letters

- **Routine claim letters**
  - **Use a direct approach.** Describe the request or problem; explain the problem clearly; close courteously, restating the action you request.
  - **Be polite and reasonable.** Your goal is not to sound off but to achieve results: a refund, a replacement, or an apology. Press your claim objectively yet firmly by explaining it clearly and by stipulating the reasonable action that will satisfy you. Do not insult the reader or revile the company.
  - **Provide enough detail to clarify the basis for your claim.** Explain the specific defect. Identify the faulty item clearly, giving serial and model numbers and date and place of purchase.
  - **Conclude by expressing goodwill and confidence in the company's integrity.** Do not make threats or create animosity.
- **Arguable claim letters**
  - **Use an indirect approach.** People are more likely to respond favorably *after* reading your explanation. Begin with a neutral statement both parties can agree to—but that also serves as the basis for your request.
  - **Once you've established agreement, explain and support your claim.** Include enough information for a fair evaluation: date and place of purchase, order number, dates of previous letters or calls, and background.
  - **Conclude by requesting a specific action.** Be polite but assertive in how you make your request.

Sales Letters

Sales letters
persuade
potential
customers

Sales letters are written to persuade a current or potential customer to buy a company's product or try its services. Because people are bombarded by sales messages—in magazines, on billboards, on television, on Facebook, on online shopping and other sites—your letter must be genuinely persuasive and must get to the point quickly. First, engage the reader immediately with an attention-grabbing statement or an intriguing question. Next, describe clearly and concisely the product or service you offer and explain its appeal. Finally, conclude by requesting immediate action.

In the letter in Figure 10.10, restaurant owner Jimmy Lekkas opens with an attention-grabbing question that is hard to ignore and has universal appeal: good food, for free, right in the neighborhood. He then makes his case by explaining the history of his restaurant (which provides immediate credibility) and offering vivid descriptions of the food. He closes by asking readers to take action by a specific date.

Figure 10.10 A sales letter

Jimmy's Greek Kitchen
24-52 28th Street, Astoria, NY 11102
Phone: (555) 274-5672   Fax: (555) 274-5671
Jimmysgreek@comcast.net
www.jimmysgreekkitchen.com

July 16, 20XX

Adriana Nikolaidis
26-22 30th Street #5
Astoria, NY 11102

Dear Ms. Nikolaidis:

Are you in the mood to sample the best Greek food in the neighborhood absolutely free of charge? We at the newly opened Jimmy's Greek Kitchen would like to say "Thank you for having us in your neighborhood" by inviting you to sample a variety of our authentic Greek specialties.

If you've heard of or visited the famous Jimmy's in Chicago, you know that our fare has been pleasing Chicago diners for over 40 years. At long last, we have opened a companion restaurant in Astoria, and we are proud to offer you the same high-quality appetizers, entrees, and desserts, prepared to perfection. In fact, I trained our Astoria chef myself.

Ranging from charbroiled meats and grilled seafoods to vegetarian specialties and Greek favorites like tzatziki, pastitsio, and moussaka, Jimmy's is truly the best in town. Please have a look at the enclosed menu to see the full range of tasty foods we offer.

Please take advantage of this special offer while it lasts. From now until August 31, just bring this letter to Jimmy's and lunch or dinner is on the house. You may choose any appetizer, entree, side order, beverage, and dessert on the menu—all free of charge. We hope that you will not only enjoy the dining experience but will tell others and come back to see us frequently.

Thank you,

Jimmy Lekkas

Jimmy Lekkas

Opens with an attention-grabbing question

Describes the long history and appeal of the restaurant

Maintains appeal by describing the menu

Ends by asking the reader to take action

Strategies

for Sales Letters

- **Begin with a question or other attention-grabbing statement.**
- **Get to the point.** People resist reading long opening passages, especially if the message is unsolicited.
- **Spell out the benefits for the recipients.** Answer this implied question: "What do I stand to gain from this?"
- **Persuade with facts and with appeals to the senses.** Facts (such as the history of your company) appeal to logic. Graphic descriptions (such as the colors of your new cars or the types of food you offer) appeal to a different part of the brain—the emotions. Use both.
- **Tell the truth.** Despite your desire to sell something, it is unethical to lie, distort, exaggerate, or underestimate to make the sale.
- **Close by asking readers to take action.** Either ask for some reasonable action (such as "like us on Facebook") or offer an incentive (such as a free sample) to encourage follow up.

Adjustment Letters

Positive and negative adjustment letters answer claim letters

Adjustment letters are written in response to a claim letter from a customer. Even though most people never make formal complaints or follow up on warranties or product guarantees, companies generally will make a requested adjustment that seems reasonable.

Rather than quibbling over questionable claims, companies usually honor the request and show how much they appreciate the customer, as in Figure 10.11. In this example, writer Jane Duval apologizes graciously for a mistake. She omits an explanation because the error is obvious: Someone sent the wrong software. Once the reader has the information and apology, Duval shifts attention to a positive feature: the gift certificate. Note the "you" perspective and friendly tone.

Of course, if a claim is unreasonable or unjustified, the recipient usually will refuse the request. In refusing to grant a refund for a 10-speed bicycle, company representative Anna Jenkins faces a delicate balance (Figure 10.12). On the one hand, she must explain why she cannot grant the customer's request; on the other hand, she must be diplomatic in how she asserts that the customer is mistaken. Although Mrs. Gower may not be pleased by the explanation, it is thorough and reasonable.

Figure 10.11 A positive adjustment letter

Software Unlimited
421 Fairview Road
Tulsa, Oklahoma 74321

May 2, 20XX

Mr. James Morris
P.O. Box 176
Little Rock AR 54701

Dear Mr. Morris:

Your software should arrive by May 15. Sorry for the mixup. We don't make a practice of sending Apple software to PC owners, but we do slip up once in a while. •————— Apologizes immediately

In appreciation for your patience and understanding, I've enclosed a $50 gift certificate. You can give it to a friend or apply it toward your next order. If you order by phone, just give the certificate number, and the operator will credit your account. •————— Offers compensation

Keep your certificate handy because you will be getting our new catalog soon. It features 15 new business and utility programs that you might find useful. •————— Looks toward the future

Sincerely,

Jane Duval

Jane Duval
Sales Manager

Encl. Gift Certificate

Strategies

for Adjustment Letters

- **If you need to apologize, do so immediately and in active voice.** Don't say "An error was made..."; instead, say "We are sorry we made an error..."
- **Be polite and professional.** Even if you must say no to a request, you can do so respectfully.
- **Use passive voice if you want to avoid sounding accusatory.** If your customer made a mistake in assembling the device, you could say "The wrong bolts were used" rather than "You used the wrong bolts."
- **If appropriate, offer an incentive.** You can create a lot of goodwill if you reach out with even a small gift certificate or in-store credit.
- **Close on a positive note.** Thank the person for writing and for being a customer.

Figure 10.12 A negative adjustment letter

People Power, Inc.
101 Salem Street, Springfield, Illinois 32456

March 8, 20XX

Mrs. Alma Gower
32 Wood Street
Lewiston, IL 32432

Dear Mrs. Gower:

Introduction starts off with the facts

When we advertise the Windspirit as the toughest, most durable ten-speed, we stress it's a racing or cruising bike built to withstand the long, grueling miles of intense competition. The bike is built of the strongest, yet lightest, alloys available, and each part is calibrated to within 1/1000 of an inch. That's why we guarantee the Windspirit against defects resulting from the strain of competitive racing.

Writer doesn't accuse; she explains in a friendly tone

The Windspirit, though, is not built to withstand the impact of ramp jumps such as those attempted by your son. The rims and front fork would have to be made from a much thicker gauge alloy, thereby increasing weight and decreasing speed. Since we build racing bikes, such a compromise is unacceptable.

Refusal is professional, direct, and reasonable

To ensure that buyers are familiar with the Windspirit's limits, in the owner's manual we stress that the bike should be carried over curbings and similar drops because even an eight-inch drop could damage the front rim. Damage from such drops is not considered normal wear and so is not covered by our guarantee.

Closing is helpful

Since your son appears to be more interested in a bike capable of withstanding the impact of high jumps, you could recoup a large part of the Windspirit's price by advertising it in your local newspaper. Many novice racers would welcome the chance to buy one at a reduced price. Or, if you prefer having it repaired, you could take it to Jamie's Bike Shop, the dealer closest to you.

Yours truly,

Anna Jenkins

Anna Jenkins
Manager, Customer Services

Checklist

for Memos and Letters

Memo

- ❏ Does my memo contain all the necessary parts (To, From, Date, Subject, body copy)?
- ❏ Is the text of my memo clear and direct?
- ❏ Does my memo follow a standard format, beginning with an introductory paragraph, explaining my points in the body of the memo, then ending with a short conclusion?
- ❏ Is the tone of my memo professional and polite?
- ❏ Have I considered whether to take a direct or an indirect approach?
- ❏ Does my memo focus on one topic?
- ❏ Is my memo directed at the right people?
- ❏ Have I considered whether the memo is more suitable to the body of an email, as an email attachment, or as a paper memo (or some combination)?

Letter

- ❏ Does my letter contain all the necessary parts (sender's address, date, inside address, salutation/attention line, body text, closing signature)?
- ❏ Is the tone of my letter professional, polite, and appropriately formal?
- ❏ Have I considered whether to take a direct or an indirect approach?
- ❏ Have I put my reader's interests first (the "you" perspective)?
- ❏ If making a difficult request, am I being tactful yet clear about what I want?
- ❏ Am I writing in clear language?
- ❏ Will my letter be delivered on paper via the mail service or as an email attachment, or both?

Applications

General Application

Write a memo as the sales director of a company to in-house sales department employees and to sales representatives. Announce and outline a new dress code policy and diplomatically explain why the policy is more strict for the sales reps. Remember to keep an informal but professional tone, format the memo properly, and keep it brief but complete. Decide whether to send the memo as the body of an email message or as a PDF email attachment (you can skip ahead to Chapter 18 for more ideas about email and memos).

Team Applications

1. In groups of two or three, assume you are co-owners of a condominium complex that has been invaded by carpenter ants. Have a meeting to discuss your plans to find a way to eliminate the ants, using an insecticide proven to be nontoxic to humans. Ask each team member to write a follow-up memo that summarizes

the meeting and recommends next steps for each team member to take. Compare memos and discuss the decisions each person made for how to organize and structure the memo.

2. Working in groups, respond to the following scenario. Appoint one group member to present the letter in class.

> Luke Harrington wants a $1,200 refund for four Douglas fir trees that have died since your workers planted them in his yard two years ago. Because you guarantee your transplants for three years, he wants his money returned. After checking Harrington's contract, you recall his problem: You wouldn't guarantee the five Douglas firs he ordered because he wanted them planted in a wet, marshy area, and Douglas firs need well-drained soil. A check of Harrington's lot confirms that four trees planted in the wet area have died of root rot. Write to him, reminding him of the contract and refusing the adjustment. As you did two years ago, suggest that he plant balsam firs in the wet area. Although balsam needles are slightly darker than the Douglas firs', both trees have the shape he wants. The balsams would retain the symmetry of his tree line. Harrington's address: 921 Daisy Lane, Churchill, MO 61516.

Global Application

Interview a person whose work takes him or her to one or more countries outside the United States. Ask that person to describe the way letters are used for international communication and whether any special issues involving grammar, forms of address, direct or indirect organizational patterns, or other features make letter writing different when addressing international audiences.

Digital and Social Media Application

Word processing programs (Microsoft Word, Google Docs, Apple Pages) offer a variety of templates for writing letters. Templates can help you get started; templates should be used wisely, however, because instead of thinking for yourself about the audience, purpose, and appropriate organizational pattern and language usage, you may end up letting the template do the thinking. Look at the various templates available in your word processing program, and make a list of ways in which the template may or may not work for your purposes. Compare the template features with those described in this chapter.

Chapter 11
Definitions

 ## Learning Objectives

11.1 Explain the audience and purpose of definitions.

11.2 Understand the legal, safety, and societal implications of definitions.

11.3 Identify parenthetical, sentence, and expanded definitions.

11.4 Use various methods to expand a definition, as the situation requires.

11.5 Place definitions in your document.

Chapter Outline

Audience and Purpose of Definitions 192

Legal, Safety, and Societal Implications of Definitions 193

Types of Definitions 194

Methods for Expanding Definitions 196

Placement of Definitions 199
  Strategies for Definitions 202
  Checklist for Definitions 202

Applications 203

Meaning and importance of definitions

Definitions explain specialized terms or concepts and may be unfamiliar to people who don't have expertise in a particular field. In many cases, a term may have more than one meaning or different meanings in different fields. Consider a word such as *atmosphere*: To a meteorologist, atmosphere refers to the envelope of gases that surrounds a planet ("the Earth's atmosphere"); to a politician or office manager, the same word would typically mean the mood of the country or workplace ("an atmosphere of high hopes"); to a geologist, it would have to do with the weather conditions in a particular area ("the atmosphere of the Hawaiian forests is lush and volcanic"); to a physicist, it would stand for a unit of pressure ("a standard atmosphere is 101,325 pascal"); and to a novelist, it would be associated with the mood of a novel ("a gothic atmosphere").

As you can see, precision is important, especially in specialized careers, in which field-specific terminology is common, and undefined terms may prevent the overall meaning of a technical document from making sense. Engineers talk about *elasticity* or *ductility*; bankers discuss *amortization* or *fiduciary relationships*. In a technical document, these terms must be defined if people inside and outside of those fields are to understand the meaning of the document as a whole. Imagine if a doctor continually used the words *myocardial infarction* in a patient brochure without ever defining the term. The fact that a myocardial infarction is the medical name for one form of *heart attack* would be lost on patients who might benefit from a clear understanding of the brochure.

Audience and Purpose of Definitions

11.1 Explain the audience and purpose of definitions.

Audience considerations

Definitions make a document usable for an audience by answering one of two questions: "What, exactly, does this definition entail?" or "What, exactly, is this process, item, concept, or technique?" The first question spells out for audience members how they are affected by the item defined. For example, a person buying a new computer needs to understand exactly what "manufacturer's guarantee" or "expandable memory" means in the context of that purchase. The second question spells out for your audience what makes an item, concept, or process unique. For example, an engineering student needs to understand the distinction between *elasticity* and *ductility*. Inside or outside any field, people have to grasp precisely what "makes a thing what it is and distinguishes that thing from all other things" (Corbett 38).

Consider the purpose of using particular terms in your document by answering the question "Why does my audience need to understand this term or concept?" The level of technicality you use must match the audience's background and experience. For a group of mechanical engineering students, your definition of a *solenoid*, for example, can be brief and to the point, and you can use highly technical language:

> A solenoid is an inductance coil that serves as a tractive electromagnet.

For general audiences, your definition will require language that is understandable by people who are not trained as engineers:

> A solenoid is a metal coil that converts electrical energy to magnetic energy capable of performing mechanical functions.

Unless you are certain your audience will grasp the exact meaning, always define a term the first time you use it.

Legal, Safety, and Societal Implications of Definitions

11.2   **Understand the legal, safety, and societal implications of definitions.**

Precise definition is essential in technical communication; inaccurate or unclear definitions have legal, safety, and societal implications. Legal implications of definitions can be seen in documents such as contracts, which are are detailed, legally binding definitions of the specific terms of an agreement. If you lease an apartment or a car, the printed contract will define both the *lessee's* and *lessor's* specific responsibilities. Likewise, an employment contract or employee handbook will spell out responsibilities for both employer and employee. In writing an employee handbook for your company, you would need to define such terms as *acceptable job performance, confidentiality, sexual harassment*, and *equal opportunity*.

Definitions also have safety implications. From areas such as food safety to the safe use of equipment to the safety of assembling a new product, definitions play a key role. For instance, the U.S. government Web site on food safety needs to define concepts and terms such as *minimum cooking temperatures, food poisoning*, and *listeria*. These definitions must be brief and to the point, accessible to a wide audience, and written with a focus on what people can do to protect themselves and stay safe.

Marginal notes:

Purpose considerations

A highly technical version

A nontechnical version

Definitions have legal implications

Definitions have safety implications

Definitions
have societal
implications

Clear and accurate definitions also help the public understand and evaluate the societal issues of specific technologies or scientific findings. For example, as a first step in helping people understanding the debate over *genetic engineering*, we need at least a very basic definition:

> Genetic engineering is the process of using recombinant DNA (rDNA) technology to alter the genetic makeup of an organism (EPA).

Of course, to follow the debate, people would need increasingly detailed information (about specific procedures, risks, benefits, and so on). But the above definition gets everyone started on course to a healthy debate by enabling us to understand the basic concept and agree on its basic meaning.

Types of Definitions

11.3   Identify parenthetical, sentence, and expanded definitions.

Three categories
of definitions

Definitions fall into three distinct categories: *parenthetical*, *sentence*, and *expanded* definitions. When you define terms within a document, decide how much detail your audience actually requires in order to grasp your exact meaning: Do you need to quickly define a word in parentheses or in a sentence, or do you need to go into significant detail explaining a complex concept?

Parenthetical Definitions

When to use
parenthetical
definitions

Often, you can clarify the meaning of a word by using a more familiar synonym or a clarifying phrase in parentheses immediately after the word. This is known as a parenthetical definition and is used when a definition is relatively simple and doesn't need detailed elaboration, as in these two examples:

Parenthetical
definitions

> The *leaching field* (sieve-like drainage area) requires crushed stone.
> The trees on the site are mostly *deciduous* (shedding foliage at season's end).

On a Web page or online help system, parenthetical definitions can be linked to the main word or phrase rather than placed in parentheses after the word. Readers who click on *leaching field*, say, would be taken to a window containing a brief definition. In a print document, words and phrases are often defined in a separate list of defined items, known as a *glossary*. (If the document is converted to PDF, those words and phrases can become links that send readers directly to the glossary.)

Sentence Definitions

When to use
sentence
definitions

A slightly longer way to define a phrase is to use the "term-class-features" method to form a sentence definition. Begin by stating the term. Then, indicate the broader class to which this item belongs, followed by the features that distinguish it from other items in that general grouping. Use a sentence definition when a concept requires further elaboration than a parenthetical definition could offer. Here are some examples:

Term	Class	Features
A carburetor	is a mixing device	in gasoline engines that blends air and fuel into a vapor for combustion within the cylinders.
Diabetes	is a metabolic disease	caused by a disorder of the pituitary gland or pancreas and characterized by excessive urination, persistent thirst, and inability to metabolize sugar.
Stress	is an applied force	that strains or deforms a body.

The previous elements may be combined into one or more complete sentences:

Diabetes is a metabolic disease caused by a disorder of the pituitary gland or pancreas. This disease is characterized by excessive urination, persistent thirst, and inability to metabolize sugar.

A complete sentence definition

Sentence definitions are especially useful if you plan to use a term frequently and need to establish a working definition that you will not need to repeat throughout the document:

Throughout this report, the term *disadvantaged student* will refer to all students who lack adequate funds to pay for on-campus housing, food services, and medical care, but who are able to pay for their coursework and books through scholarships and part-time work.

A working definition

Expanded Definitions

Brief definitions, such as parenthetical and sentence definitions, are fine when your audience requires only a general understanding of a term or when a term is not particularly complex to define. For example, the parenthetical definition of *leaching field* on page 194 might be enough to prevent reader confusion without providing excessive detail, or the above sentence definition of *disadvantaged student* might be enough to get a simple concept across. However, a document that requires more detail (such as a public health report on groundwater contamination from leaching fields) or a highly complex term would call for an expanded definition.

When to use expanded definitions

Depending on audience and purpose, an expanded definition may be a short paragraph or may extend to several pages. For example, if a device, such as a digital dosimeter (used for measuring radiation exposure), is introduced for the first time to an audience that needs to understand how this instrument works, your definition would require at least several paragraphs, if not pages.

Methods for Expanding Definitions

11.4 **Use various methods to expand a definition, as the situation requires.**

An expanded definition can be created in any number of ways as described below. The method or methods you decide to use will depend on the questions you expect the audience will want answered, as illustrated in Figure 11.1.

As you read through the following sections, refer to the following sentence definition of the word *laser*, and consider how each expansion method provides further detail in a different way:

Sentence definition

> A laser is an electronic device that emits a highly concentrated beam of light.

Etymology

Sometimes, a word's origin (its development and changing meanings), also known as the word's etymology, can help clarify its meaning. For example, *biometrics* (the statistical analysis of biological data) is a word derived from the Greek *bio*, meaning life, and *metron*, meaning measure. You can use a dictionary to learn the origins of most words. Not all words develop from Greek, Latin, or other roots, however. For example, some terms are acronyms, derived from the first letters or parts of several words. Such is the case with the word *laser* (derived from *light amplification by stimulated emission of radiation*); therefore, to expand the sentence definition of *laser*, you might phrase your definition as follows:

"How did its name originate?"

> The word *laser* is an acronym for *light amplification by stimulated emission of radiation* and is the name for an electronic device that emits a highly concentrated beam of light.

Figure 11.1 Questions to determine the best expansion approach

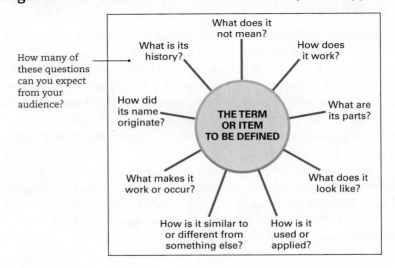

History

In some cases, the history of a term, concept, or procedure can be useful in expanding a definition. Specialized dictionaries and encyclopedias are good background sources. You might expand the definition of a laser by describing how the laser was invented:

"What is its history?"

> The early researchers in fiber optic communications were hampered by two principal difficulties— the lack of a sufficiently intense source of light and the absence of a medium which could transmit this light free from interference and with a minimum signal loss. Lasers emit a narrow beam of intense light, so their invention in 1960 solved the first problem. The development of a means to convey this signal was longer in coming, but scientists succeeded in developing the first communications-grade optical fiber of almost pure silica glass in 1970 (Stanton 28).

Negation

Some definitions can be clarified by explaining what the term *does not* mean. For example, the following definition of a laser eliminates any misconceptions an audience might already have about lasers:

"What does it not mean?"

> A laser is an electronic device that emits a highly concentrated beam of light. It is used for many beneficial purposes (including corrective eye and other surgeries), not—as science fiction might tell you—as a transport medium to other dimensions.

Operating Principle

The following example not only defines what a laser is but also shows the operating principle behind it:

"How does it work?"

> Basically, a laser [uses electrical energy to produce] coherent light: light in which all the waves are in phase with each other, making the light hotter and more intense (Gartaganis 23).

Analysis of Parts

Be sure to list all of the parts to create a complete picture, and, if necessary, define the individual parts as well, as in the following expanded definition of a laser:

"What are its parts?"

> A laser is an electronic device that emits a highly concentrated beam of light. To get a better idea of how a laser works, consider its three main parts:
>
> 1. [Lasers require] a source of energy, [such as] electric currents or even other lasers.
> 2. A resonant circuit...contains the lasing medium and has one fully reflecting end and one partially reflecting end. The medium—which can be a solid, liquid, or gas—absorbs the energy and releases it as a stream of photons [electromagnetic particles that emit light]. The photons...vibrate between the fully and partially reflecting ends of the resonant circuit, constantly accumulating energy—that is, they are amplified. After attaining a prescribed level of energy, the photons can pass through the partially reflecting surface as a beam of coherent light and encounter the optical elements.
> 3. Optical elements—lenses, prisms, and mirrors—modify size, shape, and other characteristics of the laser beam and direct it to its target (Gartaganis 23).

Visuals

"What does it look like?"

Make sure any visual you use is labeled clearly. Always introduce and explain your visual and place the visual near your discussion. If the visual is borrowed, credit the source. The following visual accompanies the previous analysis of parts:

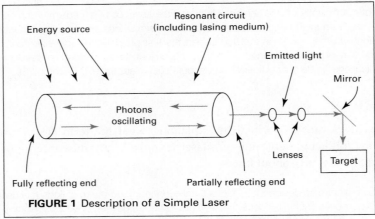

FIGURE 1 Description of a Simple Laser

SOURCE: Gartaganis, Arthur. "Lasers." *Occupational Outlook Quarterly.*

Comparison and Contrast

"How is it similar to or different from something else?"

By comparing (showing similarities) or contrasting (showing differences) between new information and information your audience already understands, you help build a bridge between what people already know and what they don't. The following example uses both comparison and contrast to expand on a more basic definition of a laser:

> Fiber optics technology results from the superior capacity of light waves to carry a communications signal. Sounds waves, radio waves, and light waves can all carry signals; their capacity increases with their frequency. Voice frequencies carried by telephone operate at 1000 cycles per second, or hertz. Television signals transmit at about 50 million hertz. Light waves, however, operate at frequencies in the hundreds of trillions of hertz (Stanton 28).

Required Conditions

"What makes it work or occur?"

In the following example, additional information on optics adds to the definition of a laser:

> In order to emit a highly concentrated beam of light, the laser must absorb energy through the reflecting end of a resonant circuit, amplify the photons produced between the reflecting and partially reflecting end of the resonant circuit, and release the photons as a beam of light via a set of lenses, prisms, and mirrors.

Examples

The following expansion using an example shows how laser light is used in medical treatment:

"How is it used or applied?"

> Lasers are increasingly used to treat health problems. Thousands of eye operations involving cataracts and detached retinas are performed every year by ophthalmologists.... Dermatologists treat skin problems.... Gynecologists treat problems of the reproductive system, and neurosurgeons even perform brain surgery—all using lasers transmitted through optical fibers (Gartaganis 24–25).

Using Multiple Expansion Methods

Depending on the complexity of what you need to define, you may need to combine multiple expansion methods, as in Figure 11.2.

Use as many expansion methods as needed

Like a good essay, this multiparagraph definition is unified and coherent: Each paragraph is developed around one main idea and logically connected to other paragraphs. Transitions emphasize the connection between ideas. The level of technicality connects with the intended audience.

Because this definition deals with a vital community issue, the author uses multiple methods to ensure that readers have a solid basis for understanding the situation: A water reservoir is threatened by chemical see page and depleted by drought. This definition forms part of the introduction to a report that analyzes the severity of the problems and explores possible solutions.

To understand the problems, readers first need to know what a water table is, how it is formed, what conditions affect its level and quality, and how it figures into town planning decisions. The concepts of *recharge* and *permeability* are vital to understanding the problem, so these terms are defined parenthetically. This audience has no interest in geological or hydrological (study of water resources) theory. Audience members simply need the broadest possible picture.

Placement of Definitions

11.5 **Place definitions in your document.**

Each time readers encounter an unfamiliar term or concept, that item should be defined in the same area on the page or screen. In a printed text, you can place brief definitions in parentheses or in the document's margin, aligned with the terms being defined. Or, as discussed earlier in this chapter, you can create a glossary; for longer reports, glossaries are placed either at the beginning or the end of a document, depending on organizational preferences. See Chapter 16, Formal Reports, for more information on creating and using a glossary. Sentence definitions should be part of the running text. Place an expanded definition either near the beginning of a long document or in an appendix (see page 306)—depending on whether

Placing printed definitions

Figure 11.2 An expanded definition

EXPANDED DEFINITION: WATER TABLE

Sentence definition ————• The water table is the level below the earth's surface at which the ground is saturated

Example ————• with water. Figure 1 shows a typical water table that might be found in the East. Wells driven into such a formation will have a water level identical to that of the water table.

FIGURE 1 A Typical Water Table (Eastern United States)

Operating principle ————•   The world's freshwater supply comes almost entirely as precipitation that originates with the evaporation of sea and lake water. This precipitation falls to earth and follows one of three courses: It may fall directly onto bodies of water, such as rivers or lakes, where it is directly used by humans; it may fall onto land, and either evaporate or run over the ground to the rivers or other bodies of water; or it may fall onto land, be contained, and seep into the earth. The latter precipitation makes up the water table.

Comparison ————•   Similar in contour to the earth's surface above it, the water table generally has a level that reflects such features as hills and valleys. Where the water table intersects the ground surface, a stream or pond results.

Operating principle ————•   A water table's level, however, will vary, depending on the rate of recharge (replacement of water). The recharge rate is affected by rainfall or soil permeability (the ease with which water flows through the soil). A water table therefore is never static; rather, it is the surface of a body of water striving to maintain a balance between the forces that deplete it and those that replenish it. In areas of Florida and some

Example ————• Western states where the water table is depleted, the earth caves in, leaving sinkholes.

Special conditions and examples ————•   The water table's depth below ground is vital in water resources engineering and planning. It determines an area's suitability for wastewater disposal or a building lot's ability to handle sewage. A high water table could become contaminated by a septic system. Also, bacteria and chemicals seeping into a water table can pollute an entire town's water supply. Another consideration in water table depth is the cost of drilling wells. These conditions obviously affect an industry's or homeowner's decision on where to locate.

Special conditions ————•   The rising and falling of the water table give an indication of the pumping rate's effect on a water supply (drawn from wells) and of the sufficiency of the recharge rate in meeting demand. This kind of information helps water resources planners decide when new sources of water must be made available.

the definition is essential to understanding the whole document or serves merely as a reference.

On a Web site, hyperlinks are a great way to make expanded definitions accessible because readers can click on an item, read about it, and then return to the original page. Figure 11.3 defines usability and then provides expanded definitions via links at the bottom of the page (usability testing; focus groups; Card Sort; and so on). The previous Web page provides a thorough definition of "usability," but the "user-centered designed" material is at a deeper level of detail; rather than disrupting the discussion of "usability," the hyperlink allows readers to jump to it if they wish.

Using hyperlinked definitions

Figure 11.3 A hyperlinked expanded definition

SOURCE: UsabilityNet

Strategies

for Definitions

- **Decide on the level of detail you need.** Definitions vary greatly in length and detail, from a few words in parentheses to a multipage document. How much does this audience need in order to follow your explanation or grasp your point?
- **Classify the item precisely.** The narrower your class, the clearer your meaning. *Stress* is classified as an applied force; to say that stress "is what..." or "takes place when..." fails to denote a specific classification. Diabetes is precisely classified as a *metabolic disease*, not as a *medical term*.
- **Differentiate the item accurately.** If the distinguishing features are too broad, they will apply to more than this one item. A definition of *brief* as a "legal document used in court" fails to differentiate briefs from all other legal documents (wills, affidavits, and the like).
- **Avoid circular definitions.** Do not repeat, as part of the distinguishing feature, the word you are defining. "Stress is an applied force that places stress on a body" is a circular definition.
- **Expand your definition selectively.** Begin with a sentence definition and select the best expansion strategy or combination of expansion strategies for your audience and purpose.
- **Use visuals to clarify your meaning.** No matter how clearly you explain, as the saying goes, a picture can be worth a thousand words—even more so when used with readable, accurate writing.
- **Know "how much is enough."** Don't insult people's intelligence by giving needless details or spelling out the obvious.
- **Consider the legal implications of your definition.** What does an *unsatisfactory job performance* mean in an evaluation of a company employee: that the employee could be fired, required to attend a training program, or given one or more chances to improve (Performance Appraisal 3–4)? Failure to spell out your meaning invites a lawsuit.
- **Consider the safety implications of your definition.** Be sure your definition of a fuzzy or ambiguous term such as *safe levels of exposure, conservative investment*, or *acceptable risk* is based on fair and accurate interpretation of the facts and makes clear to readers the safety implications for them and their families.
- **Place your definition in an appropriate location.** Allow readers to access the definition and then return to the main text with as little disruption as possible. You might use a glossary, or, for an online document, you might consider hyperlinks that define the terms or ideas but keep readers on the same document page.
- **Cite your sources, as needed.** See Appendix A.

Checklist

for Definitions

- ❏ Is the type of definition (parenthetical, sentence, expanded) suited to its audience and purpose?
- ❏ Does the definition adequately classify the item?
- ❏ Does the definition adequately differentiate the item?
- ❏ Will the level of technicality connect with the audience?
- ❏ Have I avoided circular definitions?
- ❏ Is the expanded definition developed adequately for its audience?

❏ Is the expanded definition free of needless details for its audience?
❏ Are visuals used adequately and appropriately?
❏ Are all information sources properly documented?
❏ Is the definition appropriately located in the document?

Applications

General Application

Choose a situation and an audience, and prepare an expanded definition specifically designed for this audience's level of technical understanding. Use at least four expansion strategies, including at least one visual. In preparing your expanded definition, consult no fewer than four outside references. Cite and document each source as shown in Appendix A.

Team Application

Divide into groups by majors or interests. Appoint one person as group manager. Decide on an item, concept, or process that would require an expanded definition for laypersons; some examples follow:

> *From computer science:* an algorithm, JAVA coding, or systems analysis
> *From the health sciences:* a heart ablation, coronary bypass surgery, or IV infusion

Complete an Audience and Purpose Profile (page 42). Once your group has decided on the appropriate expansion strategies, the group manager will assign each member to work on one or two specific strategies as part of the definition. As a group, edit and incorporate the collected material into an expanded definition, revising as often as needed. The group manager will assign one member to present the definition in class.

Global Application

Any definition you write may be read by someone who may not speak English as a first language. Locate an expanded definition on Wikipedia that may be difficult for a non-American or nonnative English speaker to understand for one reason or another (use of idioms, use of abbreviations, use of American metaphors such as sports metaphors not used in other countries). Explain how the definition could be reworded so that most readers would be able to understand it.

Digital and Social Media Application

If you could convert your expanded definition from the General Application into a Web page or other digital document, which items would be best suited for hyperlinks? If this expanded definition needed to be made more brief or compact so it could be posted on social media, how would you turn the expanded version into a brief 2–3 sentence version, suitable for a general readership?

Chapter 12
Descriptions

 ## Learning Objectives

12.1 Describe the audience and purpose of descriptions.

12.2 Maintain objectivity when writing descriptions.

12.3 Identify the elements and sequencing of descriptions.

12.4 Differentiate between and write product and process descriptions.

12.5 Write a set of specifications.

Chapter Outline

Audience and Purpose of Descriptions   205
Objectivity in Descriptions   206
Elements of Descriptions   207
Product and Process Descriptions   209
    Strategies for Descriptions   219
Specifications   220
    Strategies for Specifications   222
    Checklist for Descriptions and Specifications   222
Applications   223

Descriptions are essential in workplace writing because, like definitions, they help ensure that readers understand the full meaning of any technical document. Descriptions and definitions often go hand in hand. For example, to return to the *myocardial infarction* example in the previous chapter (page 192), a medical student reading a document about myocardial infarctions would need to know not only that a myocardial infarction is a form of heart attack (definition) but also what causes such a heart attack (description).

Meaning and importance of descriptions

    This chapter will explore how to write technical descriptions from a variety of angles and for a variety of purposes.

Audience and Purpose of Descriptions

12.1 Describe the audience and purpose of descriptions.

As with any technical document, consider audience and purpose carefully before writing a description.

    While definitions answer the questions "What is it?" or "What does it entail?" descriptions often include definitions first and then must answer the additional questions "What does it look like?" "What are its parts?" "What does it do?" "How does it work?" or "How does it happen?"

Audience considerations

    Assume that most readers won't be familiar with the product or process you are describing, and write your description at the appropriate level of technicality. An audience of medical technicians will easily understand jargon related to that field, but nonexperts will need familiar language. For example, the sentence "A tumor is a neoplasm" would make sense to most medical professionals; however, for an audience outside that field, you would need to use more accessible language, such as "A tumor is a growth of cells that occurs independently of surrounding tissue and serves no useful function."

Purpose considerations

Consider exactly what you want readers to know and why they need to know it. You may want to write out a purpose statement before you start writing your description, such as the following: "The purpose of this description is to help plumbing apprentices understand the parts of the Heatwave home water heater and how those parts work together to produce hot water."

Objectivity in Descriptions

12.2 Maintain objectivity when writing descriptions.

Subjective versus objective descriptions

A description can be mainly *subjective* (based on feeling) or *objective* (based on fact). Subjective descriptions do more than simply convey factual information; subjective descriptions use sensory and judgmental ideas such as "The weather was miserable" or "The room was terribly messy." In contrast, objective descriptions present an impartial view, filtering out personal impressions and focusing on details any viewer could observe ("All day, we had freezing rain and gale-force winds").

Why descriptions should be objective

Except in cases of promotional writing, descriptions should be objective. Pure objectivity is, of course, humanly impossible. Each writer filters the facts and their meaning through his or her own perspective and therefore chooses what to include and what to omit. Nonetheless, when writing descriptions, you should communicate the facts as we know and understand them. Even positive claims made in promotional writing (for example, "reliable," "rugged") should be based on objective and verifiable evidence.

Descriptions have safety implications

Being objective does not, however, mean forsaking some form of evaluation in cases in which a product or process may be unsafe or unsound. If there are important safety considerations about the product or process, be sure to include a mention or discussion of these items. (See also Chapter 13 for more information on how to include caution, warning, and danger information and visuals.)

How to be objective

One way to maintain objectivity when writing descriptions is to provide details that are visual, not emotional. Ask yourself what any observer would recognize or what a camera would record. For example, instead of saying, "His office has a depressing atmosphere" (not everyone would agree), say "His office has broken windows looking out on a brick wall, missing floorboards, broken chairs, and a ceiling with chunks of plaster missing."

A second way to maintain objectivity is to use precise and informative language. For instance, specify location and position, exact measurements, weights, and dimensions instead of using inexact and subjective words like *large, long*, and *near*.

Be careful, though, not to confuse precise language with overly complicated technical terms or needless jargon. For example, don't say *phlebotomy specimen* instead of *blood*, *thermal attenuation* instead of *insulation*, or *proactive neutralization* instead of *damage control*. General readers prefer nontechnical language—as long as the simpler words do the job.

Elements of Descriptions

12.3 Identify the elements and sequencing of descriptions.

Descriptions typically include a forecasting title, an orienting introduction, a logical sequence of topics, clarifying visuals, and a summarizing conclusion. (Based on the writing conventions of your industry or job, some of which are themselves based on regulatory and legal requirements, not all descriptions contain all of these parts.)

Title

Promise exactly what the document will deliver—no more or less. For example, assume you are describing the braking mechanism of a particular brand and type of bicycle: Be clear in your title by referring to the exact brand and type of bicycle, and be limited in your title by indicating that you will only describe the braking mechanism. The title "A Description of a Bicycle" is neither clear nor limited. A better title would be "A Description of the Velo Racing Bicycle's Center-Pull Caliper Braking Mechanism."

Provide a clear and limiting title

Introduction

Descriptions rarely call for a standard topic or thesis statement because the goal of these documents is to catalog details to help readers visualize the product or process. Any description, however, should begin by telling readers what to look for. If you have written a purpose statement to help you orient yourself prior to writing the description, simply reuse it here. For example, you might say in your introduction, "The goal of this description is to introduce apprentice road construction workers to the parts and function of a standard jackhammer." You may also simply want to start with a brief definition of what you will describe.

Provide an introduction that orients readers

Sequence of Topics

For longer descriptions, choose the sequence, or organizational pattern most logically consistent with your purpose.

Provide a logical and appropriate sequence of topics

Spatial
sequence: How
something looks

To describe how something looks, including its parts, use a *spatial* sequence. Follow the same spatial patterns readers would follow when viewing the item. Do you want to move from top to bottom, inside to outside, or right to left or follow some other pattern? For example, when describing a laptop keyboard, you might follow an outside to inside spatial sequence, first describing the "on/off" and mouse keys, then moving inward to the "page up," "page down," "shift," "tab," "caps lock," and function keys, and finally moving to the interior number, letter, and punctuation keys.

Functional
sequence: How
something
works

To describe how something works, use a *functional* sequence. Describe the workings (functions) of the device in the order in which the parts function. For example, if you want to describe how a solar home heating system works, proceed from source to outlet: from the heat collectors on the roof through intermediate components to the heating vents.

Chronological
sequence: How
something is
assembled or
occurs

To describe how something is assembled, use a *chronological* sequence. Parallel the order in which parts are assembled or stages occur. For example, if you want to describe how to put together a small desk, describe how to put together the main parts first and the smaller, more decorative parts last.

Combine
sequencing
when
appropriate

Spatial, functional, and chronological sequencing are not mutually exclusive; you can combine these sequences as needed. For example, in describing the appearance, use, and assembly of an atomic alarm clock, you would employ a spatial sequence to help readers recognize this item, a functional sequence to show how it works, and a chronological sequence to help readers assemble it correctly.

Visuals

Provide visuals
to enhance and
clarify prose
descriptions

You can explain a product or process as clearly as you like in words, but a clear diagram or other visual can show your readers the actual look and feel of the product or process. The diagram (top view) in Figure 12.1 adds a much-needed visual overview to what would be a complicated prose description. In addition to the picture, labels help readers interpret what they are seeing. The best definitions include both visuals and text combined.

Conclusion

Provide a
concise
conclusion to
give readers a
sense of finality

A conclusion should be short and to the point and not introduce any new material. Conclusions should provide readers with a brief summary of what the description has attempted to accomplish; conclusions should also give readers a sense that they now understand everything they need to know about the product or process.

Figure 12.1 A descriptive visual

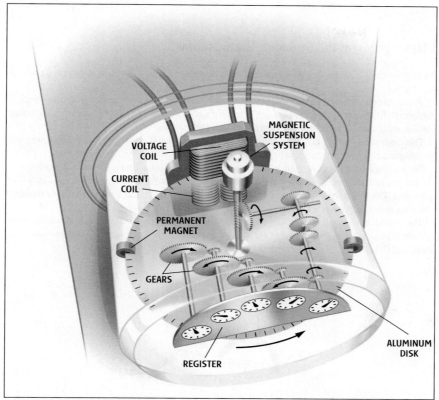

SOURCE: "Description of an Electricity Meter" illustration by George Retseck, from "Electricity Meters" by Les Rosenau, from *Scientific American*, March 2000, volume 108. Reprinted with permission.

Product and Process Descriptions

12.4 Differentiate between and write product and process descriptions.

Descriptions generally divide into two broad categories: *product descriptions* and *process descriptions*. Anyone learning the parts of a particular device (say, a standard microscope) relies on a product description. Anyone wanting to understand the steps or stages in a complex event (say, how lightning is produced) relies on a process description.

Difference between product and process descriptions

For example, the product description in Figure 12.2 gives beginning paramedical or nursing students a clear image of the overall device (a stethoscope) and its parts. The process description in Figure 12.3, on the other hand, helps surveyors or environmentalists understand the steps or stages by which contaminants may be removed from the soil using the "lasagna process."

Figure 12.2 A product description

A Description of the Standard Stethoscope

The stethoscope is a listening device that amplifies and transmits body sounds to aid in detecting physical abnormalities.

This instrument has evolved from the original wooden, funnel-shaped instrument invented by French physician R. T. Lennaec in 1819. Because of his female patients' modesty, he found it necessary to develop a device, other than his ear, for auscultation (listening to body sounds).

This description explains to the beginning paramedical or nursing student the structure, assembly, and operating principle of the stethoscope.

The standard stethoscope is roughly 24 inches long and weighs about 5 ounces. The instrument consists of a sensitive sound-detecting and amplifying device whose flat surface is pressed against a bodily area. This amplifying device is attached to rubber and metal tubing that transmits the body sound to a listening device inserted in the ear.

The stethoscope's Y-shaped structure contains seven interlocking pieces: (1) diaphragm contact piece, (2) lower tubing, (3) Y-shaped metal piece, (4) upper tubing, (5) U-shaped metal strip, (6) curved metal tubing, and (7) hollow ear plugs. These parts form a continuous unit (Figure 1).

FIGURE 1 Stethoscope with Diaphragm Contact Piece (Front View)

The seven major parts of the stethoscope provide support for the instrument, flexibility of movement for the operator, and ease in use.

In an operating cycle, the diaphragm contact piece, placed against the skin, picks up sound impulses from the body's surface. These impulses cause the plastic diaphragm to vibrate. The amplified vibrations, in turn, are carried through a tube to a dividing point. From here, the amplified sound is carried through two separate but identical series of tubes to hollow ear plugs.

Figure 12.3 A process description

The Lasagna Process

Dubbed the "lasagna" process because of its layers, this technology cleans up liquid-borne organic and inorganic contaminants in dense, claylike soils. Initial work is focused on removing chlorinated solvents.

Because clay is not very permeable, it holds groundwater and other liquids well. Traditional remediation for this type of site requires that the liquid in the soil (usually groundwater) be pumped out. The water brings many of the contaminants with it, then is chemically treated and replaced—a time-consuming and expensive solution.

The lasagna process, on the other hand, allows the soil to be remediated *in situ* (on site) by using low-voltage electric current to move contaminated groundwater through treatment zones in the soil. Depending on the characteristics of the individual site, the process can be done in either a vertical or horizontal configuration. (See figure below.)

The first step in the lasagna process is to "fracture" the soil, creating a series of zones. In a vertical configuration, a vertical borehole is drilled and a nozzle inserted; a highly pressurized mixture of water and sand (or another water/solid mix) is injected into the ground at various depths. The result: a stack of pancake-shaped, permeable zones in the denser, contaminated soil. The top and bottom zones are filled with carbon or graphite so they can conduct electricity. The zones between them are filled with treatment chemicals or microorganisms that will remediate the contaminants.

When electricity is applied to the carbon and graphite zones, they act as electrodes, creating an electric field. Within the field, the materials in the soil migrate toward either the positive or negative electrode. Along with the migrating materials, pollutants are carried into the treatment zones, where they are neutralized or destroyed.

The horizontal configuration works in much the same way, differing only in installation. Because the electrodes and treatment zones extend down from the surface, this configuration does not require the sophisticated hydraulic fracturing techniques that are used in the vertical configuration.

Schematic Diagram of the Lasagna Process

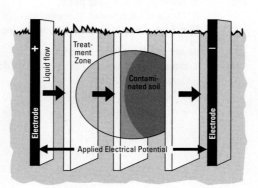

SOURCE: Based on Japikse, Catharina. "Lasagna in the making." *EPA Journal*, 20.3.

A Complex Product Description

Figure 12.4 is a complex product description. The audience for the standard bumper jack description would be car and truck owners and other general readers. This audience needs to know only the basics—what it is, what it looks like, what its parts are, and how, generally, it works—before actually using the jack safely and effectively.

To plan this description, the writer has created an outline for what details to include and how to organize the material. Also, the writer has determined what *not* to include: for example, basic dimensions and measurements are included, but they are not the precise and detailed dimensions and measurements an engineering audience might require. Finally, the writer has kept the language simple and free of jargon that this audience might not understand.

Figure 12.4 A complex product description

Writer's outline for planning the complex description

I. Introduction: General Description
    A. Definition, Function, and Background of the Item
    B. Purpose (and Audience—for classroom only)
    C. Overall Description (with general visuals, if applicable)
    D. Principle of Operation (if applicable)
    E. List of Major Parts

II. Description and Function of Parts
    A. Part One in the Descriptive Sequence
        1. Definition
        2. Shape, dimensions, material (with specific visuals)
        3. Subparts (if applicable)
        4. Function
        5. Relation to adjoining parts
        6. Mode of attachment (if applicable)
    B. Part Two in the Descriptive Sequence (and so on)

III. Summary and Operating Description
    A. Summary (used only in a long, complex description)
    B. Interrelation of Parts
    C. One Complete Operating Cycle

continued

Figure 12.4 *continued*

1

Description of a Standard Bumper Jack

Introduction- General Description
The standard bumper jack is a portable mechanism for raising the front or rear of a car through force applied with a lever. This jack enables even a frail person to lift one corner of a 2-ton automobile.

The jack consists of a molded steel base supporting a free-standing, perpendicular, notched shaft (Figure 1). Attached to the shaft are a leverage mechanism, a bumper catch, and a cylinder for insertion of the jack handle. Except for the main shaft and leverage mechanism, the jack is made to be dismantled. All its parts fit neatly in the car's trunk.

The jack operates on a leverage principle, with the operator's hand traveling 18 inches and the car only $\frac{3}{8}$ of an inch during a normal jacking stroke. Such a device requires many strokes to raise the car off the ground but may prove a lifesaver to a motorist on some deserted road.

Five main parts make up the jack: base, notched shaft, leverage mechanism, bumper catch, and handle.

FIGURE 1 A Side View of the Standard Bumper Jack

- Clear and limiting title tells readers exactly what to expect
- Introduction orients readers via a definition
- Overall description of the product uses spatial sequencing ("What does it look like?")
- Clearly labeled visual enhances prose descriptions of parts

continued

Figure 12.4 *continued*

2

Description of Parts and Their Function

Base. The rectangular base is a molded steel plate that provides support and a point of insertion for the shaft (Figure 2). The base slopes upward to form a platform containing a l -inch depression that provides a stabilizing well for the shaft. Stability is increased by a 1-inch cuff around the well. As the base rests on its flat surface, the bottom end of the shaft is inserted into its stabilizing well.

Shaft. The notched shaft is a steel bar (32 inches long) that provides a vertical track for the leverage mechanism. The notches, which hold the mechanism in position on the shaft, face the operator.

The shaft vertically supports the raised automobile, and attached to it is the leverage mechanism, which rests on individual notches.

Leverage Mechanism. The leverage mechanism provides the mechanical advantage needed for the operator to raise the car. It is made to slide up and down the notched shaft. The main body of this pressed-steel mechanism contains two units: one for transferring the leverage and one for holding the bumper catch.

The leverage unit has four major parts: the cylinder, connecting the handle and a pivot point; a lower pawl (a device that fits into the notches to allow forward and prevent backward motion), connected directly to the cylinder; an upper pawl, connected at the pivot point; and an "up-down" lever,

Description of parts uses chronological sequencing ("How is it assembled?")

Second labeled visual offers a different view of an individual part

Stabilizing well

Cuff

FIGURE 2 A Top View of the Jack Base

which applies or releases pressure on the upper pawl by means of a spring (Figure 1). Moving the cylinder up and down with the handle causes the alternate release of the pawls and, thus, movement up or down the shaft- depending on the setting ofthe "up-down" lever. The movement is transferred by the metal body of the unit to the bumper catch holder.

continued

Figure 12.4 *continued*

3

The holder consists of a downsloping groove, partially blocked by a wire spring (Figure 1). The spring is mounted in such a way as to keep the bumper catch in place during operation.

Bumper Catch. The bumper catch is a 9-inch molded plate that attaches the leverage mechanism to the bumper and is bent to fit the shape of the bumper. Its outer $\frac{1}{2}$ inch is bent up to form a lip (Figure 1), which hooks behind the bumper to hold the catch in place. The two sides of the plate are bent back 90 degrees to leave a 2-inch bumper contact surface, and a bolt is riveted between them. This bolt slips into the leverage mechanism groove and provides the attachment between the leverage unit and the car.

Jack Handle. The jack handle is a steel bar that serves both as lever and lug bolt (or lug nut) remover. This round bar is 22 inches long, $\frac{5}{8}$ inch in diameter, and bent 135 degrees roughly 5 inches from its outer end. Its outer end is a socket wrench made to fit the wheel's lug bolts. Its inner end is beveled to form a bladelike point for prying the wheel covers and for insertion into the cylinder on the leverage mechanism.

Conclusion and Operating Description
The jack is assembled by inserting the bottom of the notched shaft into the stabilizing well in the base, the bumper catch into the groove on the leverage mechanism, and the beveled end of the jack handle into the cylinder. The bumper catch is then attached to the bumper, with the lever set in the "up" position.

As the operator exerts an up-down pumping motion on the jack handle, the leverage mechanism gradually climbs the vertical notched shaft until the car's wheel is raised above the ground. When the lever is in the "down" position, the same pumping motion causes the leverage mechanism to descend the shaft.

Conclusion uses functional sequencing ("How does it work?")

A Complex Process Description

Figure 12.5 is an example of a complex process description. The writer has determined that the audience for the description of the acid rain process will be a nontechnical group of readers. The purpose of the document is to explain the threat posed by acid rain. To plan how to describe a scientific process to a nonscientific audience, the writer has created an outline and has used simple, jargon-free language.

Figure 12.5 A complex process description

Writer's outline for planning the complex description

I. Introduction
  A. Definition, Background, and Purpose of the Process
  B. Intended Audience (usually omitted for workplace audiences)
  C. Prior Knowledge Needed to Understand the Process
  D. Brief Description of the Process
  E. Principle of Operation
  F. Special Conditions Needed for the Process to Occur
  G. Definitions of Special Terms
  H. Preview of Stages

II. Stages in the Process
  A. First Major Stage
    1. Definition and purpose
    2. Special conditions needed for the specific stage
    3. Substages (if applicable)
      a.
      b.
  B. Second Stage (and so on)

III. Conclusion
  A. Summary of Major Stages
  B. One Complete Process Cycle

continued

Figure 12.5 *continued*

1

HOW ACID RAIN DEVELOPS, SPREADS, AND DESTROYS

Introduction

Acid rain is environmentally damaging rainfall that occurs after fossil fuels burn, releasing nitrogen and sulfur oxides into the atmosphere. Acid rain increases the acidity level of waterways because these nitrogen and sulfur oxides combine with the air's normal moisture. The resulting rainfall is far more acidic than normal rainfall. Acid rain is a silent threat because its effects, although slow, are cumulative.

Power plants burning oil or coal are primary causes of acid rain. The burnt fuel is not completely expended, and residue enters the atmosphere. Although this residue contains several potentially toxic elements, sulfur oxide and, to a lesser extent, nitrogen oxide are the major problems: These chemical culprits combine with moisture to form sulfur dioxide and nitric acid, which then rain down to earth.

The Process

HOW ACID RAIN DEVELOPS. Once fossil fuels have been burned, their usefulness ends. It is here that the acid rain problem begins (Figure 1).

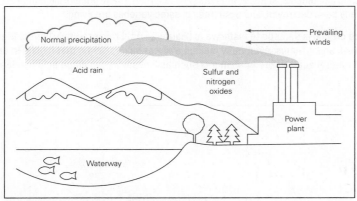

Figure 1 How Acid Rain Develops and Spreads

Acid level is measured by pH readings. The pH scale runs from 0 through 14—a pH of 7 is neutral. (Distilled water has a pH of 7.) Numbers above 7 indicate increasing alkalinity. (Household ammonia has a pH of 11.) Numbers below 7 indicate increasing acidity. Movement in either direction on the scale means multiplying by 10. Lemon juice, with a pH value of 2, is 10 times more acidic than apples, with a pH of 3, and 1,000 times more acidic than carrots, with a pH of 5.

Clear title tells readers what to expect and promotes awareness of the issue

Introduction orients readers via a definition

Description uses functional sequencing by answering "how" questions

Headers in "The Process" section mirror and follow through on the description's title

Clearly labeled visual enhances prose description of process

Additional definition introduces a new concept ("pH")

continued

Figure 12.5 *continued*

Because of carbon dioxide (an acid substance) normally present in air, unaffected rainfall has a pH of 5.6. At this time, the pH of precipitation in the northeastern United States and Canada is between 4.5 and 4. In Massachusetts, rain and snowfall have an average pH reading of 4.1. A pH reading below 5 is considered abnormally acidic and therefore a threat to aquatic populations.

HOW ACID RAIN SPREADS. Although we might expect areas containing power plants to be most severely affected, acid rain can in fact travel thousands of miles from its source. Stack gases escape and drift with the wind currents, traveling great distances before they return to earth as acid rain (Figure 1).

For roughly two to five days after emission, the gases follow the prevailing winds far from the point of origin. About 50 percent of the acid rain that affects Canada originates in the United States; conversely, 15 to 25 percent of U.S. acid rain originates in Canada.

The tendency of stack gases to drift makes acid rain a widespread menace. More than 200 lakes in the Adirondacks, hundreds of miles from any industrial center, cannot support life because their water has become so acidic.

HOW ACID RAIN DESTROYS. Acid rain causes damage wherever it falls. It erodes various types of building rock such as limestone, marble, and mortar. Damage to buildings, houses, monuments, statues, and cars is widespread. Many priceless monuments have already been destroyed, and even trees of some varieties are dying.

More crucial is damage to waterways (Figure 2). Acid rain gradually lowers the pH in lakes and streams, eventually making a waterway so acidic that it dies. In areas with natural acid-buffering elements such as limestone, the dilute acid has less

Second labeled visual provides graphic illustration of the process

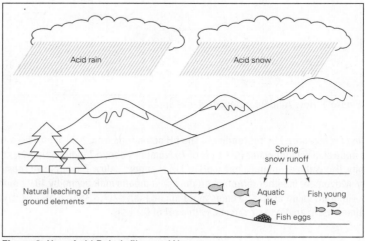

Figure 2 How Acid Rain Infiltrates Waterways

continued

Figure 12.5 *continued*

3

effect. The northeastern United States and Canada, however, lack this natural protection and so are most vulnerable.

The pH level in an affected waterway drops so low that some species cease to reproduce. A pH of 5.1 to 5.4 means that entire fisheries are threatened: Once a waterway reaches a pH of 4.5, fish reproduction ceases.

In the northeastern United States and Canada, the acidity problem is compounded by the runoff from acid snow. During winter, acid snow sits with little melting, so that by spring thaw, the acid released is greatly concentrated. Aluminum and other heavy metals normally present in soil are also released by acid rain and runoff. These concentrated toxins leach into waterways, affecting fish in all stages of development.

Summary

Acid rain develops from nitrogen and sulfur oxides emitted by the burning of fossil fuels. In the atmosphere, these oxides combine with ozone and water to form precipitation with a low pH. This acid precipitation returns to earth miles from its source, damaging waterways that lack natural buffering agents. The northeastern United States and Canada are the most severely affected areas in North America.

Conclusion summarizes the process and implicitly solicits audience support

Strategies

for Descriptions

- **Take a look at the product or process.** Study your subject. For a product description, get your hands on the item if you can; weigh it, measure it, take it apart. For a process description, observe the process yourself, if possible.
- **Analyze your audience.** Determine your primary and secondary audiences. Then ask yourself exactly what your audience needs to know: "What does it look like?" "What are its parts?" "What does it do?" "How does it work?" or "How does it happen?" Decide on the appropriate level of technicality for your audience.
- **Analyze your purpose.** Ask yourself why your audience needs your description.
- **Maintain objectivity.** Think in terms of visual (not emotional) details and specific language when describing location, measurements, weights, and dimensions.
- **Be concise.** Provide only what your audience needs.
- **Include all necessary parts.** Include a clear and limiting title, an orienting introduction, the appropriate sequence of topics (spatial, functional, chronological—or a combination), and a conclusion that brings readers full circle.
- **Incorporate visuals.** If allowable, enhance your verbal description using visuals, particularly if the product or process is too complicated to describe only in words.

Specifications

12.5 **Write a set of specifications.**

Definition and importance of specifications

Specifications (or "specs") are a type of description used by professionals. Specifications build on definitions and descriptions by asking the question "How is this process or procedure performed according to regulations?" Airplanes, bridges, computer software, medical procedures, and nearly all modern products and processes are produced according to specifications. The minimum standards are identified; then the specific methods or materials for meeting those standards are proposed, reviewed, and revised until they are approved. Specifications are vital because they prescribe standards for consistency, quality, and safety.

Specifications help ensure consistency

Specifications are important when everyone in your audience needs to understand and agree on what is to be done and how it is to be done. In other words, specifications ensure consistency, helping prevent misunderstandings that may lead to errors, slowdowns, or even lawsuits. For example, Figure 12.6 shows partial specifications drawn up by an architect designing a medical clinic (these specs are for the exterior of the building only; additional specs would be written for the interior). These specifications help ensure that contractors, architects, landscapers, and others have a consistent master plan regarding parts, materials, and designs that everyone can interpret identically.

Specifications help ensure quality

Specifications describe features such as methods for manufacturing, building, or installing a product; materials and equipment used; and size, shape, and weight. Professionals must therefore carefully consider the quality of the product they produce. They must ask themselves "Does this product exceed or at the very least meet governmental standards?" "How do the standards compare with those of others in the field?" and "How will our standards be perceived by our customers?" In the medical clinic specifications (Figure 12.6), for example, the quality of materials must meet not only government regulations but also the medical profession's requirements for quality. As a result, those specifications call for a reinforced foundation, exterior, and roof; high-quality insulated windows; and a relaxing landscape that will appeal to both highly stressed medical staff and patients.

Specifications help ensure safety

Perhaps most important, specifications are always written with public safety in mind. For example, the U.S. Department of Energy (DOE) issues specifications that prescribe minimum design requirements for the shipping containers (or casks) used to transport (via rail or road) spent nuclear fuel to permanent storage facilities. In the private sector, any product that fails to meet federal or industry specifications may provide grounds for a lawsuit.

When injury or death results (as in a bridge collapse or an airline accident), a product will be inspected to be sure it was designed and maintained according to the appropriate specifications. If not, the contractor, manufacturer, or supplier may be liable. The architectural specifications in Figure 12.6, for instance, must meet government standards for building safety as well as the medical profession's standards for a building in which patient safety is paramount.

Audience for specifications

Specifications may be written for a wide range of readers, including customers, designers, contractors, suppliers, engineers, programmers, and inspectors. If your

Figure 12.6 Specifications to ensure consistency, quality, and safety

---

Ruger, Filstone, and Grant
Architects

SPECIFICATIONS FOR THE POWNAL CLINIC BUILDING

Foundation
  footings: 8" x 16" concrete (load-bearing capacity: 3,000 lbs. per sq. in.)
  frost walls: 8" x 4' @ 3,000 psi
  slab: 4" @ 3,000 psi, reinforced with wire mesh over vapor barrier

Exterior Walls
  frame: eastern pine #2 timber frame with exterior partitions set inside posts
  exterior partitions: 2" x 4" kiln-dried spruce set at 16" on center
  sheathing: 1/4" exterior-grade plywood
  siding: #1 red cedar with a 1/2" x 6' bevel
  trim: finished pine boards ranging from 1" x 4" to 1" x 10"
  painting: 2 coats of Clear Wood Finish on siding; trim primed and finished
       with one coat of bone white, oil base paint

Roof System
  framing: 2" x 12" kiln-dried spruce set at 24" on center
  sheathing: 5/8" exterior-grade plywood
  finish: 240 Celotex 20-year fiberglass shingles over #15 impregnated felt
       roofing paper
  flashing: copper

Windows
  Anderson casement and fixed-over-awning models, with white exterior
     cladding, insulating glass and screens, and wood interior frames

Landscape
  driveway: gravel base, with 3" traprock surface
  walks: timber defined, with traprock surface
  cleared areas: to be rough graded and covered with wood chips
  plantings: 10 assorted lawn plants along the road side of the building

---

audience consists primarily of technical experts (such as architects) you can use specialized language and brief explanations. But if your audience is mixed, you may need to include more detail or refer readers to other sources of information, such as a glossary, appendix (see page 306), or Web site.

Strategies

for Specifications

- **Analyze your audience.** Determine who will be reading the specs.
- **Know the minimum governmental and industry standards.** If your product is for specific customers, also consider the standards they will expect you to meet.
- **Keep consistency, quality, and safety at the forefront.** Specifications fulfill all three purposes. Everyone who reads the document needs to be "on the same page" (consistency); the product you describe must meet minimal quality requirements; and it must also meet safety requirements.
- **Use a standard format when applicable.** If your organization uses a standard format for specifications, follow that format.
- **Include a brief introduction or descriptive title.** Include some kind of overview, be it a one- or two-sentence introduction, a brief summary, or an abstract (see Chapter 14 for more on summaries and abstracts). For an audience completely familiar with the material, a clear and descriptive title will suffice.
- **List component parts or materials.** List all the parts or materials your readers will need to know about. Group items into categories if needed.
- **Refer to other documents or specs, as needed.** Often, one set of specifications will refer to another set or to government or industry standards. If your specifications are online, link to other specifications you refer to.
- **Use a consistent terminology.** Use the same terms for the same parts or materials throughout your specifications. If you refer to an "ergonomic adapter" in one section, do not substitute "iMac mouse adapter" in a later section.
- **Include retrieval aids.** Especially in longer specifications, some readers may be interested in only one portion. For example, someone working on a subset of a larger project may want to look up technical details for his or her part of the project only. Use clear headings and a table of contents.
- **Keep it simple.** People look at specifications because they want quick access to items, parts, technical protocols, and so on. If you can, limit your specs to short lists, using longer prose passages only as necessary.
- **Check your use of technical terms.** Use terms that are standard for the field.

Checklist

for Descriptions and Specifications

Product or Process Descriptions

- ❏ Have I studied the product or process to get a clear view of how it looks or what it does?
- ❏ Have I recorded the details of the product or process objectively?

❏ Have I written a clear purpose statement on which to base my description?
❏ Does the title promise exactly what the description delivers?
❏ Have I provided an introduction based on my purpose statement (and a definition, if necessary)?
❏ Have I written the description using a spatial, functional, or chronological sequence or a combination of sequences?
❏ Are relationships among parts or stages clearly explained?
❏ Do visuals appear whenever they can provide clarification?
❏ Have I provided a conclusion to bring readers full circle?
❏ Is the use of technical terminology appropriate for this audience?

Specifications

❏ Are the specifications appropriately detailed for the audience?
❏ Do the specifications meet the requirements for consistency, quality, and safety?
❏ Do the specifications adhere to prescribed standards?
❏ Do the specifications follow a standard format, if applicable?
❏ Have I included a brief introduction or descriptive title?
❏ Have I listed the component parts or materials?
❏ Are other specifications or documents referred to, if needed?
❏ Is my terminology consistent?
❏ Are the specifications easy to navigate, with clear headings and other retrieval aids?
❏ Do I provide short lists instead of long prose passages wherever possible?
❏ Are technical terms standard for the field?

Applications

General Applications

1. Choose a product requiring a description. Identify the audience and purpose, and prepare a description for this audience's level of technical understanding. As you prepare your description, refer to the Strategies on page 219. Be sure to include a clear and limiting title; an orienting introduction; a spatial, functional, or chronological sequence of topics; at least one visual; and a conclusion. Also remain as objective as possible.
2. Select a specialized process that you understand well and that has several distinct steps. Begin by analyzing your audience and purpose. Using the process description on page 211 as a model, explain this process to classmates who are unfamiliar with it.
3. The bumper jack description in this chapter is aimed toward a general audience. Evaluate its effectiveness for this audience. In one or two paragraphs, discuss your evaluation and suggest revisions.
4. How do specifications function in your workplace or home? Find one example of specifications used in your home or workplace and analyze these specifications based on the ideas in this chapter. Are the specifications written for consistency, quality, and safety? How? What could the writers have done to improve the document?

Team Applications

1. Divide into teams. Assume your team works in the product development division of a diversified manufacturing company. Your division has come up with an idea for an inexpensive consumer item with a potentially

vast market (choose a simple mechanism, such as nail clippers or a stapler, but with some unique twist). Your group's assignment is to prepare three descriptions of this invention:

a. one for company executives who will decide whether to produce and market the item

b. one for the engineers, machinists, and so on, who will design and manufacture the item

c. one for the customers who might purchase and use the item

Before writing for each audience, complete an Audience and Purpose Profile (page 42). Appoint a group manager, who will assign tasks to members (visuals, typing, etc.). When the descriptions are prepared, the group manager will appoint one member to present the documents and explain their differences in class.

2. Select a specialized process you understand well or that you can learn about quickly by searching online (e.g., how gum disease develops, how an earthquake occurs, how steel is made, how a mirrorless camera works). Write a brief description of the process, incorporating at least one visual. Exchange your description with a classmate. Study your classmate's description for 15 minutes and then write the description in your own words. Now, evaluate your classmate's version of your original description. Does it show that your description was understood? If not, why not? Discuss your conclusions in a memo to your instructor, submitted with all samples. Be sure to document your information sources.

3. Assume your group is an architectural firm designing buildings at your college. Develop a set of specifications for duplicating the interior of the classroom in which this course is held. Focus only on materials, dimensions, and equipment (whiteboard, desk, etc.), and use visuals as appropriate. Your audience includes the firm that will construct the classroom, teachers, and school administrators. Use the same format as in Figure 12.6, or design a better one. Appoint one member to present the completed specifications in class. Compare versions from each group for accuracy and clarity.

Global Application

Descriptions, especially those for nonspecialized or nontechnical audiences, are often written by comparing the item being described to an item that is already familiar to readers. For instance, the human heart is often described as a pump and compared to a pump people already know about (the pump on a swimming pool or a car's water pump). While descriptions based on these types of comparisons can be useful, they can also be problematic if your readers are from different countries and cultures. Working with 2–3 other students, pick an item for which you'd like to write a description that will be distributed both within the United States and to at least one other country. Discuss whether to use a comparison and how you would decide which comparisons to use.

Digital and Social Media Application

Go online and search for a description of a product or process that is related to your field of study. See if you can find versions of the description in different formats (a Facebook post versus a description on a Web site versus a tweet). Consider how the writers shaped each description based on the format. Which format seems most suitable for a description? Is social media an effective way to share product or process descriptions with different audiences?

Chapter 13
Instructions and Procedures

 Learning Objectives

13.1 Discuss the audience and purpose of instructions.

13.2 Identify various types of instructions and their uses.

13.3 Understand the safety and legal implications of instructions.

13.4 Recognize the components of instructions.

13.5 Write instructions with a readable style and accessible design.

13.6 Know the audience and purpose of procedures and identify types of procedures.

13.7 Test instructions and procedures for usability.

Chapter Outline

Audience and Purpose of Instructions   227

Types of Instructional Formats   227

Safety and Legal Implications   232

Elements of Effective Instructions   233

Content, Style, and Design Considerations   236

   Strategies for Readable Instructions   236

   Strategies for Accessible Instructions   239

Procedures   239

Conducting a Usability Survey   242

   Strategies for Instructions and Procedures   244

   Checklist for Instructions and Procedures   246

Applications   246

Definition of instructions

Instructions spell out the steps required for completing a task or series of tasks (for example, installing more memory in your computer or operating an electron microscope). The audience for a set of instructions might be someone who doesn't know how to perform the task or someone who has performed the task but can't remember how or wants to perform it more effectively. In any case, well-written and carefully designed instructions enable readers to get the job done safely and efficiently.

Definition of procedures

Procedures, a special type of instructions, serve as official guidelines for people who typically are already familiar with a given task (say, firefighters who are evacuating a high-rise building). Procedures ensure that all members of a group coordinate their activities when performing a task. More so than instructions, procedures may need to be reviewed and approved by an official regulatory organization of some sort. For example, official medical procedures may need to be approved by the U.S. Food and Drug Administration and a hospital's safety and ethics board.

Formats of instructions and procedures

Instructions and procedures can be written and designed in a wide variety of formats, from detailed formats such as user manuals to shorter formats such as quick reference cards or online help. Most instructions and procedures are available as print and digital; for instance, PDF versions of consumer user manuals are typically shipped with the product and also available for download from a company's Web site. In some cases, companies are skipping the printed manual altogether: Products are shipped with a small insert that says "visit our Web site," where people can download the latest version of instructions or manuals. The format should be chosen based on the people who will be using the material (audience), what these people need to accomplish (purpose), and the environment where the material will be used. For example, instructions for connecting a battery charger to your car's battery should not be provided on a CD because most people will not have a laptop computer handy while performing this task. Instead, these instructions should be printed directly on the charger itself, with a longer brochure (containing safety information) included in the box. A shorter "getting started" version should be made available online, too, in a format suitable for viewing on a phone.

Audience and Purpose of Instructions

13.1 **Discuss the audience and purpose of instructions.**

Before writing instructions, find out how much your readers already know about the task. For instance, if you are writing for technicians who have performed a similar task but with a different piece of equipment, you may not need as much detail or context. If, on the other hand, you are writing for a general audience, such as consumers who are trying to assemble a new stereo cabinet or synch a new Bluetooth headset, you will need more details but in a less technical presentation. If you have a mixed audience (some experienced with the task, others less experienced), you will need a layered approach, offering a "quick start up" document for those in the know and a more comprehensive guide for the novices.

Audience considerations

Readers across the globe, some who may not speak English as a first language, might use your instructions. Therefore, write in a straightforward style with plenty of visuals, and remain sensitive to cultural differences.

The purpose of instructions is simply to help people perform a task or series of tasks. As you write, keep the following questions in mind: "How is the task done?" "What materials are needed to complete the task?" "In which order should the steps in the task be completed?" "What could go wrong?" and "Are any safety issues involved?" Ask yourself if the primary purpose is to allow people to complete the task quickly (as when people are trying to assemble a new stereo cabinet and don't want to take all day) or to complete the task incrementally and over a longer period (as when people are using a kit to test for radon in their homes).

Purpose considerations

Types of Instructional Formats

13.2 **Identify various types of instructions and their uses.**

As discussed above, instructions and procedures alike come in many formats. The simplest kind of instructions provide one step that corresponds to one action, such as the following instructions for using an ATM machine:

Step	Action
1. Insert ATM card	Card is swiped or goes into the machine
2. Type in the PIN	PIN is accepted, next screen is displayed
3. Select an action (cash withdraw, etc.)	User makes a selection
4. Take the receipt or cash	User takes the item(s), screen indicates the session has ended

When you begin the process of writing instructions, start with simple steps such as the above, using active verbs, where one step results in one outcome. Use this idea as a basis for expanding and creating more complicated instructional formats, including user manuals, quick reference materials, assembly guides, Web-based instructions, and online instructions.

User Manuals

User manuals are the most comprehensive instructional format. Manuals contain instructions for using a product, along with descriptions and specifications, warnings and other safety information, maintenance and troubleshooting advice, contact information (such as an 800 number, email address, Web site, and social media connections), and other information the reader is likely to need. The more complex the product, the longer the manual's size. Required regulatory information may also add to a manual's length. Still, writers should strive to write and organize the information in as concise, clear, and readable a manner as possible.

Figure 13.1 presents a user manual cover page and table of contents, in this case, for a new front load washing machine. The material is presented in a visually appealing manner, using white space to help draw the eye into the text. Each section would be written and designed in a similar manner, using active verbs, clear descriptions,

---

Figure 13.1 Table of Contents from a User Manual

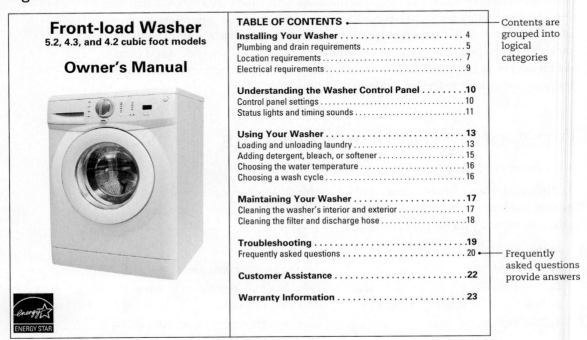

Front-load Washer
5.2, 4.3, and 4.2 cubic foot models

Owner's Manual

ENERGY STAR

TABLE OF CONTENTS

Installing Your Washer 4
Plumbing and drain requirements 5
Location requirements 7
Electrical requirements 9

Understanding the Washer Control Panel **10**
Control panel settings 10
Status lights and timing sounds 11

Using Your Washer **13**
Loading and unloading laundry 13
Adding detergent, bleach, or softener 15
Choosing the water temperature 16
Choosing a wash cycle 16

Maintaining Your Washer **17**
Cleaning the washer's interior and exterior 17
Cleaning the filter and discharge hose 18

Troubleshooting **19**
Frequently asked questions 20

Customer Assistance **22**

Warranty Information **23**

— Contents are grouped into logical categories

— Frequently asked questions provide answers

and relevant visuals. (For more on page design, layout, and the use of visuals, review Section 2, Blueprints). A "frequently asked questions" section can be written based on feedback the company receives. For instance, many companies use the content of customer phone calls and emails to create a list of the top ten consumer questions, then use these to improve the product and to give the technical writers some guidance about this section of the user manual

Given the cost of printing and distributing large printed manuals, companies are increasingly providing smaller "Getting Started" guides that contain basic operating tips and then placing the more lengthy information online as a downloadable PDF or interactive Web page. Still, in many situations, especially for consumer products, people expect to find a user manual with the product, even if the information is also available online. Online manuals are very handy when customers lose or misplace the original copy. Also, if customers register their product and provide an email address, companies can provide easy access to revised versions of the user manual and related materials. *Features of effective user manuals*

Quick Reference Materials

Quick reference materials are a form of instructions typically written and designed to fit on a single sheet of paper, a small or wallet-sized card, or a Web page. The instructions focus on the basic steps for people who only want enough information to perform a specific task. *Features of effective quick reference materials*

Figure 13.2 shows a quick reference card to help people who speak too quickly while teaching (these same tips could apply to any kind of public speaking situation). The information is brief and easy to read. The three key actions start with active verbs and are indented, using bullets and white space to draw the reader's eye to these sections. The card is available online and can be printed in different sizes, including a wallet size version, an index card size, or a full page. Readers can also cut and paste just the bulleted items to create a smaller version.

In this example, the action items do not need to take place in any particular order, so the writer used bullets. If the steps need to occur in order (such as with the ATM example, provided earlier, or with assembly guides, discussed later in this chapter), you would use a numbered format instead.

Assembly Guides

Assembly guides are a common form of instruction found with consumer products (such as furniture, home report items, appliances, and so forth). These guides describe how to assemble parts into a final product. Assembly guides can be a subsection of a larger user manual or can be a separate stand-alone document. Most assembly guides provide a brief overview, step-by-step guidelines (with substeps if required), and visuals. Readers will often skip over the text and look at the visuals first, to get an idea of what the final product our outcome should look like. For example, the visuals in Figure 13.5 show the end result of building a retaining wall. *Features of effective assembly guides*

Figure 13.2 A Quick Reference Card

Opening para- →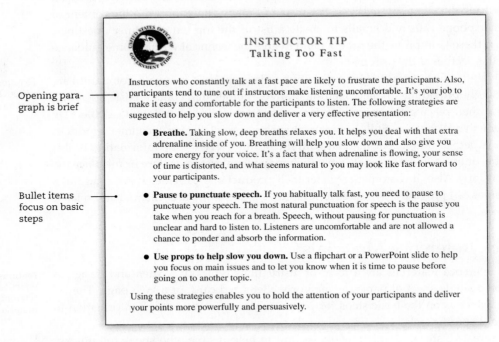
graph is brief

Bullet items
focus on basic
steps

INSTRUCTOR TIP
Talking Too Fast

Instructors who constantly talk at a fast pace are likely to frustrate the participants. Also, participants tend to tune out if instructors make listening uncomfortable. It's your job to make it easy and comfortable for the participants to listen. The following strategies are suggested to help you slow down and deliver a very effective presentation:

- **Breathe.** Taking slow, deep breaths relaxes you. It helps you deal with that extra adrenaline inside of you. Breathing will help you slow down and also give you more energy for your voice. It's a fact that when adrenaline is flowing, your sense of time is distorted, and what seems natural to you may look like fast forward to your participants.

- **Pause to punctuate speech.** If you habitually talk fast, you need to pause to punctuate your speech. The most natural punctuation for speech is the pause you take when you reach for a breath. Speech, without pausing for punctuation is unclear and hard to listen to. Listeners are uncomfortable and are not allowed a chance to ponder and absorb the information.

- **Use props to help slow you down.** Use a flipchart or a PowerPoint slide to help you focus on main issues and to let you know when it is time to pause before going on to another topic.

Using these strategies enables you to hold the attention of your participants and deliver your points more powerfully and persuasively.

SOURCE: United States Office of Government Ethics, www.oge.gov.

Visuals such as these would typically be accompanied by step-by-step instructions about selecting the rocks, preparing the soil, and so forth. For example, the steps for the example in Figure 13.5 are written as follows (abbreviated here):

1. "Measure and lay out the area…

2. Dig a trench deep enough to accommodate…the first row of boulders.

3. Set the first course of boulders into the trench…

4. Backfill soil against the back of the first course…"

(University of Minnesota Extension Service)

Substeps might be necessary if readers are novices and have never done any sort of landscaping before. For example, Step 2 might need a few substeps about how to dig a trench, which might include information on selecting the right shovels and other tools, using a level, or measuring with a tape measure. Step 4 might require substeps on how to properly backfill.

In cases where the instructions are not overly complicated and where the company has a global audience, *wordless instructions* may be the most appropriate approach. Wordless instructions are typically found with items such as furniture (a new bookshelf, for example). Usually, arrows are used to indicate action, and numbers are used to indicate steps.

Web-Based Instructions

Instructions that are set up as a Web page allow readers to click on hyperlinks to explore more information, access definitions of technical words and phrases, and learn more about topics they may not fully understand. Web-based instructions are useful in situations where your audience may be a mix of people who know something about the topic and people who don't know as much. For instance, Figure 13.3 shows Web-based instructions for how to apply for Energy Star status for a building. Some readers may already be familiar with the eligibility requirements, but people who need more information can click on the link.

Features of effective Web-based instructions

Figure 13.3 Web-based instructions

SOURCE: U.S. Environmental Protection Agency.

Web-based instructions are also useful because it's easy for organizations to keep the information updated by simply revising the Web site (rather than, say, printing thousands of new brochures).

Online Instructions

Software, apps, and other online services have largely done away with user manuals and instead provide instructions that can be accessed directly through the app. Word processing programs (Microsoft Word, e.g.) offers a good example of online instructions. If you are working on a document and forget how to create a table or set up footnotes, you simply type your question or topic into the help box to access the instructions. This content is always up to date because it is linked to the company's database of help information or is updated when your computer or software does an automatic update.

Online instructions are typically "context sensitive"—that is, the help system recognizes what you are trying to accomplish and not only provides instructions but also guides you to the menu function you are looking for.

Safety and Legal Implications

13.3 Understand the safety and legal implications of instructions.

Instructional documents carry safety and legal obligations on the part of those who prepare them. In fact, of all the various forms of technical documents, instructional materials have the strictest requirements for accurate information in an accessible format. Technical writers must be very careful to obtain all relevant safety information from the legal and engineering departments and to incorporate this information into the document, including any required notes, cautions, warnings, and danger notices (see below).

Countless injuries result from inadvertent misuse of products such as power tools, car jacks, household cleaners, and appliances; the misuse is often traced directly to defective or unclear instructions. Accurate, easy-to-follow instructions that contain just the right amount of detail and are visually clear can prove to be the difference between the unsafe and safe use of a product.

Any person injured because of unclear, inaccurate, or incomplete instructions can potentially sue the writer as well as the manufacturer. Some of the legal liabilities resulting from faulty instructions include

- Failure to provide instructions and cautions for the proper use of a product: for example, a household cleaning product that should not be mixed with other products
- Failure to warn against hazards from proper use of a product: for example, the risk of cutting one's fingers on a new type of vegetable slicer
- Failure to warn against the possible misuses of a product: for example, the danger of improperly installing a child safety seat

Elements of Effective Instructions

13.4 **Recognize the components of instructions.**

Instructions may include a combination of the following parts: a title, a brief overview or introduction, a body section (including the required steps involved in following the instructions), and a conclusion. In addition, instructions should almost always include visuals and must include notes, cautions, warnings, and/or danger notices.

Title

Be sure your title provides a clear and exact preview of the required task. For example, the title "Instructions for Cleaning a DVD Drive" tells people what to expect: instructions for a specific procedure involving one selected part. But the title "DVD drives" gives no such forecast.

Include a clear and exact title

Overview or Introduction

Explain the purpose of the instructions and describe what these instructions do and do not cover. You don't want to bury readers in an overly long overview/introduction, nor do you want to set them lose without adequate preparation. Know your audience—what people need to know and what they do not need to know. For example, you might begin with a short paragraph:

Provide a brief overview or introduction to orient readers before they begin the task

> These instructions provide complete information for the use of the lab's electron microscope. The first section explains the setup steps, and the second section describes how to create a slide and view it with the microscope.

Body

Explain each step and sub-step in the correct order. For smaller instruction sets (less than 10 steps, plus or minus, with few or no sub-steps), just list the steps simply and accurately. But if the instructions contain a large number of steps and sub-steps, "chunk" these steps into logical categories (see pages 75–77 for more on chunking). For instance, you might have sections on Preparing the Soil; Arranging the Boulders; Backfilling the Wall. You could then start each of these sections with a brief overview sentence ("This section provides the steps necessary for preparing the soil before you begin building the wall") followed by the steps and substeps.

Include a body section with task steps in correct order

Insert notes, cautions, warnings, dangers, and visuals as needed (see below for more on these elements). Keep the visuals as close as possible to the related steps or sections.

Conclusion

The conclusion of a set of instructions might summarize the main steps of the task, describe the results readers should experience, offer follow-up advice, or provide troubleshooting tips. You might do all of these things in the conclusion—or none

Wrap up with a conclusion, if appropriate

of them. If the body section has provided all the necessary information, omit the conclusion altogether.

Visuals

Provide visuals to enhance usability

Visuals in instructions play a vital role, as noted throughout this chapter. Visuals attract immediate attention, show people what to do, and help keep words to a minimum. (For more on visuals, see Chapter 8.) Visuals can illustrate any step that might be hard for people to picture. For instance, describing in words how to locate something is a lot less effective than simply showing the location with a drawing or photograph. Visuals can also help tell the whole story, offering the big picture in one glance, something that would be far less effective using words only. Figure 13.4 enables readers to visualize a task. Figure 13.5 shows readers the complete process at a glance.

Notes, Cautions, Warnings, and Danger Notices

Always include notes, cautions, and warnings for user safety

Notes provide additional information, while cautions, warnings, and danger notices prevent damage, injury, or even death. Use these items only when needed. Overuse will dull their effect, and readers may overlook their importance.

When to use notes

A note clarifies a point, emphasizes vital information, or describes options or alternatives. For example:

NOTE: If you don't name a newly initialized hard drive, the computer automatically names it "Untitled."

Notes are designed to enhance performance and prevent errors; cautions, warnings, and danger notices are used for safety reasons.

Figure 13.4 A visual that illustrates a task (how to apply weatherstrip caulking)

Seal all fixed joints of window casing.

Hold the caulking gun at a 45° angle.

Seal baseboards and quarter-round mouldings.

SOURCE: From the U.S. Department of Energy <www.nrel.gov/docs/fy01osti/28039.pdf>.

Figure 13.5 A visual that shows the full picture (how to build a boulder wall) in one glance

SOURCE: From University of Minnesota Extension Garden website, http://www.extension.umn.edu/garden/landscaping/ Copyright © 2017 Regents of the University of Minnesota. All rights reserved.

Cautions prevent possible mistakes that could result in injury or equipment damage. For example:

When to use cautions

CAUTION: A momentary electrical surge or power failure will erase the contents of internal memory. To avoid losing your work, set up the automatic backup function.

Warnings alert readers to potential hazards to life or limb. For instance:

When to use warnings

WARNING: To prevent electrical shock, always disconnect your printer from its power source before cleaning internal parts.

Danger notices identify an immediate hazard to life or limb. For example:

When to use a danger notice

DANGER: The red canister contains DEADLY radioactive material. Do not break the safety seal under any circumstances.

When you include cautions, warnings, or danger notices, be sure to provide the appropriate visual symbol or icon to indicate these conditions, as in Figure 13.6.

Figure 13.6 Caution, warning, and danger symbols

Content, Style, and Design Considerations

13.5 Write instructions with a readable style and accessible design.

In addition to including all the necessary elements in a set of instructions, you also need to decide about matters of content, style, and design.

Detail and Technicality

Provide an adequate level of detail and technicality

Readers who know a great deal about the product or task(s) to be covered don't need a lot of detail and can typically handle a high level of technical information. But readers who are new to the situation need more detail and fewer technical terms. Use the techniques described in Chapter 3 to determine how much your readers already know.

Unless you learn that your audience has the relevant background and skills, write for more general readers. For example, if you are writing instructions for providing first aid to a victim of electrical shock, you might write the following for an audience with extensive medical background:

Instructions for a technical audience

FIRST AID FOR ELECTRICAL SHOCK
1. Check vital signs.
2. Establish an airway.
3. Administer CPR as needed.
4. Treat for medical shock.

But for an inexperienced audience, not only will the above details be inadequate, but also terms such as "vital signs" and "CPR" will be too technical. Such instructions posted for workers in a high-voltage area who are not medically trained would be useless. Illustrations and explanations would be needed, as demonstrated in Figure 13.7.

Style

Write with a readable style

Instructions must always be clear and easy to follow on first reading, because people usually take immediate action. Follow the Strategies below.

Strategies

for Readable Instructions

- **Use direct address, active voice, and imperative mood.** To emphasize the reader's role, write in the second person, as direct address. Begin all steps and substeps with action verbs, using the active voice and imperative mood. In certain cases, you may want to provide a clarifying word or phrase that precedes the verb:

Say this	Not this
Insert the flash drive. *or* [To access the files] insert the flash drive.	You should insert the flash drive.
Key in your access code. *or* [To log on,] key in your access code.	The user keys in her access code.
Plug in the power cord. *or* [When you are ready to power up,] plug in the power cord.	The power cord is plugged in.

- **Use short and logically shaped sentences.** Use short sentences—one sentence for each step—so that readers can perform one step at a time. If a single step covers two related actions, describe these actions in their required sequence:

  | Before switching on the computer, insert the CD in the drive.
                                    OR
  | Insert the CD in the drive. Then switch on the computer.

- **Use parallel phrasing.** Parallelism is especially important in instructions because the repeating grammatical forms emphasize the step-by-step organization. Notice how all the sentences below are structured identically:

  To log on to the encrypted server, follow these steps:
  1. Switch the device to "on."
  2. Press the CONTROL key and the C key simultaneously.
  3. Type "logon," and then press the ESCAPE key.
  4. Type your user name, and then press the ESCAPE key.

- **Use affirmative phrasing.** Negative phrasing is harder to understand.

Say this	Not this
Examine your circuit board for dust contamination.	Verify that your circuit board is not contaminated with dust.

- **Use transitions to mark time and sequence.** Transitional expressions provide a bridge between related ideas. Some transitions ("first," "next," "meanwhile," "finally," "after," "then") mark time and sequence and are therefore especially useful in instructions, emphasizing their step-by-step nature. If your content needs to be written in prose format (for instance, if you can't use a numbered list because of concerns with how the numbers might be formatted on a different screen or device), use transitions instead.

  First, plug in the power cord, and then turn on the printer.

  After the printer warms up, insert the paper in the paper slot.

  Finally, hit the "print" button.

Design

Instructions rarely receive undivided attention. The reader, in fact, is usually doing two activities more or less at once: interpreting the instructions and performing the required task.

An effective instructional design conveys the sense that the task is within a qualified person's range of abilities. Therefore, design your instructions so that people can leave and return to the document as needed and easily find their place.

Create an accessible design

Figure 13.7 Adequate detail and technicality for a general audience

THE ABC'S OF CARDIOPULMONARY RESUSCITATION (CPR)

Cardiopulmonary resuscitation (CPR) is an emergency medical procedure for restoring breathing and heartbeat to persons who have suffered an electrical shock, heart attack, or other instance of cardiac arrest. CPR keeps oxygenated blood flowing to the brain until medical professionals arrive. Following are three simple "ABC" steps for CPR.

Step 1: A for Airway: Make sure the airway is not constricted.
- First, call 911 immediately or have someone else call.
- Check if the victim is breathing. If not, carefully roll the victim onto his or her back in one movement.
- Gently push back the forehead with one hand and lift the chin with your other hand to unblock tongue from airway.
- Listen for breathing and watch for chest movement. Move quickly to Step 2 if the victim is still not breathing.

Step 2: B for Breathing: Administer rescue breathing to keep the blood oxygenated.
- Continue to hold down the forehead and lift the neck to keep the airway open.
- Pinch the nose with the thumb and forefinger of the hand holding back the forehead.
- Take a deep breath and seal your lips around the victim's mouth.
- Blow one breath steadily into the mouth for one second; then administer a second breath.
- Do not wait to see if the victim resumes independent breathing. Move quickly to Step 3.

Step 3: C for Circulation: Perform chest compressions to keep the blood circulating.
- Kneel at the side of the victim's head and shoulders. Do not spend time checking for a pulse.
- Place the heel of one hand over the notch at the center of the victim's chest.
- Place the palm of your other hand over the first hand and, using your body weight, press down firmly and quickly, compressing the chest about two inches.
- Allow the chest to return to its original position before the next compression.
- Administer chest compressions at about two compressions per second for 20 seconds.
- Return to Step 2, first ensuring that the airway is open.
- Cycle between Steps 2 and 3 thereafter until help arrives.

Step 1

Step 2

Step 3

Strategies

for Accessible Instructions

- **Use informative headings.** Clear headings tell readers what to expect, emphasize what is most important, and provide cues for navigation. A heading such as "How to Format a DVD so You Can Record Training Videos" is more informative than "DVD Formatting."
- **Arrange all steps in a numbered list.** Unless the procedure consists of simple steps, list and number each step. Numbered steps not only announce the sequence of required actions, but also help readers remember where they left off.
- **Separate each step visually.** Single space within steps and double space between.
- **Make cautions, warnings, and danger notices highly visible.** Use ruled boxes or highlighting and plenty of white space to make these items stand out. Also, include symbols, if possible; if not, use bold text and capital letters for emphasis.
- **Make visual and verbal information redundant.** Let the visual repeat, restate, or reinforce the prose rather than provide entirely new information.
- **Place visuals and text that are connected close together.** If room allows, place a visual that goes with a step right beside the step; if not, right after the step. Set off the visual with plenty of white space.
- **Keep the design simple and easy to navigate.** Readers may be overwhelmed by an excessively complex or inconsistent design.
- **For lengthy instructions, consider a layered approach.** In a large user manual, for instance, you might add a "Getting Started" guide or quick reference page that can be used on its own.

Figure 13.8 shows instructions that have been prepared for general readers who need to make a common home repair. This example illustrates a number of features described in this chapter, including the use of visuals, numbered instructions, notes and cautions, and clear prose intended to help a novice perform this task.

Procedures

13.6 Know the audience and purpose of procedures and identify types of procedures.

Procedures provide rules and guidance for people who are required to follow accepted practice. For example, different people in your organization might perform the same task (say, monitoring groundwater pollution) at different times, with different equipment, or under different circumstances. This task may need to be standardized to ensure that all work is done with the same accuracy and precision.

Function of procedures

Figure 13.8 A complete set of instructions

1

HOW TO REPLACE A WORN FAUCET WASHER

Introduction

A leaking faucet, caused by a worn washer, can lose up to fifteen gallons of water per day. This loss can result in a higher water bill, overuse of the septic system and well pump, an increase in your hot-water bill, and rust or chlorine deposits in your sink basin. These instructions detail how to replace the washer. No special knowledge or skills are necessary.

Overview

The typical faucet consists of a round knob or a handle (Figure 1) that, when turned, causes the stem to screw down until the washer sits snugly over the seat. With the washer in place, the flow of water is stopped. A worn washer loses the ability to form a tight seal, causing a leak or drip to develop. Replacing the worn washer eliminates the leak.

Figure 1. Typical faucet in exploded view

Equipment and Material Needed

- pliers
- regular or Phillips (crossed head) screwdriver
- new washer of same size and shape as worn washer
- valve for shutting off water supply

> **Note and Caution** These instructions apply only to faucets that have washers. Avoid using any excessive force on the threaded parts because they are made of soft metal and could easily strip.

INSTRUCTIONS

1. **Shut off the water supply.** Look under the sink or fixture for the shutoff valve. If you are unable to find a valve in this location, use the main shutoff valve located in the basement or beneath the house. The water pipe (one-half to one inch in diameter) usually originates from an inside cellar wall. Locate the shutoff valve by following the pipe from the wall to an attached valve, usually within a few feet of the wall (Figure 2). Turn this valve fully clockwise. With your water supply shut off, you can take the faucet apart.

Clear title announces the document's exact purpose

Introduction provides appropriate detail for people with no experience with this task

Brief overall description and principle of operation

Visual reinforces the prose

Required items are listed

Note and caution alert readers before they take action

The body section provides step-by-step guidance

continued

Figure 13.8 *continued*

2

Figure 2. Location of main shut-off valve

2. Disassemble the faucet. Before removing the handle, open the faucet to allow remaining water in the pipe to escape. Using your screwdriver, remove the screw on top of the handle. If a cap covers the screw, pry it off (Figure 1). Remove the handle.

Next, remove the packing nut, using pliers to turn the nut counter-clockwise. The flat circular nut washer can now be lifted from the faucet base. With packing nut and washer removed, screw the stem out of the base by turning the faucet in the "open" direction. Lift the stem out of the base and proceed to step 3.

3. Replace the worn washer. Using your screwdriver, remove the screw holding the washer at the base of the stem (Figure 1). Remove the worn washer and replace it with a new one of the same size, using the washer screw to hold it in place. (Washers of various sizes can be purchased at any hardware store.) If the washer screw is worn, replace it. When the new washer is fixed in place, proceed to step 4.

4. Reassemble the faucet. To reassemble your faucet, reverse the sequence described in step 2.

Caution: Do not overtighten the packing nut!   — Caution precedes step

Using pliers, screw the stem into the base until it ceases to turn. Next, place the packing washer and nut over the threads in the collar. Tighten the packing nut using the strength of one hand. Finally, secure the handle with your screwdriver. When the faucet is fully assembled, turn the handle to the "off" position and proceed to step 5.

5. Turn on the water supply. First, check to see that your faucet is fully closed. Next, turn the water on slowly (about one-half turn each time) until the shutoff valve is fully open. These slow turns prevent a sudden buildup of pressure, which could damage the pipes. Your faucet should now be as good as new.   — Because the body section has given readers all they need, no conclusion is required

Audience and Purpose Considerations

Consider your audience

Unlike instructions, which will be read mostly by people unfamiliar with the given task, procedures may be used by people already familiar with the task but who need to follow a standard. For example, if apprentice chefs in a famous restaurant who normally prepare salads and appetizers are asked to take over on the preparation of special sauces, those workers probably already know the basics but would need more information on the specific sauces required, amounts of ingredients, reduction techniques, and so on.

Consider your purpose

Determine how your readers will use these procedures. Will they be following the procedures in a hurry while evacuating a building? Would the procedures be better distributed as a wallet-sized card, on a Web site, or as a PDF that can be printed and sent as an email attachment? Once you know exactly how the procedures will be used, you can make decisions about the document's length, format, level of detail, and medium.

Types of Procedures

The most common types of procedures are standard operating procedures (SOPs), general safety procedures, and medical or health procedures.

Standard operating procedures

Standard operating procedures are formal procedures designed to give an organization an official record of the procedure and how it should be performed. SOPs, kept up to date and in a location or format available to employees, are required by law in many workplace environments, including those that deal with chemicals or industrial waste. SOPs are also written to inform the public about how a particular procedure is performed.

Safety procedures

Safety procedures, as in Figure 13.9, are required in many settings. Hotel rooms typically list fire exit procedures on the back of the entry door. Most organizations have official procedures for dealing with emergencies.

Medical procedures

Medical procedures can be written for medical professionals or for consumers. Procedures for medical professionals might include SOPs on hand washing, surgical techniques, and other steps involved in patient care in the hospital. Today, with the vast amount of medical information available online, many medical procedures are written for nonexperts.

Conducting a Usability Survey

13.7 Test instructions and procedures for usability.

The importance of usability testing of instructions and procedures

Any technical document must be written and designed for the right audience. With instructions and procedures, however, accuracy and ease of use are especially important. Otherwise, readers could make costly and dangerous errors.

Figure 13.9 A set of procedures (safety procedures)

OSHA**FACT**Sheet

Evacuating High-Rise Buildings

The National Fire Protection Association defines "high-rise building" as a building greater than 75 feet (25 m) in height where the building height is measured from the lowest level of fire department vehicle access to the floor of the highest occupiable story. Appropriate exits, alarms, emergency lighting, communication systems, and sprinkler systems are critical for employee safety. When designing and maintaining exits, it is essential to ensure that routes leading to the exits, as well as the areas beyond the exits, are accessible and free from materials or items that would impede individuals from easily and effectively evacuating. State and local building code officials can help employers ensure that the design and safety systems are adequate.

When there is an emergency, getting workers out of high-rise buildings poses special challenges. Preparing in advance to safely evacuate the building is critical to the safety of employees who work there.

What actions should employers take to help ensure safe evacuations of high-rise buildings?

- Don't lock fire exits or block doorways, halls, or stairways.
- Test regularly all back-up systems and safety systems, such as emergency lighting and communication systems, and repair them as needed.
- Develop a workplace evacuation plan, post it prominently on each floor, and review it periodically to ensure its effectiveness.
- Identify and train floor wardens, including back-up personnel, who will be responsible for sounding alarms and helping to evacuate employees.
- Conduct emergency evacuation drills periodically.
- Establish designated meeting locations outside the building for workers to gather following an evacuation. The locations should be a safe distance from the building and in an area where people can assemble safely without interfering with emergency response teams.
- Identify personnel with special needs or disabilities who may need help evacuating and assign one or more people, including back-up personnel, to help them.
- Ensure that during off-hour periods, systems are in place to notify, evacuate, and account for off-hour building occupants.
- Post emergency numbers near telephones.

What should workers know before an emergency occurs?

- Be familiar with the worksite's emergency evacuation plan;
- Know the pathway to at least two alternative exits from every room/area at the workplace;
- Recognize the sound/signaling method of the fire/evacuation alarms;
- Know who to contact in an emergency and how to contact them;
- Know how many desks or cubicles are between your workstation and two of the nearest exits so you can escape in the dark if necessary;
- Know where the fire/evacuation alarms are located and how to use them; and
- Report damaged or malfunctioning safety systems and back-up systems

What should employers do when an emergency occurs?

- Sound appropriate alarms and instruct employees to leave building.
- Notify police, firefighters, or other appropriate emergency personnel.
- Take a head count of employees at designated meeting locations, and notify emergency personnel of any missing workers.

What should employees do when an emergency occurs?

- Leave the area quickly but in an orderly manner, following the worksite's emergency evacuation plan. Go directly to the nearest fire-free and smoke-free stairwell recognizing that in some circumstances the only available exit route may contain limited amounts of smoke or fire.

SOURCE: U.S. Occupational Safety and Health Administration.

Annotations (left margin):

Title ("Evacuating High-Rise Buildings") is clear and easy to spot

Overview/introduction section defines the issue and provides background

Headings in the form of reader questions help people find the information they need

Bullets, instead of numbered lists of steps, are appropriate for this document

To identify which parts of the document work or don't work, conduct a brief usability analysis, using the Basic Usability Survey in Figure 13.10. The survey is designed for both the writers and the readers. Essentially it asks one main question (broken into more specific questions): "Do these instructions or procedures enable you to carry out the task safely, efficiently, and accurately?" Notice how the phrasing encourages responses containing examples instead of merely yes or no answers.

In larger organizations, usability testing may take place in a formal usability lab, where engineers and technical writers can observe people using the document, sometimes using eye-tracking software to see what sections people read most closely or using a one-way mirror and keystroke capture software to provide empirical evidence about elements of the instructions that are most useful versus sections of the document that cause the most confusion.

Input from a usability survey and a more formal usability test can be used to revise the document.

Strategies

for Instructions and Procedures

- **Analyze your audience.** For instructions, assume a general audience that does not know how to perform a task. For procedures, assume that your audience does know something about the procedure but needs a set of standard guidelines.
- **Analyze your purpose.** Consider where the document will be used and how to present the information for maximum usability.
- **Become familiar with safety and legal implications.** Instructions and procedures must always be written with reader safety at the forefront.
- **Use a clear organizational format and include all needed elements.** Always include a clear and exact title; include an overview or introduction for instructions (but only if appropriate for procedures); include a body section (in list format for instructions, but not necessarily for procedures); and include visuals, notes, cautions, warnings, danger notices, and a conclusion as appropriate.
- **Provide an appropriate level of detail and technicality.** Do not give readers too much or too little detail, and use only as much technical language as your audience will understand.
- **Write with a readable style.** Refer to the Strategies for Readable Instructions (pages 236–237).
- **Design for maximum accessibility.** Refer to the Strategies for Accessible Instructions (page 239).
- **Analyze your document for usability.** Instructions and procedures must be easy to grasp in one reading, lead to successful completion of a task or procedure, and ensure reader safety. Make sure each word and image is just right by surveying readers about the usability of the document.

Figure 13.10 A basic usability survey

Basic Usability Survey

1. Briefly describe why this document is used. _____
   _____

2. Evaluate the *content:*
   - Identify any irrelevant information. _____

   - Indicate any gaps in the information. _____

   - Identify any information that seems inaccurate. _____

   - List other problems with the content. _____

3. Evaluate the *organization:*
   - Identify anything that is out of order or hard to locate or follow. _____

   - List other problems with the organization. _____

4. Evaluate the *style:*
   - Identify anything you misunderstood on first reading. _____

   - Identify anything you couldn't understand at all. _____

   - Identify expressions that seem wordy, inexact, or too complex. _____

   - List other problems with the style. _____

5. Evaluate the *design:*
   - Indicate any headings that are missing, confusing, or excessive. _____

   - Indicate any material that should be designed as a list. _____

   - Give examples of material that might be clarified by a visual. _____

   - Give examples of misleading or overly complex visuals. _____

   - List other problems with the design. _____

6. Identify anything that seems misleading or that could create legal problems or
   cross-cultural misunderstanding. _____

7. Please suggest other ways of making this document easier to use. _____
   _____

SOURCE: Adapted from Carliner 258; Daugherty 17–18; Hart 53–57.

Checklist

for Instructions and Procedures

Instructions

- ❏ Have I determined what type of instructional format I should use?
- ❏ Have I assessed the safety and legal implications of my instructions?
- ❏ Have I provided a clear and exact title?
- ❏ Have I included an orienting overview or introduction?
- ❏ Have I provided step-by-step instructions in the body?
- ❏ Have I used visuals to enhance usability?
- ❏ Have I included notes, cautions, warnings, and dangers whenever necessary?
- ❏ Have I provided the appropriate level of detail and technicality for my audience?
- ❏ Have I followed the strategies for writing with a readable style?
- ❏ Have I followed the strategies for creating an accessible design?
- ❏ Have I performed a Basic Usability Survey?

Procedures

- ❏ Have I considered my audience and purpose?
- ❏ Have I provided a clear and exact title?
- ❏ Have I provided a clear introduction and numbered steps or visuals, if appropriate?
- ❏ Have I included notes, cautions, warnings, and dangers whenever necessary?
- ❏ Have I provided a conclusion?
- ❏ Have I provided an appropriate level of detail, a readable style, and an accessible design?
- ❏ Have I performed a Basic Usability Survey?

Applications

General Application

Locate a technical manual for your field, or instructions or procedures for a general audience for a product you recently purchased. Using the Checklist above, evaluate the sample. In a memo to your instructor, discuss the document's strong and weak points, and be prepared to explain them in class.

Team Application

Divide into small groups and go online to look for a quick reference guide for something you own (your cell phone or laptop; a coffee pot or other appliance; the office copier). Look for fairly brief instructions that could use revision for improved content, organization, style, or format. Make sure the instructions cover a task that you will be able to carry out. Try out the instructions, then use the Usability Survey to review and analyze. Revise the instructions based on the survey. Submit all materials to your instructor, along with a memo explaining the improvements, and be prepared to discuss your revision in class.

Global Application

In many cultures, the use of imperative mood is considered impolite or too direct. For instance, instructions that state "Place the flash drive into the USB port" may sound bossy and inconsiderate. Find a set of instructions that use imperative mood (for example, Figure 13.10) and rewrite these for a cross-cultural audience where imperative mood might be considered too direct. But in your revisions, be sure the instructions are still clear and to the point. For instance, you might use an indirect imperative ("Be sure to insert the flash drive into the USB port").

Digital and Social Media Application

Think of a real situation in which you are trying to fix a product you own but can't find the original user manual. For instance, you might need to access the password settings for your Wi-Fi router but not remember how to do so. Go online and find the user manual (Hint: You will need the device name, brand, and model number). How easy or difficult was it to find the manual and then find the information you needed? Based on ideas from this chapter, are there other ways the information could have been made available to make your task easier? Also, see if the manufacturer has a Facebook page or Twitter feed, and look to see if any instructional document updates have been provided through these social media sites. If so, are the updates easy to find?

Chapter 14
Summaries

⌄ Learning Objectives

14.1 Understand the audience and purpose of summaries.

14.2 Identify the characteristics of successful summaries.

14.3 Summarize a long document using step-by-step strategies.

14.4 Recognize the purpose of closing summaries, informative abstracts, descriptive abstracts, and executive summaries.

14.5 Exercise caution when summarizing for social media.

Chapter Outline

Audience and Purpose of Summaries   249

Elements of Effective Summaries   250

Writing Summaries Step by Step   251

Special Types of Summaries   254

Summarizing Information for Social Media   259
    Strategies for Summaries   259
    Checklist for Summaries   260

Applications   260

A *summary* is a restatement of the main ideas in a longer document. Summaries are used to convey the general meaning of the ideas in the original source without all the specific details or examples that may appear in the original. When you write a summary, take care to provide the essential information clearly and concisely in your own words, leaving out anything that isn't absolutely central to an understanding of the original.

Definition of summary

Audience and Purpose of Summaries

14.1 Understand the audience and purpose of summaries.

Formal reports and proposals (discussed in Chapters 16 and 17) and other long documents are typically submitted to busy people: researchers, developers, managers, vice presidents, customers, and so on. For readers who must act quickly or only need to know the "big picture," reading an entire long report may not only be too time-consuming but also irrelevant. As a result, most long reports, proposals, and other long documents are commonly preceded by a summary.

Audience considerations

The purpose of summaries, then, is to provide only an overview and the essential facts. Whether you summarize your own writing or someone else's, your summary should do three things for readers: (1) describe, in short form, what the original document is all about; (2) help readers decide whether to read all of the long document, parts of it, or none of it; and (3) give readers a framework for understanding the full document that will follow if they do plan to read it.

Purpose of summaries

To get a basic idea of how summaries fulfill audience needs, consider the examples in Figures 14.1 and 14.2.

Figure 14.1 A passage to be summarized

> Scientists know with virtual certainty that human activities are changing the composition of Earth's atmosphere. Increasing levels of greenhouse gases like carbon dioxide (CO_2) since pre-industrial times are well-documented and understood. The atmospheric buildup of CO_2 and other greenhouse gases is largely the result of human activities such as the burning of fossil fuels. Increasing greenhouse gas concentrations tend to warm the planet. A warming trend of about 0.7 to 1.5°F occurred during the 20th century in both the Northern and Southern Hemispheres and over the oceans. The major greenhouse gases remain in the atmosphere for periods ranging from decades to centuries. It is therefore virtually certain that atmospheric concentrations of greenhouse gases will continue to rise over the next few decades.

SOURCE: Adapted from *State of Knowledge*, by the U.S. Environmental Protection Agency.

Figure 14.2 A summarized version of Figure 14.1

> Scientists are virtually certain that greenhouse gases largely produced by human activities are warming the planet. Temperatures have risen worldwide during the 20th century and undoubtedly will continue.
>
> *Source:* From *State of Knowledge*, by the U.S. Environmental Protection Agency.

Figure 14.2 shows a summary of the complex passage in Figure 14.1. Note how it captures the original's main ideas but in a compressed and less technical form that busy readers and general audiences would appreciate. The summary does not, however, change the essential meaning of the original—it merely boils the original down to its basic message.

Elements of Effective Summaries

14.2 Identify the characteristics of successful summaries.

Four
characteristics
of summaries

Whether you summarize your own document or someone else's, always keep in mind that all summaries have four key characteristics: accuracy, completeness, conciseness, and nontechnical style.

Accuracy

Readers expect a precise sketch of the content, emphasis, and line of reasoning used in the original document. Be careful not to alter the essential meaning of the original. For example, in Figure 14.2 above, the summary uses different wording but remains true to the original document's central point (scientists feel that global warming is "virtually certain," not "somewhat certain"), retains the emphasis made in the original (the fact that human activity is responsible), and follows the same logical sequence (global warming has occurred and will continue to occur).

Completeness

Readers will also expect your summary to include everything essential in the original document—everything they need at a glance to grasp its full meaning. For example, in Figure 14.2, nothing has been left out to prevent readers from getting a complete overview of the original. Readers will know exactly what to expect from the longer document, only in fuller detail.

Conciseness

Readers expect a summary to exclude superfluous details—as well as any new details, examples, or opinions—not found in the original. Although the summary in Figure 14.2 doesn't omit anything essential, it does omit lesser details such as statistics ("0.7 to 1.5°F"), examples (set off by "like," "such as," "and other"), and overly long passages ("in both the Northern and Southern Hemispheres and over the oceans" is replaced with "the planet"). Also, the summary in no way embellishes the original content.

Nontechnical Style

Unless your readers are all experts (and most of the time they will not be), always summarize a document using plain English rather than carrying the original's technical jargon or scientific and mathematical data into the summary. The summary in Figure 14.2, for example, omits expressions such as "atmospheric buildup" and "greenhouse gas concentrations," while also leaving out the specific temperatures mentioned.

Writing Summaries Step by Step

14.3 Summarize a long document using step-by-step strategies.

More so than for other types of documents, writing summaries involves a straightforward process: reading and rereading the original document, marking the key information, and writing and revising your summary while checking it against the original. The Strategies for Summaries on pages 259–260 provide an overview of these steps, along with audience and purpose considerations.

Step-by-step nature of summaries

Step 1: Read the Original Document

Before you can effectively summarize a document, you need a solid understanding of what it says. Read the original from start to finish, without highlighting or taking notes.

Do an initial read to get the big picture

An initial read will give you a general understanding of the document's main point and key subpoints.

Step 2: Reread and Mark Essential Material

Reread and highlight for a sharper understanding

Read the document again, this time using a highlighter or pen (if working on hard copy) or your computer's highlighting feature (after copying and pasting the document into a word processing file). Pay close attention to key words or phrases to help you identify the essential points. In Figure 14.3, key sentences are underlined, while the less important information is not.

Step 3: Cut and Paste the Key Information

Create a new document from the highlighted information

If you are working from a hard copy of the original, type the material you highlighted into a new document. If you are working from an electronic version of the original, copy and paste only the highlighted portions into a new file. Don't worry about the overall organization or sentence construction at this point; just gather everything you need.

Step 4: Redraft the Information into Your Own Organizational Pattern and Words

Turn the cut-and-paste version into your own version

At this point, reorganize the material from the original source into patterns that work well in a smaller space. Use your own wording to express the original concepts. Don't worry about length just yet. You just want to get your own wording down on paper.

Step 5: Edit Your Draft

Focus on shortening your version

In the previous step, the goal was to get your own wording down on paper. Now, edit your version. Keeping sentences clear and grammatical, cross out needless words; get rid of any asides; combine related concepts; and look for any repetitions. Note how Figure 14.4 is as pared down as it can be.

Step 6: Compare Your Version with the Original Document

Make sure you preserve the intent of the original

As a final step, double-check that you have not altered the meaning, intent, or emphasis of the original document. Reread the original and then immediately reread your own version. As you can see, Figure 14.4 remains true to the original source but is only about 25% of the original's length.

Figure 14.3 An article to be summarized

Dietary Fats and Your Health

Scientific evidence shows that consumption of <u>saturated fat, trans fat, and dietary cholesterol raises low-density lipoprotein (LDL), or "bad" cholesterol levels, which increases the risk of coronary heart disease (CHD).</u> According to the National Heart, Lung, and Blood Institute of the National Institutes of Health, more than 12.5 million Americans have CHD, and more than 500,000 die each year. That makes CHD one of the leading causes of death in the United States.

— Open with basic claim

— Omit background details

The <u>Food and Drug Administration has required that saturated fat and dietary cholesterol be listed on food labels since 1993. With trans fat added to the Nutrition Facts panel, you will know for the first time how much of all three—saturated fat, trans fat, and dietary cholesterol—are in the foods you choose.</u> Identifying saturated fat, trans fat, and dietary cholesterol on the food label gives you information you need to make food choices that help reduce the risk of CHD. This revised label will be of particular interest to people concerned about high blood cholesterol and heart disease. However, everyone should be aware of the risk posed by consuming too much saturated fat, trans fat, and dietary cholesterol.

— Include key comparison

— Omit inessential detail

But what is trans fat, and how can you limit the amount of this fat in your diet?

What Is Trans Fat?
Basically, <u>trans fat is made when manufacturers add hydrogen to vegetable oil—a process called hydrogenation.</u> Hydrogenation increases the shelf life and flavor stability of foods containing these fats. <u>Trans fat can be found in vegetable shortenings, some margarines, crackers, cookies, snack foods, and other foods</u> made <u>with</u> or fried <u>in partially hydrogenated oils.</u> Unlike other fats, the majority of trans fat is formed when food manufacturers turn liquid oils into solid fats like shortening and hard margarine. <u>A small amount of trans fat is found naturally, primarily in dairy products, some meat, and other animal-based foods.</u>

— Include essential definition

— Compress list of examples

Trans fat, like saturated fat and dietary cholesterol, raises the LDL cholesterol that increases your risk for CHD. Americans consume on average 4 to 5 times as much saturated fat as trans fat in their diets. Although saturated fat is the main dietary culprit that raises LDL, trans fat and dietary cholesterol also contribute significantly.

— Omit repetition and inessential statistic

Are All Fats Bad?
Simply put: <u>No.</u> Unsaturated fat is a major source of energy for the body and aids in the absorption of vitamins A, D, E, and K, and carotenoids. Both animal- and plant-derived food products contain fat, and when eaten in moderation, <u>unsaturated fat is important for proper growth, development, and maintenance of good health.</u> As a food ingredient, unsaturated fat provides taste, consistency, and stability and helps you feel full. In addition, parents should be aware that unsaturated <u>fats are an especially important source of calories and nutrients for infants and toddlers</u> (up to 2 years of age), who have the highest energy needs per unit of body weight of any age group.

— Include key fact

— Compress list of benefits

While <u>unsaturated fats</u> (monounsaturated and polyunsaturated) <u>are beneficial when consumed in moderation, saturated and trans fats are not.</u> Saturated fat and trans fat raise LDL cholesterol levels in the blood. Dietary cholesterol also raises LDL cholesterol and may contribute to heart disease even without raising LDL. Therefore, it is advisable to <u>choose foods low in saturated fat, trans fat, and dietary cholesterol as part of a healthful diet.</u>

— Include key comparison

— Include key point

continued

Figure 14.3 *continued*

What Can You Do About Saturated Fat, Trans Fat, and Cholesterol?

Include key instruction

Omit inessential details

When comparing foods, *look at the Nutrition Facts panel*, and choose the food with the lower amounts of saturated fat, trans fat, and dietary cholesterol. Health experts recommend that you keep your intake of saturated fat, trans fat, and dietary cholesterol as low as possible while consuming a nutritionally adequate diet. However, these experts recognize that eliminating these three components entirely from your diet is not practical because they are unavoidable in ordinary diets.

Where Can You Find Trans Fat on the Food Label?

Omit the obvious

You will find trans fat listed on the Nutrition Facts panel directly under the line for saturated fat.

How Do Your Choices Stack Up?

Omit inessential observation and advice

With the addition of trans fat to the Nutrition Facts panel, you can review your food choices and see how they stack up. Don't assume similar products are the same. Be sure to check the Nutrition Facts panel because even similar foods can vary in calories, ingredients, nutrients, and the size and number of servings in a package.

How Can You Use the Label to Make Heart-Healthy Food Choices?

The Nutrition Facts panel can help you choose foods lower in saturated fat, trans fat, and dietary cholesterol. Compare similar foods and choose the food with the lower combined saturated and trans fats and the lower amount of dietary cholesterol.

Include key fact

Omit technical detail

Include key statistics

Although the updated Nutrition Facts panel will list the amount of trans fat in a product, it will not show a Percent Daily Value (%DV). While scientific reports have confirmed the relationship between trans fat and an increased risk of CHD, none has provided a reference value for trans fat or any other information that the FDA believes is sufficient to establish a Daily Reference Value or a %DV. There is, however, a %DV shown for saturated fat and cholesterol. To choose foods low in saturated fat and cholesterol, use the general rule of thumb that 5 percent of the Daily Value or less is low and 20 percent or more is high. You can also use the %DV to make dietary trade-offs with other foods throughout the day.

Do I Have to Give Up My Favorite Fatty Foods?

Include basic advice

You don't have to give up your favorite foods to eat a healthy diet, even when they are high in saturated fat, trans fat, or dietary cholesterol. When a food you like is high in saturated fat or dietary cholesterol, balance it with foods that are low in saturated fat and dietary cholesterol at other times of the day.

SOURCE: Excerpt from *FDA Consumer* Sept.–Oct. 2003: 12–18.

Special Types of Summaries

14.4 Recognize the purpose of closing summaries, informative abstracts, descriptive abstracts, and executive summaries.

In preparing a report, proposal, or other document, you might summarize the work of other people as part of your presentation. The previous sections have described how to summarize documents written by others. But in other situations, you will often

Figure 14.4 A summary of Figure 14.3

Dietary Fats and Your Health (A Summary)

Saturated fat is a principal cause of bad cholesterol (LDL, or low density lipoprotein), but dietary cholesterol and trans fat also play a role. High LDL is a major risk factor for coronary heart disease, a leading killer in the United States. In addition to the listing of saturated fat and dietary cholesterol on food labels, the Food and Drug Administration (FDA) now requires that trans fat be listed.

Although small amounts of trans fat exist naturally in dairy products and other animal-based foods, most trans fat is a byproduct of hydrogenation, the addition of hydrogen to vegetable oil. This process increases shelf life and stabilizes the flavor of foods such as hard margarine, crackers, snack foods, and foods fried in hydrogenated oil.

Not all fats are bad. In fact, unsaturated fat serves as a major energy source, promotes vitamin absorption, enhances food taste, and helps us feel full. Consumed in moderation, unsaturated fat is essential to health and provides a vital calorie source for infants. However, saturated fats and trans fats, along with dietary cholesterol, should be avoided as much as possible.

To make wise choices about fats and cholesterol, read the Nutrition Facts label on packaged foods. Note the serving size, number of servings in the package, and the Percent Daily Value (%DV) of each ingredient. Although no Daily Value is yet established for trans fat, avoid foods with a high saturated fat or cholesterol DV (greater than 20 percent per serving), unless you can balance these with low DV foods during the day.

Source: Excerpt from FDA Consumer Sept.–Oct. 2003: 12–18.

---

need to summarize your own material. Various types of reports, proposals, and other long documents require internal summaries. Depending on the length, purpose, and audience, your document might include one or more of four special types of summaries, in different locations, with different levels of detail. These four types of summaries are (1) closing summaries, (2) informative abstracts, (3) descriptive abstracts, and (4) executive summaries. Figure 14.5 illustrates each of these types of summaries, their placement, and their purpose. The following sections discuss and illustrate each type in more detail.

Closing Summaries

A *closing summary* appears in the concluding section of a formal report or proposal. The closing summary helps readers review and remember the major findings that have preceded it. This look back at "the big picture" also helps readers appreciate the conclusions and recommendations that typically follow the closing summary. Figure 14.6 shows a closing summary at the end of a report that analyzes the feasibility of a career in technical marketing. This summary appears just before the "Recommendations" portion that ends the report.

Purpose and placement of closing summaries

Figure 14.5 Special types of summaries

*Although we take liberties with his classification, Vaughan helped clarify our thinking about the overlappling terminology that blurs these distinctions.

SOURCE: Based on Vaughan, David.

Figure 14.6 A closing summary

Summary of Findings
Technical marketing and sales requires solid technical background, motivation, communication skills, and interpersonal skills. This career offers job diversity and excellent income potential, balanced against hard work and relentless pressure to perform.

College graduates interested in this field confront four entry options: (1) direct entry with on-the-job training, (2) a formal training program, (3) prior experience in a technical specialty, and (4) graduate programs. Each option has benefits and drawbacks based on immediacy of income, rate of advancement, and long-term potential.

Informative Abstracts

Purpose and placement of informative abstracts

An *informative abstract* is a capsule version of a formal report or proposal that appears on a separate page, just after the document's title page. Informative abstracts provide readers with a snapshot of a long document—a clear picture of what is to come. Some readers, such as busy executives, may want just the "bottom line" without having to read the entire report or proposal. The informative abstract summarizes what the full document says: it identifies the need or issue that prompted the document; it describes the research methods used; it reviews the main facts and findings; and it condenses the conclusions and recommendations. (See page 296 of the formal report in Chapter 16 or page 319 of the formal proposal in Chapter 17 for an example.) An informative abstract may simply be labeled as an "abstract."

Descriptive Abstracts

More compressed than an informative abstract, a *descriptive abstract* is usually only one to three sentences long and appears on the title page of a report or proposal. A descriptive abstract merely states what a document *covers*; it doesn't get into detail about what the document contains. Such an abstract helps people decide whether to read the report. Compare, for example, the descriptive abstract in Figure 14.7 with the article summary in Figure 14.4. The descriptive abstract conveys only the basic nature and extent of the longer document.

Purpose and placement of descriptive abstracts

Figure 14.7 A descriptive abstract

> The origin of trans fat, its relation to saturated fat and dietary cholesterol, and its causative role in heart disease is explained, and advice for consumers is provided.

Executive Summaries

An *executive summary* is similar to an informative abstract; however, it not only summarizes the long document but also tells readers what they should think about it. Placed on a separate page just after a long document's title page (just like an informative abstract), an executive summary is aimed at decision makers rather than technical audiences. Unlike informative abstracts, executive summaries are written to persuade readers to act on the information. Executive summaries are crucial in cases when readers have no time to read the entire original document and when they expect the writer to help guide their thinking ("Tell me how to think about this," instead of, "Help me understand this"). Unless the readers (the organization or company) stipulate a specific format, organize your executive abstract to answer the following questions:

Purpose and placement of executive summaries

- What is the issue?
- What was found?
- What does it mean?
- What should be done?

Questions to answer in an executive summary

The executive summary in Figure 14.8 falls at the beginning of a much longer 40-page report. This one page summarizes the more detailed report. Notice how the executive summary answers all the above questions.

Figure 14.8 A one-page executive summary from a much longer (40-page) report

Status Report: Market Share for Goldilocks Breakfast Cereals (GBC)

What is the issue? —

In response to a request from GBC's Board of Directors, the accounting division analyzed recent trends in the company's sales volume and profitability.

Findings

What was found? —

- Even though GBC is the cereal industry leader, its sales for the past four years increased at a mere average of 2.5 percent annually, to $5.2 billion, and net income decreased 12 percent overall, to $459 million.

- This weak sales growth apparently results from consumer resistance to retail price increases for cereal, totaling 91 percent in slightly more than a decade.

- GBC introduces an average of two new cereal products annually (most recently, "Coconut Whammos" and "Spinach Crunchies"), but such innovations do little to increase consumer interest.

- A growing array of generic cereal brands have been underselling GBC's products by more than $1 per box, especially in giant retail outlets.

- This past June, GBC dropped its cereal prices by roughly 20 percent, but by this time the brand had lost substantial market share to generic cereal brands.

Conclusions

- Slow but progressive loss of market share threatens GBC's dominance as industry leader.

What does it mean? —

- GBC must regain consumer loyalty to reinvigorate its market base.

- Our new cereal products have done more to erode than to enhance GBC's brand image.

Recommendations

To regain lost market share and ensure continued dominance, GBC should implement the following recommendations:

What should be done? —

1. Curtail development of new cereal products, and invest in improving the taste and nutritional value of GBC's traditional products.

2. Capitalize on GBC's brand recognition with an advertising campaign to promote GBC's "best-sellers" as an "all-day" food (a healthful snack or inexpensive alternative to microwave dinners).

3. Examine the possibility of high-volume sales at discounted prices through giant retail chains.

Summarizing Information for Social Media

14.5 Exercise caution when summarizing for social media.

Information in summary format is increasingly attractive to today's readers, who often feel bombarded by more information than they can handle. Consider, for example, the numerous tweets, Facebook posts, LinkedIn announcements, email digests, and other summary formats that people receive on a daily basis. These short formats allow people to read a summary and, if an item is of interest, click on a link to read the longer form article, report, or news story. In this way, such summaries help people explore a wide range of new information, including recent research, technical updates, news stories, and medical innovations.

Yet, although summarized information on social media does provide advantages to busy readers, these short bursts maybe read so quickly that readers miss key points or ignore ideas that are not presented with the accuracy of the original published document. For instance, a Facebook feed with a catchy headline may work to grab the attention of many readers, but if that headline (or the short summary, or the visuals used) is not accurate, the summary is doing a disservice to the original study and to your audience. The challenge for technical writers who create summaries for social media is to keep the information clear and accurate but at the same time condense the information into the right size for a post or tweet. Consider the following points:

- A summary that adds material not found in the original document or omits critical information from the original can be misleading. Likewise, misrepresenting the original document's point of view is inappropriate and will not give readers a clear understanding of the full story. Remember that social media posts travel widely and quickly, so any inaccuracies in your summary may have global implications.

- A summary written and designed to grab reader attention and get more clicks or likes may end up distorting the original idea if the post uses inappropriate images or exaggerated wording. A good social media summary will maintain the original meaning but make the information accessible to a wide audience. For instance, the sentence "Certain kinds of fat can raise your bad cholesterol" is more accurate than "Eating too many French fries will cause a heart attack."

Summaries in social media formats

Social media considerations when writing summaries

Strategies
for Summaries

- **Start the summary process by reading the original document.** Read the document all the way through without highlighting or taking notes to get a clear sense of its main point and most important subpoints.
- **Reread the original while highlighting essential information.** A second read, combined with highlighting or underlining, will give you a sharper picture of important points.

- **Save only the key information.** Delete the inessential information from the original document to create a rough draft of the original document's wording.
- **Edit your version.** When you have included everything readers need, edit your work for conciseness, getting rid of wordiness, combining related ideas, and eliminating repetition.
- **Finally, check your version against the original.** Verify that you have added no personal observations (unless you are writing an executive abstract) and have not altered the meaning, intent, or emphasis of the original.
- **Indicate the exact source of the summarized material.** When you are summarizing someone else's work, immediately follow your summary with a reference to the original source.
- **Use the appropriate types of summaries in your own formal documents.** Formal reports and proposals always include informative abstracts (when the intent is simply to provide a snapshot) or executive summaries (when the intent is to persuade readers how to think about the longer document). Closing summaries are always helpful in such reports. Descriptive abstracts can be helpful when included on the title page of a formal report or proposal.
- **For social media posts, keep the information clear and accurate.** A summary that adds material not found in the original document or omits critical information from the original is misleading. Likewise, misrepresenting the original document's point of view is also inappropriate. Social media posts travel quickly; inaccuracies in your summary may have global implications.

Checklist

for Summaries

- ❏ Can the summary stand alone?
- ❏ Is the summary accurate when checked against the original?
- ❏ Is the summary free of needless details?
- ❏ Is the summary concise yet clear and comprehensive?
- ❏ Is the source of this summary documented?
- ❏ Does the descriptive abstract merely tell what the original is about?
- ❏ Is the level of technicality appropriate for its audience?
- ❏ Does the executive summary tell readers how to think about the information?

Applications

General Applications

1. Find an article about your major field or area of interest and write both an informative abstract and a descriptive abstract for the article.

2. Find a long article (at least five pages) and summarize it, following the step-by-step process described in this chapter and keeping accuracy, completeness, conciseness, and nontechnical language in mind. Capture the essence and main points of the original article in no more than one-fourth the length. Use your own words, and do not distort the original. Submit a copy of the original along with your summary.

Team Application

Organize into small groups and choose a topic for discussion: an employment problem, a campus problem, plans for an event, suggestions for energy conservation, or the like. (A possible topic: Should employers have the right to require lie detector tests or drug tests for their employees?) Discuss the topic for one class period, taking notes on significant points and conclusions. Afterward, organize and edit your notes in line with the directions for writing summaries. Write a summary of the group discussion in no more than 200 words. As a group, compare your individual summaries for accuracy, emphasis, conciseness, and clarity.

Global Application

Find a long article (longer than five pages) from a technical, scientific, financial, or similar publication. Pick an article that deals with an issue that is global in scope (for instance, an article about the use of pesticides in different countries or an article about the ways in which financial decisions have worldwide impacts). Summarize this article for an audience of nonspecialists, but for two different groups: one group of U.S. citizens and another group of citizens in a different country. Learn what you can about the other country by looking online and determining key scientific, political, or financial issues. Or bring knowledge you have from your own travel (such as a study abroad experience) or background or from a class that you took. What will you highlight in the summary for the U.S. readers, what will you highlight in the article for the non-U.S. readers, and why? Bring copies of the original article plus each summary to class to discuss with others.

Digital and Social Media Application

When used for workplace communication, Twitter, Facebook, and LinkedIn require writers to summarize complex news stories, technical information, medical research, and more into very short summaries, usually with a link where readers can find more information. Look at the Twitter feed or Facebook page for your campus or for a technical or scientific government agency (such as the National Weather Service). Or, look at your LinkedIn page for a recent summary posted by one of your contacts. How effective are these short summaries? What techniques do the writers use to keep these summaries accurate yet interesting? Summarize your findings in two to three sentences for your instructor.

Chapter 15
Informal Reports

 ## Learning Objectives

15.1 Identify the difference between informational and analytical reports.

15.2 Plan and write progress, periodic activity, and trip reports, as well as meeting minutes.

15.3 Plan and write feasibility, recommendation, and peer review reports.

Chapter Outline

Two Categories of Reports: Informational and Analytical 264

Types of Informational Reports 264
    Strategies for Progress Reports 265
    Strategies for Periodic Activity Reports 269
    Strategies for Trip Reports 269
    Strategies for Meeting Minutes 272

Types of Analytical Reports 273
    Strategies for Feasibility Reports 275
    Strategies for Recommendation Reports 277
    Strategies for Peer Review Reports 279
    Checklist for Informal Reports 279

Applications 279

When you think of reports, you probably picture long, formal documents that contain many pages of research, information, charts and graphs, footnotes, and other details. Yet in the workplace, for every long, formal report, dozens of shorter reports are written. These shorter reports typically focus on only one or two very specific issues. *Informal reports* help people make informed decisions on matters such as the most comfortable office chairs to buy or the best recruit to hire for management training. Unlike long formal reports (discussed in Chapter 16), most informal reports require no extended planning, are prepared quickly, contain little or no background information, and have no *front* or *end matter* (title page, table of contents, glossary, works cited, index).

    Despite being so focused and concise, informal reports do provide the information and analysis readers need every day on the job. Although various formats can be used, informal reports, especially those intended for internal audiences, most often take the form of a memo. (Depending on the company or organization, the words "memo" or "memorandum" may or may not be used, but a general memo format is followed.) Shorter informal reports can be sent as the body of an email message; slightly longer ones (or reports that need to appear on business letterhead) can be send as an email attachment, typically in PDF to retain proper formatting.

Definition of informal reports

Format of informal reports

Two Categories of Reports: Informational and Analytical

15.1 Identify the difference between informational and analytical reports.

In the professional world, decision makers rely on two types of informal reports: Some reports focus primarily on information ("what we're doing now," "what we did last month," "what our customer survey found," "what went on at the department meeting"), while others may also include analysis ("what this information means for us," "what courses of action should be considered," "what we recommend, and why").

The purpose of an *informational report* is to inform; that is, to provide data and other information to answer basic questions, such as how much progress has been made on a project (progress reports), what activity has taken place over the course of a certain period of time (activity reports), what activity occurred during a business trip (trip reports), or what discussions took place in a meeting (meeting minutes). These reports help keep an organization running from day to day by providing short, timely updates on important activities.

Unlike informational reports, *analytical reports* offer both information and conclusions based on the information. Analysis is the heart of technical communication. Analysis involves evaluating information, interpreting it accurately, drawing valid conclusions, and making persuasive recommendations. Although gathering and reporting information are essential workplace skills, analysis is ultimately what professionals do to earn their pay. Analytical reports analyze and evaluate whether a project or situation is feasible (feasibility reports), make recommendations on how to proceed (recommendation reports), or constructively critique the work of others (peer review reports).

Types of Informational Reports

15.2 Plan and write progress, periodic activity, and trip reports, as well as meeting minutes.

Following are the major types of informational reports, with strategies for how to plan and write each type.

Progress Reports

Organizations depend on *progress reports* (also called status reports) to monitor progress and problems on various projects. Progress reports may be written either for internal personnel or outside clients. In the case of internal audiences, managers use progress reports to evaluate projects, monitor employees, decide how to allocate funds, and keep track of delays or expense overages that could dramatically affect outcomes and project costs. In the case of external audiences, progress reports explain to clients how time and money are being spent and how difficulties have been overcome. The reports can therefore be used to assure the client that the project will be completed on schedule and on budget.

Many contracts stipulate the dates and stages when progress will be reported. Failing to report on time may invoke contractual penalties. Some organizations require regular progress reports (daily, weekly, monthly), while others use such reports only as needed, such as when a project milestone has been reached.

Figure 15.1 shows a progress report from a training manager to a company vice president. Because the audience is internal, the writer has chosen memo format. A report like this to an external client might be written in letter format and on company letterhead as a legal record. Notice also how the report provides only those details essential to the reader. In addition, it follows a timeline structure, beginning with a summary of progress on the project (or since the last progress report) and concluding with the next steps to be completed.

The next example (Figure 15.2) is a progress report written by a student. As you work on a longer report or term project, your instructor might require a progress report. In this example, the student writer documents the progress she has made on her term project: a causal analysis examining the impact of a recently formed town committee.

Elements of progress reports

Strategies

for Progress Reports

- **Choose an appropriate delivery format.** Unless the length is very short, progress reports should be written as a word processing document and delivered as an email attachment. Converting the Word file to PDF ensures that formatting will be retained. In some cases, if the report is for an external client, the document might also be sent in hard copy via surface mail.
- **Provide a clear subject line.** Progress reports should clearly identify their purpose in the subject line of a memo or email or, if written in the letter, in the introductory paragraph.
- **Present information efficiently.** Because readers of progress reports are managers or clients who want the bottom-line information as quickly as possible, chunk the information into logically headed sections and use bulleted or numbered lists. Leave out information readers will already know, but do not omit new information.
- **Make sure your report answers the anticipated questions.** First identify what has been accomplished since the last report; then discuss any important details such as outcomes of meetings, problems encountered and solutions implemented or proposed, deadlines met or missed, resources/materials needed, and so on. Conclude with steps to be completed in time for the next report, with specific dates, if available.

Figure 15.1 A Progress Report

 BETA National

Memo

To: P. J. Stone, Senior Vice President
From: B. Poret, Group Training Manager
Date: June 6, 20XX
Subject: Progress Report: Equipment for New Operations Building

Work Completed
Our training group has met twice since our May 12 report. In our first meeting, we identified the types of training we anticipate.

Types of Training Anticipated
- Loan Officer Work Experience
- Divisional Systems Training
- Divisional Clerical Training
- Divisional Management Training (Seminars)
- Special/New Equipment Training

In our second meeting, we considered various areas for the training room.

Training Room Assignment and Equipment
To conduct these trainings, we request the corporate education room on the 10th floor. We have already purchased the following equipment:

- Large flat screen monitor
- Digital video camera and tripod
- Software for computer-assisted instruction

This equipment will allow us to administer training in varied modes, ranging from programmed and learner-controlled instruction to seminars and workshops.

Work Remaining
To support the training, we need to furnish the room appropriately. Because training types will vary, the furniture should provide a flexible environment. Outlined here are our anticipated furnishing needs.

- Tables and chairs that support multiple configurations (individuals, small groups, or large seminars).
- Portable room dividers, to allow private study space as well as group training.
- Secure storage space for equipment and supplies.
- LED lighting that is suitable for presentations as well as individualized study.

The project is on schedule. As soon as we receive your approval of these specifications, we will send out bids for room dividers and have plans drawn for built-in storage.

Margin annotations:

Subject line identifies exact purpose of the report

Summarizes first achievement

Summarizes second achievement

Describes work remaining

Bulleted list breaks up dense information

Concludes with request for approval of next phase

Figure 15.2 Progress report on a term project

Progress Report

To: Dr. J. Lannon

From: T. Fitzgerald, Student

Date: April 27, 20XX

Subject: Analytical Report

"A Study of the Impact of the Sandwich Historic District
Committee on the Town's Architectural Character"

Work Completion to Date

March 22:   Completed report on Sandwich Historic District Committee.

April 11:   Obtained maps of Sandwich, legislation, certificates of appropriateness,
exemption, and appeals from Town Hall.

April 12,   Investigated district area by car, noted differences in historic
14, 15:   and nonhistoric areas.

April 18:   Photographed sampling of areas in district. Twenty photos taken, fifteen
returned by developer.

April 19:   Divided master map into sections, redefining district.

April 20:   Completed tentative outline.

April 22:   Interviewed chairman of Committee, Donald Bourne. Received new set
of rules and regulations for district.

Work in Progress   Drawing maps of present district and redefined area.

Work to be Completed

April 28:   Interview Edward Cain, committee member.

May 2:   Interview Gary Sosa committee member.

Date For Completion   May 11, 20XX

Periodic Activity Reports

Periodic activity reports resemble progress reports in that they summarize activities over a specified period. But unlike progress reports, which summarize specific accomplishments on a particular project, periodic activity reports summarize general activities during a particular period. Periodic activity reports are almost always internal, written by employees to keep their supervisors up to date on their activities as a whole in

Purpose, audience, and frequency of periodic activity reports order to help managers monitor workload. In many companies, these reports, usually written weekly or monthly, are called "status reports."

Figure 15.3 shows a periodic activity report, in the form of a weekly status report. Notice how Laura Hardin presents the most vital information first (the ongoing user manuals project) and ends with necessary but less pressing details (vacation time and "other"). The report contains only the information and level of detail her supervisor needs.

Elements of periodic activity reports

Figure 15.3 A periodic activity report

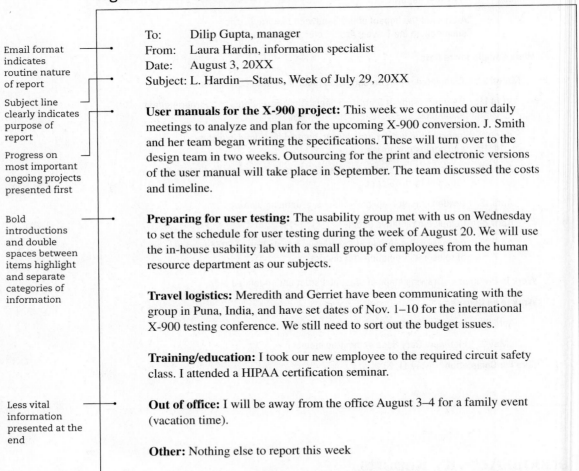

Email format indicates routine nature of report

To: Dilip Gupta, manager
From: Laura Hardin, information specialist
Date: August 3, 20XX
Subject: L. Hardin—Status, Week of July 29, 20XX

Subject line clearly indicates purpose of report

Progress on most important ongoing projects presented first

User manuals for the X-900 project: This week we continued our daily meetings to analyze and plan for the upcoming X-900 conversion. J. Smith and her team began writing the specifications. These will turn over to the design team in two weeks. Outsourcing for the print and electronic versions of the user manual will take place in September. The team discussed the costs and timeline.

Bold introductions and double spaces between items highlight and separate categories of information

Preparing for user testing: The usability group met with us on Wednesday to set the schedule for user testing during the week of August 20. We will use the in-house usability lab with a small group of employees from the human resource department as our subjects.

Travel logistics: Meredith and Gerriet have been communicating with the group in Puna, India, and have set dates of Nov. 1–10 for the international X-900 testing conference. We still need to sort out the budget issues.

Training/education: I took our new employee to the required circuit safety class. I attended a HIPAA certification seminar.

Less vital information presented at the end

Out of office: I will be away from the office August 3–4 for a family event (vacation time).

Other: Nothing else to report this week

Strategies

for Periodic Activity Reports

- **Choose an appropriate delivery format.** Short reports, such as weekly status updates, can be written as the body of an email. Longer activity reports should be written as a word processing document and delivered as an email attachment. Converting the Word file to PDF ensures that formatting will be retained.
- **Provide a clear subject line.** As with any report, identify the exact purpose of a periodic activity report by providing a subject line, such as "Monthly activity report for August."
- **Present information efficiently.** All report readers want the bottom line. Omit minor details but include all the essentials. Use headers to chunk information and bulleted and numbered lists to break up dense prose for easier reading.
- **Make sure your report answers the expected questions.** Begin by describing your most important accomplishments during the period (such as progress on an ongoing project). Then describe any other relevant activity since the last report (such as completion of one-time projects, attendance at meetings, supplies needed, conflicts or problems encountered, schedule changes, vacation time taken or upcoming, and so forth).

Trip Reports

Purpose and audience of trip reports

Trip reports resemble periodic activity reports in that they detail activities during a given period, but they focus specifically on business-related travel rather than a variety of workplace activities. These reports, like periodic activity reports, are written to help supervisors monitor employee activities. In the case of trip reports, when employers pay for employee travel, managers need to know the company is getting its money's worth. Managers also need to know what employees learn through their travels.

Elements of trip reports

Figure 15.4 shows a trip report written by an employee who has traveled to a branch office to inspect the site and interview those employees about absenteeism and hiring problems at that branch. Because the report is informational, not analytical, it sticks only to the facts. Note also that Bill Moskowicz begins the report with a purpose statement, accounts for how he spent his time, identifies the people with whom he met, offers a summary of what he learned, and provides a conclusion.

Strategies

for Trip Reports

- **Choose an appropriate delivery format.** Many organizations have template or online forms that are required when creating a trip report. If not, trip reports can be written as the body of an email or as a word processing document and delivered as an email attachment. Converting the Word file to PDF ensures that formatting will be retained.
- **Take good notes and make accurate transcriptions of interviews.** If you must interview people, either ask their permission to record the conversation or take careful notes. Transcribe interviews immediately, while the discussion is still fresh in your mind. If you investigate a location or site, take careful notes of what you observe.
- **Write down the names of people and places.** Make sure you are able to indicate who you spoke with (spelling their names correctly and getting their job titles right) and the names of places visited.

- **Account for times and locations.** Demonstrate a good use of your time by accounting for it (but not exhaustively). If you visit more than one location, be clear about what occurred at each.
- **Provide a clear title and purpose statement.** A clear title indicates exactly which trip you are referring to, including date(s), while a purpose statement at the beginning of the report prevents any possible confusion as to your reasons for taking the trip.
- **Use a format that is easy to navigate.** As you would in any report, provide clear headings to break up chunks of information and use bulleted/numbered lists, double spacing, and so on, for ease of readability.
- **Describe findings completely and objectively.** Don't omit vital information or include irrelevant information, and don't insert personal impressions—stick to the facts.

Figure 15.4 A trip report

To:	Monica Herrera, Director of Human Resources, Boston office
From:	Bill Moskowicz, Human Resources Specialist
Date:	March 30, 20XX
Subject:	Visit to the Eastfield Office

Subject line identifies trip and date

Purpose

On March 20, I visited the Eastfield office to explore these two issues:
- Higher-than-average rate of employee absenteeism at that office
- Difficulties hiring qualified employees to work and live in or near the Eastfield Fort Channel area

Starts with a purpose statement

To pinpoint the causes of these problems, I decided to interview three individuals face to face in hopes of getting more candid and detailed responses than I would via phone or email, particularly regarding the sensitive absenteeism problem.

Schedule

I spoke with the following people individually: Susan Sheehan, Director of HR (9:00 a.m.–10:00 a.m.); Sammy Lee, Marketing Manager for the gourmet desserts division (10:00 a.m.–11:00 a.m.); and Megan Fields, an Administrative Assistant in the distribution division (11:00 a.m.–12:00 p.m.). Then we all had lunch and continued the discussion between noon and 2:00 p.m., at which time I transcribed my recordings and headed back to Boston.

Provides an accounting of how time was spent

Interviews

The interviews were illuminating. Essentially all three pointed out how the absenteeism and hiring problems are not entirely separate issues; in fact, they are closely linked. While once a thriving, safe, and low-crime city (including the branch's Fort Channel area), Eastfield has now fallen upon difficult economic times, particularly in the last year. All three employees identified the following problems:

Includes discussion of what was learned

continued

Figure 15.4 *continued*

- Increased gang activity and vagrancy in the Fort Channel area
- Lack of safe public transportation to and from the office or a secure, on-site parking facility
- An increasing decline in amenities, especially lunch venues or safe public areas nearby
- Decreased security resulting from a busy police force and high security guard turnover

Uses bulleted list (and headings) to break up text and identify key points

While Susan and Sammy can both afford to occasionally take cabs and leave the Fort Channel area for lunch, Megan pointed out her limitations due to salary and an insufficient reimbursement program.

The Fort Channel area's problems have all had a direct impact on employee hiring in recent months. Both Susan and Sammy reported losing promising potential employees following interviews. According to Susan, while United Foods manufactures and distributes gourmet products, attracting those who wish to work in an upscale environment, potential employees are often frightened away, preferring employment at either the Boston office or with competitors located elsewhere in the state. At the same time, very few have opted to relocate from the Boston to Eastfield offices to help account for imbalances.

Conclusion
While the goal of this trip was not for me to make recommendations, I have some specific ideas. I would be glad to speak with you further to answer any questions and to share those ideas with you.

Provides an offer to follow up

Meeting Minutes

Many team or project meetings require someone to record the proceedings. *Meeting minutes* are the records of such meetings. Copies of minutes are typically distributed to all members and interested parties to track the proceedings and to remind members about their responsibilities. Usually, one person is appointed to record the minutes. Be sure to proofread the minutes, check the spelling of the attendees' names, and consider how you have described any politically sensitive or confidential issues before sending.

Purpose, audience, and distribution of meeting minutes

Figure 15.5 shows minutes from a personnel manager's meeting.

Figure 15.5 Meeting minutes

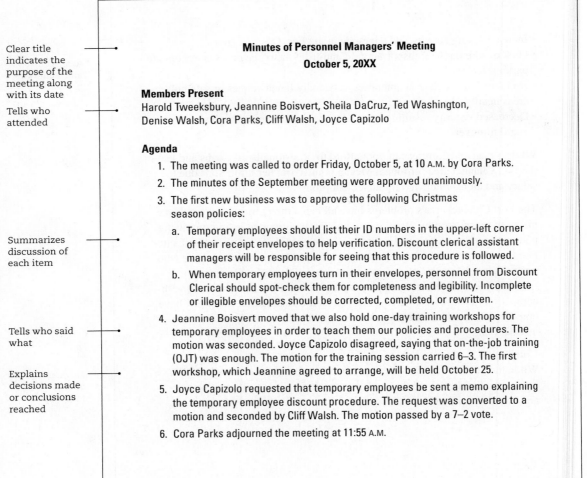

Clear title indicates the purpose of the meeting along with its date

Tells who attended

Summarizes discussion of each item

Tells who said what

Explains decisions made or conclusions reached

Minutes of Personnel Managers' Meeting
October 5, 20XX

Members Present
Harold Tweeksbury, Jeannine Boisvert, Sheila DaCruz, Ted Washington, Denise Walsh, Cora Parks, Cliff Walsh, Joyce Capizolo

Agenda
1. The meeting was called to order Friday, October 5, at 10 A.M. by Cora Parks.
2. The minutes of the September meeting were approved unanimously.
3. The first new business was to approve the following Christmas season policies:
   a. Temporary employees should list their ID numbers in the upper-left corner of their receipt envelopes to help verification. Discount clerical assistant managers will be responsible for seeing that this procedure is followed.
   b. When temporary employees turn in their envelopes, personnel from Discount Clerical should spot-check them for completeness and legibility. Incomplete or illegible envelopes should be corrected, completed, or rewritten.
4. Jeannine Boisvert moved that we also hold one-day training workshops for temporary employees in order to teach them our policies and procedures. The motion was seconded. Joyce Capizolo disagreed, saying that on-the-job training (OJT) was enough. The motion for the training session carried 6–3. The first workshop, which Jeannine agreed to arrange, will be held October 25.
5. Joyce Capizolo requested that temporary employees be sent a memo explaining the temporary employee discount procedure. The request was converted to a motion and seconded by Cliff Walsh. The motion passed by a 7–2 vote.
6. Cora Parks adjourned the meeting at 11:55 A.M.

Strategies

for Meeting Minutes

- **Choose an appropriate delivery format.** Organizations vary on how they prefer meeting minutes to be distributed. In some companies, meeting minutes are posted on the file server (intranet); in other organizations, meeting minutes may be distributed via email and then saved on shared file space for later reference.
- **Take good notes during the meeting.** Don't rely on your memory, even if you write up the minutes immediately after the meeting. Write down who said what, especially if a particularly important point was raised.

- **Complete the minutes immediately after the meeting.** Even if you take good notes, you may forget the context of a particular point if you wait too long. Write up the minutes immediately.
- **Include a clear title with the meeting date.** A clear title should indicate the meeting's exact purpose ("sales conference planning meeting") and always include the meeting date to prevent confusion with similar meetings.
- **List attendees.** List everyone who attended. If the meeting was chaired or moderated, indicate by whom.
- **Describe all agenda items.** Make sure all topics discussed are recorded. Your own memory of meeting topics and those of other meeting attendees are usually fleeting.
- **Record all decisions or conclusions.** If everyone agreed on a point or if a vote was taken, be sure to include those results in your minutes.
- **Make sure the minutes are easy to navigate, precise, and factual.** Use headings, lists, and other helpful design features. Describe each topic fully yet concisely. Don't leave out important nuances, but stick to the facts. Keep personal commentary, humor, and "sidebar" comments out of meeting minutes.

Types of Analytical Reports

15.3 Plan and write feasibility, recommendation, and peer review reports.

Following are the major types of analytical reports, with strategies for how to plan and write each type.

Feasibility Reports

Feasibility reports are used when decision makers need to assess whether an idea, plan, or course of action is realistic and practical. Sometimes an idea may make perfect sense from one perspective, but may not be feasible at the moment for one reason or another, usually because of timing. For example, a manufacturing company may want to switch to a more automated process, which would greatly reduce costs over the long term. But in the short term, the resulting layoffs would have a negative impact on morale.

Purpose of feasibility reports

A feasibility report provides answers to questions such as these:

- What is the problem or situation, and what is the best approach to solving or dealing with it?
- Is this course of action likely to succeed?
- Do the benefits outweigh the drawbacks or risks?
- What are the pros and cons, and what are the alternatives?
- Should anything be done at all? Should it wait? Is the timing right?

Typical questions about feasibility

The answers are based on the writer's careful research.

Managers and other decision makers are the primary audience for feasibility reports. These busy people want to see the recommendation or answer at or near the beginning of the document, followed by supporting evidence and reasoning. In other words, a feasibility report should use the "bottom line first" organizational pattern:

Audience for feasibility reports

here is the situation; here is our recommendation; and here is why this approach is feasible at this time.

Figure 15.6 shows a feasibility report in which a securities analyst for a state pension fund reports to the fund's manager on the feasibility of investing in a rapidly

Elements of feasibility reports

Figure 15.6 A feasibility report

State Pension Fund

Memorandum

To: Mary K. White, Fund Manager

From: Martha Mooney

Date: April 1, 20XX

Subject: The Feasibility of Investing in WBM Computers, Inc

Our Treasury bonds, composing 3.5 percent of the Fund's investment portfolio, mature on April 15. Current inflationary pressures make fixed-income investments less attractive than equities. As you requested, I have researched and compared investment alternatives based on these criteria: market share, earnings, and dividends.

Recommendation
Given its established market share, solid earnings, and generous dividends, WBM Computers, Inc., is a sound and promising company. I recommend that we invest our maturing bond proceeds in WBM's Class A stock.

Market Share
Though only ten years old, WBM competes strongly with established computer makers. Its market share has grown steadily for the past five years. This past year, services and sales ranked 367th in the industrial United States, with orders increasing from $750 million to $1.25 billion. Net income places WBM 237th nationally and 13th on return to investors.

Earnings
WBM's net profit on sales is 9 percent, a roughly steady figure for the past three years. Whereas 2006 earnings were only $.09 per share, this year's are $1.36 per share. Included in these ten-year earnings is a two-for-one stock split issued November 2, 20XX. Barring a global sales downturn WBM's outlook for continued strong earnings is promising.

Dividends
Investors are offered two types of common stock. The assigned par value of both classes is $.50 per share. Class A stock pays an additional $.25 per share dividend but restricts voting privileges to one vote for every ten shares held by the investor. Class B stock does not pay the extra dividend but carries full voting rights. The additional dividend from Class A shares would enhance income flow into our portfolio.

WBM shares now trade at 14 times earnings and current share price of $56.00, a bargain in my estimation. An immediate investment would add strength and diversity to our portfolio.

*Callouts (left margin):*
- Clear subject line leaves no doubt as to purpose of report
- Gives brief background
- Makes a direct recommendation
- Explains the criteria supporting the recommendation
- Encourages reader action

growing computer maker. Notice how it starts with background, provides a direct recommendation, provides information that supports the recommendation, and ends with a call to action.

Strategies

for Feasibility Reports

- **Choose an appropriate delivery format.** Unless the length is very short, progress reports should be written as a word processing document and delivered as an email attachment. Converting the Word file to PDF ensures that formatting will be retained. In some cases, if the report is for an external client, the document might also be sent in hard copy via surface mail.
- **Make sure the subject line is clear.** Always use the word "feasibility" (or a synonym) in the title ("Subject: Feasibility of...").
- **Provide background information.** Your readers may not always need background information, but if they do, make it short.
- **Offer the recommendation near the beginning of the report.** Because readers of feasibility reports are interested primarily in the "bottom line," state it explicitly at the very beginning of the report or just after the background information.
- **Provide the details, data, and criteria after the recommendation section.** Include supporting data, such as costs, equipment needed, results expected, and so on. Don't overdo the supporting data, but include everything directly relevant that will persuade readers to support your recommendation.
- **Explain why your recommendation is the most feasible of all the possible choices.** Your readers may prefer other choices. Persuade them that yours is the best choice.
- **End with a call to action.**

Recommendation Reports

While a feasibility report sets out to prove that a particular course of action is the right one to take, a *recommendation report* shortens or even skips the feasibility analysis (since it has already taken place or been discussed) and gets right to the point of making a recommendation. Recommendation reports, like feasibility reports, may include supporting data, but they also state an affirmative position ("Here's what we should do and why") rather than examining whether the approach will work ("Should we do it?"). Like feasibility reports, recommendation reports are for the eyes of decision makers, and these documents take a direct stance.

Figure 15.7 shows a recommendation report from a health and safety officer at an airline company to a vice president regarding the workstation comfort of the company's reservation and booking agents. Notice that it is organized similarly to a feasibility report but takes a more authoritative stance based on previous analysis, emphasizing expected rather than possible benefits. Also, a description of the problem and its causes precedes the recommendations.

Purpose and audience of recommendation reports

Elements of recommendation reports

Figure 15.7 A recommendation report

TRANS GLOBE AIRLINES

Memorandum

To: R. Ames, Vice President, Personnel

From: B. Doakes, Health and Safety

Date: August 15, 20XX

Subject line directly states exact purpose of report

Subject: Recommendations for Reducing Agents' Discomfort

Provides immediate orientation by giving brief background and main point

In our July 20 staff meeting, we discussed physical discomfort among reservation and booking agents, who spend eight hours daily at workstations. They complain of headaches, eyestrain, blurred or double vision, backaches, and stiff joints. This report outlines the apparent causes and recommends ways of reducing discomfort.

Causes of Agents' Discomfort

Statement of problem or situation precedes recommendations

Last year, we replaced all older CRT monitors with LCD screens. Ergonomics consultants have adjusted the brightness and contrast settings for each user and have advised us that the monitors themselves are not causing headaches and eyestrain. Instead, these problems seem to be caused by excessive glare from background lighting. Other concerns, such as backaches and stiffness, result from agents who are sitting in one position for up to two hours between breaks.

Recommended Changes

Makes general recommendations

We can eliminate much discomfort by improving background lighting, workstation conditions, and work routines and habits.

Expands on each recommendation

Background Lighting. To reduce the glare on display screens, I recommend these changes in background lighting:

1. Decrease all overhead lighting by installing lower-wattage LED bulbs.

2. Keep all curtains and adjustable blinds on the south and west windows at least half-drawn to block direct sunlight.

3. Install shades to direct the overhead lighting straight downward, so that it is not reflected on the screens.

Workstation Conditions. I recommend the following changes in the workstations:

1. Reposition all screens so light sources are neither at front nor back.

2. Clean the surface of each screen weekly.

3. Adjust each screen so the top is slightly below the operator's eye level.

4. Adjust all keyboards so they are 27 inches from the floor.

5. Replace all fixed chairs with pneumatic, multi-task chairs.

continued

Figure 15.7 *continued*

> **Work Routines and Habits**. These are recommended changes in agents' work routines and habits:
>
> 1. Allow frequent rest periods (10 minutes hourly instead of 30 minutes twice daily).
> 2. Provide yearly eye exams for agents as part of our routine healthcare program.
> 3. Train agents to adjust screen contrast and brightness whenever the background lighting changes.
> 4. Offer workshops on improving posture.
>
> These changes will give us time to consider more complex options such as installing hoods and antiglare filters on display screens, replacing fluorescent lighting with LED or other options, covering surfaces with nonglare paint, or other disruptive procedures.
>
> cc: J. Bush, Medical Director
>   M. White, Manager of Physical Plant

Discusses benefits of following the recommendations

This is just one example of countless short reports used to examine a workplace problem and recommend a solution.

Strategies

for Recommendation Reports

- **Choose an appropriate delivery format.** Unless the length is very short, recommendation reports should be written as a word processing document and delivered as an email attachment. Converting the Word file to PDF ensures that formatting will be retained. In some cases, if the report is for an external client, the document might also be sent in hard copy via surface mail.
- **Provide a clear subject line.** As always, make sure the subject of the report is brief and directly to the point.
- **Keep background information short.** Keep the background history brief, but do discuss how feasibility has already been determined.
- **Discuss the problem or situation prior to making recommendations.** In addition to the brief background information, outline the problem or situation that the recommended actions will resolve. Then discuss the recommendations in as much detail as necessary.
- **Use an authoritative tone.** Take a strong stance and write with confidence, knowing that the recommendation has already been determined to be feasible.
- **Use headings and make them as informative as possible.** Instead of using the vague heading "Problem," be specific ("Causes of Agents' Discomfort"). Don't forget that you are writing to a "bottom line" audience.
- **End with a list of benefits for taking action.** Rather than appealing for action, assume action will be taken by reemphasizing the benefits.

Peer Review Reports

Purpose and audience of peer review reports

Peer review reports are written between employees, providing a way for people (peers) to give each other constructive criticism and feedback. Because peer review reports are shared by colleagues wishing to preserve good workplace relationships, they must be written with tact. (Note that Figure 15.8 illustrates the use of constructive criticism in peer review and can serve as a model for reviewing the work of other students in the classroom.)

Figure 15.8 A peer review report

To:	Catie Noll, Advertising Associate
From:	David Summer, Advertising Supervisor D.S.
Date:	May 1, 20XX
Subject:	Review of your feasibility report for the Garvey account

Report starts with a friendly tone and says something positive before offering suggested changes

I have reviewed the first draft of your report for the Garvey account. Thank you for your good work! You have done a great job organizing the material and getting started. I would like to offer the following suggestions:

Voice: You use passive voice in a number of places where active voice would be more appropriate. For instance, at the bottom of page 7, you might want to

Suggested changes are clear and organized by area

change "A mistake was made" to "We made a mistake." I would recommend that you review the entire draft for this usage.

Writer provides rationale behind suggestions

Organization: As a reader, I did not know what you were recommending in this report until I reached the very end. I would suggest that you move your recommendation up to the beginning of the report, then follow it with the supporting data. Our supervisors will want to know the bottom line right away.

Writer provides specific advice to help the writer improve the reviewed document

Research: I noticed that most of your research was based on commercial Web sites. You should probably look at more reliable peer-reviewed sources, such as well-respected business newspapers, journal articles, and online publications of professional organizations.

Visuals/font: Great use of images, especially the maps on page 9. You might want to increase the font size of the base text.

Report uses a polite closing

I hope my recommendations are helpful as you complete this project. Your report is well on the way, offering solid reasons that should persuade the managers to try winning the Garvey account from our competitors. Please let me know if you have any questions.

Strategies

for Peer Review Reports

- **Choose an appropriate delivery format.** On the job, peer review reports are typically circulated via the organization's file server (intranet) or as email attachments. In class, you might be asked to upload your peer review report to the class learning management system and to bring a paper copy to class.
- **Start with the positives.** Briefly state the good points of the reviewed document as a way of leading into and balancing against the criticisms.
- **Organize by topic area.** Provide separate sections for suggestions about the reviewed document's writing style, design, use of visuals, and other areas.
- **Always provide constructive criticism.** Remember that you are reviewing the work of a colleague or colleagues. Review their work tactfully, as you would want them to review your work. However, don't ignore problem areas.
- **Support your criticisms with examples and advice.** Point to particular examples in the reviewed document as you discuss them. Suggest alternatives, if possible. Point to helpful resources, if applicable.
- **Close positively.** End with a friendly, encouraging tone. If the reviewed document is particularly problematic, state as much—but diplomatically.

Checklist

for Informal Reports

- ❏ Have I determined the right report type (status report, recommendation report, etc.) for this situation?
- ❏ When preparing a progress or status report, have I determined how much detail is necessary to include?
- ❏ When taking minutes for a meeting, have I included all the key decisions and discussion items and left out unnecessary detail?
- ❏ If I have decided to write a recommendation report, has the feasibility of the project or idea already been determined, or is a feasibility study and report more appropriate at this time?
- ❏ For all forms of informal reports, have I used a memo format?
- ❏ Is the subject line clear?
- ❏ Is the tone professional and polite but direct?
- ❏ For any report, have I done enough research so that my position is credible?
- ❏ Have I reviewed the Strategies box for my specific report type?

Applications

General Applications

1. For this or another class, write a progress report to your instructor, describing the progress you've made on a project you are working on (your final project, for instance). Use the strategies suggested in this chapter. Or write a peer review report of a classmate's draft of an upcoming assignment.

2. For a current or past job or internship, write a periodic activity report in which you report on the past week's activities (actual or typical). Be sure to follow the strategies for periodic activity reports in this chapter.

3. Take notes at the next group event or meeting you attend. Write up minutes for the meeting, thinking about how much detail to include and what kinds of information will be useful to the other members of the team.

Team Applications

1. With two or three other classmates, identify a dangerous or inconvenient area or situation on campus or in your community (endless cafeteria lines, an unsafe walkway, slippery stairs, a bad campus intersection). Observe the problem for several hours during a peak use period. Write a recommendation report to a specifically identified decision maker (the head of campus security, for example) describing the problem, listing your observations, and making a recommendation.

2. Convert the same report into a feasibility report by discussing several different approaches that might be taken and then recommending the feasibility of the approach you prefer.

Global Application

Assume that you are a team leader of a U.S.-based company with offices worldwide. You have been assigned a new manager who is a citizen of another country. This week, you need to write a report recommending that all the staff on your team receive their annual bonuses. You know the tone you would take if your manager were from the United States, but you are uncertain about what tone or level of politeness is appropriate for this new manager. Pick a country and do some research on the Internet about tone, style, and politeness in different cultures, remembering that not everyone in a country or culture is exactly alike. Write a short memo to your instructor explaining what you have learned and how you would shape your recommendation report in this situation.

Digital and Social Media Application

As this chapter illustrates, most informal reports are written for internal audiences. Yet most technical and scientific organizations use social media to publish posts about new research findings (such as new studies about highway safety), public health issues (such as influenza statistics), and current events (such as food safety recalls). These posts typically link to pages or documents that at first glance appear similar to an informal report. Use Twitter and Facebook to look at the posts of federal agencies; for example, the Centers for Disease Control (CDC) and the Department of Agriculture (USDA) or similar state-level agencies. Click on posts that link back to a report. List out the main features of the report: level of technical language and the audience you assume this report was written for; length of report; the report's title; use of headings. Compare these items with one of the information report types in this chapter (feasibility or recommendation reports would be good comparisons). Write a memo to your instructor noting the similarities and differences between the chapter examples and what you find online, and explain how these differences might relate to the online reports available to external audiences.

Chapter 16
Formal Reports

 Learning Objectives

16.1 Determine the audience and purpose of a formal report.

16.2 Identify the characteristics of an effective formal report.

16.3 Include all the essential parts in a formal report.

Chapter Outline

Audience and Purpose of Formal Reports   283

Elements of Effective Formal Reports   285

Parts of Formal Reports   288
Strategies for Formal Reports   291
Checklist for Formal Reports   307

Applications   307

Formal versus informal reports

Much like the shorter analytical reports (feasibility and recommendation reports) discussed in Chapter 15, long, formal reports are analytical reports that often lead to recommendations. The formal report format replaces the informal memo format when the topic requires lengthy discussion. Formal reports generally include a title page, a table of contents, a system of headings, a list of references or works cited, and other front-matter and end-matter supplements. An essential component of workplace problem solving, formal reports are designed to answer these questions:

- Based on the information gathered about this issue, what do we know?
- What conclusions can we draw?
- What should we do or not do?

Scenario for a formal report

For instance, imagine you work on a team of alternative energy experts (engineers, policy analysts, technical writers, lawyers), and the state department of energy has asked your organization for a report on the feasibility of producing wind energy in your state. First, you will have to learn everything you can about the nature of the energy situation in your state at this time. Then you will need to compare the advantages and disadvantages of various options based on the *criteria* you are using to assess feasibility, such as cost-effectiveness, time required versus time available to begin wind energy production, potential risks and benefits to the public and the environment, and so on. As you consider all the factors, you might find that the least expensive option might also pose the greatest environmental risk; on the other hand, the most environmentally friendly option might be too expensive.

The importance of research in formal reports

This type of situation requires critical thinking and research. Aside from the technical knowledge about wind energy that your team already has, you may need additional research about the state or about the relationship of wind energy to other sectors of the economy (for example, agricultural). Sources for this research may be available using secondary research (online or through the library), or you may need to answer these questions through primary research (surveys and interviews). For more information on how to conduct research, review Chapter 2.

Audience and Purpose of Formal Reports

16.1 Determine the audience and purpose of a formal report.

Because of their major impact on the decision-making process, formal reports are almost always written for an audience of decision makers: for example, government officials, corporate managers. You need to know whether the report will be read primarily by an individual, a team, or a series of individuals with differing roles in the company.

Audience considerations

To determine the purpose of the report, consider what question or questions it will ultimately answer. Also, consider why this particular topic is timely and useful to the intended audience. Use the Audience and Purpose Profile Sheet on page 42 to begin mapping out your audience and purpose for the report.

Purpose considerations

Next, determine which of the following three analytical categories best fits your purpose: the comparative analysis ("Which is better, X or Y?"), the causal analysis ("Why does X occur?"), or the feasibility analysis ("Is X a good idea?"). Note that not all formal reports fall neatly into one of these categories. Some reports blend two or all three. For instance, some reports will present a feasibility analysis but will also offer a great deal of comparative information.

Comparative Analysis

Comparative analysis rates similar items on the basis of specific criteria. For example, you may need to answer a question such as "Which type of security procedure—firewall or encryption—should we install in our company's computer system?"

Features of a comparative analysis

For a comparative analysis, base the comparison on clear and definite criteria: costs, uses, benefits/drawbacks, appearance, results. Identify your specific criteria, and then rank these in order of importance. Give each item balanced treatment. Support and clarify the comparison or contrast through credible examples. Use research, if necessary, for examples that readers can visualize.

In a report titled "A Comparison of Different Methods for Uploading Digital Photographs," the abstract of which is shown in Figure 16.1, Christina Romano compares three different upload methods. Romano, a freelance photographer, was asked to write this report for a local photography club. Notice how the abstract makes clear the comparative approach of the report.

Causal Analysis

Causal analysis explains the causes or the effects of an event, a problem, or a decision. For example, medical researchers may need to explain why so many apparently healthy people have sudden heart attacks. Or you might need to anticipate the possible effects of a proposed corporate merger on employee morale.

Features of a causal analysis

Figure 16.1 Abstract for a formal report that takes a primarily comparative approach

Abstract

This report compares three different methods for uploading digital photographs from camera to computer. Each method has strengths and weaknesses, depending on the needs and skill level of the photographer.

The first method involves connecting the camera to the computer with a USB cable, then uploading the photographs through whatever software is used (Google Photos; iPhoto, other). This method is the easiest but does not give users very much control on where the photo files are stored.

The second method requires users to remove the storage card from the camera, insert it into a device called a card reader, and then connect the card reader to the computer's USB or firewire port. This method is quicker than the first one described, but it is also more complicated for users not experienced with the directories on their computer.

The final method uses the camera and computer's Bluetooth wireless communication feature. This method does not require any cables or card readers, but it can be slow.

For beginning photographers, this report recommends the first method. For more advanced photographers, the second method is often preferred.

For a causal analysis, be sure the cause fits the effect. Faulty causal reasoning is extremely common, especially when people ignore other possible causes or when they confuse mere coincidence with causation. Make the links between effect and cause clear. Identify the immediate cause (the one most closely related to the effect) as well as the distant cause(s) (the ones that precede the immediate cause). For example, the immediate cause of an airplane crash might be a fuel-tank explosion, caused by a short circuit in frayed wiring. This wiring defect, it turns out, was caused by faulty design or poor quality control by the manufacturer. Discussing only the immediate cause merely scratches the surface of the problem.

The sample formal report by Crystal Cunningham, "Effects of Periodontal Disease on Preterm Low Birth Weight Babies," provided later in this chapter (see pages 292-307), takes a primarily causal approach. The writer examines the research literature on the question of whether periodontal disease in mothers might cause low birth weight in babies.

Feasibility Analysis

Features of a feasibility analysis

A feasibility analysis assesses the practicality of an idea or plan. For example, if your company needs to know whether increased business will justify the cost of maintaining a corporate blog for customers, you would do some research and describe your findings in a formal feasibility report. In some cases, you (the writer) can't actually determine the feasibility; all you can do is provide enough information so that the readers of your report can make the final decision.

For a feasibility analysis, consider the strength of supporting reasons. Choose the best reasons for supporting the action or decision being considered—based on your collected evidence. Also consider the strength of opposing reasons. Remember that people usually see only what they want to see. Avoid the temptation to overlook or downplay opposing reasons, especially for an action or decision you have been advocating. Consider alternate points of view and examine and evaluate all the evidence. After weighing the pros and cons, recommend a realistic and well-reasoned course of action.

In their report "A Study on the Feasibility of Biodiesel Production in Georgia" (the conclusion section is shown in Figure 16.2), Professor George A. Shumaker and his coauthors provide decision makers with the information needed to decide on a vital component of one state's energy policy. Their conclusion is a good example of how a feasibility study can take into account criteria that would have to be met (in this case, cost-effectiveness) for a proposed plan to be feasible.

Elements of Effective Formal Reports

16.2 Identify the characteristics of an effective formal report.

Readers expect a report that is based on thorough research, critical analysis of the evidence, and clear presentation of the material.

Figure 16.2 Conclusion of a formal report that takes a feasibility approach

Conclusion

There exist a variety of potential feedstocks both in Georgia and nearby states that could be utilized to produce biodiesel. These feedstocks vary significantly in price depending on supply and demand conditions, as well as market structural conditions. Feedstock costs represent between 50 and 75 percent of the cost of producing biodiesel, and thus a reliable source of low priced feedstocks is critical to success. A 15 million gallon biodiesel plant would require about 27% of the vegetable and animal fats currently available within the State of Georgia. This facility would produce 750 million gallons of 2% blend for approximately twice the state demand. A 20% blend will create 75 million gallons of B20 or roughly 20% of the Georgia diesel market.

The processing technology for producing biodiesel is well established and presents little technological risk. The production of biodiesel is a very efficient process, returning about 3.2 units of energy for each unit used in production. Biodiesel is thus an excellent renewable fuel source. Biodiesel can be very easily integrated into the existing petroleum distribution system from the handling, chemical, physical, and performance perspectives.

Lacking government mandates or subsidies, a feedstock cost of about 10 cents per pound or less, given current diesel fuel prices, is needed for biodiesel to be cost effective.

SOURCE: From "A Study on the Feasibility of Biodiesel Production in Georgia" by Professor George A. Shumaker et al. Copyright © 2003 by The University of Georgia's Center on Agribusiness & Economic Development. Reprinted with permission.

Accurate, Appropriate, and Clearly Interpreted Data

Choose and interpret the source material critically

Make sure your information is accurate and, to the best of your ability, unbiased. Use reputable information sources (particularly for statistical data), such as government documents, peer-reviewed sources, and sound reporting from nationally respected newspapers and similar sources. Make sure you interpret information fairly and provide valid conclusions based on your best research. Assume, for example, that you are writing a report to recommend the best brand of chain saw for a logging company. If, in reviewing test reports on various chain saw brands, you learn that one brand, Bomarc, is the easiest to operate but also has the fewest safety features, include both pieces of information in your report—even if you personally prefer this brand.

Clearly Identified Purpose Statement

Address both primary and secondary purposes in the purpose statement

Begin by defining the primary question the report will need to answer, and then identify any secondary questions. The biodiesel report discussed earlier may have begun with a question from a state legislator: "Will producing biodiesel benefit the state of Georgia?" Answering this question is the report's primary purpose (feasibility analysis); however, this question leads to others, such as "What are the advantages and drawbacks of biodiesel use versus other types of fuels?" (comparative analysis) or "How does biodiesel fuel affect the environment?" (causal analysis). Create a purpose statement that addresses both primary and secondary purpose, such as "The purpose of this report is to examine the feasibility of biodiesel production in the state of Georgia by comparing biodiesel fuels to other alternatives and assessing their environmental effects."

Understandable Structure

Use outlining, chunking, sequencing, paragraphing, and heading strategies

Structure your report for ease of navigation. Begin by outlining your report and adjusting that outline as you go. Then chunk the text so that large passages of dense information don't overwhelm your readers. Next, sequence all your data in a logical order (spatial, chronological, problem-solution, cause and effect). After that, order information within your paragraphs for maximum readability. Finally, use clarifying headings and subheadings to announce what each section contains. For example, the heading "Data Analysis" does not really say much, whereas the heading "Physiological Effects and Health Risks" offers a clear, informative preview.

Readable Style

Write clearly, concisely, fluently, and personably

Readers don't want to be bogged down with cumbersome prose. Make your writing clear by avoiding ambiguous pronoun references and modifiers, using active voice, avoiding nominalizations, unstacking modifying nouns, and avoiding unnecessary jargon. Make your writing concise by avoiding wordiness and eliminating repetition and redundancy. Make your writing fluent by combining related ideas, varying sentence construction and length, and using parallel structure. Write personally by choosing the appropriate tone and avoiding sexist and biased language. Ask a colleague or editor to copyedit your report before it is printed. Proofread the final version carefully.

Audience-Centered Visuals

Provide as much visual information as appropriate to make complex statistics and numeric data easy to understand. Graphs are especially useful for analyzing rising or falling trends, levels, and long-term forecasts. Tables and charts are helpful for comparing data. Illustrations, diagrams, and photographs are an excellent way to show a component or special feature. Place each visual near the accompanying text and be careful not to overuse visuals. The biodiesel feasibility study mentioned earlier uses visuals effectively. For instance, on page 18 of the report (see Figure 16.3), the writers

Use graphs, tables, charts, illustrations, diagrams, and photographs as appropriate

Figure 16.3 Effective use of a visual in a formal report

18

Gelling of biodiesel varies depending upon the chemical composition of the feedstock used in its production. The higher the saturated fat of the feedstock, such as in animal fats, the higher the temperature at which gelling occurs. The converse is also true. Canola oil, with low levels of saturated fats, derived biodiesel provides the lowest gelling temperature biodiesel. Pure biodiesel should be stored and transported at temperatures above 50 F and blending temperatures should be above 40 F.

Environmental Impacts of Biodiesel Use

Studies completed by the Environmental Protection Agency (NREL/TP 2001) state that a 20% blend is "basically a trade off between cost, emissions, cold weather, material compatibility and solvency issues." Researchers believe the 20% blend to be the best blend for general use without encountering major issues. Higher blends often cause problems in winter and with nitrogen oxide emissions.

Table 10. Emission Changes with Biodiesel Fuels.

Emission	100% Biodiesel*	20% Biodiesel Blend*
Carbon Monoxide	-43.2%	-12.6%
Hydrocarbons	-56.3%	-11%
Particulates	-55.4%	-18%
Nitrogen Oxides	+5.8%	+1.2%
Air Toxics	-60% to -90%	-20%
Mutagenicity	-80% to -90%	-20%
Carbon Dioxide**	-78.3%	-15.7%

* Average of data from 14 EPA FTP Heavy duty test cycle tests, variety of stock engines
** Life Cycle Emission

It would appear that the use of biodiesel can be an effective means for reducing exhaust emissions. The relevant question becomes, how does the cost of reducing emission using biodiesel compare to other means of obtaining the same level of emission reduction? The answer to that question is beyond the scope of this inquiry.

Impact Analysis

Impact analysis is a key component of any feasibility study. An impact analysis indicates the effect of a new venture on the economy. Building a new biodiesel facility in Georgia will impact the economy on two levels. The new plant will generate output as it begins selling biodiesel and its by-products. These sales will, in turn, generate additional sales as the plant purchases inputs. The suppliers to the plant will increase the purchase of their inputs, thus

The table enables readers to compare data easily

SOURCE: From "A Study on the Feasibility of Biodiesel Production in Georgia" by Professor George A. Shumaker et al. Copyright © 2003 by The University of Georgia's Center on Agribusiness & Economic Development. Reprinted with permission.

quantify the reduction in emissions when biodiesel fuel is used. In that example, a table provides an excellent way to compare information without the requirement of reading a lot of dense prose.

User-Friendly Design

Design for consistency, cohesiveness, navigation, and emphasis

Remember that a well-designed document demonstrates consistency and cohesiveness via grid patterns, margins, paragraphs, justification, line spacing, font style, and font size. A good design also aids navigation and adds emphasis via headings, color, shading, bold, italic, underlining, color, bulleted and numbered lists, and running heads and feet (see Chapter 8).

Parts of Formal Reports

16.3 Include all the essential parts in a formal report.

Most formal reports consist of the front matter, the text of the report, and the end matter. Reports may be formatted differently, depending on the instructor or the workplace setting. Use Figure 16.4 as one model, but note the items discussed below, and be sure to follow the instructions of your course instructor or workplace or internship manager.

Letter of Transmittal

Many formal reports include a letter of transmittal, addressed to a specific reader or readers, which precedes the report. This letter might acknowledge individuals or organizations that helped with the report, refer readers to sections of special interest, discuss any limitations of the study or any problems in gathering data, offer personal (or off-the-record) observations, or urge readers to take immediate action. See page 293 (Figure 16.4) for a sample letter of transmittal.

Front Matter

Preceding the text of the report is the front matter: title page, table of contents, list of tables and figures if appropriate, and abstract or executive summary.

TITLE PAGE. The title page provides the report title, the names of all authors and their affiliations (and/or the name of the organization that commissioned the report), and the date the report was distributed to readers. The title announces the report's purpose and subject by using descriptive words such as *analysis, proposal, feasibility,* or *recommendation.* Be sure the title fully describes your report, but avoid an overly long and involved title. Design the page so that the title is the most prominent item, highest on the page, followed by the name of the recipient(s), the author(s), and the date of submission. See page 294 (Figure 16.4) for a sample title page.

TABLE OF CONTENTS. The table of contents provides readers with an easy way to navigate the report. A table of contents helps readers find what they seek by page number for each major section. Do not include the letter of transmittal, title page, or table of contents itself, but do include the abstract or executive summary. Different style guides (academic and organizational) require different approaches; for example, APA style for research papers does not require a table of contents, yet for workplace reports this feature is typically included. (In Figure 16.4, the professor requested the student use a modified form of APA style by creating a running head and a table of contents.)

Number the report pages using Arabic numerals (1, 2, 3), starting with the title page. For APA style, use a running head with page numbers as shown in Figure 16.4. In some report formats, pagination is done by having the "front matter" (title page; table of contents; list of figures) numbered using lower case Roman numerals (i; ii; iii) and with Arabic numerals (1, 2, 3) beginning on the first page of the report itself.

Make sure headings and subheadings in the table of contents match exactly the headings and subheadings in the report. You can create a table of contents manually, but to ensure consistency between the table of contents and the report's headings, you should create the table of contents using Word's (or other software) table of contents tool. (Search in the help field for "create a table of contents"). This feature will connect each item to the page where the heading or sub-heading occurs and will place dot leader lines (........) between the heading and the page number. The tool will also create indentations for secondary heading levels. For a sample table of contents, see page 295 (Figure 16.4).

LIST OF TABLES AND FIGURES. If your report contains more than three tables and/or figures, on a separate page following the table of contents, list these items and their corresponding page numbers. If the report contains less than three tables/figures, you may skip this list. (Note that APA style does not require a list of figures, but different instructors, organizations, and journals will have their own rules.)

ABSTRACT OR EXECUTIVE SUMMARY. Instead of reading an entire formal report, readers interested only in the big picture may consult the abstract or executive summary that commonly precedes the report proper (see Chapter 14). APA style requires an abstract; some workplace reports will require an executive summary instead. The purpose of this summary is to explain the issue, describe how you researched it, and state your conclusions (and, in the case of an executive summary, indicate what action the conclusions suggest). Busy readers can then flip through the document to locate sections important to them.

Make the abstract or executive summary as brief as you can. Summarize the report without adding new information or leaving out critical information. Write for a general audience and follow a sequence that moves from the reason the report was written, to the report's major findings, to conclusions and recommendations. For an example of an abstract, see page 296 (Figure 16.4).

Text of the Report

The text of the report consists of the introduction, the body, and the conclusion. If the report is a scientific or technical paper to be submitted for publication, the body of the report should be broken up into other sections (methods, results, discussion, and recommendations). Figure 16.4 on pages 293–307 of this chapter illustrate a research report written by a student, which follows the basic pattern below but contains some additional items in the body section. The requirements of your class instructor or the style and format used at your workplace may vary a bit from these guidelines.

INTRODUCTION.   The introduction engages and orients the audience and provides background as briefly as possible. Readers don't generally need a long history lesson. In your introduction, identify the topic's origin and significance, define or describe the problem or issue, and explain the report's purpose. Briefly identify your research methods (interviews, literature searches, and so on). List working definitions, but if you have more than five, place definitions in a glossary. Finally, if you have not done so in the abstract or executive summary, state your conclusion. Don't make readers wade through the entire report to find out what you are recommending or advising. For a sample introduction to a formal report, see page 297 (Figure 16.4).

BODY.   The body describes and explains your findings. Present a clear and detailed picture of the evidence, interpretations, and reasoning on which you will base your conclusion. Divide topics into subtopics, and use informative headings as aids to navigation, as described earlier in this chapter. The body of your report will vary greatly, depending on the audience, topic, purpose, and situation. The body of Figure 16.4 begins after the introduction of the report and ends with the recommendation at the end the report (pages 297–303 in this book).

CONCLUSION.   The conclusion is vital because it answers the questions that originally sparked the analysis. In the conclusion, you summarize, interpret, and recommend. Although you have interpreted evidence at each stage of your analysis, your conclusion presents a broad interpretation and suggests a course of action (where appropriate). Your conclusion should provide a clear and consistent perspective on the whole document. Don't introduce new ideas, facts, or statistics. Some conclusions take the form of a recommendation. See page 303 (Figure 16.4) for a sample conclusion.

End Matter

Following the text of the report (as needed) is the end matter, which may include a list of references cited in your report, a glossary, and/or appendices. Readers can refer to any of these supplements or skip them altogether, according to their needs.

REFERENCES OR WORKS CITED LIST.   If you have used outside sources in your report (and typically you should), you must provide a list of References (per APA style) or of Works Cited (per MLA style) just after the text of the report or on a separate page. For detailed advice on documenting sources using APA or MLA style, see Appendix A of this book. The long report in Figure 16.4 uses APA style and includes a References list (page 304).

GLOSSARY.   Use a glossary if your report contains more than five technical terms that may not be understood by all intended readers. If five or fewer terms need defining, place them in the report's introduction as working definitions or use footnote definitions. If you do include a separate glossary, announce its location when you introduce technical terms defined there ("see the glossary at the end of this report").

APPENDICES.   If you have large blocks of material or other documents that are relevant but will bog readers down, place these in an appendix. For example, if your report on the cost of electricity at your company refers to another report issued by the local utility company, you may wish to include this second report as an appendix. Other items that belong in an appendix might include complex formulas, interview questions and responses, maps, photographs, questionnaires and tabulated responses, texts of laws and regulations, and the like.

Do not stuff appendices with needless information or use them to bury bad or embarrassing news that belongs in the report itself. Title each appendix clearly: "Appendix A: Projected Costs." Mention the appendices early in the introduction, and refer readers to them at appropriate points in the report: "(see Appendix A)". The sample report in Figure 16.4 includes an appendix on page 306.

Strategies

for Formal Reports

- **Choose an appropriate delivery format.** On the job, formal reports are typically circulated via the organization's file server (intranet) and/or as email attachments. Some formal reports are made available publicly, such as on the organization's Web site. In class, you might be asked to upload your formal report to the class learning management system and to bring a paper copy to class.
- **Determine your audience.** Be sure you understand what your audience needs to know or do as a result of reading your report.
- **Determine your analytical approach.** Decide whether the primary purpose of the report is to compare items, look for a cause, or determine feasibility. Because formal reports are complex, also consider if the report will have a secondary purpose or purposes.
- **Do your research and document your sources.** For a long, formal report, research is paramount. Strive for accurate, appropriate, and clearly interpreted data. Always think critically about the sources you consult during the research process. Document all your sources within the report (using parenthetical citation—see page 393 for MLA style and page 404 for APA style) and at the end of the report (in a References or Works Cited list—see page 394 for MLA Works Cited entries and page 405 for APA References).

- **Work from a clear purpose statement.** You may need to revise your purpose statement during the research process as you uncover new information, but make sure the statement is finalized before you start writing your final draft of the report.
- **Use an understandable structure.** Follow the strategies in Chapter 5 for outlining, chunking, sequencing, paragraphing, and using headings.
- **Write with a readable style.** Follow the strategies in Chapter 6 to write with a clear, concise, fluent, and personable style.
- **Include audience-centered visuals.** Follow the strategies in Chapter 7 for using graphs, tables, charts, illustrations, diagrams, and photographs as appropriate to enhance, not decorate, the report.
- **Create a reader-friendly design.** Follow the strategies in Chapter 8 for consistency, cohesiveness, navigation, and emphasis.
- **Include all appropriate front matter.** If appropriate, include a letter of transmittal. Always include a title page as well as a table of contents and an abstract or executive summary. If your report contains plentiful visuals, include a list of tables and figures.
- **Provide an introduction, body, and conclusion.** In the text of the report, include an introduction to orient readers and provide background; a body with a clear and detailed presentation of findings; and a conclusion that answers the question or questions posed by the report, possibly with recommendations.
- **Include the appropriate end matter.** Always include a list of References (APA style) or of Works Cited (MLA style) on a separate page at the report's end. If your report includes more than five technical terms to be defined, place them in a glossary after the Works Cited or References page; otherwise, define the terms in your introduction or via footnotes in the report. Relevant secondary information that will not fit within the report (surveys, complex formulas, interviews, maps, and so on) belongs in an appendix at the very end.
- **Proofread.** If possible, get someone else to read and edit your report.

A Sample Formal Report

Figure 16.4 is a formal report. Its author, Crystal Cunningham, was a student in the B.S. program in dental hygiene at the University of Minnesota. For a final project in her technical writing class, she chose a real-life research situation that fit nicely with her major. Crystal chose to examine the relationship between periodontal disease in mothers and low birth weights in their babies. Her research is aimed at other dental hygiene experts; in particular, she wants to send her report to a professor in her department who might wish to continue this research.

With this audience in mind, Crystal makes appropriate choices about technical language, statistical analysis, and reference to scientific articles. While these approaches would not be suitable for a nonexpert audience, they are just right for an audience of her professor, students in this field, and other scientists. She understands that her primary purpose is to see if the literature can show a causal relationship. Another purpose is to convince her readers to take her work seriously so that her work might be continued and possibly published in a scientific journal (such a publication would then require that she write a new paper, one that conformed to the format and style of the journal).

Figure 16.4 A sample formal report

15 Timber Drive
St. Paul, MN 55666

28 August, 20XX

Professor Janet Belding
University of Minnesota
School of Dentistry
Minneapolis, MN 55444

Dear Dr. Belding:

Thank you for providing me with this opportunity to research the potential impacts
of periodontal disease on birth weights. Enclosed in this envelope is my final report,
"Effects of Periodontal Disease on Preterm Low Birth Weight Babies." In the Appendix
to this report, I recommend that we develop a proposal to explore this potential
causal connection.

If I can provide any other information as you review this report, please don't
hesitate to contact me. I look forward to meeting with you at a later date to hear
your thoughts. I hope this report is useful in your research program.

Yours truly,

Crystal Cunningham
Crystal Cunningham, B.S., Dental Hygiene

Letter of
transmittal
targets and
thanks
specific
reader and
provides
additional
context

continued

Figure 16.4 *continued*

Running head conforms to APA style

Title is clear and encompasses entire focus of the report

Effects of Periodontal Disease

on Preterm Low Birth Weight Babies

Crystal Cunningham

University of Minnesota

Author Note

Crystal Cunningham, B.S., Department of Dental Hygiene, School of Dentistry, University of Minnesota.

This report is submitted on March 15, 20XX, to Professor Janet Belding, Department of Dental Hygiene, School of Dentistry, University of Minnesota.

continued

Figure 16.4 *continued*

EFFECTS OF PERIODONTAL DISEASE   2

Table of Contents

Abstract 3

Background 4

Methodologies of the Studies 5

Results of the Studies 8

Limitations of the Studies 9

Conclusion 10

Recommendation 10

References 11

Appendix 13

Although APA style does not require a Table of Contents, this student's professor requested one as part of the report

Table of contents helps readers find information and visualize the structure of the report

continued

Figure 16.4 *continued*

Abstract fully summarizes the content of the report

Abstract

In this report, I have assessed ten recent studies of periodontal disease and its association with preterm and low birth weight infants. A number of these studies show some correlation between periodontal disease and premature birth weight or low birth weight. Several studies, however, are limited in scope and offer contradictory results. Therefore, based on the inconclusiveness of these studies, I recommend that a new University-based study be undertaken.

Keywords: periodontal disease, infants, premature birth weight, low birth weight

continued

Figure 16.4 *continued*

In the last ten to fifteen years, interesting findings in dental and obstetric research have linked periodontal disease in mothers to preterm low birth weight conditions in their babies. Many studies have found a correlation, while adequately controlling for confounding variables; the variables include age, smoking, diabetes, and other factors already contributing to preterm low birth weight babies. However a definitive link has yet to be found. This report examines the existing studies, charting their methodologies and results, and concludes with a recommendation for future research.

— Introduction does not need a title in APA style

— Introduction sets up the problem and indicates the report's causal approach

Background

The world has seen a rise in preterm low birth weight births in the last few decades. This fact has alarmed many physicians and obstetricians because there have been so many advancements in the medical field aiming to promote the health and longevity of life. Many reasons have been proposed to explain the reasons for preterm low birth weight births, but no conclusive answers have yet emerged. In the last ten years, some researchers have suggested that gingivitis and periodontal disease may be to blame for this occurrence. One possible cause could be the increase in harmful bacteria entering the bloodstream.

— Background section provides helpful but not overly detailed context

Preterm birth is considered to be any birth that occurs before 37 weeks of gestation; low birth weight is recognized as a weight of fewer than 2,500 grams. Many studies since the mid-1990s have attempted to find a correlation between periodontal disease and preterm low birth weight babies. However, research related to the possibility that periodontal disease increases the risk for preterm low birth weight babies has varied immensely over the years.

continued

Figure 16.4 *continued*

Clear purpose statement leads into the body of the report

This report is an assessment of ten peer–reviewed journal articles that seek to examine whether periodontal disease has any correlation with preterm low birth weight babies. The goal of this report is to find a correlation between gingivitis/periodontal disease and preterm low birth weight infants in previous studies and offer a brief recommendation to conduct a new study (see Appendix).

Methodologies of the Studies

Following is a summary of the methodologies used in the various studies:

Subheads within the Methodologies section make the section easy to follow

Time

Studies by Farrell, Ide, and Wilson (2006) and Dortbudak, Eberhardt, Ulm, and Persson (2005) examined women during pregnancy. In the Farrell et al. study, pregnant women were recruited at 12 weeks of gestation (p. 116). Subjects were excluded if gestational age was below 10 weeks or above 15 weeks. The Dortbudak et al. study maintained that it was crucial to examine patients during weeks 15–20 of gestational age because a sample of amniotic fluid is needed to assess for particular bacteria (p. 46). However, most studies waited to collect fluid samples until immediately after the birth.

Setting

Sentence variety and clear prose give the report a readable style

Most of these studies were conducted in hospital settings. The remaining studies were conducted after the subjects returned home from the hospital and were either instructed to return to their dental office or wait for an examiner to visit their home within 48 hours after birth. Some studies had a lengthier time frame to collect data following the birth, such as 72 hours, or five days as in a UK study (Buduneli et al., 2005, p. 176; Moore, Randhawa, & Ide, 2005, p. 3).

continued

Figure 16.4 *continued*

EFFECTS OF PERIODONTAL DISEASE   6

Examiners

   Examiners in these studies were calibrated and blind, and often a single examiner
was used (Alves & Ribeiro, 2006, p. 322; Bassani, Olinto, & Kreiger, 2007, p. 37;
Gazolla et al., 2007, p. 844; Jarjoura et al., 2005, p. 516; Moliterno, Monteiro,
Figueredo, & Fischer, 2005, p. 887; Moore et al., 2005, p. 2). The study by Farrell et al.
(2006) involved three examiners, which allowed more subjects to be evaluated (p. 117).

Exclusion Criteria

   A questionnaire/interview was given to patients (Bassani et al., 2007, p. 32; Bosnjak,
Relja, Vucicevic-Boras, Plasaj, & Plancak, 2006, p. 712; Farrell et al., 2006, p. 117; Jarjoura
et al., 2005, p. 516; Moliterno et al., 2005, p. 888; Moore et al., 2005, p. 3). These
questions pertained to socioeconomic status, race, education, occupation, marital
status, smoking, drinking, medications, pregnancies, preterm deliveries, and prenatal
care (Gazolla et al., 2007, p. 843).

   The information gathered from questions and patients' medical records excluded
many subjects from the study. Exclusion criteria included diabetes, anemia,
cardiovascular disorders, hepatic deficiency, high blood pressure, TB, cancer, seizure
disorders, psychopathology, asthma, STD, HIV, fetal or uterine anomalies, cervical
incompetence, labor induction, and multiple birth pregnancies (Buduneli et al., 2005,
p. 177; Gazolla et al., 2007, p. 844; Jarjoura et al., p. 516; Moliterno et al., p. 887;
Moore et al., p. 4). Another common exclusion involved subjects who required
prophylactic antibiotics prior to dental treatment (Farrell et al., p. 117; Jarjoura et
al., p. 513; Moore et al., p. 3).

Writer uses accurate and clearly interpreted data

No year needed for work that follows closely after the initial reference

continued

Figure 16.4 *continued*

Data Collection

The most common measurements in each trial were pocket depths, clinical attachment levels, and bleeding on probing. A periodontal probe of varying markings was used to assess the extent of periodontal involvement. A few studies included a plaque index along with the previously mentioned tests (Farrell et al., 2006, p. 117; Jarjoura et al., 2005, p. 515; Moore et al., 2005, p. 3). One study, by Alves and Ribeiro, also included calculus detection (2006, p. 319). DMFT scores were taken into account in two other studies (Bosnjak et al., 2006, p. 712; Buduneli et al., 2005, p. 176).

Most of the studies gathered periodontal measurements from six different sites on one tooth throughout the entire dentition (Alves & Ribeiro, 2006, p. 319; Bassani et al., 2007, p. 36; Buduneli et al., 2005, p. 176; Gazolla et al., 2007, p. 845; Moliterno et al., 2005, p. 887). However other studies assessed fewer sites, for example mesial, distal, buccal, and lingual surfaces (Bosnjak et al., 2006, p. 711; Dortbudak et al., 2005, p. 47). Columbia University collected data from three sites: mesiobuccal, midbuccal, and distobuccal in two randomly selected quadrants (Jarjoura et al., 2005, p. 514). The fewest measurements were taken from one tooth at only two sites, in a UK study. These sites were midbuccal and mesiobuccal in the maxillary and midlingual and mesiolingual in the mandibular (Moore et al., 2005, p. 3).

Three studies included a subgingival plaque sample from the mesial and distal aspect of certain teeth. The sample was obtained by placing a paperpoint into the sulcus and analyzing the type of bacteria collected (Buduneli et al., 2005, p. 177; Dortbudak et al., 2005, p. 46; Jarjoura et al., 2005, p. 518).

An interesting study was conducted by Dortbudak et al. (2005). A periodontal exam was completed as in other studies; however, this study included collection of amniotic

All information from outside sources is documented in text

Writer not only describes but critiques the previous studies examined

continued

Figure 16.4 *continued*

fluid at 15–20 weeks. These women were already scheduled to have amniocentesis tests for medical purposes. Two milliliters of additional fluid were collected and analyzed for particular bacteria. The results concluded that an increased number of certain bacteria from the fluid placed these women at a higher risk for premature birth. An obvious limitation to this study, however, was that women undergoing an amniocentesis are already at an increased risk for problems during their pregnancy, or they would not be having the test in the first place (p. 51).

Results of the Studies

The research analyzed for this report demonstrates varying degrees of correlation between periodontal disease and birth weight of preterm low weight babies (PTLWB). See Table 1 for summary.

— Writer provides bottom-line results of previous studies

Table 1. Results of major studies

Correlation	Correlation percentages	Comments
High correlation:		
Alves and Ribeiro 2006, p. 323	84.21%	High correlation found.
Bosnjak et al., 2006, p. 716	73.26%	Similar correlation found between PTLWB and tobacco use (p. 716).
Dortbudak et al., 2005, p. 52	83%	No bacteria found in amniotic fluid: authors still believe maternal periodontitis could be causal.
Jarjoura et al., 2005, p. 522; Moliterno et al., 2005, p. 890	No percentages given.	Both found statistically significant casual connections.
Low correlation:		
Bassani et al., 2007, p. 39	No significant correlation.	While 59% of subjects had periodontal disease, causality was not established.
Buduneli et al., 2005, p. 181; Farrell et al., 2006, p. 120	No significant correlation.	No differences established.
Gazolla et al., 2007, p. 879	No significant correlation.	Note that the group not treated with scaling/ root planning had 79% PTLWB.

continued

Figure 16.4 *continued*

As summarized in Table 1, recent studies offer conflicting results about the relationship between periodontal disease and the birth of preterm low weight babies. The two studies to establish high, statistically significant correlations are Alves and Ribeiro (2006) and Dortbudak et al. (2005), but as noted, Dortbudak et al. did not actually find bacteria in the amniotic fluid, thus requiring the authors to make something of a casual leap. As noted in the next section, there were also other limitations to all these studies.

Limitations of the Studies

All these studies involved limitations, the most obvious being the sample size. Two studies had a sample of less than 100 subjects (Alves & Ribeiro, 2006, p. 318; Dortbudak et al., 2005, p. 45). Another limitation was the location of the studies. Many well-known studies were conducted outside the United States, in countries such as Croatia, United Kingdom, Turkey, and two in Brazil.

Almost all of these studies were conducted in lower socioeconomic areas, in developing countries, with more uniform ethnic and racial groups. Pregnant Croatian women were studied because they tend to develop more pronounced periodontal disease (Bosnjak et al., 2006, p. 710).

Limitations in only a couple cases were the ages of the subjects. It is well known that having a child above or beneath a certain age poses potential problems for the mother and child, not to mention the strong correlation between age and increased periodontal disease. Only two studies imposed a restriction on age. One study only allowed an age range of 18 to 35 years (Buduneli et al., 2005, p. 174); another only allowed an age range of 18 to 30 years (Gazolla et al., 2007, p. 842).

The writer is careful to list the limitations of previous studies

continued

Figure 16.4 *continued*

Conclusion

In conclusion, several studies found a correlation between periodontal disease and preterm low birth weight babies, even when accounting for possible confounding variables. On the other hand, many found no correlation between periodontal disease and preterm low birth weight babies. These researchers make the argument that their counterparts who did find a correlation did not account for all confounding variables.

The research conducted pertaining to the correlation between preterm low birth weight babies and periodontal disease, then, continues to result in conflicting conclusions. More research is needed in order to arrive at definitive conclusions.

Recommendation

See Appendix for a brief discussion about a proposed new study.

Conclusion provides a summary of the report

Because the report takes the causal approach, the writer is careful to show that correlation does not always equal causation

continued

Figure 16.4 *continued*

EFFECTS OF PERIODONTAL DISEASE   11

References

Alves, R. T., & Ribeiro, R. A. (2006). Relationship between maternal periodontal

    disease and birth of preterm low weight babies. *Pesquisa Odontologica Brasileira*,

    20 (4), 319–323.

Bassani, D. G., Olinto, M. T., & Kreiger, N. (2007). Periodontal disease and

    perinatal outcomes: A case-control study. *Journal of Clinical Periodontology*,

    34 (1), 32–39.

Bosnjak, A., Relja, T., Vucicevic-Boras, V., Plasaj, H., & Plancak, D. (2006). Pre-term

    delivery and periodontal disease: A case-control study from Croatia. *Journal of*

    Clinical Periodontology, *33* (10), 710–716.

Buduneli, N., Baylas, H., Buduneli, E., Turkoglu, O., Kose, T., & Dahlen, G. (2005).

    Periodontal infections and pre-term low birth weight: A case-control study.

    Journal of Clinical Periodontology, *32* (2), 174–181.

Dortbudak, O., Eberhardt, R., Ulm, M., & Persson, G. R. (2005). Periodontitis, a

    marker of risk in pregnancy for preterm birth. *Journal of Clinical Periodontology*,

    32 (1), 46–52.

Farrell, S., Ide, M., & Wilson, R. F. (2006). The relationship between maternal

    periodontitis, adverse pregnancy outcome and miscarriage in never smokers.

    Journal of Clinical Periodontology, *33* (2), 116–120.

Gazolla, C. M., Ribeiro, A., Moyses, M. R., Oliveira, L. A., Pereira, L. J., &

    Sallum, A. W. (2007). Evaluation of the incidence of preterm low birth weight

    in patients undergoing periodontal therapy. *Journal of Periodontology*, *78* (5),

    842–849.

Reference page immediately follows the report and lists all sources consulted in APA style

continued

Figure 16.4 *continued*

EFFECTS OF PERIODONTAL DISEASE   12

Jarjoura, K., Devine, P. C., Perez-Delboy, A., Herrera-Abreu, M., D'Alton, M., &
    Papapanou, P. N. (2005). Markers of periodontal infection and preterm birth.
    American Journal of Obstetrics and Gynecology, 192 (2), 513–522.

Moliterno, L. F., Monteiro, B., Figueredo, C. M., & Fischer, R. G. (2005). Association
    between periodontitis and low birth weight: A case-control study. *Journal of
    Clinical Periodontology, 32* (8), 887–890.

Moore, S., Randhawa, M., & Ide, M. (2005). A case-control study to investigate an
    association between adverse pregnancy outcome and periodontal disease. *Journal
    of Clinical Periodontology, 32* (1), 2–4.

Figure 16.4 *continued*

Appendix

Recommendation for Future Research

Overview

Content that is not central to the report goes into an appendix

Based on the existing studies described in this report, I recommend we propose a new study to explore a possible correlation between periodontal disease and preterm low birth weight babies. This study would measure six surfaces on every tooth; most importantly, it would gather a baseline periodontal reading within eight weeks after conception. Using this approach, we can measure to see if there has been any significant difference in periodontal disease during pregnancy or if the subject has always had the same level of disease. This more exacting approach should increase the accuracy and reliability of the findings. In a forthcoming proposal, I will describe this study in detail. For the purposes of this Appendix, I have outlined two key areas.

Research Design

The research design of this study would not involve any manipulation of subjects; patients are only observed for changes in their periodontal status. Therefore, the design of this study is quantitative, nonexperimental, and correlational.

Sample

The sample would include 500 women from the Twin Cities Area. Women cannot be more than eight weeks pregnant to be included in the study. Exclusion criteria include women with diabetes and other systemic illnesses, previous birth complications, and previous abuse of alcohol or other illegal substances.

Checklist

for Formal Reports

- ❏ Have I determined the audience for this report?
- ❏ Have I decided on the purpose, and have I chosen the right analytical approach (comparative, causal, feasibility) to fit this purpose?
- ❏ Did I evaluate all sources consulted while researching?
- ❏ Are my data accurate, appropriate, and clearly interpreted?
- ❏ Does my report have a clearly defined purpose statement early in the report?
- ❏ Is the structure of the report logical and appropriate for this setting?
- ❏ Is the writing style clear and professional?
- ❏ If there are visuals in my report, are the visuals supportive of what is in the text?
- ❏ Are the pages well designed and easy to follow?
- ❏ Is there a distinct introduction, body, and conclusion?
- ❏ Does the introduction provide enough of an orientation to the issue or problem without being too long?
- ❏ Does the body of the report offer a clear picture of the issue or problem?
- ❏ Does the conclusion answer the question that originally sparked the analysis?
- ❏ Have I included all the required and appropriate front and end matter?
- ❏ Have I documented all my sources both in the text and in a References or Works Cited list?

Applications

General Applications

1. Choose a specific audience and purpose, based on a real-life situation at school or at work, and write out some ideas for how you would determine whether this situation is an appropriate one for a formal report. List all possible readers (audience members) and all possible purposes. List the kinds of questions your report will need to answer, and then list the kinds of research you will need to do in order to write the report. Bring this document to class for a discussion.

2. Prepare a formal report using causal, comparative, or feasibility analysis (or some combination). As you prepare your report, refer to the Strategies for Formal Reports on pages 291–292, the Checklist, and other materials in this chapter.

Team Application

In the workplace, it is common for reports to be written not by one individual but in teams. Thinking of an idea you might have for a report for this class, ask yourself whether this report might be a team project. How would you divide the tasks and ensure the work was being done fairly? What are the advantages and disadvantages of a team approach to a report? In groups of two to three, discuss these issues. If your instructor indicates that your report is to be team-based, write a memo (as a team) to your instructor indicating the role of each team member and the timeline.

Global Application

Go online and look for reports written in English by government agencies of different countries. See if you can use the material from this chapter to determine if the reports fall into causal, comparative, or feasibility categories. Look for similarities to the reports you are familiar with within the United States (or the one you are preparing for class), as well as differences in features such as structure and organization, word choice, formatting, use of visuals, levels of politeness, and so on.

Digital and Social Media Application

Look at the Team Application above and think about ways your team could best use digital and social media to collaborate on the report. For example, you could start a shared Google document and use the document and the chat feature to brainstorm ideas. Then, once you have a draft outline and set of ideas, you could convert this file to Word and use your class learning management system or email to share drafts back and forth. Each member of the team should use track changes to edit drafts of the document, and use a system for naming the versions of your files: for instance, file names such as "ClassReport_v1" would indicate version 1; use the same naming conventions for versions 2, 3, and so forth. Finally, once the report is complete (use the Checklist in this chapter to be sure), convert the file to PDF. Explore how to use the PDF comments feature as a way readers could provide input on your report.

Chapter 17
Proposals

Learning Objectives

17.1 Define proposals and understand the audience and purpose of them.

17.2 Identify the various types of proposals.

17.3 Include all of the essential parts when organizing an informal or formal proposal.

Chapter Outline

Audience and Purpose of Proposals   310

Types of Proposals   311
Organization of Informal and Formal Proposals   316
    Strategies for Proposals   317
    Checklist for Proposals   329

Applications   329

How proposals
and reports
differ

Proposals encourage an audience to take some form of direct action: to authorize a project, purchase a service or product, or support a specific plan for solving a problem. Although often containing the same basic elements as reports (see Chapters 15 and 16), proposals have *one* specific purpose: to persuade the audience to say "Yes, let's move ahead with this plan." This purpose may sound similar to the purpose of a recommendation report. However, while a recommendation report answers the question "What should we do, and why?" a proposal maps out the steps for getting it done: "Here's what we should do, and here's how we can do it."

Proposals are called for in a variety of situations: a request to fund a training program for new employees, a suggestion to change the curriculum of your English or biology department, a bid to the U.S. Department of Energy on a solar energy project, and so on. As a student or as an intern at a nonprofit agency, you might submit a formal grant proposal requesting financial support for a research or community project. If your job depends on funding from outside sources, proposals might be the most important documents you produce. Depending on the situation, proposals may be short (informal) or long (formal) and may be written in the form of a report, a letter, or a memo.

Audience and Purpose of Proposals

17.1 Define proposals and understand the audience and purpose of them.

Audience
considerations

In science, business, industry, government, and education, proposals are written for any number of audiences: managers, executives, directors, clients, board members, or community leaders. Inside or outside the organization, these people review various proposals and then decide whether the plans are worthwhile, the projects will materialize, and the services or products are useful.

The singular purpose of proposals is to persuade your audience to say yes to your plan.

Purpose considerations

Types of Proposals

17.2 Identify the various types of proposals.

Proposals may be either *solicited* or *unsolicited*. Solicited proposals are those that have been requested by a manager, client, or customer. For example, if you represent an engineering firm specializing in highway construction, you may receive a request for proposal (RFP) from a local township asking you to bid on a road project. Typically, an RFP is issued to numerous companies, and your proposal will need to stack up against all the others. Unsolicited proposals are those that have not been requested. If you are a new advertising agency in town, you may send out short unsolicited proposals to local radio stations suggesting that they use your agency for their advertising needs.

Because the audience for a solicited proposal has made a specific request, you will not need to spend time introducing yourself or providing background on the product or service. For an unsolicited proposal (sometimes termed a "cold call" in sales), you will need to catch readers' attention quickly and provide incentives for them to continue reading: perhaps by printing a price comparison of your fees on the first page, for example.

Solicited and unsolicited proposals

Proposals may also be *informal* or *formal*. Informal proposals, like informal reports, can take the form of an email or memo (if distributed within an organization) or a letter (when sent outside an organization). Formal proposals, meanwhile, take on a similar format as formal reports (see Chapter 16), typically including front matter, the text of the report, and end matter, if applicable. Formal proposals will be discussed later in this chapter.

Informal and formal proposals

Both solicited and unsolicited proposals, whether informal or formal, fall into three categories: planning proposals, research proposals, and sales proposals.

Planning Proposals

Planning proposals offer solutions to a problem or suggestions for improvement. A planning proposal might be a request for funding to expand the campus newspaper (as in the formal proposal at the end of this chapter), an architectural plan for new facilities at a ski area, or a plan to develop energy alternatives to fossil fuels.

Characteristics of planning proposals

Figure 17.1 is a solicited, informal planning proposal that will be used by bank loan officers when deciding whether to grant a construction loan. Because this document is addressed to external readers, it is cast as a letter. For specific advice on how to approach planning proposals, read the annotations accompanying Figure 17.1 and see the Strategies for Proposals on pages 316–317.

Figure 17.1 A planning proposal

P.O. Box 185
Amherst, MA 01002

March 15, 20XX

Ambrose Savings Bank
South Haley Street
Weaton, MA 09758

Provides a clear subject line ⟶ Subject: Proposal to erect a new dwelling

Dear Mr. Smith:

Introduction states purpose, identifies plan, gives background, and provides a timetable ⟶ As we discussed in our meeting on March 6, this letter is in application for a construction loan in the amount of $300,000, on an interest-only basis, for the construction of the described residence (plans and specifications are enclosed) on Lot #6 of my Leverett property. Anticipated sales price of the completed home is $398,000, including the standard realtor's commission. I have already completed clearing work and some excavation, and I expect weather conditions to permit the commencement of foundation work within the next three weeks. Construction time is projected at approximately five months, with completion targeted for September 1, 20XX.

Body paragraph spells out details (what will be done, qualifications, obtaining permits) ⟶ The quality of construction materials and workmanship will be comparable to the adjacent three homes, which you have inspected. Exterior woodwork will be executed in Western Red Cedar, while interior finishes will comprise masonry, dry-wall, and Philippine mahogany. All sashes, doors, flooring, cabinets, and special millwork will be designed and custom fabricated. Water supply and waste disposal will be handled on-site; the appropriate permits have already been obtained. The heating system will be oil-fired hot air, ducted for the later addition of air conditioning. All windows and skylights will be double-glazed and insulation will be maximized.

Concluding paragraph thanks the reader and encourages acceptance of the proposal ⟶ Thank you for giving this proposal your immediate attention. I will be pleased to provide any additional information you may require.

Very truly yours,

Gerald A. Jackson

Gerald A. Jackson

GAJ/ch

Enclosures: architect's drawings
                    specifications

Research Proposals

Research (or grant) proposals request approval and funding for research projects. For example, a chemist at a university might address a research proposal to the Environmental Protection Agency for funds to identify toxic contaminants in local groundwater. Research proposals are solicited by many agencies, including the National Science Foundation and the National Institutes of Health. Each agency has its own requirements and guidelines for proposal format and content. Successful research proposals follow these guidelines and carefully articulate the goals of the project. In these cases, proposal readers will generally be other scientists, so writers can use language appropriate for other experts (as in the Appendix in Figure 16.4, page 306).

> Characteristics of research proposals

Figure 17.2 is a solicited, informal research proposal from an employee in the marketing and research department to her supervisor, proposing to conduct research into management-employee relations at a single location of the company that has experienced problems in this area. Because this document is addressed to an internal reader (the supervisor), it has been cast as a memo. For specific advice on how to approach research proposals, read the annotations accompanying Figure 17.2 and see the Strategies for Proposals on pages 317–318.

Sales Proposals

Sales proposals offer services or products and may be solicited or unsolicited. If solicited, several firms may be competing for the same contract, so submitted proposals may be ranked by a committee. Sales proposals can be cast as letters if the situation calls for them to be brief. If the situation requires a longer proposal, include the various parts and elements of formal proposals. A successful sales proposal persuades customers that your product or service surpasses those of any competitors. What you include in a sales proposal is determined by the guidelines from the client or by a thorough analysis of the kinds of information your audience needs.

> Characteristics of sales proposals

Figure 17.3 is an example of a solicited, informal sales proposal, in which the writer explains why her machinery is best for the job, what qualifications her company can offer, and what costs are involved. As with Figure 17.1, because this document is addressed to external readers, it is cast as a letter. For specific advice on how to approach sales proposals, read the annotations accompanying Figure 17.3 and see the Strategies for Proposals on pages 317–318.

Figure 17.2 A research proposal (memo format)

MEMORANDUM

To: James Granger, Vice President, Marketing and Research Division
From: Anne Hickett, Analyst, Marketing and Research Division
Date: March 4, 20XX
Subject: Report proposal regarding the South Dennis location

Proposed Study

In answer to your March 2 request for a research report due May 10, I propose to study the ongoing problem of low employee morale at our Foodstuff Supermarket in South Dennis. Following are the specifications:

Statement of Problem

During my two years as a part-time employee at Foodstuff, I worked at a location with similar problems. I have witnessed firsthand the high turnover and general employee dissatisfaction over the work situation and store management policies. Because we have heard continuing complaints about management–employee relations at the South Dennis location, including from top management, I propose to research the situation and offer potential solutions.

Scope of Proposed Study

My study will explore the following issues:

1. An assessment of the efficiency of Foodstuff's South Dennis management by drawing parallels and contrasts between the actual management operation and principles of effective management that I will identify and collect from my secondary sources.
2. A consideration of the direct or indirect effects that any management problem might have on employee morale.
3. An assessment of the management's effectiveness in employee motivation.
4. An assessment of the role of effective communication in all management–employee relations.

Methods and Data Sources

My secondary research will include library resources on the topic of management, as well as reliable Web resources. Primary research will include personal observation at the South Dennis site, which I will visit next Thursday; a survey (see attached) to be distributed to all of the South Dennis management and employees; and interviews with both employee and management representatives at the South Dennis location. All conclusions and any recommendations for positive change will be based on the collected evidence in my report.

If you have any further questions, I will be happy to discuss this proposal with you at your convenience.

Opens with general description of the problem and a proposed study

Describes the problem in detail as well as the writer's qualifications

Details overall scope of study

Details specific approaches to the research

Encourages reader acceptance

Figure 17.3 A sales proposal

Modern Landscaping
23–44 18th Street
Sunnyside, NY 11104

October 4, 20XX

Martin Haver
35–66 114th Avenue
Jamaica, NY 11107

Subject: Proposal to dig a trench and move boulders at Bliss site

Dear Mr. Haver:

I've inspected your property and would be happy to undertake the landscaping project necessary for the development of your farm. → Describes the subject and purpose

The backhoe I use cuts a span 3 feet wide and can dig as deep as 18 feet—more than an adequate depth for the mainline pipe you wish to lay. Because this backhoe is on tracks rather than tires and is hydraulically operated, it is particularly efficient in moving rocks. I have more than twelve years of experience with backhoe work and have completed many jobs similar to this one. → Gives the writer's qualifications

After examining the huge boulders that block access to your property, I am convinced they can be moved only if I dig out underneath and exert upward pressure with the hydraulic ram while you push forward on the boulders with your D-9 Caterpillar. With this method, we can move enough rock to enable you to farm that now inaccessible tract. Because of its power, my larger backhoe will save you both time and money in the long run. → Explains how the job will be done / Maintains a confident tone throughout

This job should take 12 to 15 hours, unless we encounter subsurface ledge formations. My fee is $200 per hour. The fact that I provide my own dynamiting crew at no extra charge should be an advantage to you because you have so much rock to be moved. → Gives a qualified cost estimate

Please phone me any time for more information. I'm sure we can do the job economically and efficiently. → Encourages reader acceptance by emphasizing economy and efficiency

Sincerely yours,
Sharon Ingram
Sharon Ingram

Organization of Informal and Formal Proposals

17.3 **Include all of the essential parts when organizing an informal or formal proposal.**

Follow a problem-solution or situation-resolution pattern

No matter the type, all proposals must move in a logical direction from problem/situation to solution/resolution. All effective proposals typically include a clear title or subject line; background information; a statement of the problem or situation; a description of how to solve the problem or resolve the situation; a breakdown of costs, timing, or qualifications (if applicable); and a conclusion that induces readers to act.

Include front matter and end matter as needed

Formal proposals typically require *front matter,* including a title page, a table of contents, an abstract or executive summary, and possibly a letter of transmittal. *End matter* would include appendices and a list of sources cited (if the formal proposal has entailed research, which it usually will). For more information on these components, see Chapter 16 (pages 288–291); front matter and end matter are presented in the same way in a formal proposal as in a formal report.

Clear Title or Subject Line

Clearly announce your proposal

State the proposal's purpose with a clear and complete title, such as "Recommended Wastewater Treatment System for the MudPie Resort and Spa," (for a formal proposal) or a subject line (in an informal proposal). Avoid being vague or overly general. An overworked decision maker facing a stack of proposals might very well decide that a proposal lacking a clear, focused title or subject line probably will be unclear and unfocused in its content, too.

Background Information

Provide your readers with background context

A background section can be brief or long. In Figure 17.1, the writer's opening sentence ("As we discussed in our meeting on March 6…") provides a quick reminder of the context for the project. This sentence is brief because the reader is already familiar with the project. For a new audience or in an unsolicited proposal, you may need to provide a longer paragraph (or, in the case of a formal proposal, a full introduction) with background information on the project. If the topic warrants, the background section may take up several pages.

Statement of Problem or Situation

Clearly describe the problem or situation

The problem or situation and its resolution form the backbone of any proposal. Describe the problem or situation statement in either the background portion of your proposal or in its own headed section. For example, a good statement of the problem or situation might be: "Complaints about noise in our college library call for a plan that will make areas of the library quiet enough for serious study."

Description of Solution or Resolution

The bulk of the proposal should map out your plan to solve the problem or resolve the situation. Include in this section as much detail as needed for your audience to evaluate the soundness of your plan. If the plan is vague or unrealistic, the proposal will be rejected.

Fully explain how you plan to solve the problem or resolve the situation

Costs, Timing, and Qualifications

If your proposal involves financial outlay, timing sensitivity, or proof of your qualifications, provide separate sections dealing with these factors. Make sure your breakdown of costs and timing is accurate, easy to understand, and realistic. If you work with an accountant or other financial specialist, ask that person to check your cost figures. If the proposal is solicited, make sure you follow the client's guidelines for establishing a budget and/or schedule.

Spell out any particulars involving money, time, and expertise

Conclusion

The conclusion reaffirms the need for your plan and induces the audience to act. A conclusion does not need to be more than a sentence or two in an informal proposal (longer, of course, in a formal proposal), but no matter the length, always end on a strong note with a conclusion that is assertive, confident, and encouraging.

End with a call to action

Strategies

for Proposals

- **Choose an appropriate delivery format.** See Chapter 16 (page 291) for this same strategy as applied to reports.
- **Consider your audience and purpose.** Remember that your audience consists of decision makers; therefore, the purpose of any proposal must be to convince the decision makers to say yes to what you propose.
- **Understand the audience's needs.** Proposal audiences want specific suggestions to meet their specific needs. Their main question will be "What will this plan do for me?" Demonstrate a clear understanding of the audience's problem or situation, and then offer an appropriate solution or resolution.
- **Perform research as needed.** Research the very latest technology for solving a problem or resolving a situation; compare the costs, benefits, and drawbacks of various approaches; contact others in your field for their suggestions; find out what competitors are up to; and so on.
- **Be sure to credit information sources and contributors.** Complex proposals rarely emerge from thin air, and proposals are often a result of a team effort. If anything in your proposal represents the work or input of others, document the sources or acknowledge fellow contributors.
- **Use an appropriate document type and delivery format.** For an informal proposal distributed internally, use the body of an email (if brief) or a memo. For an informal proposal distributed externally, use a letter. For a formal proposal distributed internally, include all the required components and use an email attachment or your company's Intranet. For a formal proposal distributed externally, include all the required components and provide a letter of transmittal.

- **Provide a clear title or subject line and background information.** Draw readers into your proposal with a title or subject line that describes the content of the proposal exactly, and orient your readers with the appropriate background information.
- **Follow a problem-to-solution or situation-to-resolution organizational pattern.** All proposals should move in this sequence from beginning to end.
- **Spell out the problem (and its causes) or situation clearly and convincingly.** Provide enough detail for your audience to appreciate the importance of the problem or situation. Answer the implied question, "Why is this such a big deal?"
- **Point out the benefits of solving the problem.** Answer the implied question, "Why should we spend time, money, and effort to do this?"
- **Offer a realistic solution or resolution.** Stick to claims or assertions you can support. Answer the implied question, "How do we know this will work?" If the solution or resolution involves accounting for costs, budgeting time, or proving your qualifications, include this information.
- **Address anticipated objections to your solution.** Decision makers typically approach a proposal with skepticism, especially if the project will cost them money and time. Answer the implied question, "Why should we accept the things that seem wrong with your plan?"
- **Include all necessary details, but don't overload.** Include as much supporting detail as you need to induce readers to say yes to your proposal. Leave nothing to guesswork. At the same time, don't overload your readers with information that is not directly relevant.
- **Write clearly and concisely.** Make sure your document is easy to read, uses action verbs, and avoids puffed-up language or terms that are too technical for your audience. If necessary for a mixed audience with differing technical levels, include a glossary.
- **Express confidence.** You are trying to sell yourself, your ideas, or your services to a skeptical audience. Be upfront about the supporting facts and state your case directly.
- **Make honest and supportable claims.** Because they often involve large sums of money, investments of time, and contractual obligations, proposals require a solid ethical and legal foundation. Don't make false promises, and if the solutions you offer have limitations, say so.
- **Induce readers to act.** Decide exactly what you want readers to do, and give reasons why they should be the ones to act. In your conclusion, answer the implied question, "What action am I supposed to take?"

A Sample Formal Proposal

Figure 17.4 was written because a state university's newspaper (SMU Torch) is struggling to meet rising costs. Because of budget cuts, the newspaper received no funding increase for three years. Bill Trippe, the Torch's business manager, must justify a requested increase of 20.6 percent. Before drafting his proposal, Bill analyzed the audience and purpose. He determined that the primary audience (the Student Fee Allocation Committee) would use the document to decide whether to grant the additional funds and that therefore, the primary purpose must be to provide a convincing rationale. Bill has thus included a detailed plan for reducing existing operating costs, a section outlining next year's projected costs, and an appendix comparing the Torch's performance with that of other nearby college newspapers. These materials demonstrate how Bill has anticipated his audience's possible objections.

Figure 17.4 A formal proposal

SMU *Torch*

Old Westport Road
North Dartmouth, Massachusetts 02747

May 1, 20XX

Charles Marcus, Chair
Student Fee Allocation Committee
Southeastern Massachusetts University
North Dartmouth, MA 02747

Dear Dean Marcus:

No one needs to be reminded about the effects of increased costs on our campus community. We are all faced with having to make do with less.

Accordingly, we at the *Torch* have spent long hours devising a plan to cope with increased production costs—without compromising the newspaper's tradition of quality service. I think you and your colleagues will agree that our plan is realistic and feasible. Even the "bare-bones" operation that will result from our proposed spending cuts, however, will call for a $6,478.57 increase in next year's budget.

We have received no funding increase in three years. Our present need is absolute. Without additional funds, the *Torch* simply cannot continue to function as a professional newspaper. I therefore submit the following budget proposal for your consideration.

Respectfully,

William Trippe

William Trippe
Business Manager, SMU *Torch*

Letter of transmittal provides additional context and persuasion

continued

Figure 17.4 *continued*

Provides a clear title

A Funding Proposal
for
the SMU *Torch*
(20XX–XX)

Prepared for
the Student Fee Allocation Committee
Southeastern Massachusetts University
North Dartmouth, Massachusetts

Writer, affiliation, and date always appear on the title page

by
William Trippe
Torch Business Manager

May 1, 20XX

continued

Figure 17.4 *continued*

ii

Table of Contents

Page

Informative Abstract iii

Introduction 1
    Overview 1
    Background 1
    Statement of Problem 1
    Need 2
    Scope 2

Proposed Plan 2
    Methods 2
    Costs 3
    Feasibility 5
    Personnel 5

Conclusion 5

Appendix (Comparative Performance) 6

Table of contents orients readers and demonstrates proposal's structure

continued

Figure 17.4 *continued*

Informative Abstract

Abstract
accurately
encapsulates
entire document

The SMU *Torch*, the student newspaper at Southeastern Massachusetts University, is crippled by inadequate funding, having received no budget increase in three years. Increased costs and inadequate funding are the major problems facing the *Torch*. Increases in costs of technology upgrades and in printing have called for cutbacks in production. Moreover, our low staff salaries are inadequate to attract and retain qualified personnel. A nominal pay increase would make salaries more competitive.

Our staff plans to cut costs by reducing page count and by hiring a new press for the *Torch*'s printing work. The only proposed cost increase (for staff salaries) is essential.

A detailed breakdown of projected costs establishes the need for a $6,478.57 budget increase to keep the paper a weekly publication with adequate page count to serve our campus.

Compared with similar newspapers at other colleges, the *Torch* makes much better use of its money. The comparison figures in the Appendix illustrate the cost-effectiveness of our proposal.

continued

Figure 17.4 *continued*

Introduction

Overview

Our campus newspaper faces the contradictory challenge of surviving ever-growing production costs while maintaining its reputation for quality. The following proposal addresses that crisis. This plan's ultimate success, however, depends on the Allocation Committee's willingness to approve a long-overdue increase in the *Torch*'s upcoming yearly budget.

Opens with an overview of the situation

Background

In ten years, the *Torch* has grown in size, scope, and quality. Roughly 6,000 copies (24 pages/issue) are printed weekly for each fourteen-week semester. Each week, the *Torch* prints national and local press releases, features, editorials, sports articles, announcements, notices, classified ads, a calendar column, and letters to the editor.

A vital part of university life, our newspaper provides a forum for information, ideas, and opinions—all with the highest professionalism. This year we published an online version as well.

Provides relevant background

Statement of Problem

With much of its staff about to graduate, the *Torch* faces next year with rising costs in every phase of production and the need to replace outdated and worn equipment.

Our newspaper also suffers from a lack of student involvement: Despite gaining valuable experience and potential career credentials, few students can be expected to work without some kind of remuneration. Most staff members do receive nominal weekly salaries: from $20 for the distributor to $90 for the Editor-in-Chief. But salaries averaging barely $5 per hour cannot possibly compete with the minimum wage. Since more and more SMU students must work part-time, the *Torch* will have to make its salaries more competitive.

The newspaper's operating expenses can be divided into four categories: hardware and software upgrades, salaries, printing costs, and miscellaneous (office supplies, mail, and so on). The first three categories account for nearly 90 percent of the budget. Over the past year, costs in all categories have increased: from as little as 2 percent for miscellaneous expenses to as much as 19 percent for technology upgrades. Printing costs (roughly one-third of our total budget) rose 9 percent in the past year, and another price hike of 10 percent has just been announced.

Describes the problem concisely

continued

Figure 17.4 *continued*

Proposes a
logical solution
to the problem,
based on
evidence

Need

Despite growing production costs, the *Torch* has received no increase in its yearly budget allocation ($37,400) in three years. Inadequate funding is virtually crippling our newspaper.

Previews the
plan before
getting into
details

Scope

The following plan includes
1. Methods for reducing production costs while maintaining the quality of our staff
2. Projected costs for technology upgrades, salaries, and services during the upcoming year
3. A demonstration of feasibility, showing our cost-effectiveness
4. A summary of attitudes shared by our personnel

Proposed Plan

This plan is designed to trim operating costs without compromising quality.

Itemizes
realistic ways to
save money and
retain staff

Methods

We can overcome our budget and staffing crisis by taking these steps:

Reducing Page Count. By condensing free notices for campus organizations, abolishing "personal" notices, and limiting press releases to one page, we can reduce page count per issue from 24 to 20, saving nearly 17 percent in production costs. (Items deleted from hard copy could be linked as add-ons in the *Torch's* online version.)

Reducing Hard-Copy Circulation. Reducing circulation from 6,000 to 5,000 copies barely will cover the number of full-time students, but will save 17 percent in printing costs. The steadily increasing hits on our Web site suggest that more and more readers are using the electronic medium. (We are designing a fall survey to help determine how many readers rely on the online version.)

Hiring a New Press. We can save money by hiring Arrow Press for printing. Other presses (including our present printer) bid at least 25 percent higher than Arrow. With its state-of-the art production equipment, Arrow will import our "camera-ready" digital files to produce the hard-copy version. Moreover, no other company offers the rapid turnover time (from submission to finished product) that Arrow promises.

continued

Figure 17.4 *continued*

Upgrading Our Desktop Publishing Technology. To meet Arrow's specifications for submitting digital files, we must upgrade our equipment. Upgrade costs will be largely offset the first year by reduced printing costs. Also, this technology will increase efficiency and reduce labor costs, resulting in substantial payback on investment.

Increasing Staff Salaries. Although we seek talented students who expect little money and much experience, salaries for all positions must increase by an average of 25 percent. Otherwise, any of our staff could earn as much money elsewhere by working only a little more than half the time. In fact, many students could exceed the minimum wage by working for local newspapers. To illustrate: The *Standard Beacon* pays $60 to $90 per news article and $30 per photo; the *Torch* pays nothing for articles and $6 per photo.

A striking example of low salaries is the $9.50 per hour we pay our student desktop publishing staff. Our present desktop publishing cost of $3,038 could be as much as $7,000 or even higher if we had this service done by an outside firm, as many colleges do. Without this nominal salary increase, we cannot possibly attract qualified personnel.

Costs

Our proposed budget is itemized in Table 1, but the main point is clear: If the *Torch* is to remain viable, increased funding is essential for meeting our projected costs.

Table 1 Projected Costs and Requested Funding for Next Year's *Torch* Budget

Projected Costs

Hardware/Software Upgrades	
27-inch Apple iMac with 16GB memory, 1TB HD (Intel Core i7)	$1,162.00
HP Pavilion IPS LED (second monitor)	355.00
Seagate 8 TB external hard drive	128.99
Olympus Stylus TC-4 digital camera	299.98
HP Scanjet 5000 sheet-feed scanner	799.00
Microsoft Office Professional Upgrade	499.00
Adobe Creative Suite 5 Master Collection	2,450.00
Subtotal	**$5,693.97**

Provides detailed breakdown of costs–the central issue in the situation

continued

Figure 17.4 *continued*

Projected Costs (*continued*)

Wages and Salaries

Desktop-publishing staff (17.5 hrs/week @ $12.00/hr x 28 wks)	$5,880.00
Editor-in-Chief	3,150.00
News Editor	1,890.00
Features Editor	1,890.00
Advertising Manager	2,350.00
Advertising Designer	1,575.00
Webmaster	2,520.00
Layout Editor	1,890.00
Art Director	1,260.00
Photo Editor	1,890.00
Business Manager	1,890.00
Distributor	560.00
Subtotal	**$26,745.00**

Miscellaneous Costs

Graphics by SMU art students (3/wk @ $10 each)	$ 840.00
Mailing	1,100.00
Telephone	1,000.00
Campus print shop services	400.00
Copier fees	100.00
Subtotal	**$3,440.00**

Fixed Printing Costs (5,000 copies/wk x 28/wk)	**$24,799.60**

TOTAL YEARLY COSTS	**$60,678.57**
Expected Advertising Revenue ($600/wk x 28 wks)	**($16,800.00)**
Total Costs Minus Advertising Revenue	**$45,109.39**

TOTAL FUNDING REQUEST	**$43,878.57**

continued

Figure 17.4 *continued*

Feasibility

Beyond exhibiting our need, we feel that the feasibility of this proposal can be measured through an objective evaluation of our cost-effectiveness: Compared with newspapers at similar schools, how well does the *Torch* use its funding?

Assesses probability of success

In a survey of the four area college newspapers, we found that the *Torch*—by a sometimes huge margin—makes the best use of its money per page. Table 1A in the Appendix shows that, of the five newspapers, the *Torch* costs students the least, runs the most pages weekly, and spends the least money per page, *despite a circulation two to three times the size of the other papers.*

The *Torch* has the lowest yearly cost of all five newspapers, despite having the largest circulation. With the requested budget increase, the cost would rise by only $0.88, for a yearly cost of $9.00 to each student. Although Alden College's newspaper costs each student $8.58, it is published only every third week, averages 12 pages per issue, and costs more than $71.00 yearly per page to print—in contrast to our yearly printing cost of $55.65 per page. As the figures in the Appendix demonstrate, our cost management is responsible and effective.

Personnel

The *Torch* staff is determined to maintain the highest professionalism. Many are planning careers in journalism, writing, editing, advertising, photography, Web design, or public relations. In any *Torch* issue, the balanced, enlightened coverage is evidence of our judicious selection and treatment of articles and our shared concern for quality.

Addresses important issue of personnel

Conclusion

As a broad forum for ideas and opinions, the *Torch* continues to reflect a seriousness of purpose and a commitment to free and responsible expression. Its role in campus life is more vital than ever during these troubled times.

Reemphasizes need and encourages action

Every year, allocations to student organizations increase or decrease based on need. Last year, for example, eight allocations increased by an average of $4,332. The *Torch* has received no increase in three years.

Presumably, increases are prompted by special circumstances. For the *Torch*, these circumstances derive from increasing production costs and the need to update vital equipment. We respectfully urge the Committee to respond to the *Torch*'s legitimate needs by increasing next year's allocation to $43,878.57.

continued

Figure 17.4 *continued*

Appendix (Comparative Performance)

Table 1A Allocations and Performance of Five Local College Newspapers

Appendix provides detailed breakdown of cost comparsions

	Stonehorse College	Alden College	Simms University	Fallow State	SMU
Enrollment	1,600	1,400	3,000	3,000	5,000
Fee paid (per year)	$65.00	$85.00	$35.00	$50.00	$65.00
Total fee budget	$104,000	$119,000	$105,000	$150,000	$325,000
Newspaper budget	$18,300	$8,580	$36,179	$52,910	$37,392
					$45,109[a]
Yearly cost per student	$12.50	$8.58	$16.86	$24.66	$8.12
					$9.00[a]
Publication rate	Weekly	Every third week	Weekly	Weekly	Weekly
Average no. of pages	8	12	18	12	24
Average total pages	224	120	504	336	672
					560[a]
Yearly cost per page	$81.60	$71.50	$71.78	$157.47	$55.65
					$67.12[a]

[a]These figures are next year's costs for the SMU *Torch*.

Source: Figures were quoted by newspaper business managers in April 20XX.

Checklist

for Proposals

- ❏ Have I identified whether my proposal is solicited or unsolicited, and have I planned accordingly?
- ❏ Have I determined whether my proposal should be informal or formal?
- ❏ Have I identified whether my proposal is a planning, research, or sales proposal?
- ❏ Does my proposal follow a problem-solution or situation-resolution pattern?
- ❏ Have I done adequate research?
- ❏ Have I provided a clear title or subject line?
- ❏ Is the problem or situation clearly identified in the introduction?
- ❏ Is the background section appropriate for this audience's needs?
- ❏ Does the proposal maintain a clear focus on benefits?
- ❏ Is the proposed solution or resolution appropriate and realistic?
- ❏ Is the cost, budget, and/or qualifications section accurate and easy to understand?
- ❏ Are my claims honest and supportable?
- ❏ Are all foreseeable limitations identified?
- ❏ Are visuals, if needed, used effectively?
- ❏ Is my writing style clear, concise, and confident?
- ❏ Does the proposal end with a call to action?

Applications

General Applications

1. After identifying your primary and secondary audience, write a short planning proposal for improving an unsatisfactory situation in the classroom, on the job, or in your dorm or apartment (e.g., poor lighting, lack of wi-fi, health hazards, poor seating arrangements). Choose a problem or situation whose solution or resolution is more a matter of common sense and lucid observation than of intensive research. Be sure to (a) identify the problem clearly, give a brief background, and stimulate interest; (b) clearly state the methods proposed to solve the problem; and (c) conclude with a statement designed to gain audience support.
2. Write a research proposal to your instructor (or an interested third party) requesting approval for your final term project (a formal analytical report or formal proposal). Verify that adequate primary and secondary sources are available. Convince your audience of the soundness and usefulness of the project.
3. As an alternate term project to the formal analytical report (Chapter 16), develop a long proposal for solving a problem, improving a situation, or satisfying a need in your school, community, or job. Choose a subject sufficiently complex to justify a formal proposal, a topic requiring research (mostly primary). Identify an audience (other than your instructor) who will use your proposal for a specific purpose. Complete an Audience and Purpose Profile.

Team Application

Working in groups of four, develop an unsolicited planning proposal for solving a problem, improving a situation, or satisfying a need in your school, community, or workplace. Begin by brainstorming as a group to come up with a list of possible issues or problems to address in your proposal. Narrow your list, and work as a group to focus on a specific issue or idea. Your proposal should address a clearly identified audience of decision makers and stakeholders in the given issue. Complete an Audience and Purpose Profile.

Global Application

For this application, interview an expert in international business (a professor in the business school; someone you met on the job; a manager from your internship; someone in the study abroad office). You can also search the Web for information on international business and find a blog or series of articles by an expert. Focus on one particular country of interest. See what you can find out about how proposals are prepared in other countries or in situations where the proposal is prepared in the United States but delivered to readers in other countries. Are there particular issues about formatting, page count, style and tone, use of visuals, and other items that need to be considered? Describe your findings in a short memo that you will share with your classmates.

Digital and Social Media Application

Solicited proposals are usually written in response to a formal "request for proposal" (RFP). Search on "solicited proposals" and then add the name of a funding agency of interest to you. For example, if you are in the sciences, you can include "NSF" (short for the National Science Foundation). Or, if you are in a health career major, try "NIH" (short for the National Institutes of Health). Also, see if that agency uses Facebook and Twitter, and find out if calls for proposals (CFPs) are ever posted to those social media sites. You can also look at other agencies (both state and federal) that deal with agriculture, public health, education, finance, and so forth. Find an RFP and examine the requirements. Does the agency's Web site offer sample proposals for you to review? How long should the proposals be? Are there any pre-proposal requirements? Write a memo to your instructor explaining what you found, why you are interested in this research, and what focus a proposal would take.

Part 4
Digital Media and Presentations

18   Email   332

19   Blogs, Wikis, and Web Pages   343

20   Social Media   355

21   Oral Presentations and Video Conferencing   367

Chapter 18
Email

 Learning Objectives

18.1 Describe the audience, purpose, components, and organization of workplace email messages.

18.2 Recognize the different types of workplace email messages.

18.3 Write stylistically and tonally appropriate workplace email messages.

18.4 Understand basic issues about copyright and privacy in digital communication.

Chapter Outline

Workplace Email   333

Types of Workplace Email   335
Strategies for Choosing and Using Email   338

Appropriate Style for Workplace Email   338
Strategies for Email Style and Tone in the Workplace   340

Copyright and Privacy in Digital Communication   341
Checklist for Email   341

Applications   342

As described in previous chapters, workplace communication typically involves a combination of both print and digital media. Email is the most common form of digital communication on the job; email can be used on its own or as a way to send an attachment.

Workplace Email

18.1 **Describe the audience, purpose, components, and organization of workplace email messages.**

Email is the primary way people communicate in today's workplace and professional settings; it has all but replaced the paper memo and letter. Email offers both rapid speed and wide reach: With one keystroke, an email can quickly reach the inboxes of thousands of people. These readers can easily forward the email (and any attachments) to others.

Email is useful when people are in different time zones or have different working schedules: You can send an email at 2:00 A.M. if you are a night owl, and your early-bird colleague can read it in the morning. Or, if you are based in the eastern United States and your colleagues are in China, the 12-hour time difference means that email is essential to your work. Email also provides written documentation—an electronic trail, so to speak—that helps track a project or conversation or that may become important for legal reasons down the road. Finally, email can be read on most devices, from laptops to tablets to phones, making it an almost universal app for workplace communication.

Advantages of workplace email

Email can be used to communicate the main message or to provide a cover note, directing readers to a longer message in an attachment (typically Word or PDF). In either case, email is best suited for straightforward messages that are not too long and that do not leave a lot of room for misunderstanding. In some jobs, people may send and receive dozens if not hundreds of emails on any given day. This speed provides efficiencies but also can cause problems if both readers and writers are not careful.

Cautions when using workplace email

On the job, email should be professional in tone and style, and messages should be precise, to avoid misinterpretation. Take your time to read and write email carefully; even writers who are usually quite professional may accidentally miss a spelling, grammar, or word choice problem.

Audience and Purpose of Email

Audience considerations

With email, you do not have total control over the final audience. You might send your message to only a small group, but because of easy forwarding, your audience could turn out to be much larger. People also tend to be more casual and off-the-cuff on email, sometimes more than in person; therefore, audience considerations become crucial.

Suppose, for example, that after a long week of work on a particularly tough engineering design project, you send a quick email to another manager. In your message, you complain about one of the engineers not holding up his end. You quickly press "Send" and head out for the weekend. At a Monday status meeting, you are surprised to find that your message was forwarded to several other engineers. Clearly, your original message was not intended for them, but—inadvertently or deliberately—someone forwarded it along.

The cardinal rule of email

Remember this cardinal rule about email: Always assume your message will travel far beyond its intended recipient, and never send anything private or confidential via email.

Purpose considerations

Email accomplishes various purposes: to schedule meetings, update team members on a project, send simple memos in electronic form, and send attached documents to colleagues both within and outside of an organization.

When not to use email

Think carefully about whether email is the best medium for the given message. If you want your message to be private or confidential or if your message is too complex for email, set up a personal meeting or phone call. You can always follow up with a brief email that summarizes the main points. Also keep in mind how much email people get on a daily basis: Important items, even if marked as such, often get ignored or accidentally deleted. Finally, be sure to check before you send large attachments, such as long reports, proposals, or legal correspondence.

Components and Organization of Email

Email components

A typical email message combines features from both memos and letters. Emails usually begin with a heading, containing "To," "From," "Date," and "Subject" fields. Most email programs also feature the courtesy copy ("cc") and blind courtesy copy ("bcc") fields. Use "cc" for people who need to know but are not central to the conversation. Use "bcc" for a very long list of recipients or for individuals who need to be in the loop but may not want their email address visible. Attachments (such as PDF files or other documents too large or too formal for the email itself) take the place of the "enclosure" notation on a paper memo or letter. Depending on the level of formality, email may sometimes be written with openings and closings ("Dear John," "Best, Linda").

Regardless of length, an effective email should contain a brief introduction (even a single sentence) that gets right to the point, a clear body section with transitions (again, this section may be only a few sentences), and a brief conclusion that might ask readers to take action (such as "Please get back to me by 5:00 P.M. on Monday"). Visually, longer emails are easier for readers to process if information is broken into chunks, such as short paragraphs and bulleted lists. However, because email can be viewed on a range of screen sizes (computer, tablet, phone), keep email messages to about the size of one screen or less.

Email organization

Types of Workplace Email

18.2 Recognize the different types of workplace email messages.

Email takes different shapes and forms, depending on where you work. A typical workplace email is shown in Figure 18.1. In this example, the writer, Rachel Byerson, sends a short message to one of her staff. Notice that this message is

Brief email messages

Figure 18.1 A Brief Email Message

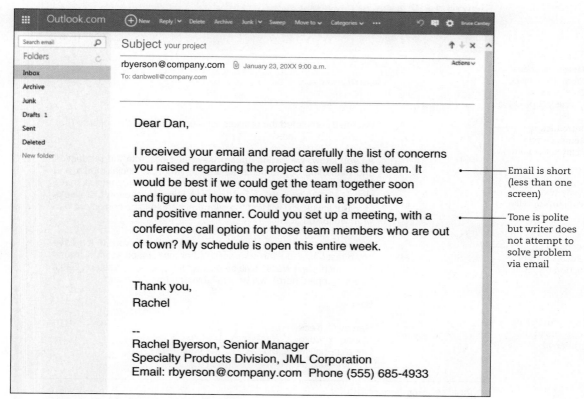

SOURCE: Microsoft Outlook 2013.

written with a professional tone and style and illustrates an important guideline: Do not use email to solve a complex situation, particularly an interpersonal one. Rachel received a long, rambling email from her employee, Dan, complaining about problems and specific people on a team project. Rachel realizes that these problems are too complicated to solve via email, so she invites Dan to set up a conference call instead. Her email doesn't "take the bait" from Dan's message, which could easily end up starting a long email chain that would only make the situation worse. Instead, she uses a considerate, polite tone and looks for a solution that involves the more personal, interactive medium of a phone call.

Cover email messages

Email is often used as a kind of cover memo to a longer attachment. In Figure 18.2, Harvey Keck writes to a consultant he wishes to hire. The email itself contains three short paragraphs (introduction; body; conclusion), which serve to provide background, some details, and context for the consultant. The longer item, a contract, is attached in PDF format. Harvey's email is professional and to the point; he knows the consultant is very busy and makes sure the email message is no longer than one screen, is easy to understand, and provides his contact information.

Figure 18.2 A Cover Email Message

Header contains From, To, Subject, Date, plus Courtesy Copy (Cc)

Introductory sentence gets right to the point

Body text explains details

Conclusion invites further action

Signature block appears at the very end

Subject Your Contract

hckeck@Lamdet.com   Sat., May 24, 20XX 2:25 p.m.
To: rdurmas@comcast.net
Cc: spkapoor@Lamdet.com

We have completed the process for hiring you as a consultant. Your contract is attached.

As you know, we had to confirm several dates with the production and marketing departments as well as with our social media and Web design group. These dates, outlined in your contract, have shifted slightly from those discussed during our meeting two weeks ago. But I think you will find the overall schedule to be consistent with what we talked about.

We are very much looking forward to working with you. If you have any questions about the contract or other matters, please feel free to be in touch. Next week, I will be on vacation, but my assistant, Sanjit Kapoor (copied here), will be available and happy to help.

Best,

Harvey C. Keck
Managing Editor
Lamdet Publishers, Inc.
Phone: (555) 682-4493

SOURCE: Microsoft Outlook 2013.

Another way email is used, particularly in large organizations, is as a formatted document that resembles company letterhead or other official communication. Unlike the examples discussed above, which are between two individuals, this type of email is sent from one part of the organization to all employees or to a large group of employees. The appearance signifies that the message is official and important. Figure 18.3 illustrates one such email; there is no attachment, rather, the email itself is formatted to look like a memo on letterhead. But because the message is digital, it contains links that readers can click on for more information. Typically, organizations will use the same visual format as a way to let readers know they should read the message. Formatting is clear, with plenty of white space, short paragraphs, and bulleted lists.

Formatted email messages

Figure 18.3 A Formatted Email Message

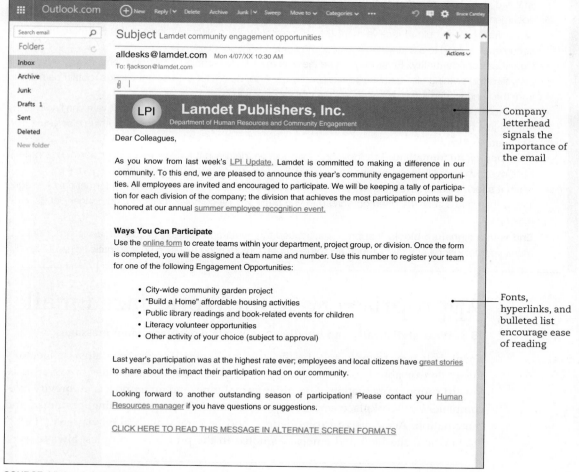

SOURCE: Microsoft Outlook 2013.

Strategies

for Choosing and Using Email

- **Consider whether your message is for one person or for a large group.** Email between individuals is usually written within the email itself, but information for large groups (such as all employees, people who have signed up for a fitness plan, and so on) should be formatted in a way to make the message appear official. Doing so helps ensure that people will read the message.
- **Determine if the situation is too complicated for email.** Solving complicated interpersonal issues (such as disagreements between team members) is not what email was designed to do. Use email in these cases to tone down the discussion and invite people to a meeting, conference call, or video chat, where employees can engage in real conversations and listen to each other.
- **Send attachments for long items or formal documents.** It's tempting to just paste the entire contents of a long document directly into an email message, but readers won't appreciate this approach. Use attachments (in Word, if you are still working on the document or don't care about precise page formatting, or in PDF if the document is complete and formatting needs to be retained). But don't send too many attachments—it can be confusing for people to receive more than three attachments with any single email. For more than three documents, upload to a shared file server or the company intranet instead.
- **Consider confidentiality.** Email may not be the best medium for sending legal documents, confidential company files, or anything else that should remain private. Also, before forwarding a message, obtain permission from the sender, who may have intended the message for you only.
- **Assume your email is permanent and readable by anyone at any time.** Forensic software can find virtually any file that has been deleted, so don't make promises you cannot keep or expect anything else you say to disappear forever.
- **Use appropriate formatting.** Provide a brief introduction, details in the body, and a conclusion. Use bullets, headings, numbered lists, italics, and other formatting features to make your message easy to read.
- **Keep it short.** Readers are impatient and don't want to scroll through long screens of information. Messages longer than one screen will often go unread. If you must send a complex message, put longer details in an attachment.
- **End with a signature block.** If appropriate, include the name and address of your organization or department, your telephone and fax number, and other contact information by using an automatic signature block.

Appropriate Style for Workplace Email

18.3 Write stylistically and tonally appropriate workplace email messages.

Workplace email style

Email between friends and family (personal email) often contains deliberately misspelled or abbreviated words, a disregard for grammatical rules, a lax attitude toward proper punctuation, a highly informal tone, and an emphasis on brevity over completeness. Workplace email, however, should use proper spelling, grammar, and punctuation. Avoid using capital letters, and be careful with abbreviations ("LOL," "imho," and the like) and emojis. As noted in the previous examples, always use a professional, respectful tone. A workplace email that is too casual (e.g., using such words as "uh huh," "whatever," and "cool") or is incomplete will undermine the writer's professionalism and confuse readers.

Be sure to avoid *flaming* (angry, sarcastic, insulting messages that will only lead to repercussions). Don't use biased language that demeans or excludes some potential readers. Do not use email for interpersonal issues, and avoid using it to blame others. Also, do not forward a particularly sensitive email without permission from the original writer, and do not edit an email to change the original meaning.

The word "netiquette" reflects the idea of Internet etiquette, the concept that online writers need to be especially careful and considerate of style, tone, feelings, and authority. Figure 18.4 shows an email lacking in professional style and overall online etiquette. Although the writer and recipient are close personal friends

Workplace email etiquette

Figure 18.4 A Workplace Email Lacking Professional Style and Tone

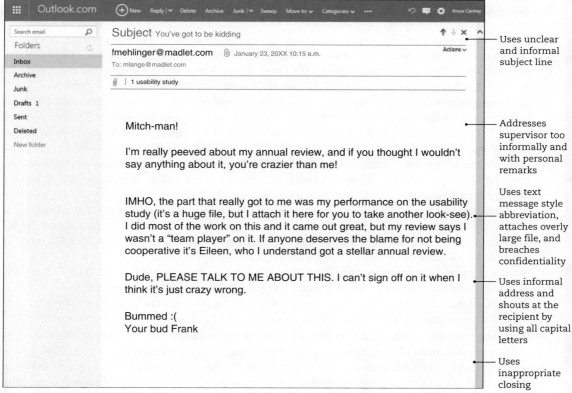

Subject You've got to be kidding

fmehlinger@madlet.com   January 23, 20XX 10:15 a.m.
To: mlange@madlet.com

1 usability study

Mitch-man!

I'm really peeved about my annual review, and if you thought I wouldn't say anything about it, you're crazier than me!

IMHO, the part that really got to me was my performance on the usability study (it's a huge file, but I attach it here for you to take another look-see). I did most of the work on this and it came out great, but my review says I wasn't a "team player" on it. If anyone deserves the blame for not being cooperative it's Eileen, who I understand got a stellar annual review.

Dude, PLEASE TALK TO ME ABOUT THIS. I can't sign off on it when I think it's just crazy wrong.

Bummed :(
Your bud Frank

Annotations:
- Uses unclear and informal subject line
- Addresses supervisor too informally and with personal remarks
- Uses text message style abbreviation, attaches overly large file, and breaches confidentiality
- Uses informal address and shouts at the recipient by using all capital letters
- Uses inappropriate closing

SOURCE: Microsoft Outlook 2013.

in addition to their employee-supervisor relationship, an email like this should never be written in the workplace. Not only does the message have legal implications in terms of the writer's job performance and future employment, but it also violates another employee's confidentiality. It is also much too informal for any workplace document

The importance of proofreading workplace email for spelling, grammar, tone, and style

Remember that email does not disappear. Your message will be backed up and saved somewhere (usually on the organization's backup system or the like) and may be brought up later in personnel or legal proceedings. Frank (the writer in Figure 18.4) did not stop to consider that his email is not just a one-time message, never to be seen again. His email could be used as part of an employment or disciplinary case later. Email may not seem permanent, but it is. Pressing "send" too quickly can be a problem down the road. Think before you type, and think again (and proofread, and wait a bit) before you send.

Strategies

for Email Style and Tone in the Workplace

- **Consider your audience.** If you are writing to a customer, client, or superior in your organization, use a more formal tone than with a coworker or immediate supervisor. If you know your recipient well, use an informal salutation ("Hello") and an informal closing ("Regards," "Best"). However, for someone you don't know or someone in authority, use a formal salutation ("Dear Dr. Gomez") and a formal closing ("Sincerely").

- **Consider your purpose.** Don't use email when a more personal medium is preferable. Sometimes an issue is best resolved by talking face to face, making a phone call, or even just leaving a voice mail. Don't use email to resign from a job, request a raise, respond to a formal letter, or respond to something that may have legal implications.

- **Write a clear subject line.** Instead of "Test Data" or "Data Request," be specific: "Request for Beta Test Data for Project 18." This line helps recipients decide whether to read the message immediately, and it helps for filing and future reference.

- **Use informal language, emojis, and abbreviations sparingly—if at all.** Even in an informal message, use proper spelling, grammar, and mechanics (avoid using only lowercase letters or all capital letters). Emojis should be avoided in workplace emails. The same goes for common abbreviations (FYI, ASAP, OMG), although technical abbreviations that are widely understood in your workplace are fine.

- **Proofread thoroughly before hitting "send."** Every message reflects your image, so double-check any email with your name on it. Also, be careful that the email goes only to your intended recipients.

- **Be professional.** Take time to read email carefully; respond in a timely manner; avoid flaming (angry or personal attacks) and biased language; do not edit forwarded emails without the sender's permission

- **Remember that there is a person on the other end of the message.** Email (and other forms of digital media) provide a shield, of sorts, between you and your reader(s). In a rush to finish up some work, or in a moment of feeling frustrated or even angry, you may write a message that makes you feel good but forgets the very real fact that a person, not a machine, will read your words. Try writing out your thoughts in a separate document, or write the email but save it in the "drafts" folder. Review it again in a few hours and revise, keeping your "reader as person" in mind.

Copyright and Privacy in Digital Communication

18.4 **Understand basic issues about copyright and privacy in digital communication.**

Because the various forms of digital communication discussed in this and the next two chapters are often written quickly and distributed widely, you need to keep in mind the importance of copyright and privacy issues.

Copyright is a system of legal protection for original works of authorship (books, photographs, user manuals, music) that are "fixed in a tangible medium." In other words, copyright applies when an idea becomes recorded or written down or otherwise fixed, as in a printed book, an email message, a Web site, or a recorded piece of music.

In technical writing and communication, especially with digital communication, there are a few key aspects of copyright to be aware of. In the workplace, if you are a full-time employee, most of what you write and create is typically owned by the company. So be careful about posting material to a blog or Web site without first obtaining permission from the company. Also, you may find a photograph or piece of music or image on a Web site and think it's the perfect visual for the report you are writing. But unless your use is for educational purposes or the piece is clearly marked as "copyright free" or "in the public domain," you probably need to seek permission to use the item. (See page 415 for more on fair use.)

If you are unsure about the copyright status of a work, it's best to consult with a librarian or with the author of the material, keeping in mind that sometimes the author is a corporate, not individual, author.

Digital communication also raises privacy issues. For example, avoid forwarding an email without checking with the sender first. Likewise, don't forward proprietary information (information that originates in your company) to unauthorized recipients outside the company.

Copyright protects many forms of work including digital communication

Digital communication and workplace privacy

Checklist

for Email

- ❏ Have I determined if email is the best medium in this situation?
- ❏ Did I write a clear subject line?
- ❏ Have I kept my message short and to the point?
- ❏ Have I included a brief introduction, details in the body, a conclusion, and a complimentary closing and signature block?
- ❏ Is my email appropriately informal or formal, depending on my audience?
- ❏ Have I used emoticons, abbreviations, and text-speak sparingly (or not at all in a formal email)?

- ❏ Does my email use a professional style?
- ❏ Have I maintained confidentiality?
- ❏ If responding to someone, did I take time to read the original email carefully?
- ❏ Did I proofread my email and check the distribution list before sending?

Applications

General Applications

1. Choose a topic and an audience, and write an email complaining about something that bothers you, written in a way that follows proper email format, includes all the required components, and avoids flaming.

2. Using Figure 18.1 as an example, come up with a situation from a group project at school or a team project at work where there have been some interpersonal concerns or complaints. Acting as team manager, write a memo similar in size, tone, and approach to the one written by Rachel Byerson, but in this case, address your email to the entire team. Offer a suggestion for how the team might communicate in this case.

Team Application

Work with a team to write a collaborative version of the complaint email (Application 1 in General Applications). Remember, a real person will be reading your email, and you are hoping for a result.

Global Application

Copyright and privacy are subject to the laws of a country or region. The Internet and other technologies complicate matters because data can easily travel around the world without regard for borders. The World Intellectual Property Organization (WIPO) is an international group that oversees the global implications of intellectual property issues. If you can, talk to a communication professional who deals with international audiences. Ask about any difficulties the person has encountered with copyright or privacy. Review the WIPO Web site with this professional, and ask how the information on this site might affect the way she or he would write, design, and distribute various digital communications.

Digital and Social Media Application

Go online and search on the word "netiquette." Compile a list of ideas, documenting which ideas came from which Web sites. Add any new ideas based on your own experience at work, at an internship, or at school. Create an informal report of your findings, and send this report to your instructor as an attachment to an email message. Be sure to cite the sources of the ideas that are not your own, and provide Web addresses for those sites. If your class is using a learning management system, your instructor may request that you and others post your report to a forum so others in class can see what you found; if so, what is the main finding that seems to be stated across all or almost all of the reports?

Chapter 19
Blogs, Wikis, and Web Pages

 ## Learning Objectives

19.1 Differentiate between internal and external blogs.

19.2 Describe the different functions of internal and external wikis.

19.3 Understand the business uses of Web pages.

19.4 Consider audience and purpose before designing and writing a Web page.

19.5 Design and write an effective Web page.

19.6 Explain credibility and privacy considerations in Web-based communication.

Chapter Outline

Blogs   344

Wikis   345

Web Pages   346

Audience and Purpose of Web Pages   347

Elements of Effective Web Pages   348

Web Page Credibility and Privacy Issues   352

> *Strategies for Blogs, Wikis, and Web Pages   352*
> *Checklist for Blogs Wikis, and Web Pages   353*

Applications   354

Advantages of blogs, wikis, and Web pages

Blogs, wikis, and Web pages are important forms of workplace communication for companies and organizations. Blogs began as forums for people to write about and discuss political topics, hobbies, and personal interests. Today, blogs have much wider uses. Wikis allow organizations to keep technical and scientific content updated and current, based on input from individual contributors. Web pages are essential for almost all organizations, large or small, as ways to advertise, maintain a visible presence, and provide information to customers.

Blogs

19.1 Differentiate between internal and external blogs.

Blogs can be either internal or external. Internal blogs help employees network with each other, while external blogs help companies stay in touch with customers and clients.

Internal Blogs

How a blog can enhance a company's internal conversation

Internal blogs enhance workflow and morale. In large organizations, blogs can provide an alternative to email for routine in-house communication. Anyone in the network can post a message or comment on other messages. In the blogging environment, meetings can be conducted without the time and location constraints of face-to-face meetings. Employee training can be delivered, and updates about company developments can be circulated. Blogs are especially useful for collaborating. For example, someone in a company's engineering department can create a forum to discuss various solutions to a technical problem.

External Blogs

While internal blogs are used for in-house communication, external blogs are written with a broader audience in mind. External blogs help organizations stay in touch with the public by providing updates on products, services, research findings, and other current and newsworthy events. Blogs offer a space for large organizations to show a more personal side, to respond amiably and quickly to customer concerns, and to allow readers to provide ideas and feedback. Tone, of course, is critical on an external blog; the writing needs to sound friendly, welcoming, and sincere.

How a blog can enhance an organization's public conversation

Increasingly, the content on a blog will often mirror what gets posted to the organization's Facebook page and Twitter feed, but blogs offer additional options such as a search function, a sign-in feature for receiving email alerts, and an RSS feed option (RSS stands for "really simple syndication" and is also known as a Web feed or a news feed.) Government and nonprofit organizations, such as the Centers for Disease Control and Prevention (CDC) and the National Wildlife Federation, as well as corporations both large and small, use external blogs for a variety of topics.

Wikis

19.2 Describe the different functions of internal and external wikis.

Wikis (from the Hawaiian phrase *wiki wiki*, meaning "quick") are used to collect information and keep this information updated. Most people are familiar with Wikipedia, an online encyclopedia for which anyone can write or revise the content. Like blogs, wikis are either internal or external.

Internal Wikis

In the workplace, wikis also allow for the sharing and updating of content, but they serve a different function: to allow employees within a company (or outside the company, if given password access) to update technical, scientific, project-related, and other information. Typically, people can log on to the wiki and make changes to content, overwriting previous versions. Despite the potential for abuse created by such alterations, most workplace wikis tend to be self-regulating: contributors notice mistakes and correct any errors. A well-managed wiki can be a valuable resource among trustworthy contributors. To ensure that serial edits do not end up distorting the original posting, copies of the original along with each subsequent edit are saved for later reference. (To see how this process works, go to Wikipedia and click on "revision history." Workplace wikis typically have similar history pages.)

How internal wikis enhance team communication

External Wikis

Advantages and
disadvantages
of using
external wikis

While some wikis are used only internally by a company or organization, others are used by external audiences in specific scientific or technical areas. Because these wikis are open to countless people with knowledge in the fields, these sites can be excellent external sources of information. But as with Wikipedia, the lack of gatekeeping by a central editor also creates the potential for inaccuracy. A well-managed wiki, one that balances open access with editorial control, can be a valuable resource. If you search for a wiki related to your undergraduate major (nursing, chemistry, engineering, technical writing), you may find some useful resources. Or you may find that a Wikipedia entry on this topic contains a link to a more specific external wiki.

Web Pages

19.3 Understand the business uses of Web pages.

Advantages of
Web pages

Most organizations, whether private or public, large or small, have a Web site. When compared with print, online information can be updated quickly and easily. Also, Web sites are interactive: People can provide input, download files, place orders, and follow hyperlinks to new or related information. Figure 19.1 shows a Web page from the U.S. Food and Drug Administration on bug bites and bee stings. Interactive features include a list of consumer updates and questions that readers can click on for more information, a search box, and a resources section.

Note that *Web site* refers to an entire site with all related pages; *Web page* refers to one single page. The rest of this section discusses elements of effective Web page writing and design.

Web site
development in
the workplace

Web site development is a complex process that changes as related technologies change. Professional Web site development requires training in visual communication, information design, and programming. Moreover, Web development is primarily a collaborative process, often involving content providers, information architects, graphic designers, computer programmers, and marketers. Nevertheless, especially in small businesses and nonprofit organizations, writing and designing for the Web often become the responsibility of everyday employees. This section introduces the basics of writing and designing Web pages. The Strategies on pages 352–353 provide a basic overview of the process.

Figure 19.1 An interactive Web page

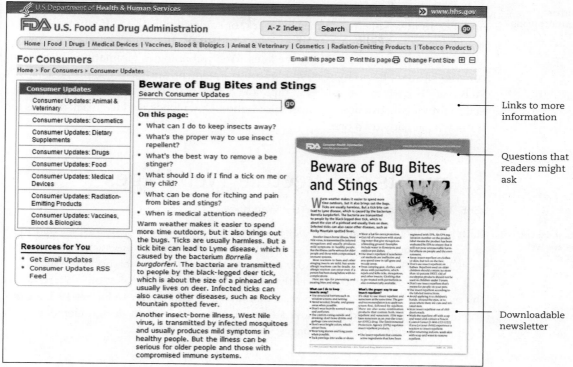

Links to more information

Questions that readers might ask

Downloadable newsletter

SOURCE: U.S. Food and Drug Administration from <http://www.fda.gov/ForConsumers/ConsumerUpdates/ucm048022.htm>.

Audience and Purpose of Web Pages

19.4 Consider audience and purpose before designing and writing a Web page.

As with any technical documents, you must first think carefully about your intended audience and purpose before designing and writing a Web page.

Consider the audience for a Web page by filling out an Audience and Purpose Profile Sheet (see Chapter 3). Does the primary audience consist of potential customers or others who are seeking information, of people buying a product or service, of customers needing product support, or of some combination? Who is the secondary audience?

Will your audience members be proficient at navigating a complex Web page, or will they need a help menu and a feedback mechanism (email address, phone number) if they have questions? Will the page be read by audiences fluent in English or nonnative speakers of English or nonspeakers of English? Unless your page is aimed at a highly technical audience, use plain, noncolloquial English that is easily

Audience considerations

understood by anyone with basic English proficiency and easily translatable into other languages.

Purpose considerations

Is the Web page's purpose to publish information, explain a task, sell a product or promote an idea, solicit customer feedback, or some combination? If you want to sell something to technologically savvy young audiences, the page will need to convey a cutting-edge image, employing the latest Web technologies (animation, interaction, complex design). Begin by writing a purpose statement, such as "The purpose of this Web page is both to sell our new mp3 and video players to a young, hip audience and to provide instructions, contact information, downloads, and feedback options for those who already own one."

Elements of Effective Web Pages

19.5 Design and write an effective Web page.

Print documents versus Web pages

Both print documents and Web pages must follow the same basic principles of understandable structure (Chapter 5), readable style (Chapter 6), audience-centered visuals (Chapter 7), and a user-friendly design (Chapter 8). However, because Web pages and print pages are read differently, some of these elements play out differently in the online environment. As you read though this section, refer to Figure 19.3, a user-friendly Web page, and note how structure, style, visual, and design elements both resemble and differ from print pages.

Structure

As discussed in Chapter 5, the three approaches in planning a print document's structure are outlining, chunking, and sequencing. This section discusses how these approaches apply to Web pages.

Create a storyboard rather than an outline

OUTLINING (STORYBOARDING). For a simple print document, you would create a basic introduction–body–conclusion outline. A longer print document would require a more detailed formal outline using alphanumeric notation, as in Figure 5.3 in Chapter 5. But instead of outlining a Web page, create a storyboard (a handwritten sketch of the page, as in Figure 19.2). This type of storyboard for a Web site is often called a site map.

Why storyboards are important

Most of us have visited Web pages that have no apparent logical organization. A well-designed Web page is storyboarded in advance so that readers can follow the information flow and locate what they seek. The page should be organized so that its main purpose stands out.

In Figure 19.3, the home page of the National Park Service Web site, the name of the organization stands out prominently on the page in white text over a black background. This header and the pull-down menus directly beneath grab readers' attention

Figure 19.2 A storyboard sketch for a home page

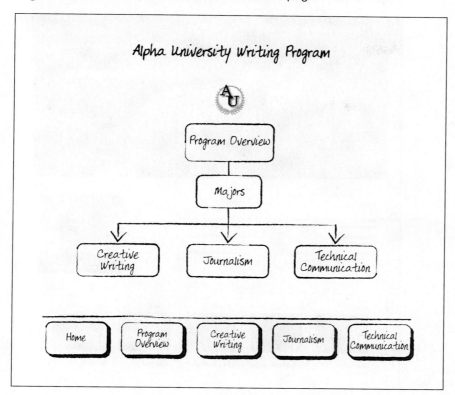

and encourage them to explore the site further. Other information on the page has been storyboarded into subcategories for further exploration.

CHUNKING. Readers expect information to be in small and easy-to-digest chunks. Computers are associated with speed, and users are impatient with long blocks of online information. Also, the flickering light patterns of computer screens tire the eyes.

Always chunk information into small segments

How you chunk the information depends on how your audience will interact with the site. Imagine you are writing text for a Web site intended to explain a medical procedure to patients. You decide to organize this information by questions users might ask: "How long will the surgery last?" or "When will I be able to return to work?" You would chunk your information into those categories, possibly making each an individual link.

Figure 19.3 chunks its content by News, Events, and Photos and Multimedia.

Figure 19.3 A user-friendly Web page

The NPS name and logo are clearly displayed at the top of the page

A search engine, pull-down menus, and other features allow for quick and easy navigation

"News" and "Events" sections take readers directly to these two popular features

The "Photos and Multimedia" feature is clearly divided into helpful subcategories

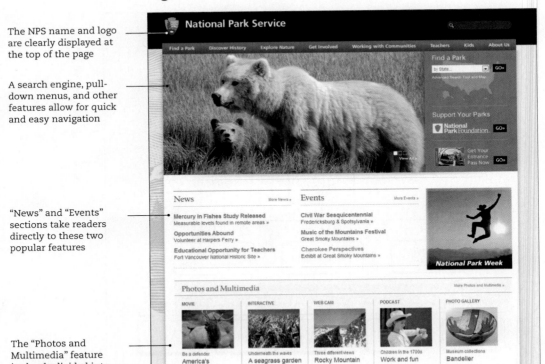

SOURCE: From the National Park Service www.nps.gov/index.htm.

Use logical sequencing, but don't expect users to follow it

SEQUENCING. A print document follows a logical, linear sequence: spatial, chronological, problem-solution, or cause-and-effect. A Web page should also follow a logical sequence, even though people tend not to read Web pages in linear fashion. A typical site displays information in a hypertext format, allowing readers to move from link to link, often randomly. Each chunk of text on a Web page must therefore make sense by itself, regardless of its order in the original sequence.

In Figure 19.3, the information is sequenced from general (Find a park) to specific (News; Events).

Style

As explained previously, information on the Web must be presented in small, easy-to-digest chunks. Be especially attentive to conciseness by avoiding wordiness and eliminating repetition and redundancy. Figure 19.3 uses short headings and phrases to help readers find the section they are looking for.

Visuals

As discussed in Chapter 8, use visuals to perform a function rather than merely dress up the page. Figure 19.3 uses photos nicely, at the top of the page and then for each section. The photos help draw the reader to the page, but they do not overwhelm with too much visual information.

Design

Like printed documents, Web pages must be designed for consistency, cohesiveness, navigation, and emphasis (see Chapter 8); however, some individual design elements serve a different function online than in print documents. The trend in Web design is toward something called "universal design," which refers to making design choices that keep the page clean, easy to navigate, accessible, and usable to people with differing levels of vision, left or right handedness, and different ages. For more details, search on "universal Web site design" or "accessible Web site design" and look for organizations such as usability.gov and the World Wide Web Consortium (WC3). Also, see the Digital and Social Media application at the end of this chapter.

GRID PATTERNS.   Web pages typically use a combination of horizontal and vertical grid patterns, as in Figure 19.3. The key information on the page is presented horizontally and takes visual precedence; other information is presented in columns.

> Combine grid patterns as needed

WHITE SPACE.   Readers get frustrated with Web pages that have a cluttered look, where too many elements are crammed together without space between. Figure 19.3, on the other hand, has an open feel. Each element is surrounded by plenty of white space.

> Provide ample white space between all page elements

FONT STYLE AND SIZE.   Use a consistent base font style and size throughout the site. In addition, choose a font style and size that will be easy on readers' eyes. In most cases, use a sans serif font in a 10- to 12-point or larger size.

> Use a readable font style and size, and use it consistently

In Figure 19.3, the font is a simple sans serif that looks professional. Note also how the font styles of various site elements complement each other.

HEADINGS.   In Figure 19.3, headings set off each item, and links enable readers to connect to separate pages they want to view.

> Use headings to chunk text on a single page and links to connect to other pages

COLOR, SHADING, ITALIC, BOLD, AND UNDERLINING.   On a Web page, use color, shading, or italics (sparingly) to emphasize particular words or phrases, but do not use bold or underlining, which signifies a hyperlink.

> Use color, shading, and italics for emphasis, but use bold or underlining for hyperlinks only

BULLETED AND NUMBERED LISTS.   Bulleted and numbered lists enhance readability by extracting from a dense paragraph interrelated items or items that fall into a sequence or process. Because the Web environment calls for small chunks of texts and ease of reading on a screen, use lists generously.

> Use bulleted and numbered lists to further chunk text

Web Page Credibility and Privacy Issues

19.6 Explain credibility and privacy considerations in Web-based communication.

The power of a Web page to convey information instantaneously and worldwide, using images, sound, and text, increases the need for sound judgment on the part of everyone involved, from technical writers to Web designers to software developers.

The power and problems of Web-based communication

Consider the speed of the Internet, its global reach, and a Web page's ability to combine sound, color, images, text, interactivity, and more. These multimedia features allow for efficient and effective communication but at the same time make it easy to create sites that are manipulative and distorted. Imagine a Web site for an herbal remedy that some people feel is helpful for anxiety. This herbal remedy may not have Food and Drug Administration approval, may never have been subjected to clinical trials or other objective research, and may have harmful side effects. But a Web site promoting this product can easily, and with very little cost, be set up to look extremely scientific and factual. Fancy logos from quasi-scientific organizations might give the page a sense of professional credibility. Statistics, charts, and links to other Web sites might create the appearance of a valid medical site. As a communicator setting up such a site, you need to question the possible risks for people reading the site who might, in turn, purchase the product.

Web site privacy statements

Web pages also raise important privacy concerns, especially in terms of behind-the-scenes technologies that gather the personal information of visitors to the site. Most credible organizations will write and display a link so readers can review the organization's Web site privacy statement. These statements let readers know how information will be used and what rights readers have. As a technical communicator, you may be asked to help write such a privacy statement. Web site privacy statements should be readily available on a site (a visible link or button), and they should be written in language anyone can understand. Updates should be noted by including a date that indicates when the privacy statement was last revised. Include a way for readers to be in touch if they have questions or concerns.

Strategies

for Blogs, Wikis, and Web Pages

Blogs and Wikis

- **Keep content brief, to the point, and concise.** Avoid wordiness and repetition.
- **Write differently for internal versus external audiences.** Internal audiences do not require as much background. External audiences may need more explanation.
- **For an external blog, focus on the customer's priorities and needs.** A friendly, encouraging tone goes a long way in good customer relations.
- **Check blog and wiki entries for credibility.** Check the content to see when the blog or wiki was last updated (usually under the "history" tab on a wiki).

Web Pages

- **Identify the intended audience.** Who is the primary audience? Who is the secondary audience? Will your audience be Web savvy? Will the audience include worldwide readers?
- **Decide on the page's purpose.** Is the purpose to inform, instruct, persuade, or some combination?
- **Decide what the page will contain.** Will it display print only or a combination of print and graphics? Will it include audio and video? Will links be provided and, if so, how many and where? Will user feedback be solicited and, if so, in what form: surveys, email comments, or other?
- **Create an understandable structure.** Map out your Web page with a storyboard that illustrates which parts of the page will go where and that provides ways to navigate. Chunk information into short passages that are easy to access and quick to read. Provide a logical sequence (even if readers won't necessarily follow it).
- **Write with a readable style.** Write clearly, concisely, fluently, and personably, with special emphasis on conciseness.
- **Use visuals.** Include visuals that serve a useful purpose, not merely a decorative one. Select simple and complementary colors.
- **Design an accessible page.** Combine grid patterns as needed; provide ample margins, consistent justification, plenty of white space, consistent line spacing, and a simple and readable font. Use headings to chunk text on a single page, color/shading/italics for emphasis, and lists whenever appropriate. Follow guidelines for universal design or accessible design, as appropriate for your project.
- **Proofread your page.** Verify the accuracy of numbers, dates, and data; check for spelling or grammar errors.
- **Attend to risk considerations.** Consider whether your page in any way exploits users. If you use copyrighted information, be aware of fair use guidelines. (see page 415 in Appendix A). When in doubt, request permission. If your page asks individuals for private information, create a privacy statement.
- **Maintain your page.** Review and update the page often and redesign as needed.

Checklist

for Blogs, Wikis, and Web Pages

Blogs and Wikis

- ❏ Have I determined if a blog or wiki should be internal (for employees only) or external (for outside audiences)?
- ❏ Are blog or wiki entries written clearly, avoiding wordiness and repetition?
- ❏ Have I checked blog or wiki entries for credibility and truthfulness?
- ❏ For external blogs or wikis, have I provided enough background and context for this audience?
- ❏ For external blogs or wikis, is the tone friendly, welcoming, and sincere?
- ❏ Have I determined if the blog or wiki should include an RSS feed?

Web Pages

- ❏ Have I assessed my audience and purpose before planning the Web page?
- ❏ Did I create a storyboard to plan the overall structure?
- ❏ Have I chunked information into small pieces for ease of reading on the Web?
- ❏ Did I sequence the information logically (even if it may not be read in its original order on the Web)?
- ❏ Did I use (but not overuse) visuals, including color?

❑ Have I used consistent grid patterns when creating multiple Web pages for the same site?

❑ Have I provided ample white space?

❑ Have I used a consistent and readable font style and size?

❑ Did I use headings to chunk text on a single Web page and links to navigate to other pages?

❑ Does the page include any color, shading, and italics to highlight key information?

❑ Have I avoided the use of bold and underlining, except to indicate hyperlinks?

❑ Have I provided a search option and links to other pages within or outside of my site?

❑ Have I attended to credibility and privacy considerations?

❑ Have I proofread the page before going "live"?

Applications

General Applications

1. Locate one or more blogs related to technical communication or to your major. Follow the discussion for a few days, and write a brief analysis of the chosen blog, its intended audience, its content areas, and its value to members in the field. On what basis did you determine the blog to be a credible source? Make a list of items that influenced your selection of this blog, and discuss this list in class.

2. With a classmate, locate one or two Web sites you might use as research sources for a project. Using the guidelines in this chapter, assess these Web sites for the quality of their structure, style, use of visuals, and design. As in the above, make notes about what items influenced your choice of this site as a credible resource. Write up your findings in an email message to your instructor. Include the Web address for each of the sites you used.

Team Application

In teams of two, find a blog written for an external audience. Analyze the writing style and tone of the blog. In what ways does the blog maintain a professional tone but still sound personal and friendly? Is the blog used mainly to provide updates, or is there also some commenting or other interaction on the site? How are visuals used on the blog? Write a short summary of your thoughts to share with class.

Global Application

Blogs, wikis, and Web pages have global reach—you can use these tools to collaborate with team members from other countries. Locate a wiki related to your major (hint: try searching on "chemistry wiki" or similar). See if the wiki is available in languages other than English. Write a memo to your instructor explaining what you found.

Digital and Social Media Application

Web designers should follow best practices on writing for the Web and on Web site design. For both topics, go online and find credible sources that provide guidelines for universal design (sometimes also called accessible design). Look at sites such as usability.gov, the World Wide Web Consortium (WC3), and the Nielsen Norman Group. These three sites will lead you to other organizations (such as groups that focus specifically on creating Web sites with seniors in mind or groups that offer guidance about sites that can be easily read by automated screen readers for people who are blind or visually impaired). Using your findings as a guide, locate three Web sites that exemplify the principles of effective Web design and style. Prepare a short presentation on your exemplary sites, and explain why you selected them as examples.

Chapter 20
Social Media

 Learning Objectives

20.1 Understand audience and purpose considerations when using social media.

20.2 Discuss the workplace uses of various popular social media.

20.3 Identify credibility and legal issues related to using social media on the job.

Chapter Outline

Considering Audience and Purpose   357

Social Media in Technical and Workplace Communication   359

Credibility and Legal Issues   363

    Strategies for Social Media   364

    Checklist for Social Media   365

Applications   365

Definition and examples of social media

Social media platforms allow people to network and share information, updates, photos, videos, and more. The most popular social media sites for workplace communication include the following:

- Customer review sites, such as Yelp and TripAdvisor, which allow individuals to post reviews of restaurants, hotels, businesses, doctors, and more
- Facebook, originally developed for college students but now used by friends, families, professional associates, businesses, nonprofits, special events, and other organizations
- Google+, a network that includes email, friends and workplace associates, document and photo sharing, and more
- Instagram, originally used for uploading and sharing personal photos, also used by businesses to share photos and coupons, promote new product lines or sales, and connect with others
- LinkedIn and other job sites, used for professional networking, job postings, job searches, and resume and job application materials
- Twitter, used for sending short messages ("tweets") to people who subscribe to a particular Twitter feed
- YouTube, where videos about how to perform a task or how to understand a technical concept or idea are posted for viewing and public comment

Blogs and wikis, and even some Web pages, might also be considered social media, depending on how they are used. This chapter focuses on the more obvious forms of social media, listed above. See Chapter 19 for information about workplace blogs, wikis, and Web pages.

As you read this chapter, keep in mind that your interactions with social media in the workplace can take two forms: as a consumer and user of such sites (using LinkedIn for the job search, for instance) and as a creator and writer of such media (writing and maintaining your organization's Facebook site or Twitter feed).

Social media are playing an increasingly important role in the workplace. In techni- cal communication, social media can serve as a resource for staying in touch with col- leagues, acquiring information from technical experts, learning more about customer preferences, sharing updated information with customers, and keeping professionals connected. On the job, you might use social media to research a report or proposal, post a job announcement, or learn more about the professional background of a job candi- date. You might also be asked to help create, maintain, update, and post to these sites. *Social media in the workplace*

Social media can help organizations disseminate cutting-edge technical and sci- entific research—and get feedback from people who may not be experts but who have firsthand experience. Public health organizations, for example, use Twitter and Facebook to get the word out about an influenza outbreak or a food safety recall. Companies might use Twitter or Instagram to announce a new product update or an upcoming seminar. These short social media posts usually contain links directing readers to a Web site with more detailed information.

Most organizations with any form of social media presence will end up hiring a social media manager, whose responsibilities are to determine the most strategic uses of social media for that organization or industry. Social media management involves not only writing and posting content but also monitoring posted responses and com- ments. Social media managers require strong writing abilities, an ability to understand the complex nature of audience and purpose in online settings, and skills with digital technology. Technical communicators, engineers, medical professionals, and others with specialized expertise may at one time or another be asked to contribute to an organization's social media sites and strategies. *Social media managers*

Considering Audience and Purpose

20.1 Understand audience and purpose considerations when using social media.

Most organizations maintain a social media site to highlight or promote a particular product or service or to provide updates and keep in touch with customers. Initially, a social media site such as Facebook may be designed with one particular audience in mind. But when set up as open to the public, Facebook and other social media sites can be viewed by thousands (if not more) people. So, your audience and purpose may soon be far more expansive than originally envisioned. For example, the Centers for Disease Control and Prevention (CDC) reports that its initial Facebook page was set up for an audience interested in health and safety updates. But as interest grew, the organization had to expand its Facebook presence, eventually supporting "multiple Facebook profiles connecting users with information on a range of CDC health and safety topics" ("CDC Social Media Guidelines," 1). *Audience and purpose for social media*

For most large organizations, it has become imperative not only to have a social media presence but also to have a social media *policy*. From government agencies to colleges and universities to businesses, social media policies describe everything from appropriate use of visuals to the tone, style, and word count best suited when writing *Social media policy*

Figure 20.1 A sample social media policy

SOURCE: Courtesy of Simon Fraser University. Used with permission.

for that organization's social media site. Simon Fraser University (see Figure 20.1), for example, suggests limiting a Facebook post to 35 words or less and keeping voice and tone professional and consistent, no matter how many people are maintaining and writing for the site (Simon Fraser University).

Audience as Contributor

Impact of audience participation

External audience members can be important contributors to social media sites. For instance, many companies encourage customers to provide feedback via a customer review site, such as Yelp or TripAdvisor. Increasingly, product instructions and user documentation (see Chapter 13) are posted online, with a comment section available so readers can report on or update the documentation if they notice problems or errors. When audience members become contributors, there are more chances to collect important information. But there is also a greater need for fact-checking.

As one technical communication expert noted:

> The challenge for the professional communicator is to contribute at a higher level, welcoming community involvement and building on it. For the technical writer, that may mean doing less writing and more curating of content—for example, identifying and promoting the best wiki contributions, correcting errors, clarifying unclear language, adding illustrations, and improving organization. (Carr)

As discussed previously, social media managers (often trained in technical communication) play an important role in encouraging community participation and checking the accuracy of what gets posted.

Personal versus Workplace Uses of Social Media

Social media posts in workplace settings need to adhere to the kind of guidelines discussed throughout this text: words and images should be professional, concise, accurate, and clear. Yet social media is a world where professional and personal lives often intersect. Your personal Facebook page, Twitter, or Instagram account may contain images and posts that are suitable for friends and family: photos of a party or vacation; political opinions; off-the-cuff remarks about a news item or a new technology. When writing these posts as a student and an individual, you probably envision your audience as only those people you have chosen to see your posts (your friends or a custom list). *Personal uses*

But it is important to keep in mind that social media posts can travel far beyond your initial audience, and they can last for years. For example, many people have come to regret a Facebook posting or a tweet when it comes time for a job interview. Remember that although you may control your "friends list," it is very easy for people with enough time on their hands (and some easy-to-use software) to dig through your online history and compile a digital profile of you and your personal opinions and habits. *Workplace uses*

Social Media in Technical and Workplace Communication

20.2 Discuss the workplace uses of various popular social media.

The most common social media sites for workplace communication are discussed below.

Customer Review Sites

For companies such as restaurants, hotels, and entertainment venues, word of mouth can be the most important—or the most damaging—form of advertising. Customer review sites (Yelp and TripAdvisor are two of the most popular) allow registered *Business uses of customer review sites* members to post feedback in the form of short reviews. People can also rate the business using a number of stars. In some cases, companies are able to write a follow-up response, which can be especially important if the customer review is not favorable.

Facebook

Facebook for organizations

As previously mentioned, Facebook is used by government agencies, nonprofit organizations, and companies both large and small, across the United States and, increasingly, around the globe. Facebook provides a way to keep readers informed about news, updates, products and services, and so forth. Like customer review sites, Facebook also allows readers to participate on the site, posting questions and comments. Social media directors and others who manage the site often need to sift through these comments to ensure accuracy and keep "flame wars" and negative information to a minimum.

Google+

Workplace uses of Google+

Google+ is a suite of applications that includes email, document collaboration and sharing, and a network of friends and workplace associates that you can use to stay in touch and share information. Google+ allows you to create special lists of people you want to communicate with: for example, business associates, friends, acquaintances, and so on. In this way, you can customize the audience for your message. Google+ also offers real-time ways to interact with your audience, such as Google Hangouts and Google Chat.

Instagram

Workplace uses of Instagram

Instagram is an app that features the use of photos and other visuals. Instagram was originally developed as a quick and easy phone-based app for people to share photos with friends, but its use has expanded as organizations notice Instagram's potential to reach customers. Businesses with a focus on visual information in particular use Instagram to share photos and coupons, promote new product lines or sales, and connect with existing and new customers.

LinkedIn and Other Job Sites

Social networking sites can help you stay connected, discover job openings, and advertise yourself. One popular professional networking site is LinkedIn (see Figure 20.2). On this and similar sites, you can keep your profile (work experience, references, and so forth) updated and make this profile available to professional contacts, potential employers, and job recruiters. Importantly, you can connect with former colleagues and classmates. These people are often your best bet for learning about job openings. Don't be shy about contacting people you don't know firsthand but with whom you have some mutual connection through a third party (a former coworker, for example).

Figure 20.2 LinkedIn, a Professional Networking Site

To keep your personal and professional contexts somewhat separate, encourage your friends and family to connect with you on Facebook, but let colleagues (both current and former) know that for professional connections, you prefer to stay in touch via LinkedIn.

Employment uses of LinkedIn

Twitter is also a popular tool for employment-related communication. Many companies use Twitter to announce job openings. By using Twitter, companies can reach hundreds of potential employees quickly and inexpensively. People can click on a link that takes them to the job posting or other information.

Twitter as an employment tool

Twitter

As mentioned, Twitter can be used for employment information. Twitter also provides real-time postings and updates in a concise format. Individuals as well as companies, government agencies, and other organizations maintain Twitter feeds to keep friends, business associates, customers, and citizens informed and updated. Called "tweets," the form of writing on Twitter is concise, with a limit of 140 characters (not counting certain character strings, such as Twitter handles, denoted with the @ symbol). A tweet may contain a Web address that people can click on for more information.

Other uses of Twitter

Twitter can be especially effective in situations that require a rapid response. For example, when a major weather event (such as a hurricane or blizzard) interrupts air travel, airlines become inundated with calls from customers. A Twitter feed can be a

Figure 20.3 Twitter feed during a weather emergency

🌲 *PineTree Airways*	**PT Airways** @PTAirways @ LauraG Sorry you can't get through by phone. Blizzard has slowed things down. Please rebook online if you can bit.ly/LGjEcl/11 ^CF
🌲 *PineTree Airways*	**PT Airways** @PTAirways @ NitaR International connections are still being rebooked. Check with a gate agent when you get in. ^CF
🌲 *PineTree Airways*	**PT Airways** @PTAirways @ AnetaD Please call us again at the new 800 no. we just posted on the website. Have your confirmation no. handy. ^MC
🌲 *PineTree Airways*	**PT Airways** @PTAirways @ greg_s Greg, did you check your flight status on our website? Here's the link bit.ly/XYZGEx ^MC
🌲 *PineTree Airways*	**PT Airways** @PTAirways @ joan_kc MSP is providing meals and blankets if you are stranded. Please see a gate agent. Thank you for your patience. ^CF
🌲 *PineTree Airways*	**PT Airways** @PTAirways @ Geoff_travels Geoff, that flight is delayed two hours. Keep checking our website if you can bit.ly/LGjEcl/11 thank you. ^CF
🌲 *PineTree Airways*	**PT Airways** @PTAirways Dear customers, as storm conditions improve, we will be updating all flight statuses so please stay tuned to Twitter and our website.

very effective method for providing customers with up-to-date information, by the minute, on flight cancellations, contingency plans, and resources for more information. See Figure 20.3—note the short, compact, informational tweets that are written with a professional, friendly tone. Those customers who are stuck at the airport or at home wondering about the flight situation can stay tuned via their phone for the latest status update.

YouTube

Using YouTube for video instructions

For workplace communication, YouTube offers an easy-to-access site where customers can watch videos that help explain a concept or demonstrate how to perform a task. Many organizations create video instructions in addition to print or online user guides. Viewers can post comments and ideas to the video's Web page; these comments provide valuable feedback on the product or idea being featured and give audience members a chance to offer their input directly to the company or organization.

Other Popular Social Media Sites

In addition to the sites mentioned above, organizations are also turning their attention to Reddit, Tumblr, and Pinterest. These sites, and other social media apps just on the horizon, illustrate the power of social media to reach audiences, especially for marketing and information-sharing purposes, with social media managers crafting information suitable for each platform. Icons are usually seen on the organization's main Web site, allowing users to click and join one of these social media feeds.

Credibility and Legal Issues

20.3 **Identify credibility and legal issues related to using social media on the job.**

Social media platforms provide powerful ways to influence human understanding. For instance, consider how social media posts can affect perceptions of credibility, truth, and accuracy. We all know of situations where a Facebook post or tweet has gone viral, circulating thousands (if not more) times, only to be discovered later to be untrue, inaccurate, or distorted.

Social media and credibility

Two factors contribute to this phenomenon. First, social media posts are typically shared by others from within a trusted network, for example, friends, family members, valued colleagues, and trusted organizations. As humans, we tend to view as credible what we hear from trusted sources. Second, social media posts combine visuals and text in short, speedy bursts. The visuals in particular play an important role in our response: Images are processed quickly and appeal to the more primitive areas of our brains—the "fight or flight" parts that want to respond (and repost) quickly. Social media images might be shared hundreds, thousands, or even more times, across numerous platforms, reinforcing their messages as the images are repeated over and over.

Because of these features, social media can be highly effective for technical and workplace communication, but the potential for problems also looms large. For example, if companies make a mistake with a social media post (say, an inaccurate claim about a product or an incorrect interpretation about a disease epidemic or medication recall), tens of thousands of Facebook, Twitter, and Yelp users can turn the mistake into a public relations nightmare (Baker 48–50) or even worse, a major health and safety situation. Or, consider the idea of "stealth marketing," in which people who publish supposedly objective product reviews fail to disclose the free merchandise or cash payments they received for their flattering portrayals. These reviews may circulate on social media appearing to be objective, factual discussions when in fact they are a form of marketing hidden behind a credible looking and sounding post.

In addition to credibility concerns, it is important to consider workplace uses of social media in relation to privacy and other legal matters. Most social media sites have privacy policies, but these documents are often difficult to find on the site and

Social media and legal issues

are dense and hard to understand. An accessible and easy-to-read privacy policy is important to help inform readers of what data the site is collecting and how the site uses this data.

Employees within the organization must maintain a professional and appropriate tone and approach when posting. Those who discuss proprietary matters or post defamatory comments on social media can face serious legal consequences— not to mention job termination. Also, like email, social media sites create the potential for violations of copyright and confidentiality (see Chapter 18 for more on email and copyright).

To reinforce legal and other standards, organizations such as IBM, the American Red Cross, Dell, Intel, and many others have created social media guidelines and policies. Recognizing the particular challenge of protecting patient privacy, the American Nurses Association and the National Council of State Boards of Nursing created special guidelines on social media and networking specific for nurses ("News Release"). These types of guidelines and policies will become increasingly important as new social media apps come online and businesses and organizations work to adapt to the changing technological environments.

Strategies
for Social Media

- **Write with a friendly yet professional tone.** It's always nice to be friendly, but a professional tone will make your message more credible.
- **Keep ideas focused and specific.** Social media let you narrow your message down to a targeted audience (say, customers who use a specific model of laptop).
- **Be discreet about what you post.** When posting to your personal Facebook or other page, remember to omit private or potentially damaging information. It may be fun to tell your friends how many parties you've attended, but when you apply for a job, this information may come back to haunt you.
- **Keep global readers in mind.** Social media can typically be viewed by readers from across many countries and cultures. Keep the content accessible to a wide audience (see Chapter 1 for more on global audiences).
- **Keep credibility and accuracy in mind.** Remember: People tend to trust what they already believe or what comes from trusted networks of friends and colleagues. Make sure your post is accurate and true, and include visuals that are appropriate for the topic but don't exaggerate or over-dramatize the point.
- **Have a social media policy.** No matter the size of your organization, having clear, accessible social media guidelines will ensure that social media communication is professional and consistent in content, tone, and style.
- **Choose the most appropriate app for your message.** A short tweet can reach thousands of readers quickly, but you'll need a link to another site (your organization's Web site, for example) to provide readers with more detailed information. Keep an eye out for new social media apps and consider how these different platforms can best support your organization's mission.

Checklist

for Social Media

- ❑ When creating a social media site for a company or organization, have I written content and used images that are professional and appropriate?
- ❑ When creating a social media site for myself, have I used the right site for the right purpose (e.g., LinkedIn for professional networking and job hunting)?
- ❑ For personal use, does the information I've posted portray me in a way that I would want a potential employer to see?
- ❑ For a workplace social media post, is my writing friendly yet professional in tone?
- ❑ Have I kept ideas focused and specific?
- ❑ For tweets that refer to a longer topic, have I included a link for more information?
- ❑ Have I used language and images appropriate for a global audience?
- ❑ Does my post or tweet adhere to the company's social media policy?
- ❑ Have I considered issues about credibility and legal matters (such as privacy and confidentiality)?

Applications

General Application

Explore several job-related social media sites (e.g., LinkedIn, Ryze, Spoke). What are the differences among these sites? For instance, all may offer to help you see your network of professional contacts, but does one of these sites offer a better visual display of connections? Do all of these sites let you upload your resume and provide a list of references? If you have an account with any of these, look at your profile to see how well it reflects your current experience and career goals. Make a list of five to six qualities that students should consider when writing and posting to professional networking sites.

Team Application

Work with a partner to look at your Facebook page and your partner's Facebook page. Imagine that you are managers interested in hiring new college students for a trainee position in your department. What do these Facebook pages tell you about these potential employees? What aspects of Facebook pages—pictures, text, connections—should college students consider during their transition from student to potential employee? Write a short summary of your thoughts, and share it with the class.

Global Application

Customer review sites are written and read by people around the globe. If you are a social media manager for a company, you'll need to read these reviews and write professional, thoughtful responses. Look up a service, restaurant, hotel, or other business using Yelp or TripAdvisor. Find one that has a mix of reviews (some good, some not so good). Did someone from the company write a response? If so, is it appropriate in tone and style for a global audience? Keeping a global audience in mind, write your own response to one or several of these (do not post it), and discuss it with a group of three to four students.

Digital and Social Media Application

Go online and search for the phrase "social media policy" and "social media guidelines." See what you can find from organizations of various sizes and content areas. (Hint: Start with your own college or university to see what they came up with). Compare the policies and guidelines you found with the posts you found on the customer review site (global application). Draft a set of social media guidelines that you think would be most effective for this customer review site (if the site has an existing policy or guidelines, see if you can add anything important based on your searches). Pay special attention to issues of word choice, tone, and privacy.

Chapter 21
Oral Presentations and Video Conferencing

Learning Objectives

21.1 Analyze the audience and purpose of an oral presentation.

21.2 Identify the five types of oral presentations.

21.3 Organize an oral presentation using an introduction–body–conclusion structure.

21.4 Prepare for an oral presentation by carefully considering various factors.

21.5 Use presentation software effectively.

21.6 Understand the workplace uses of video conferencing.

21.7 Deliver a confident, professional oral presentation.

Chapter Outline

Audience and Purpose of Oral Presentations   369

Types of Oral Presentations   369

Parts of Oral Presentations   372

Preparing Oral Presentations   373
    Strategies for Preparing Oral Presentations   379

Using Presentation Software   379

Video Conferencing   380
    Strategies for Using Presentation Software and Video Conferencing   381

Delivering Oral Presentations   382
    Strategies for Delivering Oral Presentations   382
    Checklist for Oral Presentations   383

Applications   383

The importance of oral presentations in the workplace

In addition to being excellent writers and strong visual designers, technical communicators also need to be effective at presenting their ideas in person. The skills required to give an effective oral presentation include thorough research, strong organization, and stage presence. You may be asked to make oral presentations at meetings in your department or company (status reports, team meetings, and so on), at professional conferences or meetings, to your community, or in the classroom.

The interactive nature of oral presentations

Unlike written documents, oral presentations are interactive. Face-to-face communication is arguably the richest form of interaction because you can give and receive information via body language, vocal inflection, eye contact, and other physical means. Moreover, there is room for give and take, which does not happen with written documents. Oral presentations allow you to see how your audience reacts. You can get immediate feedback, and you can change or amend your ideas on the spot.

Presentations involve careful preparation

Most professionals use software such as Microsoft PowerPoint, Apple Keynote, Google Slides, or Prezi when giving a presentation. These apps provide hundreds of easy-to-use templates, adaptable for almost any situation. However, before choosing a template, you need to begin by carefully creating a presentation that is well researched and clearly organized. Only then should you work on the slides and then practice so that your presentation is delivered with a professional yet personal style.

Audience and Purpose of Oral Presentations

21.1 Analyze the audience and purpose of an oral presentation.

Analyzing audience and purpose is a slightly different proposition when speaking rather than writing. Therefore, use the amended version of the Audience and Purpose Profile Sheet provided in Figure 21.1.

Do all you can to find out exactly who will be attending your presentation. Determine their roles within the organization. Learn about their attitudes and personal experiences regarding your subject. For example, managers may focus on the bottom line, while engineers may care more about the difficulties involved in the project you are proposing. Oral presentations are often delivered to a mixed group, so consider the attitudes of the group as a whole and speak to the needs of various factions. The group is also likely to consist of people from various cultural and linguistic backgrounds, so be sure to account for these differences.

Audience considerations

Determine whether your purpose is to inform, instruct, or persuade. Does your audience simply need some vital information? If so, provide enough detail and explanation for people to understand the information clearly. Will they use your information to perform a task? If so, focus on the task itself and send background and other information via email after the presentation. Is your goal to influence your audience's thinking or sell something? If so, be sure to have all the specifications, costs, and other data that will help audience members make their decision. In short, knowing clearly what you wish to accomplish will help you formulate a definite plan for your presentation.

Purpose considerations

Types of Oral Presentations

21.2 Identify the five types of oral presentations.

Your primary purpose will determine the type of presentation required: an informative presentation, a training presentation, a persuasive presentation, an action plan presentation, or a sales presentation.

Five types of oral presentations

Informative Presentations

Informative presentations are often given at conferences, product update meetings, briefings, or class lectures. Your goal is to be as impartial as possible and to provide the best information you can locate. If your primary purpose is informative, observe these criteria:

Informative presentations provide facts and explanations

Figure 21.1 Audience and purpose profile sheet for an oral presentation

AUDIENCE

Primary audience members: _____
(names, titles)

Secondary audience members: _____

_____

Are most attendees of this presentation members of the same team or group?
Y   N

Relationship with audience members: _____
(client, employer, other)

Technical background of audience: _____
(layperson, expert, other)

Cultural background of audience: _____

How many people will attend: 2–6   7–12   13–20   more than 20

PURPOSE

Primary purpose: _____ (informative, training,
persuasive, action plan, sales)

Secondary purpose(s): _____

Intended use of presentation: _____ (to inform or
educate; to persuade; to propose an action; to sell something)

ROOM or LOCATION for presentation

Conference tables, theater style, or other. Describe. _____

_____

EQUIPMENT AND TECHNOLOGY

Laptop or flash drive

Speakers or projector

Flip chart

Whiteboard or chalkboard

- Keep the title of the presentation clear and factual.
- Stipulate at the outset that your purpose is simply to provide information.
- Be clear about your sources of information.

Training Presentations

Training (or instructional) presentations can cover such topics as how to ensure on-the-job safety, how to use a specific software application, or how to exit a capsized kayak. Some technical communicators specialize in giving training presentations. If your primary purpose is instructional, follow these guidelines:

Training presentations show how to perform a task

- Use a title that indicates the training purpose of the presentation.
- Provide an overview of the learning outcomes—what participants can expect to learn from the presentation.
- Create slides or a handout that participants can reference later when they are trying to perform the task(s) on their own.

Persuasive Presentations

To influence people's thinking, give a persuasive presentation. For example, an engineer at a nuclear power plant may wish to persuade her peers that a standard procedure is unsafe and should be changed. In a persuasive situation, be sure to perform adequate research so you are well informed on all sides of the issue. If your primary purpose is persuasive, follow these guidelines:

Persuasive presentations attempt to gain support or change an opinion

- Be clear from the start that you are promoting a point of view.
- Use research and visual data (charts, graphs, etc.) to support your stance.
- Consider and address counterarguments in advance ("Some might say this approach won't work, but here is why it will"), and be prepared to take questions that challenge your point of view.

Action Plan Presentations

To get something done, give an action plan presentation. For example, if you wanted your company to address a design flaw in one of its products, you would give a presentation that outlined the problem, presented a specific solution, and encouraged listeners to implement the solution. If your primary purpose is to evoke action, follow these guidelines:

Action plan presentations motivate people to take action

- Be clear up front about your purpose ("My primary purpose today is to ask you to act on this matter").
- Present the research to back up the need for your plan.
- Show that you have considered other plans but that yours is most effective.
- In closing, restate what you want your audience to do.

Sales Presentations

Technical sales presentations need to be well researched. (At many high-tech companies, technical sales representatives are often scientists or engineers who understand the product's complexities and are good communicators). If your primary purpose is to sell something, observe these criteria:

- Let the facts tell the story. Use examples to illustrate why your product or service is the right one.
- Know your product or service—and those of your competitors—inside and out. Thorough knowledge and a well-researched competitive analysis will make your presentation that much more persuasive.
- Display sincere interest in the needs and concerns of your customers.
- Provide plenty of time for questions. You may think you have made an airtight case, but you will need extra face-to-face time to field questions and convince skeptical audience members.

Parts of Oral Presentations

21.3 **Organize an oral presentation using an introduction–body–conclusion structure.**

Like most technical documents, oral presentations should follow an introduction–body–conclusion structure.

Introduction

For introducing most presentations, pay attention to three main tasks:

1. Capture your audience's attention by telling a quick story, asking a question, or relating your topic to a current event or to something else the audience cares about.
2. Establish your credibility by stating your credentials or explaining where you obtained your information.
3. Preview your presentation by listing the main points and the overall conclusion.

An effective introduction might sound like this:

> How many times have you searched for medical information online, only to find that after hours of looking, you can't tell the difference between credible and questionable information? If you're like most Americans polled in a recent survey, you may feel that you are wasting time when it comes to online medical information. My name is Travis Armstrong, and I've been researching this topic for some time. Today, I'd like to share my findings with you by covering three main points: how to search for medical information, how to separate good information from bad, and how to contribute to medical discussions online.

Body

Readers who get confused or want to know the scope of a print document can look back at the headings, table of contents, or previous pages. But oral presentations have no such features. To make your presentation easy to follow, structure the material into small chunks. To signal that you are moving from one main point to another, use transition statements such as, "Now that I've explained how to separate good information from bad, let me suggest how you can contribute to medical discussions on the Internet."

Use small chunks and transitions in the body

Conclusion

Your conclusion should return full circle to your introduction. Remind your audience of the big picture, restate the main points you've just covered, and leave listeners with some final advice or tips for locating more information. You can also distribute handouts at this time.

Tie everything together

Preparing Oral Presentations

21.4 **Prepare for an oral presentation by carefully considering various factors.**

Preparing an oral presentation is a step-by-step process that requires research, planning, and rehearsal.

Research and Connect the Topic to Your Audience

Be prepared to support each assertion, opinion, conclusion, and recommendation with solid evidence. Begin gathering material well ahead of time. Use recognized sources, such as newspaper articles, peer-reviewed journals, industry fact sheets, government documents, and interviews. Check your facts for accuracy. If you will be using presentation software or handouts, you will need to indicate your information sources on the slides or handouts (typically as footnotes at the bottom of the slide or page). Keep track of your sources.

Know your topic

Even the most well-researched presentation won't be effective unless the speaker connects the topic to the interests, backgrounds, and technical levels of the audience. Look back at your Audience and Purpose Profile Sheet, and think about ways you can connect to ideas already familiar to your audience.

Relate the topic to your audience

Create an Outline or Storyboard

If your presentation is a spoken version of a written report, you can start with the outline of your written report, but modified for a presentation (Figure 21.2). Otherwise, organize your ideas in terms of A- and B-level headings. Indicate on the outline any places where you want to use a visual. If you plan to use presentation software, go to "outline mode" or "outline view" to start laying out your presentation.

Use an outline to organize your thoughts

Use a
storyboard to
accommodate
multiple visuals

If your presentation includes multiple visuals, you might create a storyboard rather than an outline. Storyboards help you see how the visuals will complement the spoken content. A simple storyboard (Figure 21.3) for an oral presentation consists of a double-column format in which your discussion is outlined in the left column and the specific supporting visuals are described in the right column.

Figure 21.2 is an outline for a short oral presentation with only a few slides and visuals, whereas Figure 21.3 is a partial storyboard for a longer oral presentation involving many visuals.

Determine a Delivery Style

Use an
appropriate
delivery style

Your presentation's effectiveness will depend largely on how well it connects with listeners. Different styles of delivery (memorized, impromptu, scripted, and extemporaneous) create different connections.

Memorized
delivery style

A memorized delivery takes a long time to prepare, offers no chance for revision during the presentation, and spells disaster if you lose your place. Avoid a memorized delivery style in workplace settings.

Impromptu
delivery style

An impromptu (off-the-cuff) delivery style can be a natural way of connecting with listeners—but only when you really know your material, feel comfortable with

---

Figure 21.2 An outline for a short oral presentation

I. Introduction
   A. Introduce myself
   B. Open with a question ("How do students use social media in college?")
   C. Give audience overview of my presentation's organization

II. Body
   A. Discuss the types of social media used most frequently by
      today's college students
   B. Talk about social media and the college experience (e.g. meeting
      your roommate via Facebook; using LinkedIn for jobs and internships)
   C. Discuss several national surveys on social media and college students
   D. Present survey findings on social media and privacy
   E. Show some of the university's social media sites that students may not be
      familiar with

III. Conclusion
   A. Restate my main points
   B. Tell audience that I will take questions for the last 15 minutes

Figure 21.3 A partial storyboard for a long oral presentation

---

Pollution Threats to Local Groundwater

1.0 Introduce the Problem

    1.1   Do you know what you are drinking when you turn on the tap and fill the glass?

    1.2   The quality of our water is good but not guaranteed to last forever.

    1.3   Cape Cod's rapid population growth poses a serious threat to our freshwater supply.   *(slide: a line graph showing 20 year population growth)*

    1.4   Measurable pollution in some town water supplies has already occurred.   *(slide: two side-by-side tables showing 20 year increases in nitrate and chloride concentrations in three town wells)*

    1.5   What are the major causes and consequences of this problem, and what can we do about it?   *(poster: a multicolored list that previews my five subtopics)*

2.0 Describe the Aquifer

    2.1   The groundwater is collected and held in an aquifer.

         2.1.1.   This porous rock formation creates a broad, continuous arch beneath the entire Cape.   *(slide: a cutaway view of the aquifer's geology)*

---

your audience, and are in an informal speaking situation. Avoid an impromptu delivery style when making complex and formal presentations, no matter how well you know the material.

In some formal settings (a speech, a keynote address, a conference paper), it may be appropriate for you to read your material verbatim from a prepared script. A scripted delivery can help you keep strict control over your material and meet time limits, but it offers little chance for audience interaction and can be boring. If you do plan to read aloud, rehearse until you are able to glance up from the script periodically without losing your place.   *Scripted delivery style*

An extemporaneous delivery style is carefully planned, practiced, and based on notes that keep you on track. In this natural way of addressing an audience, you glance at your material and speak in a conversational manner. Extemporaneous delivery is based on key ideas in sentence or topic outline form, often projected as overhead transparencies or as slides generated from presentation software.   *Extemporaneous delivery style*

An extemporaneous delivery is typically the preferred method for oral presentations in the workplace: It provides somewhat of a script for the speaker and allows the speaker to interact with the audience while following along. However, there are dangers, such as losing track, skipping over a key point, or going over a time limit.

Table 21.1 Advantages and drawbacks of delivery styles

Delivery Method	* Main Uses *	• Main Drawbacks •
IMPROMPTU (inventing as you speak)	* in-house meetings * small, intimate groups * simple topics	• offers no chance to prepare • speaker might ramble • speaker might lose track
SCRIPTED (reading verbatim from a written work)	* formal speeches * large, unfamiliar groups * strict time limit * cross-cultural audiences * highly nervous speaker	• takes a long time to prepare • speaker can't move around • limits human contact • can appear stiff and unnatural • might bore listeners • makes working with visuals difficult
EXTEMPORANEOUS (speaking from an outline of key points)	* face-to-face presentations * medium-sized, familiar groups * moderately complex topics * somewhat flexible time limit * visually based presentations	• speaker might lose track • speaker might leave something out • speaker might exceed time limit • speaker might fumble with notes, visuals, or equipment

Table 21.1 summarizes the various uses and drawbacks of the latter three delivery styles (memorized style should always be avoided and is therefore not included). In many instances, some combination of methods can be effective. For example, in an orientation for new employees, you might prefer the flexibility of an extemporaneous format but also read a scripted passage aloud from time to time.

Choose Your Technology

Use the technology that suits your audience and purpose

Although presentation software is a helpful and popular tool (see the section on presentation software in this chapter), there are other options. For example, you might opt for a more natural, extemporaneous presentation in which you use handouts or flip charts. Or you might decide to sketch on a whiteboard or show a short video clip. Think about your audience: What would work best? What would keep people active, engaged, and listening? Can you combine the use of slides with some places where you draw on a whiteboard or invite your audience to add ideas to the slides you've created?

Plan the Use of Visuals

Use visuals to enhance the presentation

Visuals not only add vigor and impact to a presentation, but they also summarize complex information and set a tone. Although visuals are an important component, they can also be overused or misused. A presentation that simply uses one visual after the other could bore or confuse an audience. Likewise, visuals that carry no real meaning or that are hard to see or decipher will frustrate the audience. Seek a balance of text/speech and visuals that enhance the presentation rather than distracting from it. Figure 21.4 uses one visual, a photograph of students using social media, to help break up the text on this slide and create visual interest.

Figure 21.4 Four slides from a short oral presentation

Note that for the full presentation, each bullet point on Slide 2 would have a corresponding slide as part of the body of the presentation

Social media and college students

Lynn N. Rice
Undergraduate research assistant
Department of Media and Communication

Title page introduces the speaker and topic

1.

Social media in college

- How do students use social media in college?
  - Commonly used forms of social media
  - Connection of social media to the college experience
  - What we know from national surveys
  - Other social media sites at the university

Overview slide previews the main points to be covered

2.

What do students use the most?

- Most commonly used sites by college students:
  - Facebook
  - Twitter
  - LinkedIn

SOURCE: Duggan, M., & Smith, A. (2013). Social media update 2013. Pew Internet & American Life Project. Retrieved from http://www.pewinternet.org/2013/12/30/social-media-update-2013/.

3.

First slide from body of the presentation

Source information is set in smaller type at the bottom of the slide

Questions and discussion

- What are your experiences with social media on campus?
- How do you feel about privacy and social media?
- Other questions

4.

Conclusion slide offers questions but invites other input

Practice the Presentation

On your own or with a volunteer viewer, practice your presentation. This process will give you an idea of how you sound and look while speaking; it will also reveal gaps or wordiness in your presentation and help you get the timing right. If possible, make an audio or video recording of yourself to see if you speak too fast or too slow or if you gesture too much or look stiff. Try to rehearse with the actual equipment you plan to use and in the actual setting.

Rehearse to fine-tune

Strategies

for Preparing Oral Presentations

- **Determine your audience.** Fill out the audience portion of an Audience and Purpose Profile Sheet. Know exactly who your listeners are (primary and secondary), what their attitude is toward the topic, what they already know, and what they need to learn. If you anticipate that different audience members will have different needs, make sure you speak to the entire audience.
- **Determine your purpose.** Is the purpose of the presentation to inform, instruct, or persuade? Adjust your presentation to suit its particular purpose.
- **Do your research.** Make sure you understand your topic. Anticipate audience questions or objections, and prepare answers or responses.
- **Decide on your delivery style.** Avoid the memorized style, as you may lose your place. Choose an impromptu, scripted, or extemporaneous style, but recognize the pros and cons of each.
- **Organize your presentation.** Include an introduction, body, and conclusion. Prepare an outline (typical presentation) or storyboard (visually complex presentation) to work out what information to discuss and when.
- **Choose your technology.** You need not always use presentation software. Consider alternatives such as handouts, flip charts, or whiteboards.
- **Use visuals.** Whenever possible, enhance your presentation by using visuals, but only when they genuinely add to the discussion. Be sure all your visuals are easy for the audience to see and understand.
- **Rehearse your presentation.** Practice, and correct any content or style problems based on your rehearsal.

Using Presentation Software

21.5 **Use presentation software effectively.**

PowerPoint, a Microsoft product, is still the most widely used presentation software, especially in the workplace (Figure 21.4 was created using PowerPoint). Yet other apps, such as Apple Keynote, Google Slides, and Prezi are also used by students and professionals alike. Each of these programs offer dozens of templates you can choose from, suitable for almost any situation. Templates can be very helpful for organizing your ideas and saving you the time involved in creating a professional design from scratch. But do not start your presentation by choosing a template.

Varieties of presentation software

Start with
research

As discussed earlier in this chapter, begin by doing careful research about your audience, the purpose of your presentation, and your topic. Use an outlining or storyboarding technique to organize your ideas. Then, choose a template that is right for your situation, considering the colors, shapes, fonts, and so forth based on guidance provided in Chapter 7 of this book. Also, keep in mind that many organizations provide in-house templates, customized with the appropriate colors, logos, and other features and information. (For instance, your college or university probably has a school template that uses the school colors and official college font.) Templates can usually be modified if you need to change a font or color but want to retain the layout.

Qualities
of effective
presentation
software slides

Keep your presentation clean, clear, and professional. Remember that what looks great on your laptop (a bright yellow font on a blue background, for example) might be unreadable on a large screen. Experiment a bit with animation and transitions, but be careful: Too much visual "noise" will distract your audience. If you are presenting as a team, transitions are a nice way to signal a shift between speakers.

If your topic involves spatial concepts (design ideas for a new office layout, for example) or visuals that are best displayed in an interactive manner, you might try Prezi, which offers many built-in features for motion and animation. Use animation, sound, and video clips only as needed to support your presentation.

For collaborative projects, consider using a cloud-based, collaborative app. Google Slides, for instance, available through Google Drive, allows multiple people to work on the project in real time, with a small chat window that you and your team can use to discuss ideas while working. The file is updated as you work on it, and the document remains on the server, not on someone's hard drive (or worse yet, attached but lost in a string of someone's emails). Microsoft Cloud, Dropbox, and your organization's internal file server also provide ways to collaborate and store files.

Whatever approach you choose, remember that good presentations must be well researched, carefully planned, well organized, and correctly timed. Excessive material crammed on one slide might help you as you speak but will frustrate your audience. Also, while presentation software helps structure your story or argument, an overreliance on bulleted items can oversimplify complex issues and distract from the deeper message. For more specific advice, see the Strategies for Using Presentation Software on pages 381–382.

Video Conferencing

21.6 Understand the workplace uses of video conferencing.

Video
conferencing
programs and
platforms

When audience members are at different job sites (around the country or in different countries), a face-to-face presentation may not be possible. Video conferencing allows team members to join the meeting but not be physically present. There are many kinds of video conferencing, including the following:

- **Webinars** allow you to deliver a presentation via the Internet. Audience members are invited to connect to the webinar via their computer and software such as

WebEx, GoToMeeting, or Adobe Connect. Most webinars display the presenter's slides on the screen while the presenter talks through each slide and controls when to change slides. You can also display video of the speaker and/or other conference participants. Audience questions are typically handled via video chat or a typed live chat feature.

- **Skype** allows people to connect via real-time audio and video from a computer, phone, or tablet. Skype software needs to be downloaded in advance, and each person needs to set up a user name and password. Skype has become quite popular, in part because it is free (and easy to use). But the sound and image quality may not always be adequate for complex technical and business presentations. Most companies prefer a webinar or other secure in-house video conferencing approach.

For video conferencing to work, everyone must be available at the same time. If you are on the east coast of the United States, for example, and some of your audience is in Europe, there could be anywhere from a five- to eight-hour time difference. Video conferencing with audiences in Asia requires even more careful time calculations. Depending on the location of team members, it may be impossible to get everyone to connect at the same time. In these cases, you may be able to record a session and allow people to view it, and your slides, later.

Special considerations for video conferencing

Strategies

for Using Presentation Software and Video Conferencing

- **Don't let the app do the thinking.** Use your own research, sense of audience and purpose, and other original ideas to shape the presentation. Then use the software to help make the material accessible and interesting. If you start with the slides, your ideas will be constrained by the template and its use of bullets and headings. Create an outline or storyboard first, then find a template that fits your thinking.
- **Have a backup plan in case the technology fails.** For smaller settings, bring handouts to the presentation. Save copies of your presentation on a flash drive and on a cloud file server (e.g. Dropbox; Google drive; Microsoft cloud; other). If allowable, email or upload your slides to the meeting organizer (or your instructor) before the presentation. If your presentation requires a connection to the Internet, check on that aspect in advance to be sure you can get on the room's wifi (in hotels or conference centers, for example, you may need a special password to connect).
- **Don't distribute handouts until you are ready to discuss the contents.** Otherwise, people will start reading the handouts instead of paying attention to you.
- **Start with an overview slide.** Orient your audience by showing an opening slide that indicates what you plan to cover and in what order.
- **Find a balance between text and visuals.** Excessive text is boring; excessive visuals can be confusing. Each visual should serve a purpose: to summarize information, to add emphasis, to set a tone, and so on. Avoid overcrowding the slides: Aim for no more than seven to nine lines per slide (including the heading) with no more than six to nine words per bulleted item.
- **Avoid using too many slides.** In general, aim for one slide per key point. If you are the kind of person who likes to embellish and enjoys speaking to a crowd, use fewer slides.

- **Don't simply read the slides.** Don't just read your slides: People in the audience can do that. Be interactive with your audience; use the slides as a guide.
- **Avoid too much flash.** Don't allow the medium (animations, color, sound) to obscure your message.
- **Keep viewers oriented.** Don't show a slide until you are ready to discuss it. Present one topic per slide, bringing bullets (subtopics) on one at a time as you discuss them. Let your audience digest the slide data *while* you speak—not before or after.
- **End with a "conclusions" or "questions" slide.** Give your audience a sense of having come full circle. On a "conclusions" slide, summarize the key points. A "questions" slide can simply provide a heading and a visual. Allow time at the end of your presentation for questions and/or comments.
- **Use video conferencing when necessary.** If people can't be in the same place at the same time, use a video conferencing solution (WebEx or another webinar platform) to allow all team members to participate in the presentation.
- **For video conferencing, keep international audience members in mind.** Remember that 9:00 A.M. your time may not work for people who live on the other side of the globe. For these people, you might need to use the "record" feature, to make your presentation and slides available to them.

Delivering Oral Presentations

21.7 Deliver a confident, professional oral presentation.

Many find that the actual delivery of an oral presentation is the most difficult hurdle. Most people experience anxiety when they must speak in public. If you are particularly nervous, seek additional advice about ways to calm your nerves, such as stretching beforehand and performing deep breathing exercises. You are likely to find that once you have actually spoken your first line, you will settle down quickly. The following Strategies offer further advice.

Strategies

for Delivering Oral Presentations

- **Be rehearsed and prepared.** The best way to calm your nerves is to remind yourself of the preparation and research you have done. Practice your delivery so that it is professional and appropriate but natural for you. Also, know your material inside and out.
- **Memorize a brief introduction.** If you begin your presentation smoothly and confidently, you won't be as nervous going forward. Do not open by saying "I'm a little bit nervous today" or "I have a slight cold. Can everyone hear me in the back?" Just begin. A memorized introduction will help you avoid having to ad lib (potentially badly) when you are most anxious.
- **Dress for success.** Wear clothes that suggest professionalism and confidence.
- **Stand tall and use eye contact.** Good posture and frequent eye contact convey a sense of poise, balance, and confidence. Practice in front of a mirror. If looking people directly in the eye makes you nervous, aim just above people's heads. Or find a friendly face or two and look at those people first. As you gain confidence, be sure to cast your gaze around the entire room or conference table.

- **Take charge.** If you get interrupted but don't want to take questions until the end, remember that you are in control. Be polite but firm: "Thank you for that good question. I'll save it and other questions until the end of my presentation."
- **Gesture naturally.** Don't force yourself to move around or be theatrical if this is not your style. But do not stand like a robot, either. Unless you are speaking from a podium or lectern, move around just a bit. And when it's time to take questions, consider moving closer to the audience. In a conference room setting, if everyone else is seated, you should stand.
- **Allow time for questions, comments, and discussion.** Announce a time limit; listen carefully; ask for clarification if necessary; provide brief but well-considered replies (if time allows—otherwise, continue later and in private). When the time is up, announce that you have time for one more question or comment, and conclude politely.

Checklist

for Oral Presentations

- ❏ Have I analyzed my audience and purpose thoroughly?
- ❏ Have I done adequate research about the topic, looking into all sides of the problem or issue?
- ❏ Have I organized my material, using an outline or storyboard?
- ❏ Have I chosen a delivery style that best suits my skills and the needs of my audience?
- ❏ Have I decided to use presentation software (e.g., PowerPoint) or to use more basic technology or no technology at all?
- ❏ Am I using an appropriate number of visuals, and do the visuals serve a specific purpose?
- ❏ Have I rehearsed my presentation and ironed out problems with content and delivery?
- ❏ If using presentation software, have I followed the strategies given in this chapter?
- ❏ Have I calmed my nerves and gained confidence by following the strategies for delivering presentations in this chapter?
- ❏ Am I prepared to allow time for questions and comments and to interact with my audience effectively when doing so?

Applications

General Applications

1. Prepare an oral presentation based on the formal report or proposal you wrote for this class. Develop an outline and a storyboard that includes at least three visuals. Ask your instructor for the time limit of the presentation (15 minutes? 20 minutes?), and practice so that you do not exceed the allotted time. (Hint: Consider the ratio of one slide per minute, then cut back to 1–2 slides if you are a slow talker.) Make note of places where you tend to struggle or places where you speak for too long.

2. At work, on an internship, or at a campus event, observe a presentation, and evaluate it according to the Strategies boxes in this chapter. In a memo to your instructor (without naming the speaker), identify strong and weak areas and suggest improvements. Note any technologies used and how much, if any, interaction the speaker had with the audience.

Team Application

In the workplace, presentations are often prepared and delivered by more teams of people. In groups of three to four students, come up with a presentation topic that everyone can work on. (You might want to base this topic on a group writing activity from the semester.) Discuss how, as a team, you will approach the research, planning, and creation of the presentation. For example, will one person be responsible for the research? Will another person put the slides together? Can you use a collaborative or cloud-based app, such as Google Slides, to work on the project? Create a brief presentation, using slides plus any other materials you deem important, describing the process you will take and the decisions your team made. Give the presentation to class. Make sure every student has a role in the presentation.

Global Application

You've been assigned to represent your company at an international conference or before international clients. As you plan and prepare your presentation, what can you do to remain sensitive to various cultural expectations? For example, some cultures might be offended by a presentation that gets right to the point without first observing formalities of politeness. Use the Internet to research issues about intercultural communication, then create a short presentation on this topic for the class.

Social and Digital Media Application

As noted in the Team Application above, presentations are often created collaboratively. What is the best way to share a presentation file and work on it as a group? Compare your options using PowerPoint, Prezi, Google drive, Microsoft cloud, and other tools or sites. Pay attention to the file sharing and collaboration features, and look at the various templates, transitions, ways of importing visual, and other features. Create a short presentation for the class recommending what would work best for students in this class.

Appendix A
Documenting Sources*

Outline

What is Plagiarism?   385

Identifying Sources and Information to be Documented   386

Taking Effective and Accurate Notes   387
    Strategies for Taking Notes   388

Quoting, Paraphrasing, and Summarizing Properly   388
    Strategies for Quoting the Work of Others   389
    Strategies for Paraphrasing the Work of Others   390
    Strategies for Summarizing the Work of Others   391

Documentation: The Key to Avoiding Plagiarism   391

MLA Documentation Style   393

APA Documentation Style   404

Other Documentation Styles   414

Recognizing Copyright Issues   414

What is Plagiarism?

When creating technical documents, especially more formal, longer documents such as reports, you will need to rely on outside research. To make your case credible, use outside sources wisely and avoid plagiarizing the work of others.

Plagiarism is using someone else's work—words, ideas, or illustrations, published or unpublished—without giving the creator of that work sufficient credit. A serious breach of scholarly ethics, plagiarism can have severe consequences in college and at work. Students risk a failing grade or disciplinary action ranging from suspension to expulsion; a record of such action can adversely affect future professional opportunities. Scholars and teachers can face public disgrace and even be forced out of a position. Elsewhere in the workplace, plagiarism can lead to a lawsuit as well as permanent career damage.

Definition and consequences of plagiarism

---

* Portions of this appendix were written by Linda Stern, Publishing School of Continuing and Professional Studies, New York University, and adapted by the authors.

Three values plagiarism violates

Plagiarism violates three significant values: preserving intellectual honesty, giving credit to the work of others, and promoting intellectual growth. First, the academic community relies on the reciprocal exchange of ideas and information to advance knowledge and research. Using material without acknowledging its source violates this expectation and consequently makes it harder for researchers to verify and build on others' results. In addition, plagiarism cheats writers and researchers of the credit they deserve for their work and creativity. Even with the writer's permission, presenting another's work as one's own is equivalent to lying: it's a form of dishonesty. Finally, and perhaps most important for students, plagiarizing negates the very reason for attending college. A student who hands in a plagiarized paper has missed an opportunity for growth and learning.

Plagiarism is easy to spot

Ethical considerations aside, it's hard to get away with plagiarism. Experienced professors can easily tell when a paper is not written in a student's own style or is more professionally prepared than they would expect. In addition, online services can now identify plagiarized papers, and academic institutions are subscribing to such services.

Most plagiarism is unintentional. To avoid plagiarism, you need to do all of the following:

Ways to avoid unintentional plagiarism

- Identify sources and information to be documented in your paper.
- Take effective and accurate notes.
- Understand how to quote, paraphrase, and summarize properly.
- Know how to document sources both in the text itself and at the end of your report.

Identifying Sources and Information to be Documented

The importance of documentation

Documentation is the key to avoiding plagiarism. The legal doctrine of *fair use* (see page 415) allows writers to quote or paraphrase a limited amount of another's work in their own papers and books. To make sure that they are not plagiarizing someone else's work, writers must therefore take care to document every source they consult accurately and clearly. Documentation involves providing readers with sufficient information about the sources you have consulted; consequently, readers may consult those sources themselves if they so desire. This sort of documentation ordinarily requires two elements: (1) an end-of-report list of sources used in the report (known as a Works Cited or References list) and (2) citations in the text of the report that link to the items in that end-of-report list.

What needs to be documented and what does not

Whenever you use information from an *outside source* (any source that isn't your own brain), you need to document that source. Some major outside sources that researchers often consult are discussed in Chapter 2 and include books, newspapers, magazines, journal articles, government sources, radio or television programs, databases and data sets, correspondence, films, plays, interviews, speeches, and surveys. These materials may be accessed in print, online, or both. The one major exception to this rule is that you do not have to document *common knowledge:* widely known information about current events, famous people, geographical facts, or familiar history. When in doubt, the safest strategy is to provide documentation. (For more on what you should document, see page 392.)

Taking Effective and Accurate Notes

Another key way to avoid unintentional plagiarism is to take notes systematically. Do not rely on your memory to keep track of the sources you consult and the information you want to use from those sources. Take detailed notes that identify the specific material and its sources; otherwise you may forget about a source you learned something from, thereby unintentionally plagiarizing.

Why note-taking is important

Because most research today is done electronically, you need to be especially careful about taking notes if you cut and paste quotations or other material from an electronic source. Whether this source is a Web page, a blog or wiki, or a journal article available in electronic format, be sure to keep track of the author (individual or organizational), Web address, and date when you accessed the information. If the publication is a traditional one in e-format (such as the electronic version of the *New York Times*), record the title, page number, and other publication information needed for the citation.

Note-taking from electronic sources

Using old-fashioned notecards is one way to record your sources and the material you want to use. Figure A.1 shows a notecard entry for a bibliographic citation.

How to take notes

Figure A.1 A bibliographic citation

Pinsky, Mark A. *The EMF Book: What You Should Know about Electromagnetic Fields, Electromagnetic Radiation, and Your Health.* Warner, 1995.

Record each bibliographic citation exactly as it will appear in your final report.

Most researchers use citation software (such as Endnote, Zotero, and Mendeley). These programs automatically download citation information directly (from a Web site, a library entry, or many other online sources). Using these programs also lets you keep notes for each entry, search and retrieve entries (by author, title, topic, date, and other fields), and generate in-text citations and references lists. These programs have cloud-based options, often functioning as an extension within popular browsers such as Chrome and Firefox, so you can access your bibliography from anywhere. A simpler option is to take notes in a word-processing file, then use the "Find" command to locate information quickly. Be careful when cutting and pasting direct quotes to mark these as such. Include all citation information.

Using citation software to take notes

Strategies

for Taking Notes

- **Keep copies of your documentation information.** For all sources that you use, keep photocopies or accurate notes of the title and copyright pages and the pages with quotations you need. Highlight the relevant citation information in color. Keep these materials until you've completed your report.
- **Create the Works Cited or References list first.** Before you start writing your report, create a working bibliography, a list of possible sources to which you add entries as they emerge. When you finalize your list, you can delete entries for sources that you've decided not to use.
- **Record bibliographical information for each source you consult.** Use the citation format that will appear in your document. Record the information accurately so you won't have to track down a source at the last minute. When searching online, print out or save the full bibliographic record for each source or copy and paste the Web address into your document, thereby ensuring an accurate citation.
- **Determine whether to quote, paraphrase, or summarize.** When quoting others directly, be sure to record words and punctuation accurately. When restating material in your own words (paraphrasing and summarizing), preserve the original meaning and emphasis. Double-check if any portions of paraphrases or summaries are actually quotations, and insert the necessary quotation marks.

Quoting, Paraphrasing, and Summarizing Properly

Three ways to use outside sources

To avoid plagiarism, you must use material from outside sources properly. You can integrate outside material into your paper in three ways: by quoting, paraphrasing, or summarizing. Each method must accurately convey the meaning expressed in the original source.

Quoting the Work of Others

Definition of a quotation

A *quotation* reproduces a portion of a source, using the exact words, for a purpose of your own: to support a statement or idea, to provide an example, to advance an argument, or to add interest or color to a discussion. A quotation can range in length from a word or phrase to several paragraphs. In general, quote the least amount that gets your point across.

In your notes, place quotation marks around all exact wording you borrow, whether the words were written or spoken (as in an interview or presentation) or appeared in electronic form. Even a single borrowed sentence or phrase or a single word used in a special way requires quotation marks, with the exact source properly cited. These sources include people with whom you collaborate. Figure A.2 shows notes for a quotation. Notes can be taken by typing your information in a word processing document.

Figure A.2 Notes for a quotation

Pinsky, Mark A. pp. 29–30
"Neither electromagnetic fields nor electromagnetic radiation causes cancer per se, most researchers agree. What they may do is promote cancer. Cancer is a multistage process that requires an 'initiator' that makes a cell or group of cells abnormal. Everyone has cancerous cells in his or her body. Cancer—the disease as we think of it—occurs when these cancerous cells grow uncontrollably."

In your notes, place quotation marks around all directly quoted material.

Strategies

for Quoting the Work of Others

- **Use a direct quotation only when absolutely necessary.** Sometimes a direct quotation is the only way to do justice to the author's words or thoughts. Use direct quotations to preserve the original line of reasoning, special phrasing or emphasis, precise meaning, or an especially striking or colorful example. Direct quotes convey the authority and complexity of expert opinion and can capture the original's voice, sincerity, or emotional intensity.
- **Copy the material from your source to your document exactly as it appears in the original.** Do not alter the original spelling, capitalization, or punctuation. If a quotation contains an obvious error, you may insert [*sic*], which is Latin for "so" or "thus," to show that the error appeared in the original. Record the exact page numbers, and double-check that you haven't altered the original expression in any way.
- **Use ellipses to keep quotations as brief as possible.** An ellipsis is three spaced periods (. . .) indicating that words have been omitted within a single sentence. Add a fourth period to indicate the end of a sentence or the omission of more than a sentence. The resulting passage must be grammatical and must not distort the original meaning. (For more on ellipses, see page 428.)
- **Use square brackets to insert your own clarifying comments or transitions.** To distinguish your words from those of your source, place them within brackets—for example, "This occupation [campus police officer] requires excellent judgment."
- **Integrate quoted material into your writing smoothly and grammatically.** Quotations must blend seamlessly into your text so that the resulting sentence is neither ungrammatical nor awkward, and punctuation must be handled properly. (For more on grammar and punctuation, see Appendix B.)
- **In your paper, set off long quotations as block quotations.** Avoid relying on long quotations except when you want to provide an extended example or definition or to analyze or discuss a particular idea or concept. Start on a separate line. Double-space and indent the entire block ten spaces. Do not indent the first line of the passage, and do not use quotation marks.
- **Cite the source of each quoted passage.** Immediately follow each quotation with a parenthetical reference (see pages 393 and 404) indicating the source.

Paraphrasing the Work of Others

Research is a process of independent thinking in which you work with the ideas of others to reach your own conclusions. Therefore, unless the author's exact wording is essential, try to paraphrase instead of quoting borrowed material. A *paraphrase* is a

Definition of a Paraphrase

restatement, in your own words and your own sentence structure, of specific ideas or information from a source. The chief purpose of a paraphrase is to *maintain your own writing style* throughout your paper. A paraphrase can be about as long as the original passage.

Paraphrasing means more than changing or shuffling a few words; it means restating the original idea in your own words—sometimes in a clearer, more direct, and emphatic way—and giving full credit to the source. To offer as a paraphrase an original passage only slightly altered is plagiarism. Equally unethical is offering a paraphrase, though documented, that distorts the original meaning.

Figure A.3 shows notes in which the quotation in Figure A.2 has been paraphrased. Paraphrased material is not enclosed within quotation marks, but it is documented to acknowledge your debt to the source.

Figure A.3 Notes for a paraphrase

Signal the beginning of the paraphrase by identifying the source and the end by citing the location.

> According to Pinsky, most researchers doubt that cancer is caused by either electromagnetic fields or electromagnetic radiation. These electrical currents, however, may "promote" cancer by initiating the "multistage process" that leads to the proliferation of cancer cells that are otherwise present in small amounts in the healthy human body (29–30).

Strategies

for Paraphrasing the Work of Others

- **Retain key words from the original to preserve its meaning.** Use quotation marks within your paraphrase to indicate quoted material.
- **Use your own words and sentence structure.** Do not duplicate the source's words (unless quoting briefly), and write the sentences in your own style.
- **Make sure your readers know when the paraphrase begins and ends.** Identify the source at the start of the paraphrase or as early into it as possible.
- **Be sure to preserve the author's original intent.** Check that your paraphrase is an accurate and objective restatement of the source's specific ideas.
- **Indicate the exact source of each paraphrased passage.** Immediately follow each paraphrase with a parenthetical reference (see pages 393 and 404) indicating the exact location of the material in the source.

Summarizing the Work of Others

Definition of a summary

Like a paraphrase, a *summary* is a restatement of the original in your own words. A summary, however, restates a large portion of the original text briefly, rather than restating a small portion of the original in about the same number of words. Figure A.4 shows notes in which the quotation in Figure A.2 has been summarized.

Figure A.4 Notes for a summary

Pinsky explains that electromagnetic waves probably do not directly cause cancer. However, they might contribute to the uncontrollable growth of cancer cells that are normally present—but controlled—in the human body (29–30).

Signal the beginning of the summary by identifying the source and the end by citing the location.

For more information on summarizing see Chapter 14.

Strategies

for Summarizing the Work of Others

- **Use your own words and sentence structure.** If you must quote a crucial word or phrase directly, use quotation marks around the quoted words.
- **Make sure your readers know when the summary begins and ends.** As with a paraphrase, identify the source early in the summary.
- **Make sure your summary is an accurate restatement of the source's main ideas.** Do not add new details or remove essential details from the original.
- **Indicate the exact source of the summarized material.** Immediately follow each summary with a parenthetical reference (see pages 393 and 404) indicating the exact location of the material in the source.

Documentation: The Key to Avoiding Plagiarism

Proper documentation satisfies professional requirements for ethics, efficiency, and authority.

Why You Should Document

Documentation is a matter of *ethics*, in that the originator of borrowed material deserves full credit and recognition. Moreover, all published material is protected by copyright law. Failure to credit a source could make you liable to legal action, even if your omission was unintentional. (For more on copyright, see page 414.)

Ethical and legal reasons

Documentation is also a matter of *efficiency*. Accurate documentation provides a network for organizing and locating the world's recorded knowledge. If you cite a particular source correctly, your reference will enable interested readers to locate that source themselves.

Efficiency reasons

Finally, documentation is a matter of *authority*. In making any claim (say, "A Mercedes is more reliable than a Ford") you invite challenge: "Says who?" Data on road tests, frequency of repairs, resale value, workmanship, and owner comments can help

Authority reasons

validate your claim by showing its basis in *fact*. A claim's credibility increases in relation to the expert references supporting it. For a controversial topic, you may need to cite several authorities who hold various views. Readers of your research report expect the *complete picture.*

What You Should Document

Document any ideas and works that are not your own

Other than ideas considered *common knowledge*, it is important to document the authors and sources of all ideas that are not your own. Specifically, you must document these sources:

Sources that require documentation

- any source from which you use exact wording
- any source from which you adapt or paraphrase material in your own words
- any visual illustration: charts, graphs, drawings, or the like

How to document a confidential source

In some instances, you might have reason to preserve the anonymity of unpublished sources—say, to allow people to respond candidly without fear of reprisal (as with employee criticism of a company) or to protect their privacy (as with certain material from email inquiries or electronic newsgroups). You must still document the fact that you are not the originator of this material. Using MLA style (see page 393), you would provide a general acknowledgment in the text ("A number of employees expressed frustration with …"), along with a general citation in your list of Works Cited ("Interviews with department employees, May 2014"). Using APA style (see page 404), you would cite the confidential source in your text itself ("During interviews with department employees in May 2014 …").

Common knowledge need not be documented

As stated previously in this appendix, you don't need to document anything considered *common knowledge* (material that appears repeatedly in general sources). In medicine, for instance, it has become common knowledge that foods containing animal fat (meat, butter, cheese, whole milk) raise blood cholesterol levels. So, in a research report on fatty diets and heart disease, you probably would not need to document that well-known fact. But you would document information about how the fat-cholesterol connection was discovered, what subsequent studies have found (say, on the role of saturated versus unsaturated fats), and any information for which some other person(s) could claim specific credit. If the borrowed material can be found in only one specific source and not in multiple sources, document it. When in doubt, document the source.

How You Should Document

Document in text and at the end of the text

Cite borrowed material twice: at the exact place you use that material and at the end of your report. Documentation practices vary widely, but all systems work almost identically in the following respect: A brief in-text reference names the source and refers readers to the complete citation at the end of the report, which allows readers to consult the source if they so desire.

This appendix illustrates citations and entries for two styles that are widely used for documenting sources in professional writing:

- Modern Language Association (MLA) style for the humanities
- American Psychological Association (APA) style for social sciences

Unless your audience or your company has a preference, any style can be adapted to most research writing. Use one style consistently throughout your document.

MLA Documentation Style

The *MLA Handbook*, 8th ed. (2016), requires that you cite a source briefly in your text (called parenthetical references or in-text citations) and fully at the end of the report (in a "Works Cited" list).

MLA Parenthetical References

For clear and informative parenthetical references, observe these guidelines:

- If you name the author in your discussion, do not repeat the name in your parenthetical reference; simply give the page or page range:

  > Lederman points out that data provided by 796 colleges indicate that violent crime on campus began increasing rapidly around 1985 (31).

  Citing page numbers only

- If you cite two or more works in a single parenthetical reference, separate the citations with semicolons:

  > (Gomez 293–94; Jones 32; Leduc 41)

  Three works in a single reference

- If you cite two or more authors with the same surname, include the first initial in your parenthetical reference to each author:

  > (R. Jones 32)
  > (S. Jones 14–15)

  Two authors with identical surnames

- If you cite two or more works by the same author, include the first significant word from each work's title or a shortened version of the title:

  > (Lamont, *Biophysics* 100–01)
  > (Lamont, *Diagnostic Tests* 81)

  Two works by one author

- If the work is by an institutional or corporate author or if it is unsigned (that is, if the author is unknown), use only the first few words of the institutional name or the work's title in your parenthetical reference:

  > (American Medical Association 2)
  > ("Distribution Systems" 18)

  Institutional, corporate, or anonymous author

Keep parenthetical references short

To avoid distracting the reader, keep each parenthetical reference as brief as possible. One method is to name the source in your discussion and to place only the page number in parentheses.

Where to place a parenthetical reference

For a paraphrase, place the parenthetical reference *before* the closing punctuation mark. For a quotation in the text, place the reference *between* the final quotation mark and the closing punctuation mark. For a quotation set off (indented) from the text, place the reference *after* the closing punctuation mark.

MLA Works Cited Entries

How to format the Works Cited list

The Works Cited list includes each source that you have paraphrased or quoted. Place your Works Cited list on a separate page at the end of the document. Arrange entries alphabetically by author's surname. When the author is unknown, list the title alphabetically according to its first word. For a title that begins with a numeral, alphabetize the entry as if the number were spelled out. Type the first line of each entry flush with the left margin. Indent the second and subsequent lines 1/2 inch. Double-space within and between entries.

How to cite individual items

Certain "core elements" of publication information, according to the *MLA Handbook*, 8th ed., should be included in every source citation, no matter what the delivery method (print or digital). These elements include the author and title of the source, the title of the larger entity (which MLA calls a *container*; for example, a journal, newspaper, website, or anthology where the source resides), the names of additional contributors when relevant, the publisher and publication date, and the page numbers or Web address (what MLA terms the *location*).

Table A.1 provides an overview of typical citation types; the rest of this section offers examples based on the MLA guidelines. The introductory section on digital sources (page 400) provides more detail on what the MLA calls the "core elements" of MLA citation style.

What to include in an MLA citation for a book

MLA WORKS CITED ENTRIES FOR BOOKS.   Book citations should contain the information shown in the following examples. Note that unlike previous MLA handbooks, the 8th edition does not require city of publication unless that information is critical for your reader. (E-books are addressed later in this chapter.)

1. Book, Single Author—MLA

Kerzin-Fontana, Jane B. *Technology Management: A Handbook.* 3rd ed. American Management Assn., 2010.

Parenthetical reference: (Kerzin-Fontana 3–4)

2. Book, Two Authors—MLA

Vogel, Werner, and Henry Kalb. *Large-Scale Solar Thermal Power: Technologies, Costs and Development.* Wiley-VCH, 2010.

Parenthetical reference: (Vogel and Kalb 71–88)

Table A.1 Index to MLA Works Cited Entries

Books

1. Book, single author
2. Book, two authors
3. Book, three or more authors
4. Book, anonymous author
5. Multiple books, same author
6. Book, one or more editors
7. Book, indirect source
8. Anthology selection or book chapter

Periodicals

9. Article, magazine
10. Article, journal with new pagination each issue
11. Article, journal with continuous pagination
12. Article, newspaper

Other Sources

13. Encyclopedia, dictionary, other alphabetical reference
14. Report
15. Conference presentation
16. Interview, personally conducted
17. Interview, published

18. Letter, unpublished
19. Questionnaire
20. Brochure or pamphlet
21. Lecture
22. Government document
23. Document with corporate or foundation authorship
24. Map or other visual aid
25. Dissertation or thesis

Digital Sources

26. Online abstract
27. Online article
28. Reference database
29. Online video (YouTube or other)
30. E-book
31. Personal email
32. Wiki
33. Blog
34. Podcast
35. Tweet
36. Web sites and other digital formats

In general, use the publisher's name as it appears on the title page. For university presses, use the abbreviation *UP*. For page numbers with more than two digits, give only the final two digits for the second number when the first digit is identical.

3. Book, Three or More Authors—MLA

Santos, Ruth J., et al. *Environmental Crises in Developing Countries.*
Harper, 2009.

Parenthetical reference: (Santos et al. 9)

et al. is the abbreviated form of the Latin *et alia*, meaning "and others."

4. Book, Anonymous Author—MLA

Structured Programming. Meredith, 2010.

Parenthetical reference: (Structured 67)

5. Multiple Books, Same Author—MLA

Chang, John W. *Biophysics.* Little Brown, 2009.

—. *Diagnostic Techniques.* Radon, 1999.

Parenthetical reference: (Chang, *Biophysics* 123–26) (Chang, *Diagnostic* 87)

When citing more than one work by the same author, do not repeat the author's name; simply type three hyphens followed by a period. List the works alphabetically by title.

6. Book, One or More Editors—MLA

Morris, A. J., and Louise B. Pardin-Walker, editors. *Handbook of New Information Technology.* Harper, 2012.

Parenthetical reference: (Morris and Pardin-Walker 34)

For more than three editors, name only the first, followed by *et al.*

7. Book, Indirect Source—MLA

Kline, Thomas. *Automated Systems.* Rhodes, 1999.

Stubbs, John. *White-Collar Productivity.* Harris, 2002.

Parenthetical reference: (qtd. in Stubbs 116)

When your source (as in Stubbs, above) has quoted or cited another source, list each source in its appropriate alphabetical place in the Works Cited list. Use the name of the original source (here, Kline) in your text, and begin the parenthetical reference with *qtd. in* (or *cited in* for a paraphrase).

8. Anthology Selection or Book Chapter—MLA

Bowman, Joel P. "Electronic Conferencing." *Communication and Technology: Today and Tomorrow,* edited by Al Williams. Assn. for Business Communication, 1994, pp. 123-42.

Parenthetical reference: (Bowman 129)

The page numbers in the complete citation are for the selection cited from the anthology.

What to include in an MLA citation for a periodical

MLA WORKS CITED ENTRIES FOR PERIODICALS.   Give all available information in this order: author, article title (in quotation marks), periodical title (in italics), volume and issue, date (day, month, year), and page numbers for the entire article—not just pages cited.

9. Article, Magazine—MLA

DesMarteau, Kathleen. "Study Links Sewing Machine Use to Alzheimer's
Disease." *Bobbin*, Oct. 1994, pp. 36-38.

Parenthetical reference: (DesMarteau 36)

Use commas to separate the title of the magazine or journal and the date, and to separate the date and the page numbers. If no author is given, list all other information:

"Video Games for the Next Decade." *Power Technology Magazine*, 18 Oct.
2009, p. 18+.

Parenthetical reference: ("Video Games" 18)

This article began on page 18 and continued on page 21. When an article does not appear on consecutive pages, give only the number of the first page, followed immediately by a plus sign. Use a three-letter abbreviation for all months except May, June, and July.

10. Article, Journal with New Pagination Each Issue—MLA

Thackman-White, Joan R. "Computer-Assisted Research." *American Library Journal*,
vol. 51, no. 1, 2010, pp. 3-9.

Parenthetical reference: (Thackman-White 4–5)

Because each issue for that year will have page numbers beginning with 1, readers need the number of this issue: Here 51 is the volume number and 1 is the issue number. Omit *The*, *A*, or *An* from a journal or magazine title.

11. Article, Journal with Continuous Pagination—MLA

Barnstead, Marion H. "The Writing Crisis." *Journal of Writing Theory*, vol. 12, 2009,
pp. 415-33.

Parenthetical reference: (Barnstead 418)

When page numbers continue from issue to issue, readers won't need the issue number because no other issue in that year repeats the same page numbers. (Include the issue number, however, if you think it will help readers retrieve the article more easily.)

If you are citing an abstract found in a bound collection of abstracts, and not the full article, include the information on the abstracting service right after the information on the original article.

How to cite abstracts

Barnstead, Marion H. "The Writing Crisis." *Journal of Writing Theory*, vol. 12, 2009, pp.
415-33. *Rhetoric Abstracts*, vol 67, 2010, p. 67.

If you are citing an abstract that appears before the printed article, add *Abstract*, followed by a period, immediately after the original work's page number or range.

12. Article, Newspaper—MLA

> Baranski, Vida H. "Errors in Medical Diagnosis." *Boston Times*, 15 Jan. 2010, evening
> ed., Sec. B, p. 3+.

Parenthetical reference: (Baranski 3)

When a daily newspaper has more than one edition, cite the edition after the date. If no author is given, list all other information.

What to include in an MLA citation for a miscellaneous source

MLA WORKS CITED ENTRIES FOR OTHER SOURCES.   Miscellaneous sources range from unsigned encyclopedia entries to conference presentations to government publications.

13. Encyclopedia, Dictionary, Other Alphabetical Reference—MLA

> "Communication." *The Business Reference Book.* 2008 ed.

Parenthetical reference: ("Communication")

Begin a signed entry with the author's name. For any work arranged alphabetically, omit page numbers in the complete citation and the parenthetical reference. For a well-known reference book, include only an edition (if stated) and a date. For other reference books, give the full publication information.

14. Report—MLA

> Electrical Power Research Institute (EPRI). *Epidemiologic Studies of Electric Utility Em-*
> *ployees.* Report No. RP2964.5, EPRI, Nov. 1994.

Parenthetical reference: (Electrical Power Research Institute [EPRI] 27)

If no author is given, begin with the organization that sponsored the report.

For any report or other document with group authorship, include the group's abbreviated name in your first parenthetical reference and then use only that abbreviation in any subsequent reference.

15. Conference Presentation—MLA

> Smith, Abelard A. "Multicultural Stereotypes in Elizabethan Prose Fiction." *First British*
> *Symposium in Multicultural Studies, London, 11–13 Oct. 2012.*

Parenthetical reference: (Smith)

For an unpublished presentation, include the presenter's name, the title of the presentation, and the conference title, location, and date. Do not italicize the conference information.

16. Interview, Personally Conducted—MLA

Nasson, Gamela. Personal interview, 2 Apr. 2010.

Parenthetical reference: (Nasson)

17. Interview, Published—MLA

Lescault, James. "The Future of Graphics." Interview by Carol Jable. *Executive Views of Automation,* edited by Karen Prell, Haber Press, 2013, pp. 216-31.

Parenthetical reference: (Lescault 218)

The interviewee's name is placed in the entry's author slot.

18. Letter, Unpublished—MLA

Rogers, Leonard. Letter to the author. 15 May 2010.

Parenthetical reference: (Rogers)

19. Questionnaire—MLA

Taynes, Lorraine. Questionnaire sent to 61 college administrators. 14 Feb. 2009.

Parenthetical reference: (Taynes)

20. Brochure or Pamphlet—MLA

Career Strategies for the 21st Century. Blount Economics Assn., 2010.

Parenthetical reference: (Career)

If the work is signed, begin with its author.

21. Lecture—MLA

Dumont, R. A. "Androgyny and the Rhetorical Tradition." University of Massachusetts at Dartmouth, 15 Jan. 2010. Lecture.

Parenthetical reference: (Dumont)

If the lecture title is not known, write *Address, Lecture,* or *Reading* and do not use quotation marks. Include the sponsor and the location if they are available.

22. Government Document—MLA

If the author is unknown, begin with the name of the government, a comma, then the name of the agency:

Virginia, Highway Department. *Standards for Bridge Maintenance.* Virginia Highway Standards Office, 2013.

Parenthetical reference: (Virginia Highway Dept. 49)

For any congressional document, identify the house of Congress (Senate or House of Representatives) before the title and the number and session of Congress after the title:

> United States Congress, House Armed Service Committee. *Funding for the Military Academies.* 108th Congress, 2nd session, U.S. Government Printing Office, 2009.

> *Parenthetical reference:* (U.S. Armed Services Committee 41)

For an entry from the *Congressional Record*, give only date and pages:

> *Cong. Rec.* 10 Mar. 2006, pp. 2178-92.

> *Parenthetical reference:* (*Cong. Rec.* 2184)

23. Document with Corporate or Foundation Authorship—MLA

> Hermitage Foundation. *Global Warming Scenarios for the Year 2030.* National Research Council, 2009.

> *Parenthetical reference:* (Hermitage Foundation 123)

24. Map or Other Visual Aid—MLA

> *Deaths Caused by Breast Cancer, by County.* Map. *Scientific American,* Oct. 1995, p. 32D.

> *Parenthetical reference:* (Deaths Caused)

If the creator of the visual is listed, list that name first. Identify the type of visual (*Map, Graph, Table, Diagram*) immediately following its title.

25. Dissertation or Thesis—MLA

Provide information in this order:

> Rose, Jordan A. "Gravitational Waves as Represented in Online News Reporting." PhD dissertation, University of Minnesota, 2016.

What to include in an MLA citation for an electronic source

MLA WORKS CITED ENTRIES FOR DIGITAL SOURCES. MLA guidelines provide flexibility for citation formats based on the medium, but as with the print source examples shown above, they should include as much information as you think your reader will need to locate your original source.

Digital sources include not only the ones listed here but also other media formats such as an Instagram posting; a discussion from a Facebook page; a YouTube or other online video; a posting to a user forum or discussion group. With so many new apps and formats coming into being every year, the following guidelines and examples provide a basis for creating source citations for new and existing media formats.

As described more generally on page 394 and illustrated in the previous examples, MLA guidelines suggest that Works Cited entries contain certain "core elements," including some or all of the following elements, as appropriate:

> Author. Title of source. Title of container, other contributors, version, number, publisher, publication date, location.

Two of these elements are especially important for documenting digital sources. *Container* refers to the place where the source resides, such as a book in a collection, a journal or magazine, a blog or Web page, or an e-book. *Location* refers to page numbers, Web address (URL), a digital library, or digital object identifier (DOI). So, for example, you might want to cite one of the Internal Revenue Services's Fact Sheets, located on their Web site. Following the core elements listed above, and the print example shown in item 22 (page 399), you would add information about the digital source in the "location" field. The citation would appear as follows (note that http:// is not required):

> Internal Revenue Service. "IRS Identity Theft Victim Assistance: How it Works." *IRS Fact Sheet FS-2016-3*, Jan. 2016, www.irs.gov/uac/Newsroom/IRS-Identity-Theft-Victim-Assistance-How-It-Works.

See the following examples for more illustrations of MLA style for digital sources; also, see style.mla.org for other examples.

26. Online Abstract—MLA

> Lane, Amanda D., et al. "The Promise of Microcircuits." *Journal of Nanotechnology*, vol. 10, no. 2, 2006, www.onlineabstracts.org/LaneA2006.

Parenthetical reference: (Lane et al.)

27. Online Article—MLA

> Jeffers, Anna D. "NAFTA's Effects on the U.S. Trade Deficit." *Sultana Business Quarterly*, vol. 3, no. 4, 2004, pp. 65-74, soltbizq.com/JeffersAD2004.

Parenthetical reference: (Jeffers 66)

28. Reference Database—MLA

> Sahl, J. D. "Power Lines, Viruses, and Childhood Leukemia." *Cancer Causes Control*, vol. 6, no. 1, Jan. 1995. PubMed Abstracts, PMID 7718739.

Parenthetical reference: (Sahl 83)

In the above example, the abstract was published as part of a journal called *Cancer Causes Control* but was accessed through a different "container," the PubMed database.

For abstracts or database entries that were not originally published in print, follow this example, providing enough information for readers to locate the source if necessary:

> Argent, Roger R. "An Analysis of International Exchange Rates for 2009." *Accu-Data*,
> Dow Jones News Service, 10 Jan. 2009, online.djnews.org/ID99783.

Parenthetical reference: (Argent)

If the author is not known, begin with the work's title. If the digital document has page numbers, include them in your entry and in your parenthetical reference.

29. Online Video—MLA

> "How to Change Your Furnace Filter." *YouTube*, uploaded by USEnergy.gov, 28 Jan.
> 2016, www.youtube.com/watch?v=XCB234-v798s.

Parenthetical reference: (How to change)

Begin with the author's name, if known.

30. E-book—MLA

> Duin, Ann Hill, et al. *Cultivating Change in the Academy*. University of Minnesota Digital
> Conservancy, 2012, purl.umn.edu/125273.

Parenthetical reference: (Duin et al. 2012)

A book published in both print and digital formats should be cited as a book, with no special mention of whether the book was read on paper or on a Kindle or other e-reader. (See items 1–8 earlier in this appendix for book citation examples in MLA format.) But books that are only available in digital formats should be cited per the example above. If possible, provide a Web address that is stable by looking for what is called a *permanent URL* or *permalink*. In the above example, this address is recognizable because it begins with "purl." Digital Object Identifiers (DOIs), discussed earlier, are another example of a stable Web address.

Another type of e-book you may encounter is a book that is either out of print or difficult to find and can best be located in a digital library, such as the HathiTrust, ProjectGuttenberg, or the Internet Archive. To help your readers understand how to access the book, cite it like a printed book but add the digital library information (location) at the very end:

> Reiss, Ira L. *Family Systems in America*. Holt, Rinehart, and Winston, 1980. HathiTrust
> Digital Library, catalog.hathitrust.org/Record/000711385.

31. Personal Email—MLA

> Wallin, John Luther. "Frog Reveries." Received by Laura Gurak, 12 Oct. 2009.

32. Wiki

"Printing Press." *Wikipedia.* Wikimedia Foundation, 2010. Accessed 1 June 2010.

Parenthetical reference: ("Printing")

Although you are not required to include the date that you accessed a source online, you may do so if you think that information might be useful to your reader.

33. Blog

Hecht, Jeff. "How Galveston Weathered the Storm." *New Scientist Environment Blog*, 15 Sept. 2008.

Parenthetical reference: (Hecht)

34. Podcast

"Countdown to Mars Touchdown." *NASA Solar System Audio Podcasts.* NASA, 16 May 2008, www.nasa.gov/multimedia/podcasting/index.html.

Parenthetical reference: ("Countdown")

For wikis, blogs, and podcasts, decide whether your readers require a Web address (URL) or other information in order to locate the item you are citing. Wikipedia (item 32) is a well-known source that anyone can locate and does not need special location information. Since readers can easily locate with a quick online search the New Scientist Environment Blog (item 33), no Web address is given. But the NASA Solar System Audio Podcasts site (item 34) is not as easily found, so in that case, you would provide a Web address.

35. Tweet

Gurak, Laura (ProfGurak). "Here's a good article on accuracy and relevance of crowd sourced content: http://goo.gl/Bs2Ah." 4 Dec. 2012, 6:48 p.m.

Parenthetical reference: (Gurak)

This tweet does not need a Web address (URL) or other location information; readers can go to the Twitter site for the author (ProfGurak) and search for the tweet by date posted.

36. Web sites and Other Digital Formats—MLA

For Web sites and other digital formats such as Facebook postings, Google maps, on-line discussion forums, and so forth, follow the "core elements" format shown on page 401, choosing items as appropriate to your citation. If the author is unknown, start with the title of source. If the source is easy to locate, omit the Web address.

"Calcium." *University of Maryland Medical Center Medical Reference Guide*, University of Maryland, 26 June 2014.

Samantha0212. "Taking Calcium Worked for Me." *WebMed Online Discussion Forum*, WebMed Online, 7 July 2016. webmed.org/forums/calcium/posting 9934.

APA Documentation Style

Another common citation style is detailed in the *Publication Manual of the American Psychological Association*, 6th ed. (2009). Because it emphasizes the publication date, APA style (or any similar author-date style) is preferred in the sciences and social sciences, where information quickly becomes outdated.

As in MLA style, APA style requires that you cite a source in text (parenthetical reference) as well as at the end of the report (where it is called a References list rather than a Works Cited list).

APA Parenthetical References

How APA and MLA parenthetical references differ

APA's parenthetical references (also called in-text reference citations) differ from MLA's as follows: the citation includes the publication date; a comma separates each item in the reference; and *p.* or *pp.* precedes the page number (which is optional in the APA system) or range, respectively. Here are specific guidelines:

- If your discussion names the author, do not repeat the name in your parenthetical reference; simply give the date and page number or range. When two authors of a work are named in your text, their names are connected by *and*, but in a parenthetical reference, their names are connected by an ampersand (&).

Author named in the text

> Lederman (1995) cites recent data provided by 796 colleges indicating that violent crime on campus is increasing (p. 31).

- If you cite two or more works in a single reference, list the authors in alphabetical order and separate the citations with semicolons:

Two or more works in a single reference

> (Gomez, 2002; Jones, 2004; Leduc, 1998)

- If you cite a work with three to five authors, try to name them in your text to avoid an excessively long parenthetical reference. In any subsequent references to this work, name only the first author, followed by *et al.* (Latin abbreviation for "and others").

A work with three to five authors

> Franks, Oblesky, Ryan, Jablar, and Perkins (2004) studied the role of electromagnetic fields in tumor formation.

- If you cite two or more works by the same author published in the same year, arrange the works alphabetically by title, and add a lowercase letter (a, b, c) to the year to differentiate them:

Two or more works by the same author in the same year

> (Lamont, 2005a, p. 135)
>
> (Lamont, 2005b, pp. 67–68)

- When a subsequent reference to a source follows closely after the initial reference, the date need not be included.

APA Reference Entries

The APA References list includes each source you have cited in your paper; it appears on a separate page at the end of the document. Arrange all entries alphabetically by the author's surname (when the author's name is unknown, alphabetize by the first word or numeral, as if the numeral were spelled out). Begin each entry flush with the left margin and indent second and subsequent lines 1/2 inch (or five spaces). Double-space within and between entries. In one notable difference from MLA style, APA style calls for only "retrievable" sources to appear in the reference list. Therefore, cite personal interviews, letters, and email messages in text only.

> How to format the References list

> How to cite nonretrievable sources

Following are examples of complete citations as they would appear in the References list. Shown immediately below each entry is its corresponding parenthetical reference as it would appear in the text. Note the capitalization, abbreviation, spacing, and punctuation in the sample entries.

> How to cite individual items

Table A.2 provides an overview of the types of citations discussed in this section.

APA ENTRIES FOR BOOKS. Any citation for a book should contain all applicable information in the following order: author, date, title, editor or translator, edition, volume number, and facts about publication—city, state (abbreviated), and publisher.

> What to include in an APA citation for a book

Table A.2 Index to APA References Entries

Books

1. Book, single author
2. Book, two to five authors
3. Book, six or more authors
4. Book, anonymous author
5. Multiple books, same author
6. Book, one to five editors
7. Book, indirect source
8. Anthology selection or book chapter

Periodicals

9. Article, magazine
10. Article, journal with new pagination for each issue
11. Article, journal with continuous pagination
12. Article, newspaper

Other Sources

13. Encyclopedia, dictionary, alphabetical reference
14. Report
15. Conference presentation
16. Interview, personally conducted
17. Interview, published

18. Personal correspondence
19. Brochure or pamphlet
20. Unpublished lecture
21. Government document
22. Miscellaneous items (unpublished manuscript, dissertation, and so on)

Electronic Sources

23. Online abstract
24. Print article posted online
25. Book or article available only online (no DOI)
26. CD-ROM abstract
27. Online encyclopedia, dictionary, handbook
28. Personal email
29. Blog posting
30. Newsgroup, discussion list, online forum
31. Wiki
32. Facebook and Twitter

Gray Literature

33. Press release
34. Technical or research report

1. Book, Single Author—APA

Kerzin-Fontana, J. B. (2010). *Technology management: A handbook* (3rd ed.). Delmar, NY: American Management Association.

Parenthetical reference: (Kerzin-Fontana, 2010, pp. 3–4)

Use only initials for an author's first and middle names. Capitalize only the first words of a book's title and subtitle and any proper names. Identify a later edition in parentheses between the title and the period. Omit the state abbreviation if the city is unambiguous.

2. Book, Two to Five Authors—APA

Vogel, W., & Kalb, H. (2010). *Large-scale solar thermal power: technologies, costs and development*. Weinheim: Wiley-VCH.

Parenthetical reference: (Vogel & Kalb, 2010)

Use an ampersand (&) before the name of the final author listed in an entry. As an alternative to a full parenthetical reference, name the authors in your text and include date (and page numbers, if appropriate) in parentheses. Give the publisher's name in full ("Yale University Press") but omit *Publisher, Company,* or *Inc.* If you are including the state (see item 1, above), use the two-letter U.S. Postal Service abbreviations for states.

3. Book, Six or More Authors—APA

Fogle, S. T., et al. (2009). *Hyperspace technology.* Boston: Little, Brown.

Parenthetical reference: (Fogle et al., 2009, p. 34)

Et al. is the Latin abbreviation for *et alia*, meaning "and others."

4. Book, Anonymous Author—APA

Structured programming. (2010). Boston: Meredith Press.

Parenthetical reference: (*Structured Programming*, 2010, p. 67)

In your list of references, place an anonymous work alphabetically by the first key word in its title (ignoring *The, A,* or *An*). In your parenthetical reference, capitalize all key words in a book, article, or journal title.

5. Multiple Books, Same Author—APA

Chang, J. W. (2010a). *Biophysics.* Boston: Little, Brown.

Chang, J. W. (2010b). *MindQuest.* Chicago: Pressler.

Parenthetical reference: (Chang, 2010a) (Chang, 2010b)

Two or more works by the same author published in different years are distinguished by their dates alone, without the added letter.

6. Book, One to Five Editors—APA

> Morris, A. J., & Pardin-Walker, L. B. (Eds.). (2012). *Handbook of new information tech-*
> *nology.* New York: HarperCollins.

Parenthetical reference: (Morris & Pardin-Walker, 2012, p. 79)

For more than five editors, name only the first, followed by *et al.*

7. Book, Indirect Source—APA

> Stubbs, J. (2010). *White-collar productivity.* Miami, FL: Harris.

Parenthetical reference: (cited in Stubbs, 2010, p. 47)

When your source has cited another source, list only this second source, but name the original source in your text: "Kline's study (cited in Stubbs, 2002, p. 47) supports this conclusion."

8. Anthology Selection or Book Chapter—APA

> Bowman, J. (1994). Electronic conferencing. In A. Williams (Ed.), *Communication and*
> *technology: Today and tomorrow* (pp. 123–142). Denton, TX: Association for
> Business Communication.

Parenthetical reference: (Bowman, 1994, p. 126)

The page numbers in the complete reference are for the entire selection cited from the anthology.

APA ENTRIES FOR PERIODICALS.   A citation for an article should give this information (as available) in this order: author, date, article title (without quotation marks), publication, volume and (when necessary) issue number, and page numbers for the entire article, not just the portion cited.

What to include in an APA citation for a periodical

9. Article, Magazine—APA

> DesMarteau, K. (1994, October). Study links sewing machine use to Alzheimer's dis-
> ease. *Bobbin, 36,* 36–38.

Parenthetical reference: (DesMarteau, 1994, p. 36)

If no author is given, provide all other information, placing the title in the author position. Capitalize only the first words in an article's title and subtitle as well as all proper nouns. Capitalize all key words in a periodical title. Italicize the periodical title and volume number.

10. Article, Journal with New Pagination for Each Issue—APA

Thackman-White, J. R. (2010). Computer-assisted research. *American Library Journal*, *51*(1), 3–9.

Parenthetical reference: (Thackman-White, 2010, pp. 4–5)

Because each issue for a given year has page numbers that begin at "1," readers need the issue number (in this instance, 1). Here 51 is the volume number, which is italicized.

11. Article, Journal with Continuous Pagination—APA

Barnstead, M. H. (2009). The writing crisis. *Journal of Writing Theory, 12*, 415–433.

Parenthetical reference: (Barnstead, 2009, pp. 415–416)

In this example, 12 is the volume number. When page numbers continue from issue to issue for the full year, readers won't need the issue number because no other issue in that year repeats the same page numbers. (You can include the issue number if you think it will help readers retrieve the article more easily.)

12. Article, Newspaper—APA

Baranski, V. H. (2010, January 15). Errors in medical diagnosis. *The Boston Times*, pp. B3, 6.

Parenthetical reference: (Baranski, 2010)

In addition to the year of publication, include the month and date. If the newspaper's name begins with *The,* include it in your citation. Include *p.* or *pp.* before page numbers. For an article on nonconsecutive pages, list each page, separated by a comma. If the entire article appeared on one page, no page number is necessary in the citation.

What to include in an APA citation for a miscellaneous source

APA ENTRIES FOR OTHER SOURCES. Miscellaneous sources range from unsigned encyclopedia entries to conference presentations to government documents. A full citation should give this information (as available): author, publication date, title of work, city, publisher (or volume and issue number), and page numbers (if applicable).

13. Encyclopedia, Dictionary, Alphabetical Reference—APA

Communication. (2008). In *The business reference book*. Upper Saddle River, NJ: Prentice Hall, p. 201.

Parenthetical reference: (Communication, 2008)

For an entry that is signed, begin with the author's name and publication date.

14. Report—APA

Electrical Power Research Institute. (1994). *Epidemiologic studies of electric utility employees* (Rep. No. RP2964.5). Palo Alto, CA: Author.

Parenthetical reference: (Electrical Power Research Institute [EPRI], 1994, p. 12)

If authors are named, list them first, followed by the publication date. When citing a group author, as in example 14, include the group's abbreviated name in your first parenthetical reference, and use only that abbreviation in any subsequent reference. When the agency (or organization) and publisher are the same, list *Author* in the publisher's slot.

15. Conference Presentation—APA

Smith, A. A. (2012). Multicultural stereotypes in Elizabethan prose fiction. In A. Hodkins (Ed.), *First British Symposium on Multicultural Studies* (pp. 106–121). London: Harrison Press.

Parenthetical reference: (Smith, 2012, p. 109)

The date of the presentation is in parentheses. The name of the symposium is a proper name, so it is capitalized. For an unpublished presentation, include the presenter's name, year and month, title of the presentation (italicized), and all available information about the conference or meeting: "Symposium held at …" Do not italicize this last information.

16. Interview, Personally Conducted—APA

This material is considered a nonrecoverable source, so it is cited only in the text, as a parenthetical reference:

Parenthetical reference: (G. Nasson, personal communication, April 2, 2010)

If you name the interviewee in your text, do not repeat the name in your citation.

17. Interview, Published—APA

Jable, C. K. (2013, June 7). The future of graphics [Interview with James Lescault]. In K. Prell (Ed.), *Executive views of automation* (pp. 216–231). Miami: Haber Press.

Parenthetical reference: (Jable, 2013, p. 218)

Begin with the name of the interviewer, followed by the interview date and title (if available), the designation (in brackets), and the publication information.

18. Personal Correspondence—APA

This material is considered nonrecoverable data, so it is cited only in the text, as a parenthetical reference:

Parenthetical reference: (L. Rogers, personal communication, May 15, 2010)

If you name the correspondent in your text, do not repeat the name in your citation.

19. Brochure or Pamphlet—APA

This material follows the citation format for book entries (pages 406–407).

20. Unpublished Lecture—APA

> Dumont, R. A. (2010, January 15). *Androgyny and the rhetorical tradition.* Lecture presented at the University of Massachusetts at Dartmouth.

> *Parenthetical reference:* (Dumont, 2010)

If you name the lecturer in your text, do not repeat the name in your citation.

21. Government Document—APA

If the author is unknown, present the information in this order: name of the issuing agency, publication date, document title, place, and publisher.

> Virginia Highway Department. (2013). *Standards for bridge maintenance.* Richmond, VA: Author.

> *Parenthetical reference:* (Virginia Highway Department, 2009, p. 49)

When the issuing agency is both author and publisher, write *Author* in the publisher's slot. For any congressional document, identify the house of Congress (Senate or House of Representatives) before the date.

> United States Congress. House. Armed Services Committee. (2010). *Funding for the military academies.* Washington, DC: U.S. Government Printing Office.

> *Parenthetical reference:* (U.S. Congress, 2010, p. 41)

22. Miscellaneous Items (Unpublished Manuscript, Dissertation, and so on)—APA

Provide information in this order:

> Author (if known). (Date of preparation). *Title of work* (italicized). Description (Unpublished manuscript, unpublished raw data, or the like).

For any work that has group authorship (corporation, committee, and so on), cite the name of the group or agency in place of the author's name.

What to include in an APA citation for an electronic source

APA ENTRIES FOR ELECTRONIC SOURCES. In 2009, the APA published the *Publication Manual of the American Psychological Association,* 6th edition. This manual provides instructions for citation of print and electronic sources. For electronic sources in particular, the APA notes that "in general… include the same elements, in the same order, as you would for a reference to a fixed-media source and add as much electronic retrieval information as needed for others to locate the sources you cited" (187).

Including the Web address is still recommended. However, one new feature is the use of digital object identifiers (DOIs). These are unique identifiers designed to last longer than Web addresses, which often disappear or get changed when Web pages are moved or renamed.

Identify the original source (printed or electronic) and give readers a path for retrieving the material. Provide all available information in the following order.

1. Author, editor, creator, or sponsoring organization.
2. Date the item was published or was created electronically. For magazines and newspapers, include the month and day as well as the year. If the date of an electronic publication is not available, use *n.d.* in place of the date.
3. Publication information of the original printed version (as in previous entries), if such a version exists. Follow this by designating the electronic medium [CD-ROM] or the type of work [Abstract], [Brochure]—unless this designation is named in the work's title (as in "Inpatient brochure").
4. Database names. Do not list database names (unless the database is obscure or the material hard to find), but do include the Web address (or DOI, discussed below).
5. Web addresses and DOIs. Provide the full electronic address. APA recommends only using home page Web address. For CD-ROM and database sources, give the document's retrieval number (see entry 23, below). Start the Web address with http://, but do not underline, italicize, use angle brackets, or add a period at the end of a Web address. When a Web address continues from one line to the next, break it only after a slash or other punctuation (except for http://, which should not be broken).

The APA now recommends using the DOI (Digital Object Identifier), when available, in place of a Web address in references to electronic texts. DOI numbers are found on some recent scholarly journals, especially in the sciences and social sciences. Here is a sample reference for a journal article with a DOI assigned:

> Schmidt, D., et al. (2009). Advances in psychotropic medication. *Boston Journal of Psychotherapy, 81*(3), 398–413. doi: 10.1037/0555-9467.79.3.483

Parenthetical reference: (Schmidt, 2009)

23. Online Abstract—APA

> Stevens, R. L. (2010). Cell phones and cancer rates. *Oncology Journal, 57*(2), 41–43. [Abstract]. Retrieved from the Dialog database. (MEDLINE Item: AY 24598).

Parenthetical reference: (Stevens, 2010)

Ordinarily an APA entry ends with a period. Entries that end with a Web address (or a DOI), however, omit the period at the end of the electronic address. If you are citing the entire article retrieved from a full-text database, delete [Abstract] from your citation.

24. Print Article Posted Online—APA

Alley, R. A. (2009, January). Ergonomic influences on worker satisfaction. *Industrial Psychology, 5*(12), 672–678. Retrieved from http://www.psycharchives/index/indpsy/2009_1.html

Parenthetical reference: (Alley, 2009)

If you were confident that the document's electronic and print versions were identical, you could omit the Web address and insert "[Electronic version]" between the end of the article title and the period.

25. Book or Article Available Only Online (no DOI)—APA

Kelly, W. (2009). *Early graveyards of New England.* Retrieved from http://www.onlinebooks.com/search/itemID=65321

Parenthetical reference: (Kelly, 2009)

This source exists only in electronic format.

26. CD-ROM Abstract—APA

Cavanaugh, H. (1995). An EMF study: Good news and bad news [CD-ROM]. *Electrical World, 209*(2), 8. Abstract retrieved from ProQuest File: ABI/INFORM database (62–1498).

Parenthetical reference: (Cavanaugh, 1995)

In this entry, 8 is the page number of this one-page article.

27. Online Encyclopedia, Dictionary, Handbook—APA

Ecoterrorism. (2012). *Ecological encyclopedia.* Washington, DC: Redwood. Retrieved May 1, 2013, from http://www.eco.floridastate.edu/index.html

Parenthetical reference: ("Ecoterrorism," 2012)

Include the retrieval date for reference works that are routinely updated.

28. Personal Email—APA

Parenthetical reference: Fred Flynn (personal communication, May 9, 2013) provided these statistics.

Instead of being included in the list of references, personal email (considered a nonretrievable source) is cited fully in the text.

29. Blog Posting—APA

Owens, P. (2010, June 1). How to stabilize a large travel trailer. Message posted to http://rvblogs.com/comm/bilge

Parenthetical reference: (Owens, 2010)

30. Newsgroup, Discussion List, Online Forum—APA

> LaBarge, V. S. (2009, October 20). A cure for computer viruses. Message posted to
>   http://www.srb/forums/frwl/webZ/m2237.html

Parenthetical reference: (LaBarge, 2009)

Although email should not be included in the list of references, postings from blogs, newsgroups, and online forums, considered more retrievable, should be included.

31. Wiki—APA

> Skull-base tumors. (n.d.). Retrieved June 10, 2009, from the Oncology wiki: http://on-
>   cology.wikia.com/wiki/Skull_base_tumors

Parenthetical reference: ("Skull-Base," n.d.)

Notice the "n.d." ("no date") designation for this collaborative Web page that can be written or edited by anyone with access.

32. Facebook and Twitter

> NASA. (2013, January 8). Astronomers have made a 3D weather map of a brown
>   dwarf using NASA's Spitzer and Hubble Space telescopes! [Facebook update].
>   Retrieved from www.facebook.com/NASA/posts/128611970637320

Parenthetical reference: (NASA, 2013)

APA ENTRIES FOR GRAY LITERATURE. The APA has new guidelines for citing so-called gray literature—material such as annual reports, fact sheets, consumer brochures, press releases, and technical reports (each type is so named in the title, in brackets, or elsewhere in the citation). In the *APA Style Guide to Electronic References*, gray literature is defined as "scientific information that falls outside the peer review process but is written by scholars or summarizes a body of scholarly work. Government departments, corporations and trade groups ... and other ... organizations produce gray literature" (p. 18). Much of this is written for the general public. In the sample citation in entry 33, the type of item is identified in brackets; in entry 34, it is part of the titling information.

What to include in an APA citation for gray literature

33. Press Release—APA

> American Natural Foods Association. (2009, January 20). *Newest food additive*
>   *poses special threat to children, according to the upcoming issue of* Eating
>   for Health [Press release]. Retrieved from http://www.anfha.org/releases/addi-
>   tives0620.html

Parenthetical reference: (American Natural Foods Association, 2009)

34. Technical or Research Report—APA

Gunderson, H., et al. (2007). *Declining birthrates in rural areas: Results from the 2005 National Census Bureau Survey* (Report No. 7864 NCB 2005-171). Retrieved from the National Center for Population Statistics: http://ncps.gov/pubs2007/pubs2007/2007171.pdf

Parenthetical reference: (Gunderson, 2007)

Notice that the report number, if available, is given after the title.

Other Documentation Styles

For class, on the job, or when writing for a specific publication, you may be required to use a documentation style different from the two described above. These other styles might include the Chicago Manual of Style, Council of Science Editors (CSE), Institute of Electrical and Electronics Engineers (IEEE), American Chemical Society (ACS), or others that are specific to a scientific, engineering, or professional field. Some of these styles use numbered citations within the text that appear almost like footnotes; references lists also have their own unique rules. You can learn more about these citation styles by searching online and at your college or university library.

Recognizing Copyright Issues

Definition of copyright

Copyright is the legal system that gives authors and owners rights over their original works of authorship. These works can include books, musical recordings, photographs, drawings, letters, memos, email, Web pages, and any other expressions of ideas that are, as the law puts it, "fixed in a tangible medium." Copyright holders have the exclusive right to reproduce, distribute, perform, display, prepare derivative works, and publish their copyrighted material. In the United States, works created after 1978 are automatically copyrighted as soon as the material is fixed; that is, the moment the idea is recorded, written down, turned into an electronic document, or otherwise.

Copyright licensing

Copyright holders have the right to grant a license (essentially, to give permission) for others to use the material in whatever way the holder deems appropriate. Online, many copyright holders are turning to putting explicit licensing statements on their websites and other work, often using parameters defined by a group called Creative Commons, which provides a range of options including "copyright by attribution," "copyright non-commercial," and so forth (search on creative commons for more information).

Purpose of copyright

The purpose of copyright is to balance the reward for the intellectual labor of the author with the importance of making information freely available to the public. If all information were covered by copyright protection forever and ever, there would be no source of public information that authors and artists could use to create new ideas. But if all information were completely free of copyright protection, creators might not have any incentive to write songs or books, for example. This is why in the United States copyright is not forever, just for a limited time. This is also why there are some conditions under which you do not need to request copyright permission.

Works in the Public Domain

Many images, sounds, books, and other materials fall into what is called the *public domain*. In these cases, you do not need to request permission for use. Public domain works include works that were published in the United States 95 years before the current year. Most government documents are also public domain, and most commonplace information, such as height and weight charts or metric conversion tables, are also public domain. Many authors and artists publish work and expressly state that the work is in the public domain. Look on the Web site or document for more information. (If you are unsure about the work's status, you may want to request permission.)

Definition of public domain

Fair Use

Fair use is a legal doctrine that allows the use of some copyrighted material, under some circumstances, without permission. Congress established fair use as a way to balance creators' rights with public access. Fair use states that under certain conditions, it is legal to use copyrighted works without permission so long as the source is clearly identified. Courts tend to ask four questions about whether a use is considered fair:

Definition of fair use

- Is the material educational or commercial? (educational use is favored)
- Has the material been previously published? (use of published works is favored)
- How much of the material is being used? (less is favored)
- How will your use of the material affect the market value of the original? (if your use does not have an impact on the value of the original, this is favored)

Determining fair use

Classroom and student use is almost always considered fair. Most use of small snippets of text, cited in a student or academic paper, is also considered fair use. Even commercial documents, such as annual reports, routinely cite information from publications such as the newspaper or research papers. These uses are all considered fair. However, if you are a consultant or employee of a for-profit organization and you wish to use a large amount of material or visuals such as photographs or graphics, fair use may not apply. In these cases, it is best to seek permission.

The Difference between Plagiarism and Copyright Infringement

If you receive permission to use someone else's material or if your use qualifies as fair use, you are probably covered when it comes to copyright. Most of the writing

Definition of copyright infringement

you will do for this class and in college generally will be situations where your use of outside material is considered educational and thus fair. But you still must document your source by providing an appropriate in-text citation as well as a reference; otherwise, you run the risk of plagiarism. Always provide a citation or caption, even if you didn't need copyright permission. Whether you use a direct quotation or a paraphrase, always include the source.

Copyright in a
digital age

In our digital age, there is a tension between the openness of the Internet, which allows people to access music, text, and images easily on the one hand, and the restrictions on such items that copyright calls for on the other. It is easy to cut and paste material online but also easy to forget that this material is probably covered by copyright protection. Creative commons, discussed earlier in this chapter, provides new ways for copyright holders to make their licensing explicit; yet, most online sources do not contain any sort of copyright information, so it is important to remember that when in doubt, you should request permission.

Appendix B
A Brief Handbook

Outline

Grammar   417

Punctuation   422

Mechanics   429

Usage   432

Transitions   432

Lists   434

Grammar

The following common grammatical errors are easy to repair.

Sentence Fragments

A sentence fragment is a grammatically incomplete sentence. A grammatically complete sentence consists of at least one subject-verb combination and expresses a complete thought. It might include more than one subject-verb combination, and it might include other words or phrases as well.

> This book summarizes recent criminal psychology research.
> The smudge tool creates soft effects.
> My dog, Zorro, ate my paper.

Complete sentences

Even though the following example contains a subject-verb combination, it doesn't express a complete thought:

> Although the report was not yet complete.

Sentence fragment

Watch out for *although* and other words like it, including *because, if, as, while, since, when,* and *unless.* These are called subordinating conjunctions. Any of these words combined with a subject-verb combination produces a subordinate clause (a clause that expresses an incomplete idea). Subordinating conjunctions leave readers waiting for something to complete the thought. The thought can be completed only if another subject-verb combination that does express a complete idea is added:

Additional
subject-verb
completes the
thought

| Although the report was not yet complete, I began editing.

This next group of words is a fragment because it contains no verb:

Fragment with
no verb

| DesignPro, a brand-new desktop publishing program.

Simply add a verb to turn the fragment into a complete sentence:

Addition of
verb corrects
fragment

| DesignPro, a brand-new desktop publishing program, will be available soon.
   or
| DesignPro is a brand-new desktop publishing program.

Avoid sentences that seem to contain a subject-verb combination but actually do not. Gerunds (verb forms ending in *-ing* that act like nouns, such as *being* in the first sentence given) and participles (verb forms ending in *-ing* that act like adjectives, such as *barking* in the second sentence given) look like verbs but actually are not:

Gerund and
participle
fragments

Dale being a document design expert
The barking dog

These fragments can be turned into complete sentences by substituting a verb for the gerund or adding a verb:

Verb
substitution
or new verb
corrects
fragment

Dale is a document design expert.
The barking dog finally stopped.

Run-on Sentences

A run-on sentence contains too many grammatically complete sentences joined together as one:

Run-on
sentence

| For emergencies, we dial 911 for other questions, we dial 088.

This sentence can be repaired in various ways. One possibility is to divide it into two sentences:

Division into
two sentences
corrects run-on

| For emergencies, we dial 911. For other questions, we dial 088.

Another possibility is to use a semicolon to join the two sentences. This option indicates a break that is not quite as strong as the period and therefore signals to the reader that the two items are closely related:

Added
semicolon
corrects run-on

| For emergencies, we dial 911; for other questions, we dial 088.

Another possibility is to add a comma followed by a coordinating conjunction (*for, and, nor, but, or, yet, so*):

| For emergencies, we dial 911, but for other questions, we dial 088.

Coordinating conjunction corrects run-on

Comma Splices

In a comma splice, two complete ideas (independent clauses) that should be *separated* by a period or a semicolon are incorrectly *joined* by a comma:

| Sarah did a great job, she was promoted.

Comma splice

There are a number of options for correcting comma splices. One option is to divide the splice into two separate sentences:

| Sarah did a great job. She was promoted.

Division into two sentences corrects comma splice

Another option is to use a semicolon to show a relationship between the two items:

| Sarah did a great job; she was promoted.

Semicolon corrects comma splice

A third option is to use a semicolon with a conjunctive adverb (an adverb, ending in *-ly*, that shows a relationship between the items, such as *consequently*):

| Sarah did a great job; consequently, she was promoted.

Semicolon with conjunctive adverb corrects comma splice

A fourth option is to use a coordinating conjunction. There are seven such conjunctions: *for, and, nor, but, or, yet, so*—you can remember them using the acronym "fanboys." Coordinating conjunctions create an equal relationship between the items:

| Sarah did a great job and was promoted.

Coordinating conjunction corrects comma splice

Finally, as on page 421 you can use a subordinating conjunction (a conjunction that creates an unequal relationship between the items):

| Because Sarah did a great job, she was promoted.

Subordinating conjunction corrects comma splice

Faulty Agreement—Subject and Verb

The subject of a sentence must agree in number with the verb. But when subject and verb are separated by other words, we sometimes lose track of the subject-verb relationship:

| The lion's share of diesels are sold in Europe.

Faulty subject-verb agreement

To correct the error, make the verb agree with its subject (*share*), not with a word that comes between the subject and the verb (in this case, the plural noun *diesels*):

| The lion's share of diesels is sold in Europe.

Correct subject-verb agreement

Some cases are trickier than others. For example, treat compound subjects connected by *and* as plural:

Compound subject takes plural verb

| Terry and Julie enjoy collaborating on writing projects.

In addition, with compound subjects connected by *or* or *nor*, the verb is singular if both subjects are singular and plural if both subjects are plural. If one subject is singular and one is plural, the verb agrees with the one closer to the verb. In the following example, the verb agrees with the closer subject, the plural *students*:

Verb agrees with closer subject in compound subject

| Neither the professor nor the students were able to see what was going on.

Also, treat most indefinite pronouns (*anybody, each, everybody*, etc.) as singular subjects:

Indefinite pronoun agrees with singular verb

| Almost everybody who registered for the class was there on the first day.

Additionally, treat collective subjects (*team, family, group, committee*, etc.) as singular unless the meaning is clearly plural. Both of the following sentences are correct. In the first sentence, the *group* is understood as a singular subject (the group is a single entity) and agrees with the singular verb *respects*, whereas in the second sentence, the *board* is understood as plural (as indicated by the plural word *authors*) and agrees with the plural verb *are*:

Collective subjects agree with singular or plural verbs depending on meaning

The group respects its leader.

The editorial board are all published authors.

Faulty Agreement—Pronoun and Referent

A pronoun must refer to a specific noun (its *referent* or *antecedent*), with which it must agree in gender and number. Faulty pronoun-referent agreement is easy to spot when the gender and number clearly don't match (e.g., "He should proceed at their own pace" should obviously read "He should proceed at his own pace"). However, when an indefinite pronoun such as *each, everyone, anybody, someone*, or *none* is the referent, the pronoun is always singular, as in the following examples:

Indefinite referents agree with singular pronouns

Everybody should proceed at his or her own pace.

None of the candidates described her career plans in detail.

Faulty Coordination and Subordination

Give equal emphasis to ideas of equal importance by joining them with one of the coordinating conjunctions: *for, and, nor, but, or, yet*, and *so* (you can memorize these by using the acronym "fanboys"). Likewise, show an unequal relationship between ideas (one idea dependent upon the other) by using a subordinating conjunction: *because, whereas, if, although, until*, and so on.

Coordination may be faulty when the ideas connected by a coordinating conjunction are not of equal importance or are not sensibly connected:

| I was late for work and wrecked my car.

Faulty coordination

To correct the problem, use a subordinating conjunction instead. Or express cause and effect or opinion in some other way, as in the following two examples:

| Because I was late for work, I backed out of my driveway too quickly into oncoming traffic, wrecking my car.

or

| Late for work, I backed out of my driveway too quickly into oncoming traffic, wrecking my car.

Corrected versions

Avoid subordinating ideas that should be of equal importance or that don't represent a genuine cause and effect relationship:

| Although John gets up early, he is never late for work.

Faulty subordination

To correct the problem and show a balanced relationship between the ideas, use a coordinating conjunction instead:

| John gets up early and is never late for work.

Corrected version

Avoid both excessive coordination and excessive subordination in complex sentences. Following are two versions of the same sentence, the first with excessive coordination and the second with excessive subordination:

| The climax in jogging comes after a few miles and I can no longer feel stride after stride and it seems as if I am floating and jogging becomes almost a reflex and my arms and legs continue to move and my mind no longer has control over my actions.

Excessive coordination

| The climax in jogging comes when after a few miles I can no longer feel stride after stride, yet it seems as if I am floating, because jogging becomes almost a reflex since my arms and legs continue to move while my mind no longer has control over my actions.

Excessive subordination

To repair either instance, blend coordination and subordination, deciding exactly which ideas should be balanced and which of the subordinated ideas is most important, as in the following revision. Here, the writer has decided to emphasize *jogging almost by reflex* as the most important idea (using the subordinating conjunction *when*) and to coordinate the four equally important sensations involved (*no longer able to feel every stride, nearly floating, my arms and legs still moving,* and *my mind no longer controlling my actions*) using commas and the coordinating conjunction *and.*

| The climax in jogging comes after a few miles, when I am jogging almost by reflex, no longer able to feel every stride, nearly floating, my arms and legs still moving, and my mind no longer controlling my actions.

Balance of coordination and subordination

Faulty Pronoun Case

A pronoun's case (nominative, objective, or possessive) is determined by its role in the sentence: as subject, object, or indicator of possession.

If the pronoun serves as the subject of a sentence (*I, we, you, she, he, it, they, who*) or follows a version of the linking verb *to be*, its case is *nominative*:

Nominative pronoun case

> She completed her graduate program in record time.
>
> Who broke the chair?
>
> The chemist who perfected this distillation process is he.

If the pronoun serves as the object of a verb or a preposition (*me, us, you, her, him, it, them, whom*), its case is *objective*:

Objective pronoun case

> The employees gave her a parting gift.
>
> To whom do you wish to complain?

If a pronoun indicates possession (*my, mine, our, ours, your, yours, his, her, hers, its, their, whose*), its case is *possessive*:

Possessive pronoun case

> The brown briefcase is mine.
>
> Whose opinion do you value most?

The following sentences are incorrect and are followed by the corrected versions in parenthesis.

Faulty pronoun case

> Whom is responsible to who? (Who is responsible to whom?)
>
> The debate was between Marsha and I. (The debate was between Marsha and me.)

Punctuation

Punctuation marks are like road signs and traffic signals. They govern reading speed and provide clues for navigation through a network of ideas. The three marks of end punctuation—period, question mark, and exclamation point—work like a red traffic light by signaling a complete stop.

Period

A period ends a declarative sentence.

Period ends declarative statement

> I see that you've all completed the essay.

It is also used as the final mark in some abbreviations, such as "Dr." and "Inc." and for certain numerical purposes ($18.43 and 26.2%).

Question Mark

A question mark follows a direct question:

| Have you all completed the essay?

A question mark should not be used to end an indirect question:

| Professor Grim asked if all students had completed the essay?
| Professor Grim asked if all students had completed the essay.

Exclamation Point

Use an exclamation point only when expression of strong feeling is appropriate:

| I can't believe you finished the essay so fast!

Semicolon

Like a blinking red traffic light at an intersection, a semicolon signals a brief but definite stop. Semicolons have several uses.

A semicolon can be used to separate independent clauses (logically complete ideas) whose contents are closely related and are not already connected by a comma and a coordinating conjunction (*and, or, but*, etc.):

| The project was finally completed; we had done a good week's work.

TO ACCOMPANY CONJUNCTIVE ADVERBS. A semicolon must accompany a conjunctive adverb such as *besides, otherwise, still, however, furthermore, moreover, consequently, therefore, on the other hand, in contrast*, or *in fact*:

| The job is filled; however, we will keep your résumé on file.
| Your background is impressive; in fact, it is the best among our applicants.

TO SEPARATE ITEMS IN A SERIES. When items in a series contain internal commas, semicolons provide clear separation between items.

| I am applying for summer jobs in Santa Fe, New Mexico; Albany, New York; Montgomery, Alabama; and Moscow, Idaho.

Colon

Like a flare in the road, a colon signals you to stop and then proceed, paying attention to the situation ahead. Colons have several uses.

TO SIGNAL A FOLLOW-UP EXPLANATION. Use a colon when a complete introductory statement requires a follow-up explanation:

| She is an ideal colleague: honest, reliable, and competent.

Do not use a colon if the introductory statement is incomplete:

Incorrect

| My plans include: finishing college, traveling for two years, and settling down in Santa Fe.

TO REPLACE A SEMICOLON. A colon can replace a semicolon between two related, complete statements when the second one explains or amplifies the first:

Colon replaces a semicolon

| Pam's reason for accepting the lowest-paying job offer was simple: She had always wanted to live in the Northwest.

TO INTRODUCE A QUOTATION. Colons can introduce quotations:

Colon introduces a quotation

| The supervisor's message was clear enough: "You're fired."

TO FOLLOW SALUTATIONS. Colons follow salutations in formal correspondence (e.g., Dear Ms. Jones:).

Comma

The comma is the most frequently used—and abused—punctuation mark. It works like a blinking yellow light, for which you slow down briefly without stopping. Never use a comma to signal a *break* between independent ideas, only a brief slow down. Use commas only in the following situations.

TO PAUSE BETWEEN COMPLETE IDEAS. In a compound sentence in which a coordinating conjunction (*and, or, nor, for, but*) connects equal (independent) statements, a comma usually precedes the conjunction.

Comma to pause between complete ideas

| This is an excellent course, but the work is difficult.

TO PAUSE BETWEEN AN INCOMPLETE AND A COMPLETE IDEA. A comma is usually placed between a complete and an incomplete statement in a complex sentence when the incomplete statement comes first.

Comma between an incomplete and complete idea

| Because he is a fat cat, Jack diets often.

When the order is reversed (complete statement followed by an incomplete one), the comma is usually omitted:

No comma needed

| Jack diets often because he is a fat cat.

TO SEPARATE ITEMS (WORDS, PHRASES, OR CLAUSES) IN A SERIES. Use commas after items in a series, including the next-to-last item:

Comma separates items in a series

| Helen, Joe, Marsha, and John are joining us on the term project.
| The new employee complained that the hours were long, the pay was low, the work was boring, and the supervisor was paranoid.

Use no commas if *or* or *and* appears between all items in a series:

| She is willing to study in San Francisco or Seattle or even in Anchorage.

No commas needed if *or* or *and* appears between all items

TO SET OFF INTRODUCTORY PHRASES.   Introductory phrases include infinitive phrases (*to* plus a simple form of the verb), prepositional phrases (beginning with *at, of, in, on,* etc.), participial phrases (beginning with an *-ing* or *-ed* form of a verb), and interjections (emotional words that have no connection with the rest of the sentence). These phrases are set off from the remainder of the sentence by a comma:

> To be or not to be, that is the question. (infinitive phrase)
> In the event of an emergency, use the fire exit. (prepositional phrase)
> Being an old cat, Jack was slow at catching mice. (participial phrase)
> Oh, is that the verdict? (interjection)

Comma sets off introductory phrases

TO SET OFF NONRESTRICTIVE PHRASES AND CLAUSES.   A *restrictive* phrase or clause modifies or defines the subject in such a way that deleting the modifier would change the meaning of the sentence. In the following sentence, "who have work experience" *restricts* the subject by limiting the category from all students to just those with work experience. Because this phrase is essential to the sentence's meaning, it is *not* set off by commas:

| All students who have work experience will receive preference.

Restrictive phrase (no comma)

A *nonrestrictive* phrase or clause could be deleted without changing the sentence's meaning ("Our new manager is highly competent") and *is* therefore set off by commas:

| Our new manager, who has only six weeks' experience, is highly competent.

Nonrestrictive phrase (use comma)

TO SET OFF PARENTHETICAL ELEMENTS.   Elements that interrupt the flow of a sentence (such as *of course, as a result, as I recall,* and *however*) are considered parenthetical and are enclosed by commas. These items may denote emphasis, afterthought, or clarification.

> This deluxe model, of course, is more expensive. (emphasis)
> Your essay, by the way, was excellent. (afterthought)
> The loss of my job was, in a way, a blessing. (clarification)

Commas to set off parenthetical elements

A direct address also interrupts a sentence and is set off by commas:

| Listen, my children, and you shall hear my story.

Commas to set off direct address

A parenthetical element at the beginning or the end of a sentence is also set off by a comma:

> Naturally, we will expect a full guarantee.
> You've done a good job, I think.

Commas to set off parenthetical elements at beginning and end

TO SET OFF QUOTED MATERIAL.   Quoted items within a sentence are set off by commas:

Comma to
set off quoted
material

| The customer said, "I'll take it," as soon as he laid eyes on our new model.

TO SET OFF APPOSITIVES.   An *appositive*, a word or words explaining a noun and placed immediately after it, is set off by commas when the appositive is nonrestrictive:

Comma to set
off appositives

Martha Jones, our new president, is overhauling all personnel policies.
Alpha waves, the most prominent of the brain waves, are typically recorded in a waking subject whose eyes are closed.

OTHER USES.   Commas are used to set off the day of the month from the year in a date (May 10, 1989), to set off numbers in three-digit intervals (6,463,657), to separate city and state in an address (Albany, Iowa), to set off parts of an address in a sentence (J. B. Smith, 18 Sea Street, Albany, Iowa, 51642), to set off day and year in a sentence (June 15, 2014, is my graduation date), and to set off degrees and titles from proper names (Roger P. Cayer, M.D., or Gordon Browne, Jr.).

Apostrophe

Apostrophes indicate the possessive, a contraction, and the plural of numbers, letters, and figures.

TO INDICATE THE POSSESSIVE.   At the end of a singular word or of a plural word that does not end in *-s*, add an apostrophe plus *-s* to indicate the possessive. Single-syllable nouns that end in *-s* take the apostrophe before an added *-s*:

Apostrophe
to indicate
possessives

The people's candidate won.
I borrowed Chris's book.

For words that already end in *-s* and have more than one syllable, add an *-s* after the apostrophe:

| Aristophanes's death

Do not use an apostrophe to indicate the possessive form of either singular or plural pronouns:

The book was hers.
Ours is the best school in the county.

At the end of a plural word that ends in *-s*, add an apostrophe only.

the cows' water supply
the Jacksons' wine cellar

At the end of a compound noun, add an apostrophe plus -*s*:

| my father-in-law's false teeth

At the end of the last word in nouns of joint possession, add an apostrophe plus -*s* if both own one item:

| Joe and Sam's lakefront cottage

Add an apostrophe plus -*s* to both nouns if each owns specific items:

| Joe's and Sam's passports

TO INDICATE A CONTRACTION.   An apostrophe shows that you have omitted one or more letters in a phrase that is usually a combination of a pronoun and a verb:

| I'm
| they're
| you'd

Apostrophes to show contractions

Be careful with faulty contractions: For example, *they're* (short for "they are" and often confused with the possessive *their* and the adverb *there*); *it's* (short for "it is" and often confused with the possessive *its*); *who's* (short for "who is" and often confused with the possessive *whose*); and *you're* (short for "you are" and often confused with the possessive *your*). See Table B.1 (pages 433–434) for further examples.

TO INDICATE THE PLURALS OF NUMBERS, LETTERS, AND FIGURES.   For example:

| The 6's on this new printer look like smudged G's, 9's are illegible, and the %'s are unclear.

Apostrophes to pluralize numbers, letters, and figures

Quotation Marks

Quotation marks have a variety of uses:

TO SET OFF THE EXACT WORDS BORROWED FROM ANOTHER SPEAKER OR WRITER.   The period or comma at the end is placed within the quotation marks:

| "Hurry up," Jack whispered.
| Jack told Felicia, "I'm depressed."

Quotation marks to set off a speaker's exact words

A colon or semicolon is always placed outside quotation marks:

| Our student handbook clearly defines "core requirements"; however, it does not list all the courses that fulfill the requirements.

When a question mark or exclamation point is part of a quotation, it belongs within the quotation marks, replacing the comma or period.

"Help!" he screamed.

Marsha asked John, "Can't we agree about anything?"

But if the question mark or exclamation point pertains to the attitude of the person quoting instead of the person being quoted, it is placed outside the quotation mark:

Why did Boris wink and whisper, "It's a big secret"?

TO INDICATE TITLES.   Use quotation marks around titles of articles, paintings, book chapters, and poems (but titles of books, journals, or newspapers should be underlined or italicized):

Quotation
marks to
indicate titles

The enclosed article, "The Job Market for College Graduates," should provide some helpful insights.

TO INDICATE IRONY.   Finally, use quotation marks (with restraint) to indicate irony.

Quotation
marks to
indicate irony

She is some "friend"!

Ellipses

Three dots … indicate that you have omitted material from a quotation. If the omitted words come at the end of the original sentence, a fourth dot indicates the period.

Ellipses to
indicate omitted
material from a
quotation

According to Beulah Montgomery, paper memorandums "… are now being … replaced with email correspondence in most workplace situations. …"

Brackets

Brackets are used within quotations to set off material that was not in the original quotation but is needed for clarification:

Brackets
to indicate
material added
to quotations

"She [Amy] was the outstanding candidate for the scholarship."

"It was in early spring [April 2, to be exact] that the tornado hit."

Use *sic* (Latin for "thus" or "so") in brackets when quoting an error from the original source:

Brackets to
indicate an error
in a quotation

The assistant's comment was clear: "He don't [sic] want any."

Italics

Use italics or underlining for titles of books, periodicals, films, newspapers, and plays; for the names of ships; and for foreign words or technical terms. Also, you may use italics *sparingly* for special emphasis.

Various uses of
italics

The *Oxford English Dictionary* is a handy reference tool.

My only advice is *caveat emptor.*

> *Bacillus anthracis* is a highly virulent organism.
>
> *Do not* inhale these fumes under any circumstances!

Parentheses

Material between parentheses, like all other parenthetical material discussed previously, can be deleted without harming the logical and grammatical structure of the sentence. Use parentheses to enclose material that defines or explains the statement that precedes it:

> An anaerobic (airless) environment must be maintained for the cultivation of this organism.
>
> The cost of running our college has increased by 15 percent in one year (see Appendix A for full cost breakdown).

Parentheses to define or explain preceding material

Dashes

Dashes can be effective to set off parenthetical material if, like parentheses, they are not overused. Parentheses deemphasize the enclosed material, whereas dashes emphasize it:

> Have a good vacation—but watch out for sandfleas.
>
> Mary—a true friend—spent hours helping me rehearse.

Dashes to set off and emphasize material

On most word processing programs, a dash is created by two hyphens, which the software will typically convert to a dash.

Mechanics

The mechanical aspects of writing a document include abbreviation, hyphenation, capitalization, use of numbers, and spelling. (Keep in mind that not all of these rules are hard and fast; some may depend on style guides used in your field.)

Abbreviation

The following should *always* be abbreviated:

- Titles such as *Ms., Mr., Dr.,* and *Jr.* when they are used before or after a proper name.
- Specific time designations (400 B.C.E., 5:15 A.M.).

Always abbreviate

The following should *never* be abbreviated:

- Military, religious, academic, or political titles (*Reverend, President*).
- Nonspecific time designations ("Sarah arrived early in the morning"—not "early in the A.M.").

Never abbreviate

Avoid abbreviations whose meanings might not be clear to all readers. Units of measurement can be abbreviated if they appear frequently in your document. However, a unit of measurement should be spelled out the first time it is used. Avoid abbreviations in visual aids unless saving space is absolutely necessary.

Hyphenation

Hyphens divide words at line breaks and join two or more words used as a single adjective if they precede the noun (but not if they follow it):

Correct use of hyphens

| Com-puter (at a line break)
| An all-too-human error (but "The error was all too human")

Other commonly hyphenated words include the following:

- Most words that begin with the prefix *self-* (*self-reliance, self-discipline*—see your dictionary for exceptions).
- Combinations that might be ambiguous (*re-creation* versus *recreation*).
- Words that begin with *ex* when *ex* means "past" (*ex-faculty member* but *excommunicate*).

Other uses of hyphens

- All fractions, along with ratios that are used as adjectives and that precede the noun and compound numbers from twenty-one through ninety-nine (*a two-thirds majority, thirty-eight windows*).

Capitalization

Uses of capitalization

Use capitalization in the following situations:

- The first words of all sentences ("This is a good idea.")
- Titles of people if the title precedes the person's name, but not after (Senator Barbara Boxer but Barbara Boxer, U.S. senator)
- Titles of books, films, magazines, newspapers, operas, and other longer works; in addition to capitalizing the first word, also capitalize all other words within the title (*A Long Day's Journey into Night*) except articles, short prepositions, and coordinating conjunctions (*and, but, for, or, nor, yet*)
- Parts of a longer work (Chapter 25, Opus 23)
- Languages (French, Urdu)
- Days of the week (Saturday)
- Months (November)
- Holidays (Thanksgiving)
- Names of organizations or groups (World Health Organization)

- Races and nationalities (Asian American, Australian)
- Historical events (War of 1812)
- Important documents (Declaration of Independence)
- Names of structures or vehicles (Empire State Building, the *Queen Mary*)
- Adjectives derived from proper nouns (Chaucerian English)
- Words such as *street, road, corporation, university*, and *college* only when they accompany a proper noun (High Street, Rand Corporation, Stanford University)
- The words *north, south, east*, and *west* when they denote specific regions (*the South, the Northwest*) but not when they are simply directions (*turn east at the light*)

Do not capitalize the seasons (*spring, winter*) or general groups (*the younger generation, the leisure class*).

Numbers and Numerals

Numbers expressed in one or two words can be written out or written as numerals. Use numerals to express larger numbers, decimals, fractions, precise technical figures, or any other exact measurements:

543
2,800,357
3.25
15 pounds of pressure
50 kilowatts
4,000 rpm

Uses of
numerals

Use numerals for dates, census figures, addresses, page numbers, exact units of measurement, percentages, times with A.M. or P.M. designations, and monetary and mileage figures.

page 14
1:15 P.M.
18.4 pounds
9 feet
12 gallons
$15

Additional uses
of numerals

Do not begin a sentence with a numeral. If the figure needs more than two words, revise your word order:

Six hundred students applied for the 102 available jobs.
The 102 available jobs attracted 600 applicants.

Uses of
numbers in
sentences

Do not use numerals to express approximate figures, time not designated as A.M. or P.M., or streets named by numbers less than 100:

When not to use numerals

> Four fifteen
> 108 East Forty-Second Street

In contracts and other documents in which precision is vital, a number can be stated both in numerals and in words:

> The tenant agrees to pay a rental fee of eight hundred and seventy-five dollars ($875.00) monthly.

Spelling

Always use the spell-check or autocorrect function in your word processing or email software. However, don't rely on these tools exclusively. Take the time to use a dictionary for all writing assignments. If you are a poor speller, ask someone else to proofread every document before you present the final version.

Usage

Be aware of the pairs of words (and sometimes groups of three words) that are often confused. Refer to Table B.1 for a list of the most commonly confused words.

Transitions

You can choose from three techniques to achieve smooth transitions within and between paragraphs.

Use Transitional Expressions

Transitional expressions

Use words such as *again, furthermore, in addition, meanwhile, however, also, although, for example, specifically, in particular, as a result, in other words, certainly, accordingly, because,* and *therefore*. Such words serve as bridges between ideas.

Repeat Key Words and Phrases

To help link ideas, repeat key words or phrases or rephrase them in different ways, as in this next paragraph (emphasis added):

Repeated key words and phrases

> Whales are among the most *intelligent* of all mammals. Scientists rank whale *intelligence* with that of higher primates because of *whales' sophisticated* group behavior. These *bright creatures* have been seen teaching and disciplining *their* young, helping *their* wounded comrades, engaging in elaborate courtship rituals, and playing in definite *gamelike patterns*. *They* are able to coordinate such *complex cognitive activities* through *their* highly effective communication system of sonar clicks and pings. Such remarkable social organization apparently stems from the *humanlike* devotion that *whales* seem to display toward one another.

Table B.1 Commonly confused words

Similar Words	Used Correctly in a Sentence
Accept means "to receive willingly."	She *accepted* his business proposal.
Except means "otherwise than."	They all agreed, *except* Bob.
Affect means "to have an influence on."	Meditation *affects* concentration in a positive way.
Affect can also mean "to pretend."	Boris likes to *affect* a French accent.
Effect used as a noun means "a result."	Meditation has a positive *effect* on concentration.
Effect used as a verb means "to make happen" or "to bring about."	Meditation can *effect* an improvement in concentration.
Already means "before this time."	Our new laptops are *already* sold out.
All ready means "prepared."	We are *all ready* for the summer tourist season.
Among refers to three or more.	The prize was divided *among* the four winners.
Between refers to two.	The prize was divided *between* the two winners.
Cite means "to document."	You must always *cite* your sources in research.
Sight means "vision."	Margarita seems to have the gift of second *sight*.
Site means "a location."	Have the surveyors inspected the *site* yet?
Continual means "repeated at intervals."	Our lower field floods *continually* during the rainy season.
Continuous means "without interruption."	His headache has been *continuous* for three days.
Council means "a body of elected people."	I plan to run for student *council*.
Counsel means "to offer advice."	Because you have experience, I suggest you *counsel* Jim on the project as it moves along.
Differ from refers to unlike things.	This plan *differs* greatly *from* our previous one.
Differ with means "to disagree."	Mary *differs with* John about the plan.
Disinterested means "unbiased" or "impartial."	Good science calls for *disinterested* analysis of research findings.
Uninterested means "not caring."	Boris is *uninterested* in science.
Eminent means "famous" or "distinguished."	Dr. Ostroff, the *eminent* physicist, is lecturing today.
Imminent means "about to happen."	A nuclear meltdown seemed *imminent*.
Farther refers to physical distance (a measurable quantity).	The station is 20 miles *farther*.
Further refers to extent (not measurable).	*Further* discussion of this issue is vital.
Fewer refers to things that can be counted.	*Fewer* than 50 students responded to our survey.
Less refers to things that can't be counted.	This survey had *less* of a response than our previous one.
Imply means "to insinuate."	This report *implies* that a crime occurred.
Infer means "to reason from evidence."	From this report, we can *infer* that a crime occurred.
It's stands for "it is."	*It's* a good time for a department meeting.
Its stands for "belonging to it."	The cost of the project has exceeded *its* budget.
Lay means "to set something down."	Please *lay* the blueprints on the desk.

(Continued)

Table B.1 (Continued)

Similar Words	Used Correctly in a Sentence
Lie means "to recline." It takes no direct object.	This patient needs to *lie* on his right side all night.
(Note that the past tense of *lie* is *lay*.)	The patient *lay* on his right side all night.
Precede means "to come before."	Audience analysis should *precede* a written report.
Proceed means "to go forward."	If you must wake the cobra, *proceed* carefully.
Principle is always a noun that means "basic rule or standard."	Ethical *principles* should govern all our communications.
Principal, used as a noun, means "the major person(s)."	All *principals* in this purchase must sign the contract.
Principal, used as an adjective, means "leading."	Martha was the *principal* negotiator for this contract.
Stationary means "not moving."	The desk is *stationary*.
Stationery means "writing supplies."	The supply cabinet needs *stationery*.
Their means "belonging to them."	They all want to have *their* cake and eat it too.
There means "at that location."	The new copy machine is over *there*.
They're means "they are."	*They're* not the only ones who disagree.

The key word *intelligent* in the preceding topic statement reappears as *intelligence* in the second sentence. Synonyms describing intelligent behavior (*sophisticated, bright, humanlike*) reinforce and advance the main idea throughout.

Use Forecasting Statements

Forecasting statements tell your readers where you are going next:

Forecasting statements

> The next step is to further examine the costs of this plan.
>
> Of course, we can also consider other options.
>
> This plan should be reconsidered for several reasons.

If you encounter a situation in which you think you need a better transition but none of these methods seems appropriate, you may need to delete or move some information.

Lists

Listed items can be presented in one of two ways: running in as part of the sentence (embedded lists) or displayed with each item on a new line (vertical lists).

Embedded Lists

An embedded list integrates a series of items into a sentence. To number an embedded list, use parentheses around the numerals and either commas or semicolons between the items, as in the following example:

In order to complete express check-in for your outpatient surgery, you must (1) go to the registration office, (2) sign in and obtain your registration number, (3) receive and wear your red armband, and (4) give your check-in slip to the volunteer, who will escort you to your room.

Embedded list

Vertical Lists

Embedded lists are appropriate for listing only a few short items. Vertical lists are preferable for multiple items. If the items belong in a particular sequence, use numerals or letters; if the sequence of items is unimportant, use bullets.

There are a number of ways to introduce vertical lists. You can introduce a vertical list with a sentence that closes with "the following" or "as follows" and ends with a colon:

All applicants for the design internship must submit the following:

- Personal statement
- Résumé
- Three letters of reference
- Portfolio

Vertical list using *following* and a colon

You can also introduce a vertical list with a sentence that closes with a noun and ends with a colon:

All applicants for the design internship must submit four items:

1. Personal statement
2. Résumé
3. Three letters of reference
4. Portfolio

Vertical list using a noun and a colon

Finally, you can introduce a vertical list with a sentence that is grammatically incomplete without the list items:

To register as a new student:

1. Take the placement test at the Campus Test Center.
2. Attend a new student orientation.
3. Register for classes by Web or telephone.
4. Pay tuition and fees by the due date.

Vertical list using grammatical incompleteness

Do not use a colon with an introductory sentence that ends with a verb, a preposition, or an infinitive, as in the following incorrect examples:

All applicants for the design internship must submit:

- A personal statement
- A résumé
- Three letters of reference
- A portfolio

Incorrect because the introductory sentence ends with a verb

Incorrect because the introductory sentence ends with a preposition

> All applicants for the design internship need to:
>
> - Submit a personal statement and résumé
> - Forward three letters of reference
> - Provide a portfolio

Incorrect because the introductory sentence ends with an infinitive

> All applicants for the design internship need to submit:
>
> - A personal statement
> - A résumé
> - Three letters of reference
> - A portfolio

If the sentence that introduces the list is followed by another sentence, use periods after both sentences. Do not use a colon to introduce the list:

Vertical list without a colon

> The next step is to configure the following fields. Consult Chapter 3 for more information on each field.
>
> - Serial port
> - Baud rate
> - Data bits
> - Stop bits

Note that some of the preceding examples use a period after each list item and some do not. As a general rule, use a period after each list item if any of the items contains a complete sentence. Do not use a period if none of the list items contains a complete sentence. Also note that items included in a list should be grammatically parallel. For more on parallelism, see page 97.

Works Cited

American Psychological Association (APA). *Publication Manual of the American Psychological Association*. 6th ed. Washington, DC: American Psychological Association, 2009.

Baker, Stephen. "Beware Social Media Snake Oil." *Bloomberg Businessweek*, 14 Dec. 2009, pp. 48–50.

Carliner, Saul. "Demonstrating Effectiveness and Value: A Process for Evaluating Technical Communication Products and Services." *Technical Communication*, vol. 44, no. 3, 1997, pp. 252–65.

Centers for Disease Control and Prevention. *Social Media Guidelines and Best Practices*. United States Department of Health and Human Services, 16 May 2012, www.cdc.gov/SocialMedia/Tools/guidelines/pdf/FacebookGuidelines.pdf.

Coe, Marlana. *Human Factors for Technical Communicators*. Wiley, 1996.

Consumer Product Safety Commission. *Fact Sheet No. 65*. U.S. Government Printing Office, 1989.

Corbett, Edward P. J. *Classical Rhetoric for the Modern Student*. 3rd ed. Oxford UP, 1990.

Crosby, Olivia. *Employment Interviewing*. U.S. Department of Labor, 2000. Daugherty, Shannon. "The Usability Evaluation: A Discount Approach to Usability Testing." *INTERCOM*, Dec. 1997, pp. 16–20.

Environmental Protection Agency (EPA). "Terminology services, definition of genetic engineering (definition 3)." United States Environmental Protection Agency website, 12 April 2017.

Environmental Protection Agency (EPA). *Climate Change, State of Knowledge*. United States Environmental Protection Agency, 29 April 1999.

Fisher, Anne. "Truth and Consequences." *Fortune*, 29 May 2000, p. 292.

Gartaganis, Arthur. "Lasers." *Occupational Outlook Quarterly*, Winter 1984, pp. 22–26.

Hart, Geoff. "Accentuate the Negative: Obtaining Effective Reviews through Focused Questions." *Technical Communication*, vol. 44, no. 1, 1997, pp. 52–57.

Hein, Robert G. "Culture and Communication." *Technical Communication*, vol. 38, no. 1, 1991, pp. 125–26.

Hoft, Nancy L. *International Technical Communication: How to Export Information about High Technology*. Wiley, 1995.

Japikse, Catharina, "Lasagna in the Making." *EPA Journal*, vol. 20, no. 3, 1990, p. 27.

Kipnis, David, and Stuart Schmidt. "The Language of Persuasion." *Psychology Today*, Apr. 1985, pp. 40–46. Reprinted in *Understanding Persuasion*. 3rd ed. Edited by Raymond S. Ross, Prentice Hall, 1990.

Modern Language Association of America. *MLA Handbook*. 8th ed., Modern Language Association of America, 2016.

Monty, Scott. "The Social Media Market Blog." 30 June 2009.

"News Release: ANA and NCSBN Unite to Provide Guidelines for Social Media and Networking for Nurses." *ANA/American Nurses Association*, 19 Oct. 2011.

Publication Manual of the American Psychological Association. 6th ed., American Psychological Association, 2010.

"Performance Appraisal—Discrimination." *The Employee Problem Solver*. Alexander Hamilton Institute, 2000.

Ross, Raymond S. *Understanding Persuasion*. 3rd ed. Prentice Hall, 1990.

Rubin, J. *Handbook of Usability Testing: How to Plan, Design, and Conduct Effective Tests*. Wiley, 1994.

Spencer, SueAnn. "Use Self-Help to Improve Document Usability." *Technical Communication*, vol. 43, no. 1, 1996, pp. 73–77.

Stanton, Mike. "Fiber Optics." *Occupational Outlook Quarterly*, Winter 1984, pp. 27–30.

University of Minnesota. Sustainable Urban Landscape Series website. "Building Boulder Walls." 26 May 2017.

Vaughan, David K. "Abstracts and Summaries: Some Clarifying Distinctions." *Technical Writing Teacher*, vol. 18, no. 2, 1991, pp. 132–41.

Victor, David A. *International Business Communication*. Harper, 1992.

Weymouth, L. C. "Establishing Quality Standards and Trade Regulations for Technical Writing in World Trade." *Technical Communication*, vol. 37, no. 2, 1990, pp. 143–47.

Wojahn, Patricia G. "Computer-Mediated Communication: The Great Equalizer between Men and Women?" *Technical Communication*, vol. 41, no. 4, 1994, pp. 747–51.

"Writing for Social Media." *SFU Editorial Style Guide*. www.sfu.ca/clf/styleguide.html.

Credits

Interior photo credits in page order: Page 2: everything possible/Shutterstock; Page 24: Sigrid Olsson/PhotoAlto/AGE Fotostock; Page 40: Monkey Business Images/Shutterstock; Page 60: corgarashu/Shutterstock; Page 70: Dotshock/123RF; Page 87: Artifacts Images/Photodisc/Getty Images; Page 103: John Lamb/Photodisc/Getty Images; Page 115: Yury Zap/Fotolia; Page 116: "Dust-Aid: DSLR Camera Sensor Cleaning Video" by Ross Wordhouse from www.youtube.com. Reproduced by permission; Page 123: Stevecoleimages/E+/Getty Images; Page 140: Mangostar/Shutterstock; Page 163: WAYHOME studio/Shutterstock; Page 191: Daniel Grill/Tetra images/Getty Images; Page 204: Blue Planet Studio/Shutterstock; Page 225: Fuse/Corbis/Getty Images; Page 228: s-cphoto/Getty Images; Page 248: Antonio Guillem/123RF; Page 262: PORTRAIT IMAGES ASIA BY NONWARIT/Shutterstock; Page 281: DragonImages/Fotolia; Page 309: Marzky Ragsac Jr./Fotolia; Page 332: Feng Yu/Shutterstock; Page 343: Ingo Schulz/imageBROKER/Alamy Stock Photo and US Food and Drug Administration FDA. https://www.fda.gov; Page 355: SDP/Alamy Stock Photo; Page 361: seewhatmitchsee/Alamy Stock Photo; Page 367: Monkey Business Images/Shutterstock; Page 378: Syda Productions/Shutterstock.

Images used throughout include: Natalia Merzlyakova/123RF (3D rendering of a laptop with icon); Marcel Mooij/Fotolia (check square 2); Blue jean images/Getty Images (three people confirming the direction).

Index

A

abbreviations, 429–430
abstracts, 32
  formal proposals, *318*
  formal reports, 284, 289
acceptance notes after job interview, 158
ACS (American Chemical Society) style, 414
action plan presentations, 371
active voice, 90–91
activity reports, periodic activity reports, 267–268
addresses, letters, 173
adjustment letters, 186
  negative adjustment letter, *188*
  positive adjustment letter, *187*
  strategies, 187
Adobe Connect, 381
alignment (justification), 129, *130*, 132
almanacs, 31
alphabetical references, MLA style citation, 398
AMWA (American Medical Writers Association)
    code of ethics, *66*
analytical categories, formal reports, 283–284
analytical reports, 264
  feasibility reports, 273–275
  peer review reports, 278–279
  recommendation reports, 275–277
antecedent/pronoun agreement, 420
APA style, 38, 99, 289–292, 298, 299, 301, 306, 393
  parenthetical references, 404
  references
  books, 405–407
    electronic sources, 410–413
    gray literature, 413–414
    miscellaneous sources, 408–410
    periodicals, 407–408
appendices
  formal proposals, *328*
  formal reports, 291, *306*
Apple Keynote, 368, 379–380
application letters
  checklist, 160
  solicited application letter, *149*
  solicited letters, 148
  strategies, 150
  unsolicited letters, 150
arguable claims letters, 181, *183*

assembly guides, 229–231
attention line, letters, 173
audience
  analysis questions, 42
  analyzing, 46
  connection, 48–51
  cultural background, 45–46
  definitions and, 192–193
  email, 334
  FDA main page example, *44–45*
  formal reports, 287–289
  instructions, 227
  oral presentations, 369, *370*
  persuasion and, 48–51
  primary, 42–43
  procedures and, 242
  profile sheet, *42*
  proposals, 310–311
  purpose of descriptions and, 205–206
  relationship, 43
  secondary, 42–43
  social media and, 357–359
  summaries, 248–249
  technical background, 43–44
  Web pages, 347–348
audience-centered visuals, 104–105
  accuracy, 119–120
  appropriateness, 118–119
  checklist, 120
  color use, 119
  cross-references, 119
  cultural considerations, 118
  diagrams, 114–115, 117
  figures, 105
  formal reports, 287–288
  graphs, 108–110
  icons, 116–118
  illustrations, 114–115, 117
  photographs, 115, 117
  placement, 119
  presentation, 119
  stand-alone, 107
  to support text, 106–107
  symbols, 116–118
  tables, 106–107
  videos, 116, 117

B

background information, formal proposals, *223*
background information, informal proposals, 316
bar graphs, 108, *109*
biased language, 99
bibliographic citations, 387
bibliographies, 31
block format, letters, 175
blogs, 21, 29
   checklist, 353
   external, 345
   internal, 344
   MLA citation style, 402
   strategies, 352
body text
   email, *336*
   instructional documents, 233–234
   letters, 173
   oral presentations, 373
boldface font, 131, 133, 136, 351
books
   APA style citations, 405–407
   MLA style citations, 394–396
brochures, 13
   MLA style citation, 399
budget, usability and, 54
bulleted lists, 133, *135*
   email, *333*
   Web pages, 351

C

callouts, color, *134*
capitalization, 430–431
causal analysis, 283–284
cause-and-effect sequencing, 78
cautions, instructional documents, 234–235
CFPs (calls for proposals), 13
charts. *See also* graphs
   flowcharts, 111, *112*, 113
   organization charts, 111, 113, *113*
   pie charts, 111, *112*, 113
   strategies, 113
Chicago Manual of Style, 414
chronological sequencing, 78, 208
chunking information, 77, 349
citations
   ACS (American Chemical Society) style, 414
   Chicago Manual of Style, 414
   CSE (Council of Science Editors) style, 414

IEEE (Institute of Electrical and Electronics Engineers) style, 414
   places to cite, 392–393
   quotations, 388–389, *389*
   software, 387
claim letters
   arguable claims, 181, *183*
   routine claims, 181, *182*
   strategies, 184
claims, persuasion and, 48
closings, 255–256
   persuasive documents, *11*
coherence
   paragraphing and, 78, 79–80
   structure and, 72
collaboration, 14–15
   conflict management, 17–18
   cultural differences and, 18
   digital communication and, 17–18
   editing documents, 19–20
   interpersonal styles and, 17
   meetings and, 15–17
   project organization, 15
   project planning form, *16*
   reviewing documents, 19–20
   strategies, 15
color, 133, 136
   callouts, *134*
   cross-references, *134*
   headings, *134*
   leader lines, *134*
   ruled boxes, *134*
   rules, *134*
   screens, *134*
   sidebars, *134*
   tabs, *134*
   Web pages, 347
comma splices, 419
common knowledge, documentation and, 387, 392
comparative analysis, 283
complex process descriptions, 216–219
complex product descriptions, 212–215
compliance, audience connection and, *49*
complimentary closing, letters, 173
conclusions
   descriptions and, 208
   email, *336*
   formal proposals, *327*
   formal report, *285*, *304*
   informal proposals, 317

instructional documents, 233–234
  oral presentations, 369
conference presentations, MLA style citation, 398
conflict management, 17–18
confused words, *433–434*
conjunctions, 420–421
connection to audience
  approaches, 49
  compliance and, *49*
  identification and, *49*
  internalization and, *49*
  power connection, 48, 49
  rational connection, 48, 50
  relationship connection, 48, 49–50
consistency, specifications
      and, *221*
containers, MLA style, 394
  digital sources, 401
context sensitivity, online instructions, 232
coordinating conjunctions, 420–421
copy notation in letters, 175
copyrights, 414–415
  fair use and, 415
  plagiarism *versus* copyright infringement,
      415–416
  public domain works, 415
corporate authored documents, MLA style
      citation, 400
costs, informal proposals, 317
cover letters, 148
cover messages, email, *336*
critical thinking, 26
cross-references, color, *134*
CSE (Council of Science Editors) style, 414
cultural differences
  audience and, 45–46
  collaboration and, 18
customer review social media sites, 359–360
  Facebook, 360
  Google+, 360
  Instagram, 360
  job sites, 360–361
  LinkedIn, 360
  Twitter, 361–362
  YouTube, 362

D

danger notices, instructional documents, 235
data interpretation, formal reports and, 286
databases, periodicals, 30
date, letters, 173

definitions, 192
  analysis of parts and, 197
  audience and, 192–193
  checklist, 202–203
  comparisons and contrasts, 198
  etymology and, 196
  examples and, 199
  expanded, 195, *200, 201*
  history and, 197
  legal implications, 193–194
  multiple expansion methods, 199
  negation and, 197
  operating principles and, 197
  parenthetical, 194
  placement, 199–202
  purpose of terms, 193
  required conditions and, 198
  safety implications, 193–194
  sentence, 194–195
  societal implications, 194
  specifications, 220–222
  strategies for, 202
  visuals and, 198
  working definitions, 195
descriptions
  audience and, 205–206
  checklist, 222–223
  conclusion, 208
  formal proposals, *320–322*
  introduction, 207
  objectivity in, 206–207
  process descriptions, *211*
    complex, 216–219
  product descriptions, 209, *210*
    complex, 212–215
  resolution, informal proposals, 317
  solution, informal proposals, 317
  strategies, 219
  titles, 207
  topic sequence, 207–208
  visuals, 208
descriptive abstracts, 257
design, 71
  characteristics of good design, 125–128
  checklist, 137
  cohesiveness, 128–132
  consistency, 128–132
  emphasis and, 133–136
  font size, 131
  font style, 131
  formal reports, 288

design (*continued*)
  grid patterns, 128, *129*
  importance, 124–125
  indentation, 130
  instructional documents, 237
  justification (alignment), 129
  line spacing, 130
  margins, 128
  navigation and, 133, 136–137
  paragraphs, 129
  Web pages, 348–350
  white space, 129–130
diagrams, 115, 117
dictionaries, 31
  MLA style citation, 398
digital communication
  blogs, 21
  collaboration and, 17–18, 20–21
  digital whiteboards, 21
  editing software, 21
  email, 20
  IM (instant messaging), 20
  intranets, 21
  privacy issues, 337
  project management software, 20
  teleconferencing, 20
  web conferencing, 21
  wikis, 21
digital employment materials *versus* print, 151
digital sources
  APA style citations, 410–413
  MLA citations, 398–400
digital whiteboards, 21
directories, 31
dissertations, MLA style citation, 400
documentation
  ACS (American Chemical Society) style, 414
  APA style, 392, 405–414
  authority and, 391
  bibliographic citations, 387
  Chicago Manual of Style, 414
  citation software, 387
  citations, 392–393
  common knowledge and, 387, 392
  CSE (Council of Science Editors) style, 414
  efficiency and, 391
  ethics and, 391
  IEEE (Institute of Electrical and Electronics Engineers) style, 414
  inclusion, 392
  in-text citations, 386

  MLA style, 392
    parenthetical references, 393–394
  note taking and, 387–388
  outside sources and, 386–387
  references list, 386
  works cited list, 386
documents
  audience, 42–46
  audience profile sheet, *42*
  brochures, 13
  design, 5
  editing, 19–20
  email, 12
  formats, 5
  headings, *8*
  illustrations, *8, 9*
  instructions, 12
  intended use, 47
  introduction, *9*
  letters, 12
  manuals, 12
  memos, 12
  numbered steps, *9*
  preparation, 41
  procedures, 12
  proofreading, 56–57
  proposals, 13
  purpose, 46–47
  purpose profile sheet, *42*
  reports, 13
  reviewing, 19–20
  revising, 56–57
  task analysis, 51–52
  testing, 56–57
  text, *8*
  titles, *8*
  usability, 41–52
  user centered, 4–5
  warning box, *9*
dossiers, 152, 154
  strategies, 155

E
e-books, MLA citation style, 402
editing documents, 19–21
email, 12, 20
  advantages, 333
  audience, 334
  body text, *336*
  brief messages, *335*, 335–336
  bulleted lists, *337*

cardinal rule, 334
cautions, 333–334
checklist, 341–342
components, 334–335
conclusion, *336*
cover messages, *336*
etiquette, 339
fonts, *337*
formatted messages, *337*
header, *336*
hyperlinks, *337*
introductory sentence, *336*
letterhead, *337*
lists, 29
organization, 334–335
permanence, 340
purpose, 334
readability, *337*
signature block, *336*
strategies, 338, 340
style, 338–340, *339*
tone, 338–339, *339*
when not to use, 334
embedded lists, 434–435
emphasizing information
boldface, 131, 136
bulleted lists, 135, 136
color, 133–136
font style, 131–132
headings, 136
italics, 131, 136
numbered lists, 135, 136
shading, 136
underlining, 136
employment materials. *See also* resumes
application letters, 148–150, 160–161
cover letters, 148
digital, strategies for, 152
digital *versus* print, 151
dossiers, 152, 154
e-portfolios, 154–155
follow-up communication, 157–159
interviews, 156–157
job market research, 142–143
portfolios, 154–155
skills assessments, 142
unsolicited application letters, 150
enclosure notation in letters, 175
encyclopedias, 31
MLA style citation, 398
end matter, 263

appendices, 291, *302*
glossary, 291
informal proposals, 312
references, 290–291, *301*
works cited list, 290–291
Endnote citation software, 387
e-portfolios, 154–155
ethics, 61
abuse, strategies for avoiding, 67
AMWA code of ethics, *66*
banking and retail and, 62
checklist for effectiveness, 67–68
communication checklist, 67–68
downplaying information, 64
environmental pollutants and, 62
exaggeration, 65
exploitation of cultural differences, 65
fabrication, 64
falsification, 64
images, truthfulness, 65
information suppression, 64
medical technologies and, 62
misuse of electronic information, 65
omissions, *63*
plagiarism and, 64, 385–386
proprietary information and, 65
workplace pressures and, 62–64
etiquette in email, 339
evidence, persuasive documents, *10*
executive abstracts, 257–258
executive summary, formal reports, 289
expanded definitions, 195, *200*
analysis of parts and, 197
comparisons and contrasts, 198
etymology and, 196
examples and, 199
history and, 197
hyperlinks, *201*
multiple expansion methods, 199
negation and, 197
operating principles and, 197
questions to ask, 196
required conditions and, 198
visuals and, 198
experiments, 36–37
external blogs, 345
external wikis, 346

F
Facebook, 352
feasibility analysis, 284–285

feasibility reports, 273–275
feasibility statement, formal proposals, *327*
figures, 105
flowcharts, 111, *112*
fluent writing
   parallel structure, 97
   sentence construction, 96–97
   sentence length, 96–97
follow-up memos, 168–169, *170*
font size, 131, 132, 351
font style, 131, *131*, 132
   boldface, 131
   italics, 131
   sans serif, 131
   serif, 131
   Web pages, 351
fonts
   decorative, 131
   email, *333*
footers/headers, 135
formal outlining, 75
   alphanumeric notation, *76*
   decimal notation, *77*
formal proposals, 311
   abstracts, *322*
   appendices, *328*
   background, *323*
   conclusion, *327*
   descriptions, *324–326*
   feasibility statement, *327*
   introduction, *323*
   letter of transmittal, *319*
   sample, *318–328*
   statement of problem, *323–324*
   tables of contents, *321*
   title, *320*
formal reports, 282
   abstracts, 284, *296*
   appendices, *306*
   audience-centered visuals, 287–288
   causal analysis, 283–284
   checklist, 307
   comparative analysis, 283
   conclusion, *285, 304*
   data interpretation, 286, *298*
   design, 288
   end matter, 290–291
   feasibility analysis, 284–285
   front matter, 288–289
   introduction, *297*
   letter of transmittal, 288, *293*
   purpose, 283
   purpose statement, 286, *297*
   readability, 286–287, *301–302*
   references, *304*
   sample, 292–306
   strategies, 291–292
   structure, 286, *301–303*
   style, 286–287
   tables of contents, *295*
   text, 290
   titles, *294*
   visuals, 287–288
formats, 5
   block format, letters, 175
   formatted email messages, *337*
   informal reports, 263
   instructions, 227–232
   memos, 165
   usability and, 53
foundation authored documents, MLA
      style citation, 400
front matter, 263
   abstract, 289
   executive summary, 289
   informal proposals, 316
   list of tables and figures, 289
   table of contents, 289
   title page, 288
functional sequence, 208

G

global communication, 13–14
glossary, formal reports, 291
Google, secondary sources and, 28
Google+, 356
Google Books, 28
Google Scholar, 28
Google Slides, 370, 379–380
GoToMeeting, 381
government documents, MLA style citation,
   399–400
grammar
   comma splices, 419
   conjunctions, 420–421
   coordinating conjunctions, 420–421
   pronoun case, 422
   pronoun/antecedent agreement, 420
   run-on sentences, 418–419
   sentence fragments, 417–418
   subject/verb agreement, 419–420
   subordinating conjunctions, 420–421

graphs. *See also* charts
    bar graphs, 108, *109*
    line graphs, 108, *110*
    strategies, 111
gray literature, 32
    APA style citations, 413–414
grid patterns, 128, *129*, 131
    Web pages, 351

H

handbooks, 31
HathiTrust, 402
headers, email, *336*
headers/footers, 135
headings, *8*, 81, *82–83*, 136
    color, *134*
    levels of headings, 133
    Web pages, 351
hyperlinks
    definitions and, *201*
    email, *337*
    permalinks, digital sources and, 402
hyphenation, 430

I

icons, 116–118
    cautions, 235
    danger notices, 235
    warnings, 235
identification, audience connection
        and, *49*
IEEE (Institute of Electrical and Electronics
        Engineers) style, 414
illustrations, *8*, *9*, 114–115, 117
IM (instant messaging), 20
indentation, 130, 132
indexes, 31, 136, 137
Inernet Public Library, 29
informal proposals, 311
    background information, 316
    conclusion, 317
    costs, 317
    description of resolution, 317
    description of solution, 317
    end matter, 316
    front matter, 316
    qualifications, 317
    statement of problem, 316
    statement of situation, 316
    strategies, 317–318

    subject line, 316
    timing, 317
    title, 316
informal reports, 263, 264
    analytical, 264
    checklist, 279
    informational, 264
    meeting minutes, 271–273
    periodic activity reports, 267–268, *269*
    progress reports, 264–267
    trip reports, 268–271
information
    persuasion balance, 6
    relevance, 6
    visual hierarchy, 126–128
information plan, 54–56
informational documents, 7, *8*
informational interviews, 34–35
informational memos, 169, *171*
informative abstracts, 256–257
informative oral presentations, 371
inquiries, research and, 33–34
inquiry letters
    solicited *versus* unsolicited, 179
    strategies, 181
    unsolicited, *180*
Instagram, 352
instructional documents, *5*, *7*, *9*, 12, 226
    assembly guides, 229–231
    audience and, 227
    body, 233
    cautions, 235
    checklist, 246
    conclusion, 233–234
    content considerations, 236
    danger notices, 235
    design, 237
    formats, 227–232
    introduction, 233
    legal implications, 232
    notes, 234–235
    online instructions, 232
    overview, 233
    quick reference materials, 229
    safety and, 232
    style, 236
    title, 233
    usability, 242–245
    user manuals, 228–229
    visuals, 234
    warnings, 235

instructional documents (*continued*)
  web-based instructions, 231–232
  wordless instructions, 230–231
instructions
  checklist, 246
  strategies, 236–237, 239, 244
internal blogs, 344
internal wikis, 34
internalization, audience connection and, *49*
International Organization for Standardization, 118
international readers, letter tone, 178
Internet Archive, 29
interpersonal styles, collaboration and, 17
interviews
  acceptance notes, 158
  employment, 156–157
  informational, 34–35
  refusal notes, 158
  strategies, 159
interviews, MLA style citation, 399
intranets, 21
introductions, *9*
  descriptions and, 207
  email, *336*
  formal proposals, *323*
  instructional documents, 233–234
  oral presentations, 373
italics, 131, 133, 136, 351

J
jargon, 93–94
job application. *See* employment materials
job market research, 142–143
journal articles, MLA style, 397–398
justification (alignment), 129, *130*, 132

K
key word repetition, 428
Keynote, 364, 375–376

L
leader lines, color, *134*
lectures, MLA style citation, 395
legal implications
  of instructional documents, 232
  of terminology, 194
length, usability and, 53
letter of transmittal, 288
  formal proposal, *315*

letterhead, *10*
  email, *337*
letters, 12, *174*
  addresses, 173
  adjustment letters, 186–188
  attention line, 173
  block format, 175
  body text, 173
  checklist, 189
  claim letters, 181–184
  complimentary
    closing, 173
  copy notation, 175
  date, 173
  directness *versus* indirectness, 178
  enclosure notation, 175
  inquiry, 179–181
  international readers, 178
  MLA style citation, 395
  optional parts, 175
  plain English, 177–178
  sales, 184–186
  salutation, 173
  signature, 175
  strategies, 178–179
  subject lines, 173
  tact, 177
  templates, 172–173
  tone, 175–179
  typist notation, 175
  you perspective, 175, 177
libraries
  Internet Public Library, 29
  OPAC (online public access
    catalog), 28
  secondary sources and, 28
line graphs, 108, *110*
line spacing, 130, 132
LinkedIn, 143, 356
  resume templates, 151
lists
  bulleted lists, 133, *135*
  embedded lists, 434–435
  list of reasons, persuasive
    documents, *10*
  list of tables and figures, formal
    report, 289
  numbered lists, 133, *135*
  vertical lists, 435–436
locations, MLA style, 394
  digital sources, 401

M

magazine articles, MLA style, 397
manuals, 12. *See* user manuals
    usability, 41–52
maps, MLA style citation, 400
margins, 128, 132
meetings
    minutes, 271–273
    strategies for running, 17
memos, *5*, 12, 164–165
    checklist, 189
    direct approach, 167
    example, *166*
    follow-up, 168–169, *170*
    format, 165
    indirect approach, 167
    informational, 169, *171*
    strategies, 172
    summary, 168–169, *170*
    tone, 165–168
    transmittal, 168, *169*
Mendeley citation software, 387
Microsoft PowerPoint, 368, 379–380
minutes of meetings, 271–273
MLA style, 392–394
    containers, 394
    core elements, 394
    locations, 394
    parenthetical references, 393–394
    qtd. in, 396
    Works Cited, 38, 291, *395*
        alphabetical references, 398
        books, 394–396
        brochures, 399
        conference presentations, 398
        corporate authored documents, 400
        dictionaries, 398
        digital sources, 400–404
        dissertations, 400
        encyclopedias, 398
        foundation authored documents, 400
        government documents, 399–400
        interviews, 399
        lectures, 399
        letters, 399
        maps, 400
        pamphlet, 399
        periodicals, 396–398
        questionnaires, 399
        reports, 398
        theses, 400
        visual aids, 400

modifiers, ambiguity, 90
Monster.com, 143
    resume templates, 151

N

navigating documents, 133, 135–136
    headings, *8*
    indexes, 136, 137
    page numbers, 137
    running, 136–137
    running headers/footers, 135
    tables of contents, 136, 137
netiquette, email, 339
networking, job search and, 143
newspaper articles, MLA style, 398
nominalizations, 92–93
note taking, documentation and, 387–388
    strategies, 388
notes, instructional documents, 234–235
nouns
    nominalizations, 92–93
    stacked, 93
numbered lists, 133, *135*, 351
numbered steps, *9*
numbers/numerals, 431–432
numeric tables, 107, *108*

O

objectivity in descriptions, 206–207
observations, 36–37
omissions, ethics and, *63*
online abstracts, MLA citation style, 401
online articles, MLA citation style, 401
online forums, 29
online instructions, 232
online videos, MLA citation
    style, 402
OPAC (online public access catalog), 28
opening paragraphs, *10*
oral presentations
    See also presentations
    action plans, 371
    audience, 369, *400*
    body, 373
    checklist, 383
    conclusion, 373
    delivery strategies, 382–383
    delivery style, 374–376
    informative, 369, 371
    introduction, 372
    outlining, 373–374

oral presentations *(continued)*
  persuasive presentations, 371
  purpose, 369
  purpose profile sheet, *370*
  rehearsal, 379
  research, 373
  sales, 373
  slide examples, *377–378*
  storyboarding, 373–374
  strategies, 379
  technology used, 376
  topic, audience and, 373
  training presentations, 371
  visuals, 376
organization charts, 111, *113*
outlining, 72–73
  alphanumeric notation, 75, *76*
  chunking information and, 77
  decimal notation, 75, *77*
  email example, *73*
  essential information list, 73–74
  formal, 75–76
  Roman numerals, 75
  strategies, 75–76
  Web pages, 348–349
outside sources, 386–387
overviews, *85*
  instructional documents, 233–234
  longer documents, 81–84

P
page numbers, 137
pamphlet, MLA style citation, 399
paragraphing, 129, 132
  coherence, 78, 79–80
  sequence of thoughts, 80
  support paragraphs, 78
  topic sentence, 78
  unified paragraphs, 78, 79
parallelism, 97
paraphrasing, 389–390
parenthetical definitions, 194
parenthetical references
  APA style, 404
  MLA style, 393–394
passive voice, 91–92
peer review reports, 278–279
periodic activity reports, 267–268, *269*
periodicals
  APA style citations, 407–408

databases, 30
  MLA citations, 396–398
permalinks, digital sources and, 402
personable writing
  biased language, 99
  tone, 98
personal email, MLA citation style, 402
persuasion
  information balance, 6
  strategies, 51
persuasive documents, 7
  closings, *11*
  evidence, *10*
  letterhead and, *10*
  list of reasons, *10*
  opening paragraph, *10*
  statistics, *11*
persuasive elements, 47
  audience connection, 48–51
  claims, 48
persuasive presentations, 401
photographs, 115, 117
phrase repetition, 432
pie charts, 111, *112*
Pinterest, 363
plagiarism, 385–386. *See also* documentation
  versus copyright infringement, 415–416
  paraphrasing and, 389–390
  quotations and, 388–389
  summarizing and, 390–391
planning proposals, 311, *312*
podcasts, MLA citation style, 402
portfolios, 154–155
  strategies, 155
power connection, 48, 49–50
PowerPoint, 368, 379–380
presentations
  Apple Keynote, 370, 379–380
  Google Slides, 370, 379–380
  Microsoft PowerPoint, 368, 379–380
  Prezi, 368, 379–380
Prezi, 368, 379–380
primary audience, 42–43
primary purpose of document, 47
primary sources for research, 27, 33–37
privacy, digital communications and, 341
problem-solution sequencing, 78
procedures, 5, 12, 226, 239
  audience and, 242
  checklist, 246

general safety procedures, 242
health procedures, 242
medical procedures, 242
purpose and, 242
SOPs (standard operating procedures), 12, 242
strategies, 244
usability, 242–245
process descriptions, *211*
   complex, 216–219
product descriptions, 209, *210*
   complex, 212–215
progress reports, 264–267
Project Guttenberg, 402
project management software, 20
projects
   meetings and, 15–17
   planning form, *16*
   strategies, 15
   team organization, 15
pronouns
   case, 418
   pronoun/antecedent agreement, 420
pronouns, ambiguity, 89–90
proofreading, 56–57
   strategies, 57
proposals, 13, 310
   audience, 310–311
   CFPs (calls for proposals), 13
   checklist, 329
   formal, 401
      abstracts, *322*
      appendices, *328*
      background, *323*
      conclusion, *327*
      descriptions, *324–326*
      feasibility statement, *327*
      introduction, *323*
      statement of problem, *323–324*
   informal, 311
      background information, 316
      conclusion, 317
      costs, 317
      description of resolution, 317
      description of solution, 317
      end matter, 316
      front matter, 316
      qualifications, 317
      statement of problem, 316
      statement of situation, 316
      strategies, 317–318

subject line, 316
   timing, 317
   title, 316
planning proposals, 311, *312*
purpose, 310–311
research proposals, 313, *314*
RFPs (requests for proposals), 13, 311
sales proposals, 313, *315*
solicited, 311
strategies, 317–318
unsolicited, 311
punctuation
   apostrophe, 426–427
   brackets, 428
   colon, 423–424
   comma, 424–426
   dashes, 429
   ellipses, 428
   exclamation point, 423
   italics, 428–429
   parenthesis, 429
   period, 422
   question mark, 423
   quotation marks, 427–428
   semicolon, 423
purpose
   descriptions, audience and, 205–206
   documents
      intended use, 47
      primary, 47
      secondary, 47
   email, 334
   formal reports, 283
   oral presentations, 369, *370*
   procedures, 242
   profile sheet, *42*
   proposals, 310–311
   social media, 357–358
purpose statement, formal reports and, 286
purpose summaries, 248–249

Q

qualifications, informal proposals, 317
quality, specifications and, *221*
questionnaires, 36, 37
   MLA style citation, 399
quick reference card, *230*
quick reference materials, 229
quotations, 388–389, *389*
   paraphrasing, 389–390

R

rational connection, 48, 50
readable style, 88–89. *See also* writing clearly
    email, *337*
    formal reports, 286–287
readers, document focus, 4–5
recommendation reports, 275–277
Reddit, 363
redundancy, conciseness and, 95
reference databases, MLA citation
        style, 401–402
reference materials, 229
references, 30
    abstracts, 32
    ACS (American Chemical Society) style, 414
    almanacs, 31
    APA style, 290
        books, 405–407
        electronic sources, 410–413
        gray literature, 413–414
        miscellaneous sources, 409–410
        periodicals, 407–408
    bibliographies, 31
    Chicago Manual of Style, 414
    CSE (Council of Science Editors) style, 414
    dictionaries, 31
    directories, 31
    encyclopedias, 31
    formal reports, 290–291, *305*
    handbooks, 31
    IEEE (Institute of Electrical and Electronics
        Engineers) style, 414
    indexes, 31
refusal notes after job interview, 158
relationship connection, 48, 49–50
repetition, conciseness and, 95
reports, *5*, 13
    analytical
        feasibility reports, 273–275
        peer review reports, 278–279
        recommendation reports, 275–277
    formal, 282
        abstracts, 284
        audience-centered visuals, 287–288
        causal analysis, 283–284
        comparative analysis, 283
        conclusion, *285*
        data interpretation, 286
        design, 288
        end matter, 290–291

        feasibility analysis, 284–285
        front matter, 288–289
        letter of transmittal, 288
        purpose, 283
        purpose statement, 286
        readability, 286–287
        sample, 292–302
        strategies, 291–292
        structure, 286
        style, 286–287
        text, 290
        visuals, 287–288
    informal, 263
        analytical reports, 264
        informational reports, 264
        meeting minutes, 271–273
        periodic activity reports, 267–268, *269*
        progress reports, 264–267
        trip reports, 268–271
    MLA style citation, 398
research, 6–7, 25–26
    blogs, 29
    books, hard copy, 30
    checklist, 38
    critical thinking and, 26
    depth of, 26
    digital collections, 29–30
    digital libraries, 29–30
    email lists, 29
    experiments, 36–37
    global communication and, 14
    Google searches, 28
    government Web sites, 28
    gray literature, 32
    informational interviews, 34–35
    inquiries, unsolicited, 33–34
    interpretation of findings, 26
    library searches, 28
    locating, 27–28, 32–33
    magazines, 28–29
    observations, 36–37
    online forums, 29
    online news outlets, 28–29
    periodical databases, 30
    periodicals, 30
    primary sources, 27, 33–37
    questions, 26
    reference works, 30–32
    secondary sources, 27–33
    source evaluation, 26

strategies, 26
surveys, 35–36
Web sites, 28
Wikipedia, 29
wikis, 29
research proposals, 313, *314*
resumes. *See also* employment materials
activities, 144, 146
career objectives, 144
checklist, 160
contact information, 144
description, 143–144
dossiers, 152, 154
education, 144
example, *145, 147*
leadership experience, 144, 146
organization, 146
printed *versus* digital, 151
references, 146
skills assessments, 142
strategies, 146
templates, 151
work experience, 144
reviewing documents, 19–20
revising, 56–57
RFPs (requests for proposals), 13, 311
Riley Guide, employment and, 143
routine claims letters, 181, *182*
RSS (really simple syndication)
feeds, 345
ruled boxes, color, *134*
rules, color, *134*
running headers/footers, 135
run-on sentences, 418–419

S

safety implications of instructional
documents, 232
safety implications of terminology, 194
specifications and, *221*
sales letters, 184–187
sales presentations, 372
sales proposals, 313, *315*
salutation, letters, 173
screens, color, *134*
secondary audience, 42–43
secondary purpose of document, 47
secondary sources for research, 27–33
blogs, 29

books, hard copy, 30
digital collections, 29–30
digital libraries, 29–30
email lists, 29
Google searches, 28
government Web sites, 28
gray literature, 32
library searches, 28
locating, 27–28, 32–33
magazines, 28–29
online forums, 29
online news outlets, 28–29
periodical databases, 30
periodicals, 30
reference works, 30–32
strategies, 32–33
Web sites, 28
Wikipedia, 29
wikis, 29
sentence fragments, 417–418
sentences
construction, 96–97
definitions, 194–195
length, 96–97
sequencing
cause-and-effect, 78
chronological, 78, 208
functional, 208
problem-solution, 78
spatial, 77–78, 208
topic sequence, 207–208
Web pages, 346
setting, usability and, 53
shading, 133
Web pages, 351
sidebars, color, *134*
signature block, email, *336*
Skype, 381
social media
audience and, 357–358
checklist, 365
credibility and, 363–364
customer review sites, 359–363
Facebook, 356
Google+, 356
Instagram, 356
legal issues, 363–364
LinkedIn, 356
personal use, 359
Pinterest, 363

social media (*continued*)
   policies, 357–358
   purpose and, 357–358
   Reddit, 363
   strategies, 364
   summaries and, 259
   TripAdvisor, 356
   Tumblr, 363
   Twitter, 356
   workplace use, 359
   Yelp, 356
   YouTube, 356
societal implications of terminology, 194
software
   citations, 387
   editing, 21
   project management, 20
solicited application letters, 148
solicited proposals, 311
SOPs (standard operating procedures), 12
sources
   bibliographic citations, 387
   citation software, 387
   electronic, 387
   outside sources, 386–387
   photographs, 115
   plagiarism and, 385–386
   quotations, 388–389, *389*
spatial sequencing, 77–78, 208
specialized questions, 4
specifications, 220–222
   checklist, 223
   strategies, 222
spelling, 432
stacked nouns, 93
stand-alone visuals, 107
statement of problem
   formal proposals, *323–324*
   informal proposals, 316
statement of situation, informal proposals, 316
statistics, persuasive documents, *11*
steps, numbered steps, *9*
storyboarding, Web pages, 348–349, *349*
strategies, 317–318
structure, 71, *74*
   checklist, 84
   chunking information, 77
   coherence, 72
   formal reports, 286
   headings, 81, *82–83*
   outlining, 72–77

   overviews, 81–84, *85*
   paragraphing, 78
   questions to ask, 72
   sequencing, 77–78
   unity and, 72
   Web pages, 348–350
style, 71
   checklist, 100
   email, 338–340
   formal reports, 286–287
   instructional documents, 236
   summaries, 251
   Web pages, 348–350
subject line
   informal proposals, 316
   letters, 173
subject/verb agreement, 419–420
subordinating conjunctions, 420–421
summaries, 254–255
   accuracy and, 250–251
   audience, 248–249
   checklist, 260
   closing summaries, 255–256
   completeness and, 251
   conciseness and, 251
   descriptive abstracts, 257
   executive summaries, 257–258
   informative abstracts, 256–257
   nontechnical style, 251
   purpose, 248–249
   social media and, 259
   steps for, 251–254
   strategies, 259–260
summarizing, plagiarism and, 390–391
summary memos, 168–169, *170*
support paragraphs, 78
surveys
   questionnaires, 36, 37
   samples, 36
   strategies, 36
   target population, 35
symbols, 116–118
   cautions, 235
   danger notices, 235
   warnings, 235

T
tables
   numeric, *106*, 108
   textual, *107*, 108
tables of contents, 136, 137

formal proposals, *321*
formal report, 289
user manuals, 228
tabs, color, *134*
target population for surveys, 35
task analysis, 51–52
teamwork, 14. *See also* collaboration
   conflict management, 17–18
   cultural differences and, 18
   digital communication and, 17–18
   interpersonal styles and, 17
   meetings and, 15–17
   project planning form, *16*
   strategies, 15
   team organization, 15
technical background of audience, 43–44
technical communication. *See also*
      documents
   versus academic writing, 4
   applications, 22–23
   checklist, 21–22
   description, 3
   global issues, 13–14
   information relevance, 6
   informational documents, *7, 8*
   instructional documents, *7, 9*
   persuasion, 6
   persuasive documents, *7, 10–11*
   primary purposes, 7–11
   research, 6–7
   truthfulness, 6–7
   workplace benefits, 4
   writing style, 5–6
technical documents. *See* documents
technical information, specialized
      settings, 3–4
teleconferencing, 20
templates
   letters, 172–173
   resumes, 151
terminology. *See also*
      definitions
   expanded definitions, 195
   legal implications, 193–194
   purpose of terms, 193
   safety implications, 193–194
   societal implications, 194
testing, usability and, 56–57
text, *8*
textual tables, *107*, 108
thank you notes after job interview, 158

theses, MLA style citation, 400
timing
   informal proposals, 317
   usability and, 54
titles, *8*
   descriptions and, 207
   formal proposal, *320*
   informal proposals, 316
   instructional documents, 233–234
   title page, report front
      matter, 288
tone
   email, 338–339
   letters, 175–179
   strategies, 98
topic sentence, 78
topic sequencing, descriptions and, 207–208
training presentations, 371
transitional expressions, 432
transmittal memos, 168, *169*
trip reports, 268–271
TripAdvisor, 356
Tumblr, 363
Twitter, 356
   tweets, MLA citation style, 402
typist notation in letters, 175

U

underlining, 133, 136, 351
unity, structure and, 72
unsolicited proposals, 311
usability
   audience and, 42–46
   budget and, 54
   checklist, 57–58
   format and, 53
   information plan and, 54–56
   instructional documents, 242–245
   length and, 53
   persuasion and, 47–51
   potential problems, 53
   procedures, 242–245
   proofreading and, 56–57
   purpose and, 46–47
   revising and, 56–57
   setting and, 53
   task analysis and, 51–52
   testing and, 56–57
   timing and, 54
   writing and, 56–57

user manuals, *5*, 228–229
user-centered documents, 4
   instructions, *5*
   memos, *5*
   procedures, *5*
   reports, *5*
   user manuals, *5*

V

values, plagiarism and, 386
verb/subject agreement, 419–420
vertical lists, 435–436
video conferencing, 380–382
videos, 116, 117
visuals, 104
   accuracy, 119–120
   appropriateness, 118–119
   charts, 111–113
   checklist, 120
   color use, 119
   cross-references, 119
   cultural considerations, 118
   descriptions and, 208
   diagrams, 114–115, 117
   figures, 105
   formal reports, 287–288
   graphs, 108–110
   icons, 116–118
   illustrations, 114–115, 117
   instructional documents, 234
   MLA style citation, 400
   photographs, 115, 117
   placement, 119
   presentation, 119
   stand-alone, 107
   to support text, 106–107
   symbols, 116–118
   tables, 106–108
   videos, 116, 117
   Web pages, 348–350

W

warning boxes, *9*, 307
warnings, instructional documents, 235
Web conferencing, 21
Web development, 346
Web pages, 346
   audience, 347–348
   bold text, 351
   bulleted lists, 351
   checklist, 353–354
   chunking, 349
   color, 351
   credibility issues, 352
   design, 351
   font style and size, 351
   grid patterns, 351
   headings, 351
   interactive, 347
   italic text, 351
   numbered lists, 351
   outlining, 348–349
   privacy issues, 352
   sequencing, 350
   shading, 351
   storyboarding, 348–349, *345*
   strategies, 353
   structure, 348–350
   style, 350
   underlining, 351
   user-friendliness, *350*
   visuals, 351
   white space, 351
Web sites, 346
   MLA citation style, 402
Web-based instructions, 231–232
WebEx, 382
Webinars, 380–381
white space, 129–130, *130*, 132
   Web pages, 351
Wikipedia, 29, 345
wikis, 21, 29
   checklist, 353
   external, 346
   internal, 345
   MLA citation style, 402
   strategies, 352
word usage
   confused words, *433–434*
   forecasting statements, 434
   key word repetition, 432
   phrase repetition, 432
   transitional expressions, 432
wordiness, 94–95
wordless instructions, 230–231
workplace
   benefits, 4
   social media use, 359
workplace email
   advantages, 333
   audience, 334

cardinal rule, 334
cautions, 333–334
purpose, 334
when not to use, 334
Works Cited list. *See also* plagiarism; sources
books, 394–396
digital sources, 400–404
formal reports, 290–291
MLA style, 291, *395*
periodicals, 396–398
writing clearly
active voice, 90–91
jargon, 93–94
modifiers, ambiguity, 90
nominalizations, 92–93
nouns, stacked, 93
passive voice, 91–92
pronouns, ambiguity, 89–90
writing concisely
redundancy, 95–96
repetition, 95–96
wordiness, 94–95
writing fluently
parallel structure, 97
related ideas, combining, 96
sentence construction, 96–97
sentence length, 96–97
writing personably
biased language, 99
tone, 98
writing style, 5–6
paraphrasing and, 390

Y
Yelp, 356
YouTube, 356

Z
Zotero citation software, 387